Linguistic Semantics: An Introduction is the successor to Sir John Lyons's textbook *Language, Meaning and Context* (1981). While preserving the general structure of the earlier book, the author has substantially expanded its scope to introduce several topics that were not previously discussed, and to take account of new developments in linguistic semantics over the past decade. The resulting work is an invaluable guide to the subject, offering clarifications of its specialized terms and explaining its relationship to formal and philosophical semantics and to contemporary pragmatics. With its clear and accessible style it will appeal to a wide student readership.

LINGUISTIC SEMANTICS

LINGUISTIC SEMANTICS

An Introduction

JOHN LYONS

CAMBRIDGE
UNIVERSITY PRESS

CAMBRIDGE UNIVERSITY PRESS
Cambridge, New York, Melbourne, Madrid, Cape Town, Singapore, São Paulo

Cambridge University Press
The Edinburgh Building, Cambridge CB2 2RU, UK

Published in the United States of America by Cambridge University Press, New York

www.cambridge.org
Information on this title: www.cambridge.org/9780521433020

First published 1995
Reprinted 2002, 2005

Linguistic Semantics: An Introduction succeeds and replaces *Language, Meaning and Context,*
first published by Fontana/Collins in 1981.

A catalogue record for this publication is available from the British Library

Library of Congress Cataloguing in Publication data
Lyons, John, 1932–
Linguistic semantics: an introduction/John Lyons.
p.   cm.
Includes bibliographical references and index.
ISBN 0 521 43302 9 (hardback) –
ISBN 0 521 43877 2 (paperback)
1. Semantics. I. Title.
P3325.L9595 1995
401′.43–dc20   95-49736   CIP

ISBN-13 978-0-521-43302-0 hardback
ISBN-10 0-521-43302-9 hardback

ISBN-13 978-0-521-43877-3 paperback
ISBN-10 0-521-43877-2 paperback

Transferred to digital printing 2006

Contents

Preface

This book started life as a second edition of *Language, Meaning and Context* (1981) and, regrettably, in several places has been announced as forthcoming under that title. It now appears with a completely different title because, in the event, it has turned out to be a very different book. It is much longer; it deals with several topics that were not dealt with at all in the earlier book; and, above all, it is written at a different level and in a different style.

Many of these differences derive from the fact that *Linguistic Semantics* (*LS*), unlike its predecessor (*LMC*), is intended to be used as a textbook for courses in semantics given in departments of linguistics (and related disciplines) in colleges and universities. Although *LMC* was not conceived as a textbook, it was quite widely used as such, until it went out of print some years ago. I hope that *LS*, being written especially for students of linguistics, will prove to be much more satisfactory for this purpose.

In revising the original text, apart from taking account of such recent developments as seemed to me to be relevant to what is presented as an introduction to the subject, I have found myself obliged to add several new sections and to rewrite or expand others. I have, however, kept to the same general plan; as before, I have divided the book into four parts and ten chapters (amending the chapter titles when it appeared to be appropriate to do so); as far as possible, I have used the same examples to illustrate the same points, even though the points being made may now be formulated somewhat differently; much of the original text is still here (albeit with minor stylistic changes); and, finally, I have maintained (and explained in greater detail) the notational conventions used in *LMC* (which were first used in my two-volume *Semantics*, 1977). It should be possible therefore for those who are familiar with *LMC*, especially instructors and lecturers who have used it for their own courses, to find their way through *LS* without difficulty.

Much has happened in linguistic semantics in the last decade or so. Apart from anything else, the term 'linguistic semantics' is now more commonly used than it was when I employed it in the Preface to *LMC*; and this implies that it is now more widely recognized than it was at one time that there are several legitimately different kinds of semantics, each of which has its own disciplinary orientation or focus: linguistic, philosophical, anthropological, psychological, literary, etc. Recognition of this fact does not of course imply that the boundaries between these different kinds of semantics are impermeable or eternal or that everyone engaged in semantics will agree as to where the interdisciplinary boundaries should currently be drawn. My own view is essentially the same as it was when I wrote *LMC* (and *Semantics*).

For me, semantics is by definition the study of meaning; and linguistic semantics is the study of meaning in so far as it is systematically encoded in the vocabulary and grammar of (so-called) natural languages. This definition of linguistic semantics, as far as it goes, is relatively uncontroversial. But it is also almost wholly uninformative unless and until one goes on to say, first, what one means by 'meaning' and, second, what exactly is meant by 'encoded' in this context.

As I explain in greater detail in Chapter 1, I take a rather broader view of meaning than many linguists do. It follows that I include within the subject-matter of semantics – and therefore, if it is systematically encoded in the structure of natural languages, within the subject-matter of linguistic semantics – much that many linguists who take a more restrictive view of meaning than I do would exclude. In particular, I include much that they would deal with, not within semantics, but within what has come to be called pragmatics.

Those who draw a terminological distinction between 'semantics' and 'pragmatics' and take a narrower view of meaning than I do will see this book as an introduction to what they think of as the broader, combined, field of linguistic semantics-and-pragmatics, and I have no objection to their tacitly retitling it accordingly. As far as the major substantive issues that are involved in drawing the distinction between semantics and pragmatics are concerned, these have to be discussed anyway, regardless of how broadly or narrowly one defines the term 'meaning' and in whatever way one maps out the field of linguistic semantics. Such issues, which include the distinction between meaning and use, between propositional (or representational) and non-propositional meaning, between competence and performance, between sentences and utterances, are fully discussed in the present book. I think it is true to say that there is now more agreement among linguists than there used to be about the relevance of the distinctions that I have mentioned and greater sophistication in drawing them. But there is as yet no consensus about the relative importance of particular topics.

I have described this book as an introductory textbook and have deliberately used the term 'Introduction' in its subtitle. This does not mean that I expect everything in it to be immediately comprehensible to those who come to it without any previous background in linguistics and with no previous knowledge of semantics. It is introductory in the sense that my *Introduction to Theoretical Linguistics* (1968) was introductory: although it presupposes no previous specialized knowledge of its subject-matter, it is based on the assumption that those who use it, with or without an instructor, will have read, or will read in conjunction with it, some of the other works referred to in 'Suggestions for further reading'. I realize that some sections of the book, especially in the later chapters, will be quite demanding, even for students with some previous knowledge of linguistics, unless they also have, or are prepared to acquire, some knowledge of the relevant parts of logic and of the philosophy of language. But I would argue that no-one can hope to understand modern linguistic semantics without some knowledge of its philosophical underpinnings. I have tried to make everything as clear as possible in context and to give, non-technically, as much of the philosophical background as is necessary for the purpose in hand.

My treatment of what I call linguistic semantics (which others, as I have explained, might refer to as a combination of linguistic semantics and pragmatics) is necessarily selective. It is also somewhat personal. In choosing the topics that I have chosen and in allotting to each of them the space that I have allotted to them, I have relied upon my own evaluation of their intrinsic or relative long-term importance, rather than upon the consensus of my colleagues (even where there is such a consensus). I have deliberately included several topics which are not dealt with at all, or in my view are dealt with unsatisfactorily, in otherwise comparable works. Students who use this book in class with an instructor will of course have the benefit of the instructor's commentary and criticism. However, in the interests of those who are reading the book without such guidance, I have tried to make it clear in the text itself when and in what respect I am presenting a non-standard view of a particular topic and why I think the standard view is defective, incomplete, or (as is frequently the case) imprecisely formulated. In saying this, however, I do not wish to exaggerate the differences between one view of linguistic semantics and another. Very often these differences are more apparent than real, and I shall be pleased if students using this book in conjunction with others come to the same conclusion.

No-one embarking upon the study of linguistic semantics these days can afford to be ignorant of at least the rudiments of formal semantics. One of my principal aims in writing this book, as it was in writing its predecessor, has been, on the one hand, to show how formal semantics, conceived as the analysis of a central part of the meaning of sentences – their propositional content – can be integrated within the broader field of linguistic semantics and, on the other, to demonstrate that formal, truth-conditional, semantics, as currently practised, fails to handle satisfactorily the non-propositional meaning that is also encoded, whether lexically or grammatically, in the sentences of particular natural languages. There are now available, as there were not when I wrote *LMC*, good textbooks of formal

semantics (which I mention in 'Suggestions for further reading'): I trust that my own book will be seen as complementary
to these and, at certain points, will serve as an introduction to
them. It is far less technical as far as the formalization of semantics is concerned. But at times I have provided rather more of
the historical and philosophical context than they do.

It is because I have had the particular purpose of relating the
content of this book to formal semantics that I have given proportionately more space to sentence-semantics and to utter-
ance-semantics than I have to lexical semantics. It is only
recently that linguists have been seriously concerned with the
contribution that is made by grammatical structure to the
meaning of sentences (and utterances), whereas this concern
has always been central in formal semantics. There are aspects
of lexical semantics that I do not deal with at all in the present
book. These can be followed up in the other works to which readers are referred in 'Suggestions for further reading'. What I
have tried to do is to show how lexical and non-lexical meaning
fit together and are interdependent.

I should now say something about terminology. When it
comes to the introduction of technical terms, non-specialists are
often put off by what they see, initially, as esoteric and unnecessary jargon. Admittedly, specialists in any field of study are
often guilty of using the jargon of their trade in contexts where
it is inappropriate – in contexts where preciseness of reference
is unimportant and where the esoteric jargon serves only to mys-
tify those who are not familiar with it. There are other contexts,
however, where the use of specialized terminology is essential if
misunderstanding is to be avoided.

It is very difficult to write clearly and unambiguously about
language in non-technical language and without a certain
amount of formalism; and most authors who attempt to do so
fail badly. What look, at first sight, like straightforward, plain-
English, statements, when examined critically, usually turn out
to be riddled with ambiguities or to be uninterpretable. The
issues with which we shall be concerned, even at the level at
which they are presented in this book, are inevitably rather technical in places; and there is a certain amount of specialized ter-

minology to be mastered. I have done my best to avoid the
unnecessary use of specialized terms, but whenever clarity of
exposition and precision are in conflict with the treacherous
pseudo-simplicity of so-called plain English, I have almost
always sacrificed the latter to the former.

I have also systematically avoided the use of many devices –
such as near-synonyms for the sake of variety – which students
are often taught to cultivate as hallmarks of a lively and attractive style and which are often deliberately exploited by writers
of introductory textbooks in all subjects. Semanticists, more
than most, must train themselves to identify and to control the
ambiguities, the vagueness and the indeterminacy of everyday
language. One way of doing so is by being deliberately and resolutely pedantic in one's use of terms and, as we shall see later,
in one's use of particular notational conventions.

I am very grateful to Jean Aitchison for the help she gave me
with the earlier book (*LMC*), as general editor of the series in
which it appeared, and for the comments she made on the
pre-final draft of the present book. I am similarly indebted to
Rodney Huddleston for his invaluable critical comments on
several points of detail. Since I have not always taken their
advice (and may yet come to regret that I have not), they are
not to be blamed for any errors, infelicities or inconsistencies
that remain in the final text.

As always, I am greatly indebted to the editors that I have
worked with at Cambridge University Press for their highly pro-
fessional guidance at all stages (and for their patience), in this
case to Marion Smith, who commissioned the book for the
Press, and to Judith Ayling who, several years later, saw it
through to completion. I owe a special debt of gratitude to
Julia Harding, who has once again acted as my copy editor and
has dealt cheerfully and competently with a difficult and messy
typescript, eliminating many inconsistencies and errors.

December 1994

John Lyons
Trinity Hall, Cambridge

Symbols and typographical conventions

&	conjunction
$\vee$	disjunction
$\rightarrow$	implication
$\Rightarrow$	entailment
$\Leftrightarrow$	symmetrical entailment
$\equiv$	equivalence operator
$\sim$	negation operator
(x) or $(\forall x)$	universal quantifier
(E) or $(\exists)$	existential quantifier
N or $\square$	necessity
M or $\diamond$	possibility
t_0	temporal zero-point

SMALL CAPITALS
For sense-components and other more abstract elements, or correlates, of meaning.

Italics
1. For forms (as distinct from lexemes or expressions) in their orthographic representation.
2. For certain mathematical and logical symbols, according to standard conventions.

'Single quotation-marks'
1. For lexemes and expressions.
2. For the citation of sentences (i.e. system-sentences).
3. For book titles.

"Double quotation-marks"
1. For meanings.
2. For propositions.
3. For quotations from other authors.

Bold type
For technical terms and for emphasis

PART I

Setting the scene

CHAPTER I

Metalinguistic preliminaries

1.0 INTRODUCTION

In this chapter, which constitutes the whole of Part 1, we deal with a number of concepts which are fundamental to the whole enterprise of putting linguistic semantics on a sound theoretical footing. Although it is one of the longest chapters in the book and includes several sections containing material which, at times, is quite demanding for those who are new to the subject, I have deliberately not divided it into two (or more) chapters, because I wish to emphasize the fact that everything that is dealt with here hangs together and is equally relevant throughout.

Readers who find some of the material difficult on a first reading should not be too concerned about this. They can come back to it as they proceed through the following three parts of the book and see how the various technical distinctions that are drawn here are actually used. Indeed, this is the only way of being sure that one has understood them. The fact that I have brought together, at the beginning of the book, some of the more fundamental terminological and notational distinctions which are relevant throughout should make it easier for readers to refer back to them. It should also make it easier for them to see how the conceptual and terminological framework that I am adopting compares with that adopted in other works that are referred to in 'Suggestions for further reading'.

We begin and end the chapter with the most fundamental question of all, the question to which semantics, linguistic and non-linguistic, seeks to provide a theoretically and empirically satisfying answer: what is meaning? This question is posed non-technically in section 1.1; in section 1.7, we look briefly at some of the general answers that have been proposed by philosophers, linguists and others in the past and more recently.

Between these two sections I have inserted a section (1.2) on what I have called the metalanguage of semantics and a section (1.3) which sets out in greater detail than I have done in the Preface the scope of linguistic semantics. That there should be a section dealing with the relation between linguistic and non-linguistic semantics is only to be expected. It is important that readers should realize that there are various ways in which the subfield of linguistic semantics is defined by specialists as part of the broader fields of semantics, on the one hand, and of linguistics, on the other, and that they should be able to see from the outset the way in which my definition of 'linguistic semantics' differs from that of other authors.

The term 'metalanguage' and the corresponding adjective 'metalinguistic', as we shall see in the later chapters of this book, are quite commonly employed nowadays in the discussion of particular issues in linguistic semantics. (The two terms are fully explained in section 1.2.) It is not often, however, that theorists and practitioners of linguistic semantics discuss explicitly and in general terms the relation between the every-day metalanguage of semantics and the more technical metalanguage that they use in the course of their work. I have devoted some space to this topic here because its importance, in my view, is not as widely acknowledged as it ought to be.

The next three sections introduce a number of distinctions – between language and speech, 'langue' and 'parole', 'competence' and 'performance'; between form and meaning; between sentences and utterances – which, nowadays, are all more or less generally accepted as part of the linguist's stock-in-trade, though they are not always defined in exactly the same way. Once again, I have given rather more space to some of these distinctions than is customary. I have also sought to clarify what is often confused, especially in the discussion of sentences and utterances, on the one hand, and in the discussion of competence and performance, on the other. And I have explained these distinctions, of course, in the present context with particular reference to their application in semantics (and pragmatics) and to the use that is made of them in the organization of this book.

1.1 THE MEANING OF 'MEANING'

Semantics is traditionally defined as the study of meaning; and this is the definition which we shall initially adopt. But do all kinds of meaning fall within the scope of semantics, or only some? What is meant by 'meaning' in this context?

The noun 'meaning' and the verb 'mean', from which it is derived, are used, like many other English words, in a wide range of contexts and in several distinguishable senses. For example, to take the case of the verb: if one says

(1) *Mary means well,*

one implies that Mary is well-intentioned, that she intends no harm. This implication of intention would normally be lacking, however, in an utterance such as

(2) *That red flag means danger.*

In saying this, one would not normally be implying that the flag had plans to endanger anyone; one would be pointing out that it is being used (in accordance with a previously established convention) to indicate that there is danger in the surrounding environment, such as a crevasse on a snowy hillside or the imminent use of explosives in a nearby quarry. Similar to the red-flag use of the verb 'mean', in one respect at least, is its use in

(3) *Smoke means fire.*

In both (2) and (3) one thing is said to be a **sign** of something else: from the presence of the sign, a red flag or smoke, anyone with the requisite knowledge can infer the existence of what it **signifies**, danger or fire, as the case may be.

But there is also an important difference between (2) and (3). Whereas smoke is a **natural** sign of fire, causally connected with what it signifies, the red flag is a **conventional** sign of danger: it is a culturally established **symbol**. These distinctions between the intentional and the non-intentional, on the one hand, and between what is natural and what is conventional, or symbolic, on the other, have long played a central part in the theoretical investigation of meaning and continue to do so.

That the verb 'mean' is being employed in different senses in the examples that I have used so far is evident from the fact that

(4) *Mary means trouble*

is ambiguous: it can be taken like (1) *Mary means well* or like (3) *Smoke means fire*. Indeed, with a little imagination it is possible to devise a context, or scenario, in which the verb 'mean' in (4) *Mary means trouble* can be plausibly interpreted in the way that it would normally be interpreted in (2) *That red flag means danger.* And, conversely, if we are prepared to suspend our normal **onto-logical assumptions** – i.e., our assumptions about the world – and to treat the red flag referred to in (2) as an animate being with its own will and intentions, we can no less plausibly interpret (2) in the way in which we would normally interpret (1).

Most language-utterances, whether spoken or written, depend for their interpretation – to a greater or less degree – upon the context in which they are used. And included within the context of utterance, it must not be forgotten, are the ontological beliefs of the participants: many of these will be culturally determined and, though normally taken for granted, can be challenged or rejected. The vast majority of natural-language utterances, actual and potential, have a far wider range of meanings, or interpretations, than first occur to us when they are put to us out of context. This is a point which is not always given due emphasis by semanticists.

Utterances containing the verb 'mean' (or the noun 'meaning') are no different from other English utterances in this respect. And it is important to remember that the verb 'mean' and the noun 'meaning' are ordinary words of English in other respects also. It must not be assumed that all natural languages have words in their everyday vocabulary which can be put into exact correspondence with the verb 'mean' and the noun 'meaning' grammatically and semantically. This is a second important

point which needs to be properly emphasized, and I will come
back to it later (1.2).

Let us now take yet another sense (or meaning) of the verb
'mean'. If one says

(5) *'Soporific' means "tending to produce sleep"*,

one is obviously not imputing intentionality to the English word
'soporific'. It might be argued, however, that there is an essential, though indirect, connexion between what people mean, or
intend, and what the words that they use are conventionally
held to mean. This point has been much discussed by philosophers of language. Since it is not relevant to the central concerns
of this book, I will not pursue it here. Nor will I take up the
related point, that there is also an intrinsic, and possibly more
direct, connexion between what people mean and what they
mean to say. On the other hand, in Chapters 8 and 9 I shall be
drawing upon a particular version of the distinction between
saying what one means and meaning what one says – another
distinction that has been extensively discussed in the philosophy
of language.

Intentionality is certainly of importance in any theoretical
account that one might give of the meaning of language-
utterances, even if it is not a property of the words of which
these utterances are composed. For the moment, let us simply
note that it is the meaning of the verb 'mean' exemplified in
(5), rather than the meaning exemplified in

(6) *Mary didn't really mean what she said,*

which is of more immediate concern in linguistics.

We have noted that the noun 'meaning' (and the corresponding verb 'mean') has many meanings. But the main point that I
want to make in this section is, not so much that there are many
meanings, or senses, of 'meaning'; it is rather that these several
meanings are interconnected and shade into one another in various ways. This is why the investigation of what is referred to as
meaning (in one sense or another of the English word 'meaning')
is of concern to so many disciplines and does not fall wholly
within any single one of them. It follows that, if semantics is

defined as the study of meaning, there will be many different, but intersecting, branches of semantics: philosophical semantics, psychological semantics, anthropological semantics, logical semantics, linguistic semantics, and so on.

It is **linguistic semantics** with which we are primarily concerned in this book; and, whenever I employ the term 'semantics' without further qualification, it is to be understood as referring, more narrowly, to linguistic semantics. Similarly, whenever I employ the term 'language' without qualification, it is to be understood as referring to what are commonly called **natural languages**. But what is linguistic semantics and how does it differ from non-linguistic semantics? And how do so-called natural languages differ, semantically and otherwise, from other kinds of languages? These are the questions which we shall address in section 1.3. But something should first be said about terminology and style, and more generally about the technical and non-technical **metalanguage** of semantics.

1.2 THE METALANGUAGE OF SEMANTICS

We could have gone on for a long time enumerating and discussing examples of the different meanings of 'meaning' in the preceding section. It we had done so and if we had then tried to translate all our examples into other natural languages (French, German, Russian, etc.), we would soon have come to appreciate the force of one of the points made there, that 'meaning' (and the verb from which it is derived) is a word of English which has no exact equivalent in other, quite familiar, languages. We would also have seen that there are contexts in which the noun 'meaning' and the verb 'mean' are not in correspondence with one another. But this is not a peculiarity of English or of these two words. As we shall see later, most everyday, non-technical, words and expessions in all natural languages are like the noun 'meaning' or the verb 'mean' in that they have several meanings which cannot always be sharply distinguished from one another (or alternatively a range of meaning within which several distinctions can be drawn) and may be somewhat vague or indeterminate. One of the most important tasks that we have to accomplish in the course of this book is to furnish ourselves with a technical vocabulary which is, as far as possible, precise and unambiguous.

In doing so, we shall be constructing what semanticists refer to as a **metalanguage**: i.e., a language which is used to describe language. Now it is a commonplace of philosophical semantics that natural languages (in contrast with many non-natural, or artificial, formal languages) contain their own metalanguage: they may be used to describe, not only other languages (and language in general), but also themselves. The property by virtue of which a language may be used to refer to itself (in whole or in part) I will call **reflexivity**. Philosophical problems that can be caused by this kind of reflexivity will not be of direct concern to us here. But there are other aspects of reflexivity, and more generally of the metalinguistic function of natural languages, which do need to be discussed.

The metalanguage that we have used so far and shall continue to use throughout this book is English: to be more precise, it is more or less ordinary (but non-colloquial) **Standard English** (which differs in various ways from other kinds of English). And whenever I use the term 'English' without further qualification this is the language (or dialect) to which I am referring. Ordinary (Standard) English is not of course absolutely uniform throughout the world or across all social groups in any one English-speaking country or region, but such differences of vocabulary and grammatical structure as there are between one variety of Standard English (British, American, Australian, etc.) and another are relatively unimportant in the present context and should not cause problems.

We have now explicitly adopted English as our meta-language. But if we are aiming for precision and clarity, English, like other natural languages, cannot be used for metalinguistic purposes without modification. As far as the metalinguistic vocabulary of natural languages is concerned, there are two kinds of modification open to us: **regimentation** and **extension**. We can take existing everyday words, such as 'language', 'sentence', 'word', 'meaning' or 'sense', and subject them to strict control (i.e., **regiment** their use), defining them or re-defining them for our own purposes (just as physicists re-define 'force' or 'energy' for their specialized purposes). Alternatively, we can **extend** the everyday vocabulary by introducing into it technical terms which are not normally used in everyday discourse.

In the preceding section, we noted that the everyday English word 'meaning' has a range of distinguishable, but interconnected, meanings. It would be open to us at this point to do what many semanticists writing in English do these days: we could **regiment** the use of the word 'meaning' by deliberately assigning to it a narrower, more specialized, sense than it bears in normal everyday discourse. And we could then employ this narrower, more specialized, definition of 'meaning' to restrict the field of semantics to only part of what is traditionally covered by the term 'semantics' in linguistics, philosophy and other disciplines. In this book, we shall adopt the alternative strategy. We shall continue to use both the noun 'meaning' and the verb 'mean' as non-technical terms, with their full range of everyday meanings (or senses). And for the time being we shall continue to operate with a correspondingly broad definition of 'semantics': until such time as it is re-defined, semantics for us will continue to be, by definition, the study of meaning. It should be mentioned, however, that nowadays many authorities adopt a rather narrower definition of 'semantics', based on the regimentation of the word 'meaning' (or one of its near-equivalents) in other languages. I will come back to this point (see 1.6).

Although the ordinary-language word 'meaning' will be retained without re-definition in the metalanguage which we are now constructing, several composite expressions containing the word 'meaning' will be introduced and defined as we proceed and will be used thereafter as technical terms. For instance, later in this chapter distinctions will be introduced between **propositional** and **non-propositional meaning**, on the one hand, and between **sentence-meaning** and **utterance-meaning**, on the other; and these will be subsequently related, with various other distinctions, to the distinction that is commonly drawn nowadays between **semantics** (in the narrow sense) and **pragmatics**. In Chapter 3, **sense** and **denotation** will be distinguished as interdependent aspects or dimensions of the meaning of words and phrases. **Reference** will be distinguished from denotation initially in Chapter 3 and then in more detail in Chapter 10. Once again, until they are formally defined or re-defined these three terms – and especially the word 'sense' – will be used non-technically. So too will all other words and expressions of ordinary everyday English (including the nouns 'language' and 'speech' and such semantically related verbs as 'speak', 'say' and 'utter', which will be dealt with in some detail in section 1.4).

As will be explained in a later chapter, in recent years linguists and logicians have constructed various highly **formalized** (i.e., mathematically precise) **non-natural** metalanguages in order to be able to describe natural languages as precisely as possible. It will be important for us to take a view, in due course, about the relation between the formal, non-natural, metalanguages of logical semantics and the regimented and extended, more or less ordinary, metalanguage with which we are operating. Which, if either, is more basic than the other? And what does 'basic' mean in this context?

It is of course written English that we are using as our metalanguage; and we are using it to refer to both written and spoken language, and also (when this is appropriate) to refer to languages and to language-utterances considered independently of the **medium** in which they are realized. In our regimentation of ordinary written English for metalinguistic purposes, it will be useful to establish a number of notational conventions, which will enable us to refer unambiguously to a variety of linguistic units. Such more or less ordinary notational conventions as are employed metalinguistically in this book (italics, quotation marks, etc.) will be formally introduced in section 1.5 (see also the list of symbols and typographical conventions on p. xvii).

As far as the everyday metalinguistic use of the spoken language is concerned, there are certain rules and conventions which all native speakers follow without ever having been taught them and without normally being conscious of them. But these have not been fully codified and cannot prevent misunderstanding in all contexts. Phoneticians have developed special notational systems for the representation of spoken utterances with great precision. However, in the everyday, non-technical, use of English (and other natural languages) there is no conventionally accepted written representation of intonation, rhythm, stress and other non-verbal features, which are a normal and essential part of speech. As we shall see later, such features have many communicative and expressive functions.

Here, I want to draw attention to the fact that they may also have a metalinguistic function. For example,

(7) *John said it was raining*

can be pronounced in various ways. In particular it can be uttered with a characteristic prosodic transition between *said* and *it*, which would distinguish in speech what is conventionally distinguished in the written language as

(8) *John said [that] it was raining*

and

(9) *John said, "It was raining".*

In this case, there is a more or less generally accepted convention – the use of quotation-marks – which serves to distinguish direct from indirect discourse in written English. But there are recognized alternatives to the use of quotation-marks. And even when quotation-marks are used, the conventions for using them are not fully codified or universally accepted: for example, different writers and different printing houses have their own rules for the use of single and double quotation-marks. As I have already mentioned, my own conventions for the metalinguistic use of single and double quotation-marks (and for the metalinguistic use of italics) will be explained in a later section (1.5).

There are many ordinary-language metalinguistic statements which are unambiguous when spoken, but not necessarily when written. Conversely, because there is nothing in normal speech that is in direct one-to-one corespondence with the punctuation marks and **diacritics** of written language (underlining, italics or bold type for emphasis, quotation-marks, capital letters,

etc.), there are many ordinary-language metalinguistic statements which are unambiguous when written, but not when spoken. For example,

(10) *I can't stand Sebastian*

differs from

(11) *I can't stand 'Sebastian',*

in that (10) might be interpreted as a statement about a person
whose name happens to be 'Sebastian' and (11) as a statement
about the name 'Sebastian' itself. But the conventional use of
quotation-marks for such purposes in ordinary written English
is not obligatory. And, as we shall see presently, it needs to be
properly regimented (as does the use of other notational diacritics) if it is to do the job we want it to do as part of the metalanguage of semantics.

1.3 LINGUISTIC AND NON-LINGUISTIC SEMANTICS

The English adjective 'linguistic' is ambiguous. It can be understood as meaning either "pertaining to language" or "pertaining
to linguistics".

The term 'linguistic semantics' is correspondingly ambiguous.
Given that semantics is the study of meaning, 'linguistic semantics' can be held to refer either to the study of meaning in so far
as this is expressed in language or, alternatively, to the study of
meaning within linguistics. It is being employed here, and
throughout this book, in the second of these two senses. Linguistic semantics, then, is a branch of linguistics, just as philosophical
semantics is a branch of philosophy, psychological semantics is
a branch of psychology, and so on.

Since linguistics is generally defined as the study of language,
it might be thought that the distinction which I have just
drawn between the two senses of 'linguistic semantics' is a distinction without a difference. But this is not so. Linguistics does
not aim to deal with everything that falls within the scope of the
word 'language'. Like all academic disciplines, it establishes its
own theoretical framework. As I have already explained in

respect of the word 'meaning', linguistics reserves the right to re-
define for its own purposes everyday words such as 'language'
and does not necessarily employ them in the way in which they
are employed, whether technically or non-technically, outside
linguistics. Moreover, as we shall see in the following section,
the English word 'language' is ambiguous, so that the phrase
'the study of meaning in language' is open to two quite different
interpretations. There are therefore, in principle, not just two,
but three, ways in which the term 'linguistic semantics' can be
interpreted. And the same is true of the phrase 'linguistic meaning' (for the same reason). This point also will be developed in
the following section. Meanwhile, I will continue to employ the
everyday English word 'language' without specialized restriction or re-definition.

Of all the disciplines with an interest in meaning, linguistics is
perhaps the one to which it is of greatest concern. Meaningfulness, or **semanticity**, is generally taken to be one of the defining
properties of language; and there is no reason to challenge this
view. It is also generally taken for granted by linguists that natural languages are, of their essence, communicative: i.e., that
they have developed or evolved – that they have been, as it
were, designed – for the purpose of communication and interaction and that their so-called **design-properties** – and, more
particularly, their grammatical and semantic structure – fit
them for this purpose and are otherwise mysterious and inexplic-
able. This view has been challenged recently within linguistics
and philosophy. For the purposes of this book we can remain
neutral on this issue. I will continue to assume, as most linguists
do, that natural languages are properly described as **communi-
cation-systems**. I must emphasize however that nothing of
consequence turns on this assumption. Although many kinds of
behaviour can be described as meaningful, the range, diversity
and complexity of meaning expressed in language is unmatched
in any other kind of human or non-human communicative behaviour. Part of the difference between communication by
means of language and other kinds of communicative behaviour
derives from the properties of intentionality and conventionality, referred to in section 1.1.

A non-human animal normally expresses its feelings or attitudes by means of behaviour which appears to be non-intentional and non-conventional. For example, a crab will signal aggression by waving a large claw. Human beings, on the other hand, will only rarely express their anger, whether intentionally or not, by shaking their fist. More often, they will convey feelings such as aggression by means of language-utterances such as

(12) *You'll be sorry for this*

or

(13) *I'll sue you*

or

(14) *How dare you behave like that!*.

True, the tone of the utterance will generally be recognizably aggressive; and it may also be accompanied with a recognizably aggressive gesture or facial expression. But as far as the words which are used are concerned, it is clear that there is no natural, non-conventional, link between their form and their meaning: as we noted in the preceding section, the words are, in this sense, **arbitrary**. So too is much of the grammatical structure of natural languages which serves to express meaning. And, as we shall see throughout this book, there is much more to accounting for the semanticity of language – its capacity to express meaning – than simply saying what each word means.

It should also be emphasized at this point that, although much of the structure of natural-language utterances is arbitrary, or conventional, there is also a good deal of non-arbitrariness in them. One kind of non-arbitrariness is commonly referred to these days as **iconicity**. Roughly speaking, an iconic sign is one whose form is explicable in terms of similarity between the form of the sign and what it signifies: signs which lack this property of similarity are non-iconic. As linguists have been aware for centuries, in all natural languages there are words which are traditionally described as **onomatopoeic**, such as *splash, bang, crash* or *cuckoo, peewit*, etc. in English; they are nowadays classified under the more general term 'iconic'. But these are relatively few in number. More important for us is the fact that, although much of the grammatical structure of natural languages is arbitrary, far more of it is iconic than standard textbooks of linguistics are prepared to concede. Most important of all, however, from this point of view, is the partial iconicity of the **non-verbal** component of natural-language utterances.

Spoken utterances, in particular, will contain, in addition to the words of which they are composed, a particular intonation-contour and stress-pattern: these are referred to technically as **prosodic features**. They are an integral part of the utterances in which they occur, and they must not be thought of as being in any sense secondary or optional. Prosodic features, in all natural languages, are to a considerable degree (though not wholly) iconic. Spoken utterances may also be accompanied by what are called **paralinguistic features** – popularly, but inaccurately, called body-language (gestures, posture, eye movements, facial expressions, etc.). As the term 'paralinguistic' suggests, these are not regarded by linguists as being an integral part of the utterances with which they are associated. In this respect, they differ from prosodic features. But paralinguistic features too are meaningful, and, like prosodic features, they serve to **modulate** and to **punctuate** the utterances which they accompany. They tend to be even more highly iconic, or otherwise non-arbitrary, than prosodic features. In both cases, however, their non-arbitrariness is blended with an equally high degree of conventionality: that is to say, the prosodic features of spoken languages and the paralinguistic gestures that are associated with spoken utterances in particular languages (or dialects) in particular cultures (or subcultures) vary from language to language and have to be learned as part of the normal process of language-acquisition.

Written language does not have anything which directly corresponds to the prosodic or paralinguistic features of spoken language. However, punctuation marks (the full stop, or period, the comma, the question-mark, etc.) and capitals, italics, underlining, etc. are roughly equivalent in function. Hence my use of the term 'punctuation' as a technical term of linguistic semantics for both spoken and written language.

Another kind of non-arbitrariness, to which semanticists have given increasing attention in recent years, is **indexicality**. An **index**, as the term was originally defined, is a sign which, in some sense, calls attention to – **indicates** (or **is indicative of**) – what it signifies (in the immediate situation) and which thereby serves as a clue, as it were, to the presence or existence (in the immediate situation) of whatever it is that it signifies. For example, smoke is an index of fire; slurred speech may indicate drunkenness; and so on. In these two cases there is a causal connexion between the index and what it indicates. But this is not considered to be essential. In fact, the term 'index', as it was originally defined, covered a variety of things which have little in common other than that of focusing attention on some aspect of the immediate physical situation. One of the consequences is that the term 'indexicality' has been used in several conflicting senses in the more recent literature. I will select just one of those senses and explain it in Chapter 10. Until then, I will make no further use of the terms 'index', 'indexical' or 'indexicality'.

I will however employ the verb 'indicate' (and also 'be indicative of') in the sense in which I have used it of smoke and slurred speech in the preceding paragraph. When one says that smoke means fire or that slurred speech is a sign of drunkenness, one implies, not merely that they call attention to the presence of fire or drunkenness (in the immediate situation), but that fire is the source of the smoke and that it is the person whose speech is slurred who is drunk. If we make this a defining condition of **indication**, in what I will now adopt as a technical sense of the term, we can say that a good deal of information that is expressed in spoken utterances is indicative of the biological, psychological or social characteristics of their source. For example, a person's accent will generally be indicative of his or her social or geographical provenance; so too, on occasion, will the selection of one, rather than another, of two otherwise synonymous expressions.

How then do linguists deal with the meaning of language-utterances? And how much of it do they classify as linguistic (in the sense of "falling within the scope of linguistics") rather than as paralinguistic (or extralinguistic)? Linguists' ways of dealing with any part of their subject-matter vary, as do those of specialists in other disciplines, in accordance with the prevailing intellectual climate. Indeed, there have been times in the recent past, notably in the United States in the period between 1930 and the end of the 1950s, when linguistic semantics was very largely neglected. One reason for this was that the investigation of meaning was felt to be inherently subjective (in the pejorative sense of the word) and, at least temporarily, beyond the scope of science.

A more particular reason for the comparative neglect of linguistic semantics was the influence of behaviourist psychology upon some, though not all, schools of American linguistics. Largely as a result of Chomsky's criticisms of behaviourism in the late 1950s and the subsequent revolutionary impact of his theory of generative grammar, not only upon linguistics, but also upon other academic disciplines, including philosophy and psychology, the influence of behaviourism is no longer as strong as it was a generation ago. Not only linguists, but also philosophers and psychologists, are now prepared to admit as data much that was previously rejected as subjective (in the pejorative sense of the word) and unreliable.

This book concentrates upon linguistic semantics, and it does so from what many would classify as a traditional point of view. But it also pays due attention to those developments which have taken place as a consequence of the increased collaboration that there has been, in recent years, between linguists and representatives of other disciplines, including formal logic and the philosophy of language, and examines the strengths and weaknesses of some of the most important notions which linguistic semantics currently shares with various kinds of non-linguistic semantics.

1.4 LANGUAGE, SPEECH AND UTTERANCE; 'LANGUE' AND 'PAROLE'; 'COMPETENCE' AND 'PERFORMANCE'

The English word 'language', like the word 'meaning', has a wide range of meaning (or meanings). But the first and most important point to be made about the word 'language' is that (like 'meaning' and several other English nouns) it is **categorially ambivalent** with respect to the semantically relevant property of **countability**: i.e., it can be used (like 'thing', 'idea', etc.) as a count noun (which means that, when it is used in the singular, it must be combined with an article, definite or indefinite, or some other kind of **determiner**); it can also be used (like 'water', 'information', etc.) as a mass noun (i.e., noncount noun), which does not require a determiner and which normally denotes not an individual entity of set or entities, but an unbounded mass or aggregate of stuff or substance. Countability is not given grammatical recognition – is not **grammaticalized** (either morphologically or syntactically) – in all natural languages (cf. 10.1). And in those languages in which it is grammaticalized, it is grammaticalized in a variety of ways.

What is of concern to us here is the fact that when the word 'language' is used as a mass noun in the singular (without a determiner) the expression containing it can be, but need not be, semantically equivalent to an expression containing the plural form of 'language' used as a count noun. This has the effect that some statements containing the word 'language' in the singular are ambiguous. One such example (adapted from the second paragraph of section 1.2 above) is

(15) *A metalanguage is a language which is used to describe language.*

Another is

(16) *Linguistics is the scientific study of language.*

Do (15) and (16) mean the same, respectively, as

(17) *A metalanguage is a language which is used to describe languages*

and

(18) *Linguistics is the scientific study of languages?*

This question cannot be answered without reference to the context in which (15) and (16) occur, and it may not be answerable even in context. What should be clear however, on reflection if not immediately, is that (15) and (16), as they stand and out of context, are ambiguous, according to whether they are interpreted as being semantically equivalent to (17) and (18), respectively, or not.

The reason for this particular ambiguity is that, whenever the word 'language' is used as a mass noun, as in (15) and (16), the expression containing it may be referring, not to a set of languages, each of which is (or can be described as) a **system** of words and grammatical rules, but to the spoken or written **products** of (the use of) a particular system or set of systems. What may be referred to as the **system–product ambiguity** of many expressions containing the English word 'language' correlates with the fact, which has just been noted, that the English word 'language' (like many other nouns in English) is syntactically ambivalent: i.e., it belong to two syntactically distinct subclasses of nouns (count nouns and mass nouns). And it so happens that, when it is used as a mass noun in the singular, the expression containing it can refer either to the product of (the use of) a language or to the totality (or a sample) of languages.

Expressions containing the words 'English', 'French', 'German', etc. exhibit a related, but rather different, kind of system–product ambiguity when they are used as mass nouns in the singular (in certain contexts). For example,

(19)   *That is English*

may be used to refer either to a particular text or utterance as such or, alternatively, to the **language-system** of which particular texts or utterances are the products. That this is a genuine ambiguity is evident from the fact that in one interpretation of (19), but not the other, the single-word expression 'English' may be replaced with the phrase 'the English language'. It is obvious that one cannot identify any particular English utterance with the English language. It is also obvious that, in cases like this, the syntactic ambivalence upon which the ambiguity turns, is not between count nouns and mass nouns, as such, but between proper (count) nouns and common (mass) nouns.

What I have referred to as the system–product ambiguity associated with the categorial ambivalence of the word 'language' is obvious enough, once it has been explained. But it has been, and continues to be, the source of a good deal of theoretical confusion. One way of avoiding at least some of this confusion is to adopt the policy of never using the English word 'language' metalinguistically as a mass noun when the expression containing it could be replaced, without change of meaning, with an expression containing the plural form of 'language' used as a count noun. This policy will be adhered to consistently in all that follows; and students are advised to adopt the same policy themselves.

Another way of avoiding, or reducing, the ambiguity and confusion caused by the syntactic (or categorial) ambivalence of the everyday English word 'language' and by its several meanings is to coin a set of more specialized terms to replace it. Such are the now widely used 'langue' and 'parole', which were first employed technically by Saussure (1916), writing in French, and 'competence' and 'performance', which were introduced into linguistics as technical terms by Chomsky (1965).

In everyday, non-technical, French the noun 'langue' is one of two words which, taken together, have much the same range of meaning or meanings as the English word 'language'. The other is 'langage'. The two French words differ from one another grammmatically and semantically in several respects. Two such differences are relevant in the present context: (i) 'langue', in contrast with 'langage', is always used as a count noun; (ii) 'langue' denotes what are commonly referred to as natural languages and, unlike 'langage', is not normally used to refer (a) to the artificial (i.e., non-natural) formal languages of logicians, mathematicians, and computer scientists, (b) to such extralinguistic or paralinguistic communication systems as what is popularly called body-language, or (c) to non-human systems of communication. The fact that French (like Italian, Portuguese, Spanish and other Romance languages) has two semantically non-equivalent words, one of which is much more general than the other, to cover what is covered by the English word 'language' is interesting in itself. It reinforces the point made earlier about the English word 'meaning': the everyday metalanguage that is contained in one natural language is not necessarily equivalent semantically, in whole or in part, to the metalanguage contained in other natural languages. But this fact has been mentioned here in connexion with the Saussurean distinction between 'langue' and 'parole'.

Expressions containing the French word 'langage' are subject to the same kind of system–product ambiguity as are expressions containing the English word 'language'. But expressions containing the word 'langue' are not. They always refer to what I am calling language-systems (and by virtue of the narrow range of 'langue', in contrast with the English word 'language', to what are commonly called natural languages). This holds true regardless of whether 'langue' is being used technically or non-technically in French.

The word 'parole' has a number of related, or overlapping, meanings in everyday French. In the meaning which concerns us here it covers part of what is covered by the French word 'langage' and the English word 'language' when they are being used as mass nouns. It denotes the product or products of the use of a language-system. Unlike 'langage' and 'language', however, it is restricted to spoken language: i.e., to the product of speech. Consequently, the Saussurean distinction between 'langue' and 'parole' has frequently been misrepresented, in English, as also in several other European languages including German and Russian, as a distinction between language and speech.

The essential distinction, as we have seen, is between a system (comprising a set of grammatical rules and a vocabulary) and the products of (the use of) the system. It will be noted that here, as earlier in this section, I have inserted in parentheses the phrase 'the use of'. This brings us to a second point which must be made, not only about the Saussurean distinction between 'langue' and 'parole', but also about the Chomskyan distinction between 'competence' and 'performance', which has also given rise to a good deal of theoretical confusion.

By 'competence' (more fully, 'linguistic competence' or 'grammatical competence') Chomsky means the language-system which is stored in the brains of individuals who are said to know, or to be competent in, the language in question. Linguistic competence in this sense is always competence in a particular language. It is normally acquired by so-called native speakers in childhood (in normal environmental conditions) by virtue of the interaction of (i) the specifically human and genetically transmitted language-faculty (to which Chomsky applies the term 'universal grammar') and (ii) a sufficient number of sufficiently representative sample utterances which can be analysed (with the aid of the child's innate knowledge of the principles and parameters of universal grammar) as products of the developing language-system. There is much in the detail of Chomsky's theory of language-acquisition and universal grammar which is philosophically and psychologically controversial. But this is irrelevant to our present concerns. It is, or ought to be, by now uncontroversial that what Chomsky calls competence in particular natural languages is stored neurophysiologically in the brains of individual members of particular language-communities. And Chomsky's 'competence', thus explicated, may be identified for present purposes with Saussure's 'langue'.

As Chomsky distinguishes 'competence' from 'performance', so Saussure distinguishes 'langue' from 'parole'. But 'performance' cannot be identified with 'parole' as readily as 'competence' can be identified with 'langue'. Strictly speaking, 'performance' applies to the use of the language-system, whereas 'parole' applies to the products of the use of the system. But this terminological distinction is not always maintained. The Chomskyan term 'performance' (like the term 'behaviour') is often employed by linguists to refer indifferently, or equivocally, both to the use of the system and to the products of the use of the system. 'Parole', in contrast, is rarely, if ever, employed to refer to anything other than the products of the use of particular language-systems. What is required, it should now be clear, is not a simple two-term distinction between a system and its products, but a three-term distinction, in which the products ('parole') are distinguished, not only from the system, but also from the process ('performance','behaviour', 'use', etc.). Whether we employ specialized metalinguistic vocabulary for this purpose or not, it is important that what is produced by the process of using a language should be carefully distinguished from the process itself.

Many everyday English nouns derived from verbs are like 'performance', in that they can be used to refer both to a process and to its product or products. These include the noun 'production' itself and a host of semantically related nouns, such as 'creation', 'composition' and 'construction'. They also include such ordinary-language (i.e., ordinary-metalanguage) words as 'speech', 'writing' and 'utterance' (and many others). The two senses of these terms must not be confused, as they have been confused – and continue to be confused – in many textbooks of linguistics. This point, as we shall see, is of special importance when it comes to the definition of 'pragmatics'.

Much that has been said in this section is relevant, not only to the problems which can arise if we do not exercise great care in the use of such everyday words as 'language' and 'speech', but to a range of other issues which will come up later. It is essential that those who are new to the study of semantics should be made aware of what I will refer to here as the **system–process–product trichotomy**. Students who are already familiar with the principles of modern generative grammar and formal semantics will know that there are further refinements to be made to the system–process–product analysis of language and of the use of language which has been presented here. In particular, there is a more abstract, mathematical, sense of 'process' and 'product' in terms of which sentences are said to be produced – or generated – by a grammar operating upon an associated vocabulary. This more abstract sense of 'process' (like the more abstract sense of 'sentence' which depends upon it and will be explained in due course) is logically independent of use and context and can be considered as system-internal. But technical questions of this kind do not concern us for the present. We can make a good deal of progress in semantics before we need to take account of recent advances in theoretical linguistics and formal logic.

1.5 WORDS: FORMS AND MEANINGS

At this point it will be convenient to introduce the notational convention for distinguishing between form and meaning with which we shall be operating throughout this book. It is readily explained, in the first instance, with respect to the form and meaning of words. It may then be extended, as we shall see, to phrases, sentences and other expressions.

One of the tacit assumptions with which we have been operating so far and which may now be made explicit is that words (and other expressions, including phrases and sentences) have meaning. They also have **form**: in fact, in English and any other natural language which is associated with a writing-system, whether alphabetic or non-alphabetic, and is in common use, words have both a spoken form and a conventionally accepted written form. (In certain cases, the same spoken language is associated with different writing-systems, so that the same spoken word may have several different written forms. Conversely, and more strikingly, phonologically distinct spoken languages may be associated, not only with the same writing-system, but with the same written language, provided that, as is the case with the so-called dialects of Modern Chinese, there is a sufficient degree of grammatical and lexical **isomorphism** among the different spoken languages: i.e., a sufficient degree of structural identity in grammar and vocabulary.) We shall not generally need to draw a distinction between written and spoken forms, although some of the conventions for doing so, when necessary, are well enough established in linguistics (including the use of symbols from the International Phonetic Alphabet within square brackets or obliques for the phonetic or phonological representation of forms). But it will certainly be necessary to distinguish the word (considered as a composite unit) from both its form and its meaning. And for this purpose we can employ the ordinary written form of a word to stand, not only for the word itself as a composite unit with both form and meaning, but also for either the form or the meaning considered independently of one another. This is what is done in the everyday metalinguistic use of English and other languages. However, in order to make it clear which of these three different metalinguistic functions the written form of a word is fulfilling on a particular occasion we need to establish distinctive notational conventions.

Regrettably, the notational conventions most commonly used by linguists fail to distinguish clearly and consistently between words (and other expressions), on the one hand, and their form or their meaning, on the other. In this book, **single quotation-marks** will be employed for words, and for other composite units with both form and meaning; **italics** (without quotation-marks) for forms (whether spoken or written); and **double quotation-marks** for meanings (or senses).

A moment's reflection will show that all we have done so far is to systematize and codify (i.e., to regiment), for our own special purposes, some of the ordinary metalinguistic conventions of written English. When ordinary users of English (or other natural languages) wish to refer to a word, they do so by **citing** it in either its written or spoken form, as the case may be. For example, they might say

(20) *Can you tell me what 'sesquipedalian' means?*

and one possible response would be

(21) *I'm sorry, I can't: look it up in the dictionary,*

where 'it', in context, both refers to and can be replaced by the word 'sesquipedalian'. Similarly, conventional dictionaries of English and of other languages that are associated with an alphabetic writing-system identify words by means of their form, listing them according to a purely conventional ordering of the letters of the alphabet, which is taught for this very purpose at school.

We have now explicitly adopted a notational convention for distinguishing words (and other expressions) from both their meaning and their form. But in many languages, including English, words may also have more than one form. For example, the noun 'man' has the grammatically distinct forms *man, man's, men* and *men's*; the verb 'sing' has the grammatically distinct forms *sing, sings, singing, sang* and *sung*; and so on. These grammatically distinct forms of a word are traditionally described as **inflectional**: the noun 'man', like the vast majority of count nouns in English, is inflected for the grammatical (more precisely, **morphosyntactic**) properties of singularity/plurality and possession; the verb 'sing', like the majority of verbs in English, is inflected for the grammatical category of tense (present versus past), etc. Some languages are much more highly inflected than others. English in contrast with Russian or Latin, or even French, Italian, Spanish, etc., or German, does not have much inflectional variation in the forms of words; and certain languages (so-called analytic, or isolating, languages), notably Vietnamese and Classical Chinese, have none. It is nevertheless important to draw a distinction between a word and its form, even if it has no distinct inflectional forms.

Among the inflectional forms of a word, in English and other languages, one is conventionally regarded as its **citation-form**: i.e., as the form which is used to cite, or refer to, the word as a composite whole. And it is usually the citation-form which appears, in alphabetical order, at the head of an entry in conventional dictionaries of English and of other languages that are associated with an alphabetic writing-system.

The conventionally accepted everyday citation-form of a word is not necessarily the form of the word that a linguist might identify as its root or stem. Generally speaking, in English, as it happens, the everyday citation-form of most words – except for verbs – is identical with their stem-form. But this is not so in all languages. Throughout this book, for all languages other than English, we shall use whatever citation-form is most generally accepted in the mainstream lexicographical tradition of the languages being referred to. In English, as far as verbs are concerned, there are two alternative conventions. The more traditional everyday convention, which is less commonly adopted these days by linguists, is to use the so-called infinitive-form, composed of the particle *to* and the stem-form (or, in the case of irregular verbs, one of the stem-forms): e.g., 'to love', 'to sing', 'to be', etc. The less traditional convention, which is the one I will follow, is to use the stem-form (or one of the stem-forms), not only for nouns, pronouns, adjectives and adverbs, but also for verbs: e.g., not only 'man', 'she', 'good' and 'well', etc., but also 'love', 'sing', 'be', etc. There are undoubtedly good reasons for choosing the stem-form (or one of the stem-forms) as the citation-form in languages such as English. But, in principle, the fact that one form rather than another is used for metalinguistic reference to the word of which it is a form is arbitrary and a matter of convention.

Not only do most English words have more than one form. They may also have more than one meaning; and in this respect English is typical of all natural languages. (Although there are natural languages in which every word has one and only one form, it is almost certainly the case that there are no natural languages, and never have been, in which every word has one and only one meaning.) For example, the noun 'foot' has several meanings. If we wish to distinguish these notationally, we can do so by numbering them and attaching the numbers as subscripts to our symbolic representation of meaning: "$foot_1$", "$foot_2$", "$foot_3$", etc. More generally, given that X is the citation-form of a word, we refer to that word as 'X' and to its meaning (i.e., to the set of its one or more meanings) as "X"; and if it has more than one meaning, we can distinguish these as "X_1", "X_2", "X_3", etc.

Of course, this use of subscripts is simply a convenient notational device, which tells one nothing at all about the meaning or meanings of a word. When it comes to identifying the different meanings other than symbolically in this way, we can do so by means of definition or paraphrase. For example, in the case of the word 'foot', we can say that "$foot_1$" is "terminal part of a leg", that "$foot_2$" is "lowest part of a hill or mountain", etc. How one decides whether a particular definition or paraphrase is correct or not is something that will be discussed in Part 2. Here I am concerned simply to explain the metalinguistic notation that I am using. But I should also make explicit the fact that the use that I am making of the notation at this point rests upon the assumption that the meanings of words are both (i) discrete and (ii) distinguishable. This assumption is one that is commonly made by lexicographers (and linguists) and is reflected in the organization of most standard dictionaries.

But it is a salutary experience for students who have not previously done this to take a set of common English words – e.g., 'foot', 'game', 'table', 'tree' – and to look them up in half-a-dozen comprehensive and reputable dictionaries. They will find many differences of detail, not only in the definitions that are offered, but also in the number of meanings that are recognized for each word. They will also find that some dictionaries, but not all, operate with a further level of differentiation, such that, not only is "X_1" distinguished from "X_2", "X_3", etc., but "X_{1a}" is distinguished from "X_{1b}", "X_{1c}", etc. and so on. At the very least, the experience of comparing a number of different dictionaries in this way should have the effect of making it clear that it is not as easy to say how many meanings a word has as casual reflection might initially suggest. It should also cast doubt upon the view that all dictionaries are equally authoritative and upon the alternative view that one particular dictionary (the *Oxford English Dictionary*, *Webster's*, etc.) is uniquely authoritative and unchallengeable. Indeed, it might even promote the suspicion that in many cases it is not just difficult in practice, but impossible even in principle, to say how many distinct meanings a word has. This suspicion, as we shall see, would be confirmed by further experience of the theory and practice of lexicography.

Something should now be said, briefly, about **homonyms**: different words with the same form (to use the traditional definition). Most dictionaries distinguish homonyms by assigning to them distinctive numbers (or letters) and giving to each of them a separate entry. We shall use numerical subscripts. For example, 'bank$_1$', one of whose meanings is "financial institution", and 'bank$_2$', one of whose meanings is "sloping side of a river", are generally regarded as homonyms (see Figure 1.1). The fact that they have been classified by the editor or compilers of a particular dictionary as homonyms – i.e., as separate words (and

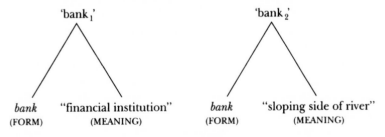

Figure 1.1

most dictionaries of English do so classify them) – is evident from the very fact that they have been given separate entries (whether or not they are also furnished with a distinctive number or letter). It is taken for granted that those who consult the dictionary will have some intuitive understanding of the traditional notion of homonymy, even if they do not know the traditional term for it: it is taken for granted, for example, that those consulting the dictionary will agree that 'bank$_1$' is a different word from 'bank$_2$' and know, intuitively, what it means to say that they are different words. As we shall see in Part 2, however, the traditional notion of homonymy is not as straightforward as it might appear to be at first sight and needs to be clarified. Although our more comprehensive discussion of homonymy may be postponed until then, it may be helpful to answer, in advance of that discussion, a question which will have occurred to some readers in relation to one or two of the examples that I have used in this section. If homonyms are words which have the same form but differ in meaning, why did I say that, for example, "terminal part of a leg" and "lowest part of a hill or mountain" are two different meanings of the same word, 'foot'? Should we not say as we did for 'bank$_1$' and 'bank$_2$' that two different words, 'foot$_1$' and 'foot$_2$', are involved?

Briefly, there are two reasons why 'bank$_1$' and 'bank$_2$' are traditionally regarded as homonyms. First of all, they differ **etymologically**: 'bank$_1$' was borrowed from Italian (cf. the Modern Italian 'banca') in the fifteenth century; 'bank$_2$' can be traced back through Middle English, and beyond, to a Scandinavian word (related ultimately to the German source of the Italian 'banca', but differing from it in its historical development). Second, they are judged to be **semantically unrelated**: there is assumed to be no connexion – more precisely, no synchronically discernible connexion – between the meanings of 'bank$_1$' and the meanings of 'bank$_2$'. The two (or more) meanings of 'foot', on the other hand, are etymologically and semantically related; and the order in which they are numbered and listed in a dictionary will generally reflect the editor's view of how closely one meaning is related to the other (or others), either historically or synchronically.

We shall be looking more closely later at the notion of related-ness of meaning, independently of the question of how (or indeed whether) the notion of homonymy has a role to play in modern linguistic semantics. For the moment, it is sufficient to note that, due allowance having been made for what is traditionally regarded as homonymy, we can usually identify one meaning of a word as being more central (or, alternatively, as being contex-tually more salient) than the others. This is the meaning that I expect the reader to have in mind whenever I refer to the mean-ing of a word (without further qualification) by means of the notational device of double quotation-marks introduced above. When necessary, one meaning can be distinguished from another with subscripts or by enclosing in double quotation-marks a paraphrase or (partial) definition that is sufficient for the purpose in hand. As we have seen, homonyms may be distin-guished from one another in the same way: for example, we may distinguish 'sole$_1$' from 'sole$_2$' (on the assumption that this is indeed a case of homonymy: readers' intuitions may well dif-fer) by saying that the former means (roughly) "bottom of foot or shoe" and the latter "kind of fish". It must be realized, how-ever, that symbolic notation of itself is no more than a tool, which, like other tools, needs to be used with care and the appro-priate skill. This point is worth making here in relation to the comparatively simple – almost trivial – task of regimenting the use of italics and quotation-marks for different kinds of meta-linguistic reference. It is far more important when it comes to the use of some of the more specialized notation that will be introduced in the following chapters.

As I said earlier, homonymy is not as readily determinable in many cases as may have been implied in this section with refer-ence to the examples 'bank$_1$' and 'bank$_2$', or 'sole$_1$' and 'sole$_2$'. It will be discussed in greater detail in Chapter 2. So too will the differences among the various senses in which the term 'word' is used both technically and in everyday discourse. Until then, the word 'word' will be employed loosely and, as we shall see presently, ambiguously (as it often is in everyday usage). Meanwhile, readers are advised to bear constantly in mind the importance of not confusing natural-language expressions, such as words, phrases or sentences, with their form (or any one of their forms). Careful attention to the notational conventions introduced above should help them to do this.

In conclusion, readers' attention is also drawn to the fact: (i) that (as was mentioned at the beginning of this section without discussion) that there may be a mismatch between the spoken and the written form (or forms) of words; and (ii) that there are different ways in which forms may be identical with one another or not. The use of the term 'form' (and even more so of its derivative 'formal') in linguistics is at times both confused and confusing (see Lyons, 1968: 135–7). For present purposes it is sufficient for me to explain briefly, with reference to (i) and (ii), how the various senses of the term 'form' are related to one another and can be distinguished if and when it is necessary to do so.

We started from the more or less everyday, non-technical, metalinguistic distinction between form and meaning, saying that words (and other expressions) have, not only form, but a form. We then saw that, in some instances and in some languages, words (and other expressions) may have more than one form, which, typically though not necessarily, differ from one another in grammatical function. Let us temporarily disregard the fact that words may have more than one grammatically (or inflectionally) distinct form: this is tantamount to assuming that we are (temporarily) concerned solely with isolating, or analytic, languages, such as Classical Chinese or Vietnamese.

Trading on the possibility of using the word 'form' both as a count noun and as a mass noun (as I have done in the preceding paragraph and throughout this section), we can now say that two forms are identical (in one sense of 'identical') if they have the same form. For example, two spoken forms will be phonetically identical if they have the same pronunciation; and two written forms (in a language written with an alphabetic script) will be orthographically identical if they have the same spelling. (Orthographic identity needs to be formulated somewhat differently for languages with a non-alphabetic script, but this does not affect the application to such languages of the notion of orthographic identity.) A further distinction can be drawn, as far as the spoken language is concerned, between phonetic and phonological identity. Students who are familiar with this distinction will see the implications of drawing it in particular instances; those who are not need not be troubled by it here. It is normally phonological identity that is at issue in linguistic semantics. But, for simplicity of exposition, I will not draw the distinction between phonetic and phonological identity at this point: I will talk simply about forms being phonetically identical or not (in this or that accent or dialect).

The fact that two (or more) written forms may be phonetically identical is readily illustrated from English (in many, if not all, dialects): cf. *soul* and *sole*, *great* and *grate*, or *red* and *read* (in one of its two different pronunciations). The fact that two or more phonetically different forms may be orthographically identical is also readily illustrated from English: cf. *read* (in *have read* vs *will read*), *blessed* (in *The bishop blessed the congregation* vs *Blessed are the peacemakers*). The kind of identity that has just been discussed and exemplified may be called **material identity**. As I have explained it here, it is dependent on the physical medium in which the form is realized. Extensions and refinements of the notion of material identity are possible, but the somewhat simplified account that I have given of it here will suffice for the deliberately restricted purposes of the present book.

Let us now bring into the discussion the fact that in many natural languages, including English, referred to technically as non-isolating, or (morphologically) synthetic languages, words may have two or more grammatically distinct forms: cf. *man* (singular, non-possessive), *man's* (singular, possessive), *men* (plural, non-possessive) and *men's* (plural, possessive). Typically, as with the four forms of 'man', the grammatically distinct – more specifically, the inflectionally distinct – forms of a word (or other expression) are materially different (non-identical). But material identity is neither a sufficient nor a necessary condition of the grammatical (and, more specifically, the inflectional) identity of forms. For example, the form *come* serves as one of the present-tense forms of 'come' (*they come*) and also as what is traditionally called its past-participle form (*they have come*). Is *come* the same form in both cases? The answer is: in one sense, yes; and, in another sense, no. The *come* of *they come* is the same as the *come* of *they have come* in the sense that it is materially identical with it (in both the spoken and the written language). But the *come* of *they come* and the *come* of *they have come* are different **inflectional forms** of the verb 'come'. Conversely, given that some speakers of what is otherwise the same variety of Standard English say (and write) *have learned* and that others say (and write) *have learnt* (and that yet others alternate between the two), the two materially different forms *learned* and *learnt* can be regarded as grammatically identical (or equivalent). To make the point more precisely: (in this variety of Standard English) the same grammatical – or, more specifically in this case, the same inflectional form – of the word 'learn' is realized by two materially different (phonetic and orthographic) forms.

What has just been said, in conclusion, about different kinds of identity will be helpful later. It should also reinforce the point made earlier about the importance of establishing a set of technical terms and notational conventions, whether by regimentation or extension, for the purpose of precise metalinguistic reference. Generally speaking, the sense in which I am using the term 'form' at various places in this book will be clear in context. Whenever this is not so, I will invoke the distinction that has been drawn here between forms considered from the point of view of their material composition and forms considered from the point of view of their grammatical function.

1.6 SENTENCES AND UTTERANCES; TEXT, CONVERSATION AND DISCOURSE

We have been assuming (and shall continue to assume) that all natural languages have words, which have both form and meaning (1.5). Let us now make explicit two further working assumptions: (i) that all natural languages also have sentences, which similarly have form and meaning; and (ii) that the meaning of a sentence is determined, at least partly, by the meanings of the words of which it is composed. Neither of these assumptions is controversial. Each of them, however, will need to be looked at carefully later. None of the general points which are made in the first few chapters will be seriously affected by any refinements or qualifications that are brought in subsequently.

The meaning of a sentence is determined not only by the meaning of the words of which it is composed, but also by its grammatical structure. This is clear from the fact that two sentences can be composed of exactly the same words (each word being interpreted in the same way) and yet differ in meaning. For example, the following two sentences, (22) and (23), contain the same words (in the same form) but differ grammatically. One is a declarative sentence and the other is the corresponding interrogative sentence, and the grammatical difference between them is matched with a corresponding difference of meaning:

(22) 'It was raining yesterday'

and

(23) 'Was it raining yesterday?'.

So too, do (24) and (25). In this case, however, the two sentences are both declarative, and they are not related to one another as corresponding members of two matched and grammatically definable classes of sentences:

(24) 'John admires Mary'

and

(25) 'Mary admires John'.

It will be noted that I am using single quotation-marks for sentences (even when they are numbered and displayed), as well as for words and other expressions with form and meaning. This is in accord with the notational convention introduced in the preceding section, which will be adhered to throughout this book. Whether sentences are expressions in the same sense that words and phrases are expressions is a question that we need not be concerned with in Parts 1 and 2 of this book.

For simplicity of exposition, I am making the distinction between **word-meaning** (or, to be more precise, **lexical meaning**) and **sentence-meaning** one of the main organizing principles of this book, dealing with the former in Part 2 and the latter in Part 3. It must be emphasized however that this method of organizing the material carries with it no implication whatsoever about the logical or methodological priority of lexical meaning over sentence-meaning. There is no point in addressing the question of the priority of the one over the other until we have built up rather more of the theoretical and terminological framework. And when we have done so, we shall see that, like many such apparently straightforward questions, it does not admit of a simple, straightforward, answer.

The distinction between sentence-meaning and **utterance-meaning** provides us with a further organizing principle. This distinction cannot be taken for granted in the way that the one between word-meaning and sentence-meaning can. Not only is it less familiar to non-specialists. It is also the subject of a good deal of controversy among specialists. Most of the details may be left for Part 4. But a few general points must be made here.

In everyday English, the word 'utterance' is generally used to refer to spoken language (as also are the words 'discourse' and 'conversation'). The word 'text', in contrast, is generally used to refer to written language. Throughout this book, both 'utterance' and 'text' will be used neutrally with respect to the difference between spoken and written language.

It would have been possible to extend our metalanguage, at this point, by introducing a whole set of specialized **medium-neutral** terms. A certain number of such terms will be introduced in later chapters. Meanwhile, however, we shall use such ordinary-language terms as 'speaker' and 'hearer', as well as 'utterance', 'text' and 'discourse' in a medium-neutral sense.

But language must not be confused with speech. Indeed, one of the most striking properties of natural languages is their relative independence of the **medium** in which they are realized. Language is still language, whether it is realized as the product of speech or of writing and, if it is the product of writing, regardless of whether it is written in the normal alphabet or in braille, morse-code, etc. The degree of correspondence between written and spoken language varies somewhat, for historical and cultural reasons, from one language to another. But in English, and in other languages that are associated with an alphabetic writing-system, most, if not all, sentences of the spoken language can be put into correspondence with written sentences. The fact that this is not a one-to-one correspondence will occupy us later.

Nothing further needs to be said, at this point, about text, discourse and conversation. Indeed, I shall have nothing to say about them until we get to Chapter 9. In the meantime we can think of utterances as minimal (spoken or written) texts and of discourses and conversations as sequences of (one or more) utterances.

But, as we have seen, the terms 'utterance', 'discourse' and 'conversation' (unlike 'text') have both a process-sense and a product-sense: in their process-sense, they denote a particular kind of behaviour, or activity; in their product-sense, they denote, not the activity itself, but the physical product or products of that activity (1.4). Obviously, the two senses are related; but the nature of the relation is not self-evident, and it will be discussed in Part 4.

Meanwhile, we will establish the terminological convention that, whenever the term 'utterance' is used in this book without further qualification and in contexts in which the process-sense is excluded for syntactic reasons, it is to be interpreted as denoting the product or products of what in Chomskyan terminology may be referred to as performance. Utterances, in this sense of the term, are what some philosophers of language have called **inscriptions**: i.e., sequences of symbols inscribed in some physical medium. For example, a spoken utterance is normally inscribed (in this technical sense of 'inscribed') in the medium of sound; a written utterance is inscribed in some other suitable medium which makes it visually identifiable. In so far as languages are used, typically if not necessarily, for communication, utterances may be regarded as **signals** which are transmitted from speaker to hearer – more generally, from a sender to a receiver – along some appropriate **channel**. Utterances (i.e., utterance-inscriptions or utterance-signals) will be distinguished notationally from sentences (as the forms of a word are distinguished from the word itself) by using italics for the former and single quotation-marks for the latter. This implies that utterances are forms; and this is the view of utterances (in the sense

of inscriptions) that is taken throughout this book. As we shall
see in Part 4, a case can also be made for the view that they may
in many instances be regarded as the context-dependent forms
of particular sentences. But at this stage we do not need to take
one view rather than another on the controversial issue of the
relation between utterances and sentences.

Natural-language utterances, it must be emphasized, are not
just sequences, or **strings**, of word-forms. As we have already
seen, superimposed upon the **verbal component** of any spoken
utterances (the string of words of which it is composed), there is
always and necessarily a **non-verbal component**, which linguists further subdivide into a **prosodic** subcomponent and
paralinguistic subcomponent (1.3). Just where the line should
be drawn between these two subcomponents need not concern
us here. Let us merely note that the prosodic contour of an utterance includes its intonation, and perhaps also its stress-pattern;
and that paralinguistic features include such things as tone of
voice, loudness, rhythm, tempo, etc. These non-verbal features
of an utterance are just as relevant to the determination of the
meaning of the utterance as are the meanings of the words it contains and its grammatical meaning, both of which are **encoded**
in the verbal component.

It is only the verbal component of a spoken utterance that is
independent of the medium in which it is realized and is
medium-transferable, in that it can, in principle, be held constant under the conversion of speech to writing. As we have
noted already, some writing systems do include more or less
conventionalized principles for the punctuation of written
utterances. But these never match significant differences of
intonation in the spoken language. Even when the normal
conventions of punctuation are supplemented with such typographical devices as the use of capitals, italics, bold print,
accent-marks, etc., there may be some part of the **prosodic
contour** of an utterance that is left unrepresented.

This is an important point. Almost every written utterance
cited in this and other books on language can be put into
correspondence with significantly different spoken utterances.
The written utterance *Mary won't come*, for example, can be

pronounced, or read aloud, in several different ways, indicative of boredom, surprise, certainty, etc. I will try to choose my examples so that, with sufficient explanation at the time, it does not matter, for the particular issue that is under discussion, which of several significantly different spoken utterances is chosen by the reader.

I am taking for granted, for the time being, the reader's ability to identify the sentences of any language in which he or she is competent: i.e., to distinguish them from other combinations of words that are not sentences. I will now make the further assumption that some non-sentences are not sentences because they are grammatically incorrect and others because they are grammatically incomplete, or elliptical; and that, once again, those who are competent in the language, whether they are native speakers or not, can identify these two subclasses of non-sentences. As we shall see later, many everyday utterances are grammatically incomplete, but, in context, both acceptable and interpretable. On the other hand, there are sentences which, though fully grammatical, for one reason or another cannot normally be uttered: the difference between grammaticality and acceptability (including semantic acceptability) is critically important in linguistic semantics and will be dealt with in Part 2 (5.2).

Throughout Parts 2 and 3 of this book we shall be restricting our attention to utterances whose relation to sentences is relatively straightforward. We shall leave for Part 4 the task of specifying in some detail what exactly is meant by the expression 'to utter a sentence' and explaining how it can be extended to cover grammatically correct, but incomplete, utterances, which constitute a particular subclass of non-sentences. As I have already said, most everyday utterances may well fall into this subclass of non-sentences.

The difference between sentence-meaning and utterance-meaning will be dealt with in Part 4. At this stage it will be sufficient to make two general points. First, sentence-meaning is (to a high degree) **context-independent**, whereas utterance-meaning is not: that is to say, the meaning of an utterance is (to a greater or less degree) determined by the context in which it is uttered. Second, there is an intrinsic connexion between the meaning of a sentence and the **characteristic use**, not of the particular sentence as such, but of the whole class of sentences to which the sentence belongs by virtue of its grammatical structure This connexion may be formulated, for one class of sentences, as follows: a **declarative** sentence is one that belongs, by virtue of its grammatical structure, to the class of sentences whose members are used, characteristically, to make **statements**, as in

(26) 'Exercise is good for you'

or

(27) 'I prefer mine with ice'.

Similarly for another class of sentences, which is distinguished from declaratives in English and in many languages: an **interrogative** sentence is one that belongs, by virtue of its grammatical structure, to the class of sentences whose members are used characteristically to ask **questions**, as in

(28) 'What time is lunch?';

and so on. When I said earlier of the sentences (22) 'It was raining yesterday' and (23) 'Was it raining yesterday?' that their meaning was determined, in part, by their grammatical structure, I was tacitly appealing to the reader's knowledge of the characteristic use of declarative and interrogative sentences. It is of course the recognition of this as their characteristic use which accounts for the traditional terms 'declarative' and 'interrogative'. Much traditional grammatical terminology similarly reveals assumptions, whether correct or incorrect, about the characteristic use of particular grammatical categories and constructions.

It should be noted that the notion of characteristic use (which is also intrinsically connected with the notion of literal meaning) has been associated here with classes of sentences, rather than with each and every member of a particular class. This is important, even though some sentences are never, or very rarely, used in normal circumstances with the function that characterizes the grammatically defined class to which they belong; and, as we shall see later, all sentences can be used occasionally in the performance of what have come to be called **indirect speech acts** (declarative sentences being used to ask questions, interrogative sentences to issue requests, etc.). However, it is obviously impossible that most declarative sentences should normally be used to ask questions, most interrogative sentences to make statements, and so on. For declarative and interrogative sentences are, by definition, sentences with the characteristic use that is here ascribed to them. If a language does not have a grammatically distinct class of sentences with one or other of these characteristic uses, then it does not have either declarative or interrogative sentences, as the case may be.

It must not be thought that all languages have the same grammatical structure. As we shall see later, there are many natural languages which do not have interrogative or declarative sentences. This does not mean, of course, that it is impossible to ask questions or to make statements in those languages. Questions might be distinguished from statements, as utterances, by superimposing upon the same string of words a distinctive prosodic or paralinguistic contour in speech and distinctive punctuation-marks or diacritics in writing. For example, (29) – the product of the utterance of sentence (26) – may be uttered in the spoken language with a particular intonation-pattern which marks the utterance as a question (indicative perhaps also of surprise or indignation, etc.) and in the written language with a question-mark:

(29)   *Exercise is good for you?*

But exactly the same sentence can be uttered with a different intonation pattern in the spoken language or differently punctuated in the written language (e.g., with a full stop, or period, rather than a question-mark) in order to make a statement.

Sentence-meaning, then, is related to utterance-meaning by virtue of the notion of characteristic use, but it differs from it in that the meaning of a sentence is independent of the particular context in which it may be uttered. To determine the meaning of an utterance, on the other hand, we have to take contextual factors into account. This point will be developed in greater detail later. But what has been said here will do for the purpose of organizing the content of this book between Parts 3 and 4. Meanwhile, the notational distinctions we have adopted will enable us to keep distinct sentences and utterances and to distinguish the meaning of the sentence itself from the meaning of an utterance which results from the use of that sentence in particular contexts.

1.7 THEORIES OF MEANING AND KINDS OF MEANING

There are several distinguishable, and more or less well-known philosophical, theories of meaning: theories which seek to provide an answer to the question *What is meaning?* Among them, one might mention the following:

(i)   the **referential** (or **denotational**) theory ("the meaning of an expression is what it refers to (or denotes), or stands for"; e.g., 'Fido' means Fido, 'dog' means either the general class of dogs or the essential property which they all share);

(ii) the **ideational**, or **mentalistic**, theory ("the meaning of an expression is the idea, or concept, associated with it in the mind of anyone who knows and understands the expression");

(iii) the **behaviourist** theory ("the meaning of an expression is either the stimulus that evokes it or the response that it evokes, or a combination of both, on particular occasions of utterance");

(iv) the **meaning-is-use** theory ("the meaning of an expression is determined by, if not identical with, its use in the language");

(v)   the **verificationist** theory ("the meaning of an expression, if it has one, is determined by the verifiability of the sentences, or propositions, containing it");

(vi) the **truth-conditional** theory ("the meaning of an expression is its contribution to the truth-conditions of the sentences containing it").

None of these, in my view, will serve alone as the basis for a comprehensive and empirically well-motivated theory of linguistic semantics. But each of them has contributed in one way or another to the background assumptions of those who are currently working towards the construction of such a theory. I will not go into the details of any of those theories of meaning listed above. However, I will make reference to some of the key-concepts which distinguish them in the course of the chapters that follow, and I will explain these concepts in the context in which they are invoked and applied. Limitations of space will prevent me from discussing the historical connexions among the several theories or the philosophical issues associated with them. I should add that the list I have given is by no means complete and that the definitions in brackets have in certain cases been deliberately simplified.

It is now worth noting that one philosophically defensible response to the question *What is meaning?* is *There is no such thing as meaning*. This was the response, for example, of the later Wittgenstein (1953); and it has to be taken seriously. It clearly makes sense to enquire about the meaning of words, sentences and utterances, just as it makes sense to ask what they mean. In doing so, we are using the English words 'meaning' and 'mean' in one of their everyday metalinguistic functions. As we saw earlier, there are also other everyday meanings, or uses, of the noun 'meaning' and the verb 'mean'; and some philosophers at least have held these to be intimately connected with and perhaps more basic than the one that has just been exemplified. Interestingly enough they cannot always be matched one-to-one with the meanings or uses of otherwise comparable expressions in such familiar European languages as French, German, Italian, Russian or Spanish. For example, the following two English sentences,

(30) 'What is the meaning of 'concept'?'

and

(31) 'What do you mean by the word 'concept'?',

might be translated into French as

(30a) 'Quel est le sens de 'concept' [en anglais]?'

and

(31a) 'Qu'est-ce que tu veux dire par le mot [anglais] 'concept'?'

(and comparably into Italian and Spanish), respectively; into German as

(30b) 'Was ist die Bedeutung von 'concept' [auf Englisch]?'

and

(31b) 'Was meinst du mit dem [englischen] Wort 'concept'?';

into Russian as

(30c) 'Čto znacit [anglijskije slovo] 'concept'?'

and

(31c) 'Čto vy podrazumyvaete pod [anglijskym] slovom 'concept'?';

and so on.

In supplying these translations I have not translated the English word 'concept', because I have assumed that French, German and Russian are being used metalinguistically with reference to English. There are, of course, other possibilities, especially in the case of (31a–c). In fact, there is a whole range of possibilities, as anyone who has any practical experience of translation will be aware. But we need not go into these in the present context. What these examples show, on the basis of translation into just a few other languages, is that, in each case, the second of the two translated examples, (31a–c), uses an expression which reveals, at least etymologically, a sense of the English verb 'to mean' – **utterer's meaning**, as it is sometimes called – which relates it either to communicative intention (French 'vouloir dire', German 'meinen') or to understanding and interpretation (Russian 'podrazumevatj'). There are those who have seen utterer's meaning as being, ultimately, the basis for linguistic meaning.

For the present, however, I am concerned to make the simple point that we cannot infer the existence of meaning or meanings from the existence and meaningfulness of the everyday English word 'meaning'. Moreover, even if there is such a thing as meaning (whatever 'thing' means in this context), its onto-logical and psychological status is surely more questionable than that of form. We shall come back to this point.

It was part of the later Wittgenstein's purpose to emphasize the diversity of the communicative functions fulfilled by language. His slogan "Don't look for the meaning, look for the use" (which does not necessarily lead to the meaning-is-use theory, though it is commonly so interpreted) must be under-stood with reference to this purpose. Like the so-called ordinary-language Oxford philosophers, such as J. L. Austin (whose theory of **speech acts** we shall be looking at in Part 4), he pointed out that the question *What is meaning?* tends to attract answers which are either so general as to be almost vac-uous or so narrow in their definition of meaning as to leave out of account much of what ordinary users of a language think is relevant when one puts to them more specific questions about the meaning of this or that expression in their language.

In this book we are taking a fairly broad view of meaning. We are also assuming that there is an intrinsic connexion between meaning and communication. As was noted earlier, this assump-tion is not uncontroversial. It has been strongly challenged, for example, by Chomsky, but it is one that is commonly made by philosophers, psychologists and linguists. It enables us to give a better account of the relation between form and meaning in nat-ural languages than does any currently available alternative. And I would emphasize that, although I have referred here to various philosophical theories of meaning and shall draw freely upon them throughout, I am not concerned with philosophical issues as such but with the theoretical and practical problems that arise in the description of natural languages.

So far we have been talking, in a preliminary way, about the meaning of words, sentences and utterances. We have also seen that there are distinguishable senses of the English word 'mean-ing' which may well correspond to different, but related, kinds of meaning. But how many kinds of meaning are there? Are they all of concern to the linguist? And how do they correlate with the distinction we have drawn between lexical meaning and sentence-meaning (including, as we shall see, grammatical meaning), on the one hand, and between sentence-meaning and utterance-meaning, on the other?

In this book, I will make no attempt to provide a comprehensive classification of the different kinds of meaning that a linguistic theory of semantics (and pragmatics) should cover. However, it might be helpful to draw even now one very broad distinction which can be developed in more detail later. This is the distinction between **descriptive** (or **propositional**) and **non-descriptive** (or **non-propositional**) **meaning**. (Alternative terms, more or less equivalent with 'descriptive' and 'propositional', are 'cognitive' and 'referential'.) With regard to descriptive meaning, it is a universally acknowledged fact that languages can be used to make descriptive statements which are true or false according to whether the **propositions** that they express are true or false. This fact is given particular prominence in the truth-conditional theory of semantics, which has been extremely important in recent years.

Non-descriptive meaning is more heterogeneous and, in the view of many philosophers and linguists, less central. It includes what I will refer to as an **expressive** component. (Alternative more or less equivalent terms are 'affective', 'attitudinal' and 'emotive'.) Expressive meaning – i.e., the kind of meaning by virtue of which speakers express, rather than describe, their beliefs, attitudes and feelings – is often held to fall within the scope of stylistics or pragmatics. It will be demonstrated in Part 3, however, that some kinds of expressive meaning are unquestionably a part of sentence-meaning. It follows from this fact that for anyone who draws the distinction between semantics and pragmatics in terms of the distinction between sentences and utterances, expressive meaning falls, at least in part, within semantics. It also follows, as we shall see in due course, that sentence-meaning is not wholly truth-conditional.

Natural languages vary considerably in the degree to which they grammaticalize expressive meaning. English does so to a relatively low degree. For example, it does not have a rich system of grammatical moods (subjunctive, optative, dubitative, etc.) as many languages do. Like all natural languages, however, it encodes expressive meaning in much of its vocabulary and in the prosodic structure of spoken utterances. We are, of course, taking the view (which, as I have noted, is not widely shared) that the meaning of sentences (in contrast with the meaning of utterances) is independent of the prosodic contour with which they are uttered: i.e., that the same sentence can be uttered with various, significantly different, prosodic contours. It can also be argued that exclamatory and contextualizing particles of the kind that one finds in many languages, are not constituents of the sentence, but of utterances which result from the use of the sentence. But expressive meaning is also lexicalized in combination with descriptive meaning, as we shall see, in many ordinary nouns, verbs and adjectives.

Other kinds of non-propositional meaning may be left until later. It is worth emphasizing, however, that the expressive functions of language cannot be sharply differentiated from their social and instrumental functions. Human beings are social beings with socially prescribed and socially sanctioned purposes. They may not always be consciously projecting one kind of self-image rather than another; they may not be deliberately expressing the feelings and attitudes that they do express in order to manipulate the hearer and achieve one goal rather than another. Nevertheless, it is impossible for them to express their feelings and attitudes in language, however personal and spontaneous these attitudes and feelings might be, otherwise than in terms of the distinctions that are encoded in particular language-systems. As we shall see throughout this book, but more especially in Part 4, expressive meaning necessarily merges with what many authors have referred to as **interpersonal**, **instrumental**, **social** or **conative**, **meaning**. In other words, as far as the structure and function of natural languages are concerned, the expressive is necessarily **socio-expressive** and the personal is necessarily **interpersonal**. Unless this fact is appreciated, it would seem to be impossible to give a proper semantic account of even such common, though not universal, grammatical categories as tense, pronouns or mood.

PART 2

Lexical meaning

CHAPTER 2

Words as meaningful units

2.0 INTRODUCTION

As we saw in the preceding chapter, it is generally agreed that the words, phrases and sentences of natural languages have meaning, that sentences are composed of words (and phrases), and that the meaning of a sentence is the product of the words (and phrases) of which it is composed.

But what is a word? And do all natural languages, in fact, have words? These questions are not as easy to answer as they might appear to be at first sight. One reason is that the term 'word' is ambiguous, both in everyday usage and also as it is employed technically by linguists. Words may be considered purely as **forms**, whether spoken or written, or, alternatively, as composite **expressions**, which combine form and meaning. To complicate matters further, the term 'form' is employed in several different, though related, senses in linguistics. One of my principal aims in this chapter is to sort out these different senses of 'word' and 'form' and to establish notational and terminological conventions for avoiding ambiguity and confusion.

Another reason why it is not as easy to say whether something is or is not a word as non-linguists might think – or to say whether all natural languages have words – is that several different criteria come into play in the definition of words, both as forms and as expressions, and these criteria are often in conflict. Moreover, some of the criteria employed by linguists, taken separately, are such that they do not sharply divide words from non-words.

In this book, we are concerned primarily with words as expressions: i.e., as composite units that have both form and meaning (more precisely, as we shall see, as units which have, typically, a set of forms and a set of meanings). Whenever the term 'word' is used without further qualification, this is the sense in which it is to be understood. In fact, as will be explained in this chapter, the term 'word' will generally be used throughout this book, and especially in Part 2, to refer to what may be called, non-technically, dictionary-words (or vocabulary-words): i.e., in the sense in which it is used in the everyday metalanguage when one says, for example, that a comprehensive dictionary of a given language contains, in the ideal, all the words in the vocabulary of that language. In this sense of 'word', all languages do have words.

The technical term that we shall be using for what I have just called dictionary-words is 'lexeme'. The noun 'lexeme' is of course related to the words 'lexical' and 'lexicon'. (We can think of 'lexicon' as having the same meaning as 'vocabulary' or 'dictionary'.) A lexeme is a lexical unit: a unit of the lexicon. The lexical structure of a language is the structure of its lexicon, or vocabulary; and the term 'lexical meaning', which has been used as the title of Part 2, is therefore equivalent to the commonly used, less technical (but ambiguous), term 'word-meaning'. The reasons for extending our metalanguage by introducing the more technical terms 'lexeme' and 'lexical meaning' (in accordance with the principles outlined in section 1.2) will be explained in this chapter. As we shall see, not all words are lexemes and, conversely, not all lexemes are words. We shall also see that, far from being novel or paradoxical, this is something which anyone who consults a conventional dictionary simply takes for granted, without necessarily reflecting upon its implications for semantic (and grammatical) theory.

When we look at words (and phrases) as meaningful units we also have to deal with the fact that, on the one hand, a single form may be combined with several meanings and, on the other, the same meaning may be combined with several word-forms. This fact is well recognized in traditional grammar and lexicography and will be discussed here from a fairly traditional point of view, in terms of the concepts of **homonymy**, **poly-semy** and **synonymy**.

Finally, as far as this chapter is concerned, we shall look at the distinction between lexical and grammatical meaning, which derives from the distinction that is traditionally drawn between the vocabulary of a language and its grammar. The way in which this distinction is developed and formalized will vary according to the particular theoretical framework within which it is elaborated. There will be a major difference, for example, between formulations of the distinctions that operate with a morpheme-based grammar and those that operate with the more traditional word-based grammar (which we are using). But at the relatively elementary level at which we are discussing the question in this book, nothing is seriously affected by the differences between these two different models, or theories, of grammatical structure; and it would be a useful exercise for students who have a sufficient background in grammatical theory, traditional and modern, to check that this is so and to reformulate what I have to say about form and meaning with reference to morphemes (and combinations of morphemes), rather than words.

As to the effect of adopting a model of linguistic analysis which draws the distinction between the vocabulary (or lexicon) and the grammar at a different place from the place at which it is drawn in traditional grammar and lexicography, this too is relatively unimportant in the context of the present book. Adjustments can easily be made by those who are familiar with current developments in grammatical theory. The really important point is that, however one draws the distinction between grammar and vocabulary, in general linguistic theory and in the description of particular languages, the two must be seen as complementary and interdependent. That this is so will be made clear as we move from Part 2 to Part 3.

2.1 FORMS AND EXPRESSIONS

One of the assumptions that was made explicit in Chapter 1 was that the meaning of a sentence depends, in part, upon the meaning of the words of which it is composed (1.6). This assumption now needs to be considered more carefully. We have already noted that the word 'word' is ambiguous: that words may be considered either as forms or as expressions (1.5). Let us begin then by asking in what sense of 'word' it is true to say that sentences are composed of words.

There are, in fact, two quite different distinctions to be taken into account, as we address this question. It is important not to confuse the one with the other. The first is what the American philosopher C. S. Peirce (1839-1914) referred to as the distinction between words as **tokens** and words as **types**. This is readily explained by means of a simple example. Consider the following sentence:

(1) 'He who laughs last laughs longest'.

From one point of view, it can be said to contain six words: it is six words long. From another point of view, however, it can be said to contain only five words, since two of the words – the third and the fifth (*laughs*) – are identical: they are different tokens (or **instances**) of the same type. Put like this, the notion of type/token identity is not difficult to grasp. And, generally speaking, it is clear enough in everyday life when the term 'word' is to be understood in the one sense rather than the other with respect to Peirce's distinction.

There is, however, a second distinction to be taken into account, which is more relevant to our present concerns. This distinction too may be explained by means of a simple example. How many words are there in the following sentence:

(2) 'If he is right and I am wrong, we are both in trouble'?

Once again, there are two correct answers to the question. But the fact that this is so has nothing to do with the type/token distinction (although it is sometimes confused with it in general works on semantics). It rests upon the difference between words as **forms** and words as **expressions**. There are thirteen forms in the sentence in question, and each of them **instantiates** (is an instance, or token, of) a different type. From this point of view, however, three of the words – *is*, *am*,

and *are* – would traditionally be regarded as different forms of
the same word. In one sense of 'word', therefore, sentence (2) is
composed of thirteen words; in another, equally common and
equally correct, sense of the term, it is composed of only eleven
words. Let us express this difference in the meaning of 'word' by
saying that the sentence is composed of thirteen **word-forms**
and eleven **word-expressions**. It is word-expressions, not
word-forms, that are listed and defined in a conventional dictionary. And they are listed, as we saw in Chapter 1, according to an
alphabetic ordering of their **citation-forms**: i.e., what are commonly referred to as the **headwords** of dictionary entries (1.5).

In order to assign a meaning to the word-forms of which a sentence is composed, we must be able to identify them, not merely
as tokens, or instances, of particular types, but as forms of particular expressions. And tokens of the same type are not necessarily forms of the same expression. For example, in the sentence

(3) 'They have found it impossible to found hospitals or chari-
    table institutions of any kind without breaking the law',

the third and seventh word-tokens (*found*) are tokens of the same
type, but not forms of the same expression.

It is the distinction between forms and expressions, rather
than the distinction between forms as tokens and forms as types,
which I had in mind when I drew attention to the ambiguity of
the word 'word'. As I have already mentioned, whenever it is
used without further qualification, 'word' will mean "word-
expression", rather than "word-form", throughout the present
work.

Not all the expressions listed in a dictionary, however, are
words. Some of them are what are traditionally called **phrases**;
and phrasal expressions, like word-expressions, must be distinguished in principle from the form or forms with which they are
put into correspondence by the inflectional rules of the language.
For example, 'pass muster' is a phrasal expression, whose forms
are *pass muster, passes muster, passed muster*, etc. It is tokens of these
forms that occur in utterances of the language.

The expressions of a language fall into two sets. One set,
finite in number, is made up of **lexically simple** expressions:

lexemes. These are the expressions that one would expect to find listed in a dictionary: they are the vocabulary-units of a language, out of which the members of the second set, **lexically composite** expressions, are constructed by means of the grammatical (i.e., syntactic and morphological) rules of the language. In terms of this distinction, 'pass muster' is a lexeme, whereas 'pass the examination' is lexically composite. Most word-expressions, in all languages that have words, are lexically simple. However, in many languages, there are productive (**derivational**) rules for what is traditionally called **word-formation**, which enable their users to construct new word-expressions out of pre-existing lexically simpler expressions. For example, 'politeness' is constructed from the lexically simpler expression, 'polite', by means of a productive rule of English word-formation. Although many conventional dictionaries do in fact list 'politeness' as a vocabulary-unit (i.e., provide for it a separate entry with its own headword and definition), it is unnecessary to do so, since both its meaning and its grammatical properties (as well as its pronunciation) are fully predictable by rule.

Most phrasal expressions, in contrast with word-expressions, are lexically composite. Indeed, all natural languages would appear to contain rules for the construction of an infinite number of lexically composite phrasal expressions. And, as we shall see later, it is an important principle of modern formal semantics that the meaning of all such lexically composite expressions should be systematically determinable on the basis of the meaning of the simpler expressions of which they are composed. Lexically simple phrasal expressions (i.e., phrasal lexemes) include, not only such examples as 'pass muster' mentioned above (which has no corresponding lexically composite homonym formed by productive rules of the language), but also idiomatic phrasal lexemes such as 'red herring', which is formally identical with the lexically composite phrase 'red herring' (formed by the productive rules of the language) meaning "herring which is red". The meaning of the lexically simple, idiomatic, phrase (let us call it 'red herring$_1$'), like that of 'pass muster', but unlike that of the lexically composite, non-idiomatic, phrases 'red herring$_2$'

and 'pass the examination', is not systematically determinable (by rule) from the meaning of its constituent lexemes.

The distinction that has just been drawn between lexically simple expressions (lexemes) and lexically composite expressions is not as straightforward, in practice, as I have made it appear. Just where the distinction is drawn will depend upon the model or theory of grammar with which the linguist is operating. But at whatever point the distinction is drawn between the grammar of a language and its vocabulary (or lexicon), there will always be borderline cases of expressions which can be classified, with equal justification, as lexically simple or lexically composite. But some such distinction is, and must be, drawn in the grammatical and semantic analysis of natural languages.

It is lexemes and lexical meaning that will be at the centre of our attention in this and the next two chapters. But forms, in so far as they are forms of particular lexemes, are also of concern to the semanticist. Different forms of the same lexeme will generally, though not necessarily, differ in meaning: they will share the same **lexical meaning**, but differ in respect of their **grammatical meaning**. For example, the forms *girl* and *girls* have the same lexical meaning (or meanings); but they differ in respect of their grammatical meaning, in that one is the singular form (of a noun of a particular subclass) and the other is the plural form (of a noun of a particular subclass); and the difference between singular forms and plural forms, or – to take another example – the difference between the past, present and future forms of verbs, is semantically relevant: it affects sentence-meaning. The meaning of a sentence, it will be recalled, is determined partly by the meaning of the words (i.e., lexemes) of which it is composed and partly by its grammatical meaning.

As we shall see in Part 3, the relation between lexical and grammatical meaning varies from language to language: what is encoded lexically (**lexicalized**) in one language may be encoded grammatically (**grammaticalized**) in another. The grammaticalization of meaning, as we shall also see later, is not simply, or primarily, a matter of inflection (even in languages which, unlike English, have a very rich inflectional system). Far more important are the **syntactic** differences between one grammatical construction and another.

At this point, however, it may be noted that, when word-forms are considered, not just as forms, but as forms invested with grammatical meaning, yet another sense both of 'form' and of 'word' comes to light. Consider, for example, the following sentences:

(4) 'That sheep over there belongs to the farmer next door'
(5) 'Those sheep over there belong to the farmer next door'.

Is the second word-form of (4) the same as the second word-form of (5)? The distinction that we have drawn between forms and expressions does not, of itself, suffice to answer the question in a case like this. Let us grant immediately that the two word-forms are identical in respect both of their phonological form (in the spoken language) and of their orthographic form (in the written language): they are **formally identical**. But they are not **grammatically identical**. Whether we say that the second word-form of (4) is the same as the second word-form of (5) depends, therefore, on whether, in putting this question, we are concerned with formal identity alone – phonological or orthographic, as the case may be – or with both formal and grammatical identity. The two word-forms that occur in the second position of (4) and (5) are formally identical, but grammatically distinct, forms of the same lexeme. More precisely, they are inflectionally, or **morphosyntactically**, distinct forms of the same lexeme. The way in which this phenomenon is handled by grammarians will differ according to the model of grammar which they adopt.

What has been said in this section about Peirce's type/token distinction, about the different senses in which 'word' is used both technically and non-technically in linguistics, about the distinction between forms and expressions and about lexical and grammatical meaning is sufficient for the time being. It may seem at first sight that, in this section, I have been unnecessarily pedantic in my regimentation and extension of the everyday metalanguage. This is not so. Whatever terms we use to draw the distinctions that have been drawn here, the distinctions themselves must be drawn if we are to avoid the confusion and equivocation which is almost inevitably associated with what I referred to in the Preface as the pseudo-simplicity of so-called plain English.

All the points that I have made could be developed at great length, and would need to be, in a fuller account of what is commonly, but imprecisely, referred to as word-meaning. They would also need to be formulated somewhat differently in relation to particular theories of phonology, syntax and morphology. I have deliberately adopted a rather traditional view of the grammatical and lexical structure of languages. There are two reasons why I have done this. The first is that this view is the one that is reflected in the most widely used authoritative dictionaries and reference grammars of English and other languages and is also the view that is taught or taken for granted in most schools: it may therefore be assumed to be a view which is familiar to most readers of this book (even if they are not in command of all the technical terminology). The second reason is that, although various refinements and qualifications have to be made to this traditional view in the light of developments in modern grammatical theory, so-called traditional grammar (with the necessary refinements and qualifications to which I have referred) serves better than any alternative so far available as an established standard system into which and out of which other competing systems can be translated. Students who have already had some training in modern grammatical theory will find it instructive to carry out this exercise in translation from one metalanguage to another as we proceed through this and the following chapters.

2.2 HOMONYMY AND POLYSEMY; LEXICAL AND GRAMMATICAL AMBIGUITY

What is traditionally described as **homonymy** was illustrated in Chapter 1 by means of the no less traditional examples of 'bank$_1$' and 'bank$_2$', the former meaning "financial institution" and the latter "sloping side of a river". The examples are appropriate enough. But the traditional definition of homonymy is, to say the least, imprecise.

Homonyms are traditionally defined as different words with the same form. We can immediately improve this definition, in the light of what was said in the preceding section, by substituting 'lexeme' for 'word'. But the definition is still defective in that it fails to take account of the fact that, in many languages, most lexemes have not one, but several, forms. Also, it says nothing about grammatical equivalence.

Let us begin, therefore, by establishing a notion of **absolute homonymy**. Absolute homonyms will satisfy the following three conditions (in addition to the necessary minimal condition for all kinds of homonymy – identity of at least one form):

(i)   they will be unrelated in meaning;
(ii) all their forms will be identical;
(iii) the identical forms will be grammatically equivalent.

Absolute homonymy is common enough: cf. 'bank$_1$', 'bank$_2$'; 'sole$_1$' ("bottom of foot or shoe"), 'sole$_2$' ("kind of fish"); etc.

But there are also many different kinds of what I will call **partial homonymy**: i.e., cases where (a) there is identity of (minimally) one form and (b) one or two, but not all three, of the above conditions are satisfied. For example, the verbs 'find' and 'found' share the form *found*, but not *finds, finding*, or *founds, founding*, etc.; and *found* as a form of 'find' is not grammatically equivalent to *found* as a form of 'found'. In this case, as generally in English, the failure to satisfy (ii) correlates with the failure to satisfy (iii). However, it is important to realize that the last two conditions of absolute homonymy made explicit in the previous paragraph are logically independent. They are usually taken for granted without discussion in traditional accounts of the topic.

It is particularly important to note the condition of grammatical equivalence, and the fact that this is a matter of degree. Although *found* as a form of 'find' is not grammatically equivalent to *found* as a form of 'found', it is in both cases a transitive-verb form. Consequently, there are certain contexts in which

found may be construed, grammatically, either as a form of
'found' or as form of 'find'. For example (see (3) in section 2.1):

(6)   *They found hospitals and charitable institutions*

can be construed as a present-tense sentence containing a form of
the verb 'found' or, alternatively, as a past-tense utterance containing a form of 'find'. The fact that 'found' and 'find' are transitive verbs – and to this degree (though not fully)
grammatically equivalent – means that they can both take a
noun-phrase such as 'hospitals and charitable institutions' as
their direct object. And since 'hospitals and charitable institutions' is, not only grammatically, but also semantically, acceptable as the direct object of both verbs, (6) is ambiguous.

The ambiguity of (6) is partly lexical and partly grammatical.
It is lexically ambiguous in so far as its ambiguity depends upon
a difference in the lexical meaning of the two partially homon-
ymous lexemes 'found' and 'find'. It is grammatically ambiguous in so far as its ambiguity depends upon the (semantically
relevant) grammatical non-equivalence of *found* construed as a
form of 'found' and of *found* construed as a form of 'find'.

The reason why it is important for the semanticist to take note
of grammatical equivalence, is that in general, it is this which
determines whether homonymy (absolute or partial as the case
may be) results in ambiguity. If *have* is inserted before *found* in
(6), to yield

(7)   *They have found hospitals and charitable institutions,*

the ambiguity disappears. The effect of putting the form *have*
before the form *found* is to change the morphosyntactic identity
of the latter: on the assumption that (7) is indeed fully grammatical in English, *found* must now be construed as a past participle.
The past-participle form of 'find' happens to be formally identical with the past-tense form of 'find' (both phonologically and
orthographically). The past-participle form of 'found', on the
other hand, is formally identical with its past-tense form: *founded*.
(In this respect, 'found' is like most other English verbs; 'find',
in contrast, belongs to a particular subclass of what are traditionally described as irregular, or strong, verbs.)

The ambiguity that is manifest in (6) also disappears if *he* or *she* is substituted for *they*:

(8) *He/she found hospitals and charitable institutions.*

The reason now is that in English, whereas there is formal identity (except for the verb 'be') between singular and plural forms in all simple past-tense verb-forms, what are traditionally called third-person singular and plural forms are formally distinct in the simple present tense of the indicative (in all verbs other than modals, such as 'may' or 'can'): cf. *finds* : *find* and *founds* : *found*. It follows that in (8) *found* must be construed as a form of 'find' and therefore as a past-tense form. To be contrasted with (6) are, on the one hand,

(9) *He/she founds hospitals and other charitable institutions*

and, on the other,

(10) *He/she founded hospitals and other charitable institutions.*

Ambiguity which results from absolute homonymy cannot be eliminated by manipulating the grammatical environment in this way. But, it is quite possible for the partial homonymy of two lexemes rarely or never to result in ambiguity: ambiguity is forestalled, as it were, if the shared forms are prohibited from occurring in the same grammatical environments. For example, the partial homonymy of the adjective 'last$_1$' (as in 'last week') and the verb 'last$_2$' (as in 'Bricks last a long time') rarely produces ambiguity. Their sole shared form, *last*, is almost always readily identifiable as a form of the one or the other by virtue of the grammatical environment in which it occurs.

We shall return to the question of ambiguity in a later chapter. We shall then see that the kind of grammatical ambiguity (combined with lexical ambiguity) which has been exemplified here in connexion with the traditional notion of homonymy is just one kind of grammatical ambiguity. It has been mentioned at this point because many general accounts of homonymy, both traditional and modern, fail to draw attention to the complexity and variety of the grammatical conditions that must be satisfied if partial homonymy is to result in ambiguity.

Many accounts of homonymy also fail to point out that partial homonymy does not necessarily involve identity of either the citation-forms or the underlying base-forms of the lexemes in question. For example, the noun 'rung' and the verb 'ring' are partial homonyms:

(11) *A rung of the ladder was broken*;
(12) *The bell was rung at midnight.*

The reason why this kind of partial homonymy is often not recognized in standard treatments, traditional or modern, is that the former tend to concentrate on citation-forms, whereas the latter frequently restrict their discussion of homonymy to base-forms. It so happens, of course, that in English the citation-form coincides with the base-form in all morphologically regular lexemes. But this is not so in all languages, as far as the traditional ordinary-language citation-forms of lexemes are concerned. For the semanticist, as we have seen, the question at issue is whether and to what degree homonymy produces ambiguity. From this point of view there is nothing special about either citation-forms or base-forms.

Let us now turn to **polysemy**. Whereas homonymy (whether absolute or partial) is a relation that holds between two or more distinct lexemes, polysemy ("multiple meaning") is a property of single lexemes. This is how the distinction is traditionally drawn. But everyone who draws this distinction also recognizes that the difference between homonymy and polysemy is not always clear-cut in particular instances. It has been demonstrated, for English, that there is a good deal of agreement among native speakers, in most cases, as to what counts as the one and what counts as the other. But there are also very many instances about which native speakers will hesitate or be in disagreement. What, then, is the difference in theory between homonymy and polysemy?

The two criteria that are usually invoked in this connexion have already been mentioned in Chapter 1: etymology (the historical source of the words) and relatedness of meaning. In general, the etymological criterion supports the native speaker's untutored intuitions about particular lexemes. For example,

most native speakers of English would probably classify 'bat₁'
("furry mammal with membranous wings") and 'bat₂' ("imple-
ment for striking a ball in certain games") as different lexemes;
and these two words do indeed differ in respect of their historical
source, 'bat₁' being derived from a regional variant of Middle
English 'bakke', and 'bat₂' from Old English 'batt' meaning
"club, cudgel".

To say that etymology generally supports the intuitions of
native speakers is not to say that this is always the case. It sometimes happens that lexemes which the average speaker of the
language thinks of as being semantically unrelated have come
from the same source. The homonyms 'sole₁' ("bottom of foot
or shoe") and 'sole₂' ("kind of fish"), which I mentioned above,
constitute a much-quoted example; and there are others, no less
striking, to be found in the handbooks. Less common is the converse situation where historically unrelated meanings are perceived by native speakers as having the same kind of connexion
as the distinguishable meanings of a single polysemous lexeme.
But there are several examples of what, from a historical point
of view, is quite clearly homonymy being reinterpreted by later
generations of speakers as polysemy. It falls within the scope of
what is commonly referred to by linguists as **popular etymology**. Today, for example, a number of speakers assume that
'shock₁' as in 'shock of corn' is the same as 'shock₂' as in 'shock
of hair'. Yet historically, they have different origins.

There are exceptions, then, of both kinds. Nevertheless, the
generalization that I have just made is undoubtedly correct: in
most cases, etymology supports the average native speaker's
intuitive sense of the distinction between homonymy and polysemy. And we shall see presently that there are good reasons
why this should be so. One of the principal factors operative in
semantic change is metaphorical extension, as when 'foot' meaning "terminal part of a leg" also came to mean "lowest part of a
hill or mountain". And it is metaphorical extension as a synchronic process that is at issue when one refers to the related
meanings of polysemous lexemes. There are, of course, other
kinds of relatedness of meaning which are relevant in this connexion. But metaphorical creativity (in the broadest sense of

'metaphorical') is part of everyone's linguistic competence. In the last resort, it is impossible to draw a sharp distinction between the spontaneous extension or transfer of meaning by individual speakers on particular occasions and their use of the pre-existing, or institutionalized, extended and transferred meanings of a lexeme that are to be found in a dictionary. This fact has important implications for linguistic theory that go way beyond the traditional, and perhaps insoluble, problem of distinguishing polysemy from homonymy.

2.3 SYNONYMY

Expressions with the same meaning are **synonymous**. Two points should be noted about this definition. First it does not restrict the relation of synonymy to lexemes: it allows for the possibility that lexically simple expressions may have the same meaning as lexically complex expressions. Second, it makes identity, not merely similarity, of meaning the criterion of synonymy.

In this latter respect, it differs from the definition of synonymy that will be found in many standard dictionaries and the one with which lexicographers themselves customarily operate. Many of the expressions listed as synonymous in ordinary or specialized dictionaries (including *Roget's Thesaurus* and other dictionaries of synonyms and antonyms) are what may be called **near-synonyms**: expressions that are more or less similar, but not identical, in meaning. Near-synonymy, as we shall see, is not to be confused with various kinds of what I will call **partial synonymy**, which meet the criterion of identity of meaning, but which, for various reasons, fail to meet the conditions of what is generally referred to as absolute synonymy. Typical examples of near-synonyms in English are 'mist' and 'fog', 'stream' and 'brook', and 'dive' and 'plunge'.

Let me now introduce the notion of **absolute synonymy**, in contrast not only with near-synonymy, but also with the broader notion of synonymy, just defined, which covers both absolute and partial (i.e., non-absolute) synonymy. It is by now almost a truism that absolute synonymy is extremely rare – at least as a relation between lexemes – in natural languages. (It is not rare of course as a relation between lexically composite expressions.) Two (or more) expressions are absolutely synonymous if, and only if, they satisfy the following three conditions:

(i)   all their meanings are identical;
(ii) they are synonymous in all contexts;
(iii) they are semantically equivalent (i.e., their meaning or meanings are identical) on all dimensions of meaning, descriptive and non-descriptive.

Although one or more of these conditions are commonly mentioned in the literature, in discussions of absolute synonymy, it is seldom pointed out that they are logically independent of one another; and non-absolute, or partial, synonymy is not always clearly distinguished from near-synonymy.

This being so, I wish to insist upon the importance of: (a) not confusing near-synonyms with partial synonyms; and (b) not making the assumption that failure to satisfy one of the conditions of absolute synonymy necessarily involves the failure to satisfy either or both of the other conditions. Let us take each of the conditions of absolute synonymy in turn.

Standard dictionaries of English treat the adjectives 'big' and 'large' as polysemous (though they vary in the number of meanings that they assign to each). In one of their meanings, exemplified by

(13) 'They live in a big/large house',

the two words would generally be regarded as synonymous. It is easy to show, however, that 'big' and 'large' are not synonymous in all of their meanings: i.e., that they fail to satisfy condition (i) and so are only partially, not absolutely, synonymous. The following sentence,

(14) 'I will tell my big sister',

is lexically ambiguous, by virtue of the polysemy of 'big', in a way that

(15) 'I will tell my large sister'

is not. All three sentences are well-formed and interpretable. They show that 'big' has at least one meaning which it does not share with 'large'. There are many such examples of polysemous lexemes that are synonymous in one or more, but not all, of their meanings.

Let us now turn to condition (ii). What is at issue here is the **collocational range** of an expression: the set of contexts in which it can occur (its **collocations**). It might be thought that the collocational range of an expression is wholly determined by its meaning, so that synonyms must of necessity have the same collocational range. But this does not seem to be so. Once again, 'big' and 'large' will serve as an example. There are many contexts in which 'large' cannot be substituted for 'big' (in the meaning which 'big' shares with 'large') without violating the collocational restrictions of the one or the other. For example, 'large' is not interchangeable with 'big' in

(16) 'You are making a big mistake'.

The sentence

(17) 'You are making a large mistake'

is, presumably, not only grammatically well-formed, but also meaningful. It is however collocationally unacceptable or un-idiomatic. And yet 'big' seems to have the same meaning in (16) as it does in phrases such as 'a big house', for which we could, as we have seen, substitute 'a large house'.

It is tempting to argue, in cases like this, that there must be some subtle difference of lexical meaning which accounts for the collocational differences, such that it is not synonymy, but near-synonymy, that is involved. Very often, undoubtedly, collocational differences can be satisfactorily explained, in terms of independently ascertainable differences of meaning. But this is not always so. We must be careful therefore not to assume that the collocational range of a lexeme is predictable from its meaning. Indeed, there are cases where it can be argued that the collocations of a lexeme are part of its meaning. This, regrettably, is one of many aspects of lexical semantics that cannot be dealt with in this book.

The third of the conditions of absolute synonymy listed above was identity on all dimensions of meaning. The most widely recognized dimension of meaning that is relevant to this condition is descriptive (or propositional) meaning (see section 1.7). In fact, many theories of semantics would restrict the notion of synonymy to what I will call **descriptive synonymy**: identity of descriptive meaning. What precisely is meant by identity of descriptive meaning is a question that will be taken up in Part 3. For the present, it will be sufficient to say that two expressions have the same descriptive meaning (i.e., are descriptively synonymous) if, and only if, propositions containing the one necessarily imply otherwise identical propositions containing the other, and vice versa. By this criterion (which will be reformulated in Part 3 in terms of the truth-conditional equivalence of sentences), 'big' and 'large' are descriptively synonymous (in one of their meanings and over a certain range of contexts). For instance, one cannot without contradiction simultaneously assert that someone lives in a big house and deny that they live in a large house.

One of the classic examples of descriptive synonymy is the relation that holds (or perhaps used to hold) in English between 'bachelor' (in one of the meanings of 'bachelor') and 'unmarried man'. (There are those who would deny that these two expressions are descriptively synonymous, nowadays, on the grounds that a divorced man, though unmarried, is not a bachelor. The point is debatable; and, since it can be exploited for more general theoretical purposes, I will return to it in a later chapter. But the principle that the example is intended to illustrate is clear enough.) One tests for descriptive synonymy, in this case, by investigating whether anyone truly, or correctly, described as a bachelor is truly describable as an unmarried man, and vice versa. It may well be that for some speakers the expressions are synonymous and for others they are not, and that for a third group the situation is unclear. (Those who hold that 'unmarried' means, not simply "not married", but "never having been married", and cannot be correctly applied to divorcees – together with those, if any, who would readily apply both 'bachelor' and 'unmarried' to divorcees – will presumably treat 'bachelor' and 'unmarried man' as descriptively synonymous.)

When it comes to **expressive** (or socio-expressive) **meaning** – and this is the only kind of non-descriptive meaning that we will take into account here – there is no readily available and reasonably objective criterion which enables us to decide between identity and difference. But it is none the less possible, in particular instances, to determine that two or more descriptively synonymous expressions differ in respect of the degree or nature of their expressive meaning. For example, it is intuitively obvious that a whole set of words including 'huge', 'enormous', 'gigantic' and 'colossal' are more expressive of their speakers' feelings towards what they are describing than 'very big' or 'very large', with which they are perhaps descriptively synonymous. It is more difficult to compare 'huge', 'enormous', 'gigantic' and 'colossal' among themselves in terms of their degree of expressivity. But speakers may have clear intuitions about two or more of them; and the question is, in principle, decidable by means of relatively objective psychological tests.

As to expressions which differ in the nature of their expressive meaning, the most obvious difference is between those which imply approval or disapproval and those which are neutral with respect to expressivity. Textbooks of linguistic semantics are full of examples, such as 'statesman' versus 'politician', 'thrifty' versus 'mean', 'stingy' versus 'economical', 'stink' versus 'stench' versus 'fragrance' versus 'smell', 'crafty' versus 'cunning' versus 'skilful' versus 'clever', and so on. In many cases, the fact that an expression implies approval or disapproval is much more readily ascertainable than is its descriptive meaning (if it has any). This is true, for example, of words such as 'bitch' or 'swine' used in what was once, but is perhaps no longer for most speakers of English, their metaphorical sense. Under what conditions can one truly describe a person as a bitch or swine? In cases like this it is surely the expressive, rather than the descriptive, component of meaning that is dominant.

Most of the lexemes in everyday use have both a descriptive and an expressive meaning. Indeed, as certain philosophers of language have pointed out in respect of the vocabulary of moral and aesthetic statements, it may be even theoretically impossible at times to separate the descriptive from the expressive. However that may be, knowing the expressive (or socio-expressive) meaning of a lexeme is just as much part of one's competence in a language as knowing its descriptive meaning. This point should be constantly borne in mind throughout this book, even though we shall be concerned almost exclusively with descriptive meaning in our discussion of lexical structure in Chapter 3 and in several of the later chapters.

Synonymy has been discussed and richly exemplified, from many points of view, not only in works devoted to linguistic semantics as such, but also in handbooks of stylistics, rhetoric and literary criticism. My main purpose, in the brief account that has been given here, has been to emphasize the theoretical importance of distinguishing the several kinds of partial, or non-absolute, synonymy from one another and from near-synonymy. In doing so, I have been obliged to gloss over a number of difficulties and complications that a more comprehensive discussion of synonymy would require us to deal with. Some of these will be mentioned in Chapter 4, as far as descriptive synonymy is concerned, in connexion with the notion of entailment.

2.4 FULL AND EMPTY WORD-FORMS

The word-forms of English, like the word-forms of many languages, can be put into two classes. One class consists of full forms such as *man, came, green, badly*; the other of empty forms such as *the, of, and, to, if*. The distinction between the two classes is not always clear-cut. But it is intuitively recognizable in the examples that I have just given. And it has been drawn on non-intuitive grounds by grammarians, by applying a variety of criteria. Essentially the same distinction was drawn, centuries ago, in the Chinese grammatical tradition; at the end of the nineteenth century, by the English grammarian Henry Sweet; and at the height of post-Bloomfieldian structuralism, in the 1950s, by the American linguist C. C. Fries (1952). It subsequently found its way into many of the textbooks of applied linguistics and practical teaching-grammars of English and other languages in the period preceding the rise of Chomskyan generative grammar in the 1960s. It correlates with the distinction between **open-class** and **closed-class** word-forms which is drawn (in these or other terms) in many modern schools of grammatical theory.

The terms that I have chosen, taken from the Chinese tradition, emphasize the intuitively evident semantic difference between typical members of one class and typical members of the other. Empty word-forms may not be entirely devoid of meaning (though some of them are in certain contexts). But, in an intuitively clear sense of 'meaningful', they are generally less meaningful than full word-forms are: they are more easily predictable in the contexts in which they occur. Hence their omission in headlines, telegrams, etc., and perhaps also in the utterances of very young children as they pass through early stages of language-acquisition. Full word-forms in English are forms of the major parts of speech, such as nouns, verbs and adjectives; empty word-forms (in languages that have them) belong to a wide variety of classes – such as prepositions, definite and indefinite articles, conjunctions, and certain pronouns and adverbs – which combine with the major parts of speech in grammatically well-formed phrases and sentences and which (unlike the major parts of speech) tend to be defined mainly in terms of their syntactic function, rather than semantically.

Other terms found in the literature, more or less equivalent to 'empty word-form', are 'form word', 'function word', 'grammatical word' and 'structural word'. All these terms reflect the view that what I am here calling empty word-forms differ grammatically and semantically from full word-forms. They are usually defined within the framework of Bloomfieldian and post-Bloomfieldian (including Chomskyan) morpheme-based grammar on the basis of Bloomfield's definition of the word (in the sense of 'word-form') as a minimal free form. We are operating throughout this book within the more traditional framework of what has been called word-and-paradigm grammar. But what I have to say here, and indeed throughout this book, could be reformulated without difficulty in the terminology of any of several different schools of grammatical theory, old and new, and is intended to be, as far as possible, theory-neutral. I have chosen to use 'empty word-form' and 'full word-form' because these terms emphasize the semantic dimension of the difference between the two classes.

Looked at from a grammatical point of view, empty word-forms can be seen as playing much the same role in non-inflecting, or lowly inflecting, languages as do prefixes, suffixes, etc. in highly inflecting languages. For example, a prepositional phrase such as *to John* when it occurs in the indirect-object position after the verb 'give' in English can be matched, semantically and grammatically, in many highly inflecting languages, such as Latin or Russian (and many other languages belonging to many different language-families throughout the world), with what is traditionally referred to as the dative (or allative) form of the noun, which contrasts with other syntactically and/or semantically distinct forms of the same lexeme in having the dative (or allative) suffix, rather than the nominative, accusative, genitive, etc. suffix, attached to the base-form. Similarly, for the definite article *the*. The vast majority of the languages of the world do not have a separate word-form which can be identified grammatically and semantically with the English definite article.

Indeed, most natural languages do not encode a category of definiteness as such at all, either grammatically or lexically. Some languages which do encode definiteness (in so far as this is identifiable and separable from other semantic categories across languages) do so inflectionally, in much the same way that the indirect-object function is expressed inflectionally by the dative case in Latin. In view of the attention that twentieth-century English-speaking logicians, beginning with Russell (1905), have given to the analysis of noun-phrases containing the definite article, it is worth noting the non-universality, not just of the definite article, but also of anything that might be called a semantic category of definiteness, in natural languages. But this is an issue which does not concern us for the moment. I have mentioned the English definite article at this point as an example of the class of what I am calling empty word-forms.

It will be noted that, although I have referred to empty word-forms as word-forms, I have not said that they are forms of lexemes (as *dog* is a form of 'dog', *ran* is a form of 'run', and so on). It is a moot point whether forms such as *the* or *to* (in its indirect-object function or its infinitive-forming function at least) should be listed in the dictionary of a language or accounted for within the grammar. This is an issue which cannot be settled except within the framework of one grammatical theory or another. But whatever view is taken on this issue, the main point to be made here is that, even if they are listed in dictionaries of the language (whether for reasons of practical convenience or on the basis of a theoretically defensible notion of the distinction between grammar and lexicon), empty word-forms, such as *the, of, and, to* and *if* in English, are not fully lexical. They may be words in the sense of 'word-form', but they are not words in the full sense.

Not only do empty word-forms tend to be less meaningful than full word-forms. Their meaning seems to be different from, and more heterogeneous than, that of full word-forms. The difference between the two classes of word-forms comes out immediately in relation to some of the theories of meaning mentioned in Chapter 1. For example, it might seem reasonable enough to say that the meaning of 'dog' is some kind of concept or behavioural response, which can be described or explicated without taking into account the phrases and sentences of English in which 'dog' can occur. But it hardly makes sense to discuss the meaning of *the, of, and, to* and *if* in such terms. Nor does it seem reasonable to say that their meaning, however we describe or explicate it, is independent of their grammatical function. This difference between full forms and empty forms is consistent with the fact that (as was mentioned above) the major parts of speech – especially nouns and verbs – are traditionally defined, either wholly or mainly, in terms of their meaning and independently of one another, whereas the minor parts of speech – the definite and indefinite articles, prepositions, conjunctions, etc. – are always defined in terms of their grammatical function and in relation to their potential for combining with one or other of the major parts of speech or with such higher-level units as phrases and clauses.

The grammatical distinction between full word-forms and empty word-forms that I have explained informally and non-technically in this section is, in fact, the product of several more technical distinctions, for which readers may consult the text books referred to in the Bibliography.

Since we are not concerned here with grammatical theory for its own sake, we shall not go into the details. What is really at issue, as far as we are concerned, is the distinction between the **grammar** of a language and its vocabulary, or **lexicon**, and the distinction between grammatical and lexical meaning, which depends upon it. This is a topic that will be taken up in the following section.

There is one point that can be usefully made, however, before we proceed, on the basis of the distinction drawn in this section between full word-forms and empty word-forms. This has to do with one of the questions raised in section 1.6: which is more basic than, or logically prior to, the other, the meaning of words or the meaning of sentences? One argument for the logical priority of sentence-meaning over word-meaning, which is often presented by advocates of truth-conditional semantics, runs as follows.

(i) The meaning associated with such words as *if, to* and *and* in English cannot be defined otherwise than in terms of the contribution that they make to the meaning of the larger units – phrases, clauses and sentences – in which they occur. The meaning of such words at least is logically secondary to (i.e., dependent upon) the meaning of the sentences in which they occur.

(ii) But the meaning of a sentence is the product of the meaning of the words of which it is composed. So, all words, both empty and full, can (and must) be brought within the scope of the general principle that the meaning of a form is the contribution it makes to the meaning of the sentences in which it occurs.

(iii) It is methodologically preferable to have a single notion of
       word-meaning applicable to all words.
(iv)   If the meaning of words such as *if, to* and *and*, whose mean-
       ing is defined as the contribution that they make to the
       meaning of the sentences in which they occur, is logically
       secondary to sentence-meaning, the meaning of all words
       is logically secondary to sentence-meaning, for the mean-
       ing of all words can be (and by methodological decision is)
       defined as the contribution that they make to the meaning
       of the sentences in which they occur.

Now, it may or may not be the case that sentence-meaning is
logically prior to, or more basic than, what is here being referred
to as word-meaning. But the argument that is commonly presented to support this conclusion is fallacious. It rests upon the
spurious methodological principle that so-called word-meaning
is homogeneous: that the meaning associated with empty word-
forms such as *if, to* and *and* is in all relevant respects comparable
with that of full word-forms. It also trades upon the fact that
the term 'word' denotes both forms and expressions and that
some forms are, as it were, more fully words than others. Fullness
and emptiness, in the sense in which I have been using these
terms in the present section, are, in any case, a matter of degree.
The emptiest of word-forms, such as *if, the* and *and* in English,
are neither expressions nor forms of expressions: as we have
seen, they are semantically and, to a certain extent grammatically, comparable with the morphologically bound prefixes and
suffixes of inflected word-forms. To call them 'words' and then
to make generalizations about word-meaning on the basis of
this classification merely confuses the issue.

Confusion is further confounded by what is arguably an equi-
vocal use of the term 'word-meaning'. As we shall see in the following section, 'word-meaning' does not necessarily mean the
same as 'lexical meaning'. The meaning of full word-forms combines both lexical and grammatical meaning. Empty word-
forms may not have any lexical meaning at all; and this is what
is implied by saying that they are semantically empty. It may
also be mentioned here that, as we shall see later, much of the

discussion of the logical priority of sentence-meaning over word-meaning that is to be found in otherwise reliable and authoritative works on linguistic semantics, traditional and modern, is further confused by the failure to draw the distinction between sentences and utterances. For example, it is often asserted that sentences, not words, are from the outset – in the period of language-acquisition as also in adulthood – the basic units of communication. This assertion must be challenged. Utterances, not sentences (in the relevant sense), are the units by means of which speakers and hearers – interlocutors – communicate with one another. Some of these utterances, being grammatically complete and well-formed, are traditionally called sentences, in what, as we shall see in Part 3, is a secondary and derivative sense of 'sentence'. Increasingly complex utterances are produced by children as they pass through the several distinguishable stages of language-acquisition; but it is a long time before any of the child's utterances can reasonably be described as sentences (in what is, in any case, an irrelevant sense of the ambiguous term 'sentence').

It is lexical meaning that we are discussing in Part 2. Grammatical meaning, not all of which can be assigned to word-forms, is largely a matter of sentence-meaning, and will therefore be dealt with in Part 3.

2.5 LEXICAL MEANING AND GRAMMATICAL MEANING

As was noted in the preceding section, what were there referred to as full word-forms are forms of the major parts of speech, such as nouns, verbs and adjectives. Empty word-forms, in contrast, in English (and in other languages which in this respect are typologically similar to English) belong to a wide variety of smaller form-classes, which are defined, traditionally, in terms of their syntactic function, rather than semantically.

It is for this reason that empty word-forms are traditionally described by logicians, not as independent terms or **categories**, but as **syncategorematic**: i.e., as forms whose meaning and logical function derives from the way in which they combine with (*syn-*) the independently defined major categories. I have deliberately introduced the traditional term 'category' here (together with its less familiar derivative 'syncategorematic') because in later chapters I shall be appealing frequently to an updated version of the traditional notion of **categorial meaning**. (The term 'categorial' bears the same sense here as it does in the phrase 'categorial ambivalence', which was employed in the preceding chapter.) As we shall see, categorial meaning is one part of grammatical meaning: it is that part of the meaning of lexemes (and other expressions) which derives from their being members of one category rather than another (nouns rather than verbs, verbs rather than adjectives, and so on).

The distinction between full word-forms and empty word-forms has served its purpose. I now want to introduce the distinction between the **grammar** of a language and its vocabulary, or **lexicon**. Grammar and lexicon are complementary; every grammar presupposes a lexicon, and every lexicon presupposes a grammar.

The grammar of a language is traditionally regarded as a system of rules which determines how words are put together to form (grammatically well-formed) phrases, how phrases are put together to form (grammatically well-formed) clauses, and how clauses are put together to form (grammatically well-formed) sentences. Grammatically ill-formed combinations of words, phrases and clauses – i.e., combinations which break the rules of the grammar – are traditionally described as ungrammatical. One of the major issues that has divided twentieth-century theorists in their discussion of the relation between semantics and grammar is the degree to which **grammaticality** (grammatical well-formedness) is determined by **meaningfulness**. This issue will be addressed in Chapter 5.

Modern linguistic theory has produced a large set of more or less traditional, alternative approaches to the grammatical analysis of natural languages, which differ from one another in various ways. Some of these are morpheme-based (rather than word-based), in that they take the morpheme to be the basic unit of grammatical analysis (for all languages). Some recognize no distinction between clauses and sentences (and use the term 'sentence' for both). Some respect the traditional bipartite analysis of all clauses into a subject and a predicate; others do not, or, if they do, make this a matter of secondary, rather than primary, determination. This list of differences between rival approaches could be extended almost indefinitely. The differences are by no means unimportant. But most of them are irrelevant to the issues that will confront us in this book. Such of them as are both important and relevant will be identified as we proceed.

The lexicon may be thought of as the theoretical counterpart of a dictionary, and it is frequently so described. Looked at from a psychological point of view, the lexicon is the set (or network) of all the lexemes in a language, stored in the brains of competent speakers, with all the linguistic information for each lexeme that is required for the production and interpretation of the sentences of the language. Although the so-called mental lexicon has been intensively studied in recent years from a psychological (and neuropsychological) point of view, relatively little is known so far about the way in which it is stored in the brain or about the way it is accessed in the use of a language. Relatively little is known, similarly, about the mental grammar that all speakers of a language, presumably, also carry around with them in their heads. In particular, it is not known whether there is a clear-cut psychological distinction to be drawn between grammar and lexicon.

Linguists have so far found it impossible to draw any such distinction sharply in the description of particular languages. And this is one reason for the controversy and lack of consensus that currently exists among linguists as to the way in which grammar and lexicon should be integrated in the systematic description of languages. This is one of the controversies that we do not need to get involved with in a book of this kind. For simplicity of exposition, I will adopt a deliberately conservative view of the relation between grammar and lexicon: the view that is reflected in standard textbooks of linguistics and in conventional dictionaries of English and other languages. Adjustments can easily be made by those readers who are familiar with recent grammatical theory (which, in this and other respects, has in any case not completely superseded traditional grammar and can still profitably draw upon it for many of the concepts that it seeks to formalize and explicate).

Although we are not concerned with grammatical theory as such in this book, we are concerned with the way in which meaning is encoded in the grammatical (i.e., the syntactic and the morphological) structure of languages. It was in that connexion that, in the preceding section, I introduced the distinction between what I called full word-forms and empty word-forms. Some, though not all, empty word-forms, in English and other typologically similar languages, will have a purely grammatical meaning (if they have any meaning at all). All full word-forms, on the other hand, will have both a lexical and a grammatical, and more particularly a categorial, meaning. For example, *child* and *children*, being forms of the same lexeme ('child') have the same lexical meaning (which I am symbolizing, notationally, as "child"). In so far as the lexeme has certain semantically relevant grammatical properties (it is a noun of particular kind), the two word-forms also share some part of their categorial meaning. But they differ, of course, grammatically (more precisely, morphosyntactically) in that the one is a singular and the other a plural noun-form. The difference between singular and plural (in those languages in which it is grammaticalized) is another part of the categorial component of grammatical meaning. And it is of course accounted for traditionally, both grammatically and semantically, in terms of what may be thought of as the **secondary** grammatical category of **number**. Other such semantically relevant secondary grammatical categories (not all of which are to be found in all languages) are **tense**, **mood**, **aspect**, **gender** and **person**. Reference will be made to some of these categories in later chapters.

CHAPTER 3

Defining the meaning of words

3.0 INTRODUCTION

How does one set about defining the meaning of words? In this chapter, we shall see that different answers can be given to this question. We shall also see that different answers can be given for different kinds of words.

For some words, especially nouns such as 'table' or 'chair' in English, one might think that a version of the so-called referential theory of meaning, mentioned in Chapter 1, is perfectly satisfactory: one might think that they can be readily defined by identifying what they stand for. Some theorists have taken this view; and it is well represented in the literature of both linguistic and philosophical semantics. It is undoubtedly a reasonable view to take, at least for words that stand for such things as dogs and cats, or tables and chairs; and it is commonly such words that are used to exemplify, not only the referential theory, but also complementary or alternative theories of lexical meaning.

But how does one define or identify what a word stands for? Is it possible to say what one word stands for without employing other semantically related words in doing so and without saying in what respect these semantically related words are similar to one another in meaning and in what respects they differ? And what exactly does the traditional expression 'stand for' mean in this context? As we shall see in the following section, we have to distinguish what expressions denote from what they can be used to refer to: we have to distinguish **denotation** from **reference**. These two ways in which words (and other expressions) can stand for things are commonly confused in presentations of the so-called referential theory of lexical meaning. They are, in fact, two quite different ways in which (to use a fashionable metaphor) language hooks on to the world. We shall also see that there is another dimension of the lexical meaning of words such as 'table' and 'chair', which I will call their **sense**, and that sense and denotation are interdependent.

Another question that needs to be addressed is whether some words in the vocabularies of natural languages are more basic than others. Once again, it is a reasonable view to take that they are, and that less-basic words can be defined in terms of more-basic words. For example, 'puppy' is intuitively less basic than 'dog': one would not normally define 'dog' by saying that it means "grown-up puppy", whereas, in the appropriate context, it would be quite normal to define 'puppy' by saying that it means "young dog". This is the way in which one might explain the meaning of puppy to a young child learning English (on the assumption that he or she already knows the meaning of the defining words 'dog' and 'young'). Similarly, for 'kitten', 'lamb', 'calf', 'foal', etc., in relation to 'cat', 'sheep', 'cow', 'horse', etc. In cases like this, it is intuitively clear that one of a pair of semantically related words is more basic than the other. But is this intuition valid? And, if it is, how do we know that it is?

Granted that some words are more basic than others, is there in natural languages a relatively small set of what might be referred to as absolutely basic words: a set of words in terms of which it is theoretically possible to define the meaning of all other words in the vocabulary? And, if there is, is the meaning of these absolutely basic words qualitatively different from the meaning of the non-basic words? Questions of this kind will occupy us in section 3.2.

We shall then move on, in section 3.3, to consider another apparent difference between words: the difference between words which (independently of whether they are absolutely basic, or more or less basic) denote what are traditionally called **natural kinds** and those that do not. What is meant by this

traditional term will be explained later. Here it is sufficient to
note that a strong case can be made for the view that such words,
which include 'dog', cannot be satisfactorily defined by means of
the classic type of genus-and-species definition: i.e., in terms of
the common properties of what they stand for. We shall also see
that, in linguistic semantics, there is no reason to distinguish so-
called natural-kind words, in respect of the kind of meaning they
have, from words such as 'table' or 'chair' (or 'king', 'priest',
etc.): i.e., words that denote culture-specific classes of things
(including persons, animals, etc.) that are not given in nature
and would not be classified as they are (and might not be held to
exist) if it were not for the prior existence of particular languages
operating in particular cultures.

A currently popular theory of lexical meaning, as we shall see
in section 3.4, is the theory of **semantic prototypes**. This was
first invoked in connexion with the definition of natural-kind
words, but it has now been applied more widely and has inspired
a good deal of interesting research on various areas of the vocabulary in several languages.

The general purpose of this chapter is to show that, although
many proposals for the definition of words (or, to be more precise, lexemes) have been proposed in the literature, none of
them to the exclusion of the others is acceptable. Each of them
has its problems. Nevertheless, we can still learn a lot from
them, and more particularly from trying to formulate them precisely within the framework of modern theories of the grammatical and lexical structure of languages.

3.1 DENOTATION AND SENSE

Standard monolingual dictionaries of a language explain the
meaning of words by providing them with metalinguistic definitions in which the object language is used as its own metalanguage (see 1.2). The format of these definitions will vary
somewhat from dictionary to dictionary. It will also vary from
one class of words to another, especially in the case of so-called
function words, or lexically empty word-forms, such as prepositions (*of*, *in*, etc.) or the definite and indefinite articles (*the*, *a*): it

is notoriously difficult to devise satisfactory dictionary definitions for such forms, whose meaning is primarily grammatical,
rather than lexical (see 2.4). In this chapter we are concerned
with lexically full words: lexemes that belong to the major parts
of speech (nouns, verbs and adjectives, and some subclasses of
adverbs).

In the definition of such words, bilingual dictionaries rely
heavily on the notion of interlingual synonymy: e.g., by saying,
in an English–French dictionary, that (the English word) 'dog'
has (more or less) the same meaning as (the French word)
'chien'. Monolingual dictionaries also make use of the notion
of synonymy (intralingual, rather than interlingual). But
monolingual-dictionary definitions will usually combine paraphrase, in terms of partial intralingual synonymy, with analysis
and description. For example, in defining the word 'dog' (in
one of its meanings) a dictionary entry might tell us that dogs
are animals belonging to a particular genus and species and
that they are carnivorous, have been domesticated, and so on.
We shall look at two examples of such definitions in the following section. Here I want to point out that traditional dictionary definitions can be seen as defining (in the case of words
such as 'dog') two different, but complementary, aspects of
lexical meaning: denotation and sense.

To say what the word 'dog' **denotes** is to identify all (and
only) those entities in the world that are correctly called dogs.
How one goes about identifying, in practice, everything and
anything that is denoted by 'dog' is a question that we will take
up presently. The important point for the moment is that some
(though not all) words may be put into correspondence with
classes of entities in the external world by means of the relation
of **denotation**.

Denotation, as we shall see later, is intrinsically connected
with **reference**. Indeed, many authors (especially those who
subscribe to a referential theory of meaning: see section 1.7)
draw no distinction between them, subsuming both under a
broader notion of reference than the one which we shall be
adopting. However, it is intuitively obvious that 'dog' does not
stand for the class of dogs (or, alternatively, for some defining

property of this class) in quite the same way that 'Fido' can be used to **stand for**, or **refer to**, some particular dog.

The crudest version of the referential theory of meaning, which has been aptly dubbed the 'Fido'-Fido theory, will not work for anything other than proper names; and, as we shall see later, it does not work all that well even for proper names. There are more sophisticated and philosophical versions of the referential theory of meaning, which would justify the adoption of a broader notion of reference than the one we shall be employing in this book. But whatever terms are used and whatever theory of meaning is adopted, it is important to take account of the difference in the two ways in which language hooks on to the world. This difference, which I am associating with a terminological distinction between 'reference' and 'denotation', is all too often obscured by a loose use of the term 'reference'.

The crucial difference between reference and denotation is that the denotation of an expression is invariant and **utterance-independent**: it is part of the meaning which the expression has in the language-system, independently of its use on particular occasions of utterance. Reference, in contrast, is variable and **utterance-dependent**. For example, the word 'dog' always denotes the same class of animals (or, alternatively, the defining property of the class), whereas the phrases 'the dog' or 'my dog' or 'the dog that bit the postman' will refer to different members of the class on different occasions of utterance. Reference, as distinct from denotation, will be dealt with (as part of utterance-meaning) in a later chapter. The important point to note, for the present, is that lexemes, as such, do not have reference, but may be used as referring expressions or, more commonly, as components of referring expressions in particular contexts of utterance.

The lexeme 'dog', then, denotes a class of entities in the external world. But it is also related, in various ways, to other lexemes and expressions of English, including 'animal', 'hound', 'terrier', 'spaniel', etc. Each such relation that holds between 'dog' and other expressions of the same language-system, may be identified as one of its **sense-relations**. Descriptive synonymy, which we discussed in the last chapter, is one kind of sense-relation. We shall look briefly at some of the other sense-relations exemplified above for 'dog' in Chapter 4. Meanwhile, the examples themselves will suffice for the purpose of explaining both the distinction between denotation and sense and, no less important, their interdependence.

The **sense** of an expression may be defined as the set, or network, of sense-relations that hold between it and other expressions of the same language. Several points may now be made in respect of this definition.

First, sense is a matter of **interlexical** and **intralingual** relations: that is to say, of relations which hold between a lexical expression and one or more other lexical expressions in the same language. Sense, as I have defined it here, is wholly internal to the language-system. This distinguishes it clearly from denotation, which relates expressions to classes of entities in the world.

What has just been said is not invalidated by the existence, in all natural languages, of various kinds of metalinguistic expressions; and this point must be emphasized (see 1.2). The distinction between sense and denotation applies to metalinguistic expressions such as 'lexeme', 'word' or 'linguistic expression' in exactly the same way as it applies to other expressions. Admittedly, it is much harder to keep one's thinking straight in the case of metalinguistic expressions than it is in respect of expressions that denote dogs and cats (or shoes, ships, sealing wax, cabbages and kings) and other such denizens of the external world. Nevertheless, it should be clear that linguistic expressions such as 'linguistic expression' and 'lexeme' are related to one another in terms of sense exactly as 'animal' and 'dog' are, whereas 'linguistic expression' and 'lexeme' are related to one another in terms of denotation in the same way as 'animal' is related to some particular dog or other animal. For example, just as 'animal' denotes a class of entities whose members are the dogs Fido, Rover, etc., as well as other subclasses of the class of animals (cows, tigers, camels, etc.), so the English-language expression 'linguistic expression' denotes a class of entities whose members are the linguistic expressions 'linguistic expression', 'lexeme', 'word', etc., as well as, say, 'dog', 'animal', etc.

Denotation, as we have seen, is a relation which holds primarily, or basically, between expressions and physical entities in the external world. But many, if not all, natural languages also contain expressions which denote various kinds of non-physical entities. Although metalinguistic expressions are not the only such expressions, they are of particular interest to the semanticist.

The second point that needs to be made explicit about sense and denotation is that both notions apply equally to lexically simple and lexically composite expressions. For example, 'domesticated canine mammal' is a lexically composite expression, whose sense and denotation is determined by the sense and denotation of its component lexemes. To make the point more technically: the sense and denotation of the composite expression is a **compositional function** of the sense and denotation of its component parts. What is meant by this will be explained in Chapter 4.

A third point, which is perhaps obvious but, like the preceding one, will be important later and needs to be clearly stated, is that sense and denotation are, in general, interdependent in that (in the case of expressions that have both sense and denotation) one would not normally know the one without having at least some knowledge of the other. This raises the possibility that either sense or denotation should be taken to be logically or psychologically more basic than the other. I will take up this question in the following section.

Sense and denotation are not only interdependent: they are inversely related to one another. The nature of this inverse relation can be explained informally as follows: the larger the denotation, the smaller the sense, and conversely. For example, the denotation of 'animal' is larger than, and includes, that of 'dog' (all dogs are animals, but not all animals are dogs), but the sense of 'animal' is less specific than, and is included in, that of 'dog'.

A comparable inverse relation is well recognized in traditional logic in terms of the difference between extension and intension. Roughly speaking, the **extension** of a term, or expression, is the class of entities that it defines, and the **intension** is the defining property of the class. Modern formal semantics, as we shall see later, has exploited and developed the distinction between extension and intension in various ways. And some scholars have actually identified the sense of an expression with its intension. For reasons which become clearer later, I prefer to treat extension and intension as complementary aspects of denotation. Regardless of the view that one takes of the ontological status, or reality, of properties, it is convenient to be able to say that an expression denotes (extensionally) a class of entities and (intensionally) its defining property (i.e. the property which all members of the class share and by virtue of which they are members of the class in question). For example, it is convenient to be able to say that the word 'red' denotes, not only the class of red things, but also the property of redness. This is intended to be a philosophically neutral way of talking: neutral with respect to the long-standing philosophical controversy between nominalists and realists and neutral with respect to the typically empiricist thesis of extensionality, which has been so influential in twentieth-century logic and philosophical semantics.

Finally, as far as this section is concerned, it must be emphasized that nothing said here about sense and denotation is to be taken as implying that either the one or the other is fully determinate in the case of all, or even most, lexemes in the vocabularies of natural languages. On the contrary, the sense of most lexemes, and therefore of most lexically composite expressions, would seem to be somewhat fuzzy at the edges. Similarly, it is very often unclear whether a particular entity falls within the denotation of an expression or not. What then does it mean to say that someone knows the descriptive meaning of particular expressions in his or her native language? Indeed, how do we manage to communicate with one another, more or less successfully, by means of language, if the descriptive meaning of most lexemes – their sense and denotation – is inherently fuzzy or indeterminate? This question will be taken up in section 3.4.

3.2 BASIC AND NON-BASIC EXPRESSIONS

About half-a-century ago, Bertrand Russell drew a distinction, which has subsequently been much discussed by semanticists (in these or other terms), between what he called object-words and dictionary-words. The distinction itself was by no means original. But Russell expressed himself with characteristic lucidity, and the way in which he developed the underlying, initially appealing, principle makes his formulation of the distinction particularly interesting. Object-words, he tells us, "are defined logically as words having meaning in isolation, and psychologically as words which have been learnt without its being necessary to have previously learnt any other words". Dictionary-words, in contrast, "are theoretically superfluous", since they are definable, and may be learned, in terms of the logically and psychologically more basic object-words (Russell, 1940: 62–3).

Leaving the non-basic dictionary words on one side for the moment, we may now ask how one comes to know the descriptive meaning of the allegedly basic object-words. Russell is quite clear on this point. Object-words are learned by demonstration or, as philosophers say, **ostension**: that is, by showing the learner a sufficient number of entities that fall within the denotation, or extension, of each object-word. At its most explicit, **ostensive definition** – definition by ostension – would involve pointing at one or more entities denoted by the word in question and saying,

(1) *That is a(n) X.*

For example, pointing at one or more dogs, one might say,

(2) *That is a dog.*

Ostensive definition plays a prominent role, in theory if not always in practice, in the empiricist tradition, to which Russell belonged. So too does denotation. And Russell's definition of object-words makes it clear that their meaning, in contrast with that of dictionary words, is wholly a matter of denotation.

But the notion of ostensive definition has come in for a lot of criticism. In fact, it is readily shown to be indefensible in the form in which Russell and other empiricist philosophers have assumed it to operate. First of all, those for whom an expression is being defined ostensively must understand the meaning of the demonstrative pronoun 'that' in the utterance *That is a(n) X*, or alternatively of the gesture that serves the same purpose. They must also realize what more general purpose is being served by the utterance or gesture in question; it is easy to overlook the importance of this component of the process of ostensive definition. Finally, they must not only appreciate that the entity to which their attention is being drawn, ostensively, is to be considered as an example of some class, but also either know in advance or infer the intension (defining property) of the class that is being exemplified. Every entity exemplifies a potentially infinite set of classes. For example, given that Fido is a member of the class of dogs, it is also a member of indefinitely many of its subclasses (spaniels, dogs with drooping ears, dogs with short legs, dogs with a doleful expression, dogs with reddish-brown hair, etc.); of indefinitely many of the larger classes of entities of which dogs are a subclass (mammals, four-legged creatures, animals, physical entities, etc.); and, most important of all, of indefinitely many classes of entities to which few, if any, other dogs, but lots of non-dogs may belong (e.g., the class of mobile entities that make a recognizable sound and cause little Johnny to coo with pleasure: a class which also includes Mummy, Daddy, the cat, the vacuum cleaner, etc.). How can one tell just which of this potentially infinite set of classes is the one that is being defined?

The problem is not insoluble, if we assume that the person learning the extension of an expression (the class of entities it denotes) has prior knowledge of what its intension is likely to be. For the out-and-out – **tabula rasa** – empiricist, however, who assumes that the mind is initially an empty slate (a *tabula rasa* in Latin) upon which post-natal experience, and more especially sensation, writes what it will, the problem does seem to be insoluble. And Russell was an out-and-out empiricist, as have been most philosophers who have made ostensive definition the foundation stone of lexical semantics.

Let us now drop what I will refer to as Russell's **condition of atomicity**: the condition imposed upon basic expressions that their meaning should be logically and psychologically independent of the meaning of other expressions. It is much easier to get people to see what is being pointed to and to give them some idea of the class that is intended to be exemplified by the entity indicated, if one is allowed to use other expressions, basic or non-basic, that are related in sense to the word that is being defined. For example, if one says, not (2), but

(3) *That animal is a dog,*

one is less likely to be taken to be pointing at the vacuum cleaner or the hearth rug. If one says

(4) *That is a dog – not a cat,*

one thereby draws the addressee's attention to those features, both **phenomenal** and **functional**, which distinguish dogs from cats. In short, ostensive definition is much more likely to be successful if the condition of atomicity is dropped.

Anyway, regardless of whether it is in principle possible to learn the denotation of one expression without knowing (or simultaneously learning) the denotation of other expressions to which it is related in sense, it seems clear that human beings do not operate in this way in practice. They do not, as children, first learn the full extension of, let us say, 'red' without knowing anything of the extension of 'brown' or 'pink'. They do not learn the full extension of 'dog' without knowing anything of the extension of some of the more commonly occurring expressions that are related to it in sense. Russell claimed, it will be recalled, that basic words "are defined ... psychologically, as words which have been learnt without its being necessary to have previously learnt any other words". If 'psychologically' in Russell's definition is understood to make reference to the acquisition of languages by children under normal conditions, then the sense and denotation of what Russell and others might think of as basic words are certainly not psychologically independent of one another. (Incidentally, Russell's own examples, from English, include 'man', 'dog', 'yellow', 'hard', 'sweet', 'walk', 'run', 'eat', 'drink', 'up', 'down', 'in', 'out', 'before', 'after'. All of these are plausibly regarded by rationalists, in the rationalism-versus-empiricism debate, as words whose meaning might well be acquired on the basis of innate, biologically transmitted, knowledge, interacting with experience.) The acquisition of language by children has been intensively investigated in recent years, and it is clear that children do not learn the meaning of words atomistically (one at a time) in the way that Russell suggests. They generally learn the denotation of one word only by simultaneously learning the denotation of other, semantically related, words and over a period of time making adjustments to their understanding of the sense and denotation of sets of semantically related words.

Where does this leave us, then, as far as the distinction between basic and non-basic expressions is concerned? It has a long history and, as I said earlier, it is intuitively appealing. Obviously, if the argument of the last few paragraphs is accepted, we cannot go along with Russell and say that basic expressions are those whose sense is fully determined by their denotation and that non-basic expressions are those whose sense (which subsequently determines their denotation) is fully determined by the sense of the basic expressions used to define them.

But this does not mean that the distinction itself falls to the ground. After all, it is the very foundation stone of the eminently practical system known as Basic English, invented by C. K. Ogden in the 1930s and intended as an international second language. Basic English has a vocabulary of 850 lexemes; and these are held to be sufficient for the definition of the other lexemes of other languages. And Basic English is one of several such systems which derive ultimately from the philosophical speculations of Leibniz, Bishop Wilkins and other seventeenth-century scholars, whose works inspired the tradition of logical empiricism to which Russell belonged and exerted a powerful influence upon Roget, when he compiled his famous *Thesaurus of English Words and Phrases* in 1852. Also, without making any philosophical claims for the allegedly basic vocabulary with which they operate, many foreign-language manuals deliberately restrict themselves to what they consider to be basic, in the sense of being necessary and sufficient for everyday purposes. In some countries, and for some languages, lists of basic words of this kind have been officially promulgated, and textbooks and examinations are geared to them.

As for so-called dictionary-words, it is interesting to return now to the lexically composite expressions taken from the entries for 'dog' in two recent dictionaries of English: 'domesticated canine mammal' and 'common four-legged flesh-eating animal'. The former comes from the *Collins Dictionary of the English Language* (1979); the latter from the *Longman Dictionary of Contemporary English* (1978). The most striking difference between them is that the Longman definition is written in words selected from "a controlled vocabulary of approximately 2000 words which were selected by a thorough study of a number of frequency and pedagogic lists" and conforms to the principle that "definitions are always written using simpler terms than the words they describe" (pp. viii-ix), whereas the Collins definition is written with respect to the different, but not incompatible, principle that the definition should be "in lucid English prose" and should be written with words each of which "is itself an entry in the dictionary" (p. vx). Another difference, which will be relevant in the following section, is that the Collins expression is closer to being synonymous with 'dog' (in one of its meanings) than the Longman expression is.

Here I want to emphasize the fact that there are at least two different senses of 'basic' (or 'simple') in which one lexeme may be more basic (or simpler) than another. The more obvious sense of 'basic' is that which depends upon frequency of occurrence in everyday, non-technical, usage. By this criterion the Longman entry clearly contains more basic (and simpler) words than the Collins entry does – though it also requires the user to interpret the lexically composite expressions 'four-legged' and 'flesh-eating'. The deliberately restricted vocabulary of the foreign-language manuals referred to above can be called basic in the same sense.

In principle, however, there is another sense of 'basic'. In this second sense, it is by no means clear that familiar, everyday words, such as 'dog' or 'wolf', are necessarily more basic than less familiar words, such as 'mammal' or 'domesticated'. Some words might be more basic than others in that they can be used to define a greater proportion of the total vocabulary or can be used to construct a more elegant and systematic set of inter-connected definitions. And they might be thought to be more directly associated with what Leibniz and other seventeenth-century philosophers have thought of as **atomic concepts**: the building blocks, as it were, of the conceptual system which guides and constrains all thinking and rational discourse. This is the sense of 'basic', or 'primary', that is dominant in the philo-sophical tradition, though Russell and others frequently talk as if the two senses will determine much the same class of expres-sions. It is also this second sense of 'basic' that has been domi-nant, as we shall see in Chapter 4, in a good deal of recent theorizing in linguistic semantics. There is no reason to believe that the two senses of 'basic' should be applicable to exactly the same lexemes. But it is perhaps reasonable to assume that many of the lexemes in the vocabularies of all natural languages should be basic in both senses. We shall keep this point in mind in our discussion of natural kinds and semantic prototypes.

In this section, I have deliberately introduced and empha-sized some philosophical ideas which are rarely mentioned in introductions to semantics written by linguists. I have done this because, in my view, it is impossible to evaluate even the most down-to-earth and apparently unphilosophical works in descriptive semantics unless one has some notion of the general philosophical framework within which they are written. This holds true regardless of whether the authors themselves are aware of the philosophical origins or implications of their work-ing principles.

It remains to add that the empiricist tradition has been immensely important in the development of modern formal semantics and continues to influence the thinking of many who declare themselves to be rationalists and are most vociferous in their rejection of empiricism. Empiricist philosophers have always tended to give priority to the **phenomenal** attributes of entities in their discussion of denotation: i.e., to those attributes that can be known or perceived through the senses. We must be careful not to accept this point of view uncritically, simply because it has been passed on to us, often no less uncritically, by tradition. The **functional** attributes – those attributes that make things useful to us for particular purposes – are no less important in the determination of what is, or might be, basic in the vocabulary of human languages. For example, edibility is likely to be as important as colour or shape, and just as likely to serve as one of the properties which we recognize as criterial in establishing the denotation of whole sets of lexemes; and edibility for human beings is not only biologically, but also culturally, determined. I have chosen edibility as an example because edibility – i.e., culturally determined edibility – demonstrably serves as a major determinant of the lexical structure of all natural languages.

It may also be added, though I will not go into this here, that edibility, together with shape, size, animacy, sex, etc., is often grammatically (or semi-grammatically) encoded in the **classifiers** or **genders** of languages that have such categories. One can hardly discuss the question of basic and non-basic expressions in natural languages properly without doing so in relation to what is grammaticalized, as well as lexicalized, in particular languages.

3.3 NATURAL (AND CULTURAL) KINDS

Naive monolingual speakers of English, or of any other language, are often surprised when they are told that there are lexemes in their language that cannot be matched with descriptively equivalent lexemes in other languages. And yet it is true. Nor should it be thought that it is only words denoting culturally or geographically restricted classes of entities (e.g., 'shrine', 'boomerang', 'monsoon', 'willow', etc.) that lack their descriptive equivalents in other languages. There is plenty of snow in Greenland; there is no dearth of sand in the Australian desert; and camels are ubiquitous in most of the Arabic-speaking countries. Nevertheless, there is no single, general word for snow in Eskimo, no word for sand in many of the aboriginal languages of Australia, no word for camels as such in Arabic.

Examples like this have now become commonplace and are widely cited in textbooks of linguistics.

But we do not have to take our examples from what many would regard as exotic languages. Despite the impression that might be given by standard bilingual dictionaries, such common English words as 'brown', 'monkey', 'chair', 'jug', 'carpet' – to take but a few – cannot be translated into French, out of context, without making more or less arbitrary choices. According to context, 'brown' is to be translated into French sometimes with 'brun' and sometimes with 'marron', not to mention 'beige' and similar more specific words. There are even occasions, notably with reference to men's shoes, when 'brown' (if we know that it refers to a particularly light shade) might well be translated with 'jaune', which we usually think of as meaning "yellow". And there are numerous other examples cited in the literature. These lexical differences between languages are frequently summarized by linguists in the following generalization: every language divides up the world, or reality, in its own way. A more controversial formulation of the same point, associated in recent years with the names of the American linguists Edward Sapir and Benjamin Lee Whorf, is that what we think of as the world, or reality, is very largely the product of the categories imposed upon perception and thought by the languages we happen to speak. Essentially the same view was taken, at the turn of the century, by the Swiss linguist Ferdinand de Saussure, and is a common, though not essential, component in various kinds of **structuralism**, both European and American.

Structuralism may be contrasted, in this respect, with **atomism** (note the condition of atomicity and the notion of atomic concepts mentioned in the previous section): structuralism emphasizes the interdependence of entities, rather than their individual and separate existence. Indeed, structuralism as a philosophical doctrine maintains in its extreme form that entities have no essence or existence independently of the structure that is imposed by thought or language upon some otherwise undifferentiated world-stuff. It is a heady doctrine, and many semanticists have been intoxicated by it. Diluted with a sufficient measure of naive realism, it is not only philosophically and psychologically defensible, but provides, in my view, an empirically sounder basis for linguistic semantics than does any atomistic theory of meaning.

Naive realism may differ from philosophical realism. But supporters of each are at one in their belief that the external world exists independently of the mind and of language. Moreover, many philosophical realists would agree with naive realists in saying that the external world is made up of physical entities whose existence is similarly independent of the mind and of language and that some or all of these entities (human beings, animals, things) can be grouped into what are traditionally called **natural kinds**: i.e., classes whose members have the same nature or essence. ('Kind' in this context is to be understood as meaning "genus" or "class".) The most obvious candidates for the status of natural kinds are, of course, living species, which reproduce themselves, as the traditional expression has it, each according to its kind. It is a matter of experience that human beings beget and give birth to human beings; tigers produce new tigers; oak trees reproduce their kind essentially unchanged; and so on. According to the naive realist, the external world also contains (in addition to different kinds of entities) aggregates of different kinds of matter or stuff – water, gold, salt, etc. – such that any two aggregates of stuff are wholly or partly of the same kind or not. Traditional grammar, which was strongly realist in philosophical inspiration throughout most of its history, would say that, whereas proper names denote individual entities, common (i.e., non-proper) nouns denote natural kinds. English, like some but not all languages, draws a grammatical distinction between entity-denoting words, so-called **count nouns** ('man', 'tiger', 'oak tree') and stuff-denoting words, **mass nouns** ('water', 'gold', 'salt'). We have already invoked the distinction between count nouns and mass nouns, it will be recalled, in connexion with the two senses of the English word 'language' (see 1.4).

Until recently, most philosophers of language who have subscribed to the traditional doctrine of natural kinds have interpreted it in terms of the distinction between intension and extension (see 1.3). They have said that to know the meaning of any expression that denotes a natural kind (i.e., to know its sense) is to know its intension: its defining property, or, in philosophical terms, the necessary and sufficient conditions that must be satisfied by any entity or stuff that falls within the extension of the expression in question. In the last few years, an interestingly new version of the doctrine of natural kinds has been proposed, notably by Saul Kripke (1972) and Hilary Putnam (1975), which severs the connexion between intension and essence. We need not go further into the philosophical issues in this book. It may be noted, however, that the theory of natural-kind expressions, as developed by Putnam and Kripke, transcends the age-old dispute between nominalism and realism: it is like nominalism in that it identifies meaning with naming and takes the association between a natural-kind expression and its extension to be, in all crucial respects, identical with the association between a proper name and its bearer; it is like realism in that it does not deny that members of the same natural kind share the same properties. The arguments deployed by Putnam, Kripke and their followers are subtle and (up to a certain point at least) persuasive. They have been very influential, not only in philosophy, but also in linguistic semantics.

Ideally, any good theory of semantics should fit in with everyday, non-technical accounts of descriptive meaning; it should not be in conflict with commonsense accounts of the kind which non-philosophers and non-linguists give; and it should be empirically plausible and should – to use a traditional expression – **save the appearances**. In one important respect, the Kripke–Putnam approach, mentioned above, does indeed meet these conditions: it does not require that the intension of common natural-kind words (whose meaning, on a commonsense view of the matter, is known to all ordinary native speakers) should be determinate and known to everyone competent in the language. If knowing the descriptive meaning of 'dog' involves knowing the defining characteristics of the natural kind that it denotes, few, if any, speakers of English can be said to know the meaning of 'dog'. There are experts, recognized as such in the culture to which we belong, who can arbitrate for us in dubious cases. For example, if one is prosecuted on the grounds that one has wilfully allowed one's dog to foul the pavement or sidewalk and one denies that it is a dog, an expert witness can be called to settle the matter or, in the last resort, the judge trying the case can give a ruling either arbitrarily or in terms of precedent.

A further important point made by Kripke and Putnam has to do with the conditions under which one is prepared to revise one's previously held view of the meaning of words in the light of new information or of scientific discoveries which change one's view of the world. Let us suppose (to adapt a by now famous example) that biologists one day discover that what we currently think of as the natural kind, or class, of dogs is not a unitary class distinguishable from, let us say, foxes, badgers and cats, or even, more radically, that dogs are not in fact animals, despite all appearances to the contrary, but inanimate auto-mata, skilfully contrived by some supernatural or extraterres-trial being in order to deceive us. Will the word 'dog' have changed its meaning if speakers of English continue to use it in order to refer to what they now know is a heterogeneous class of inanimate entities?

The answer to this question is not self-evident. But one thing is clear. On the assumption that the word 'dog' continues to denote all and everything that it previously denoted, at least this part of its meaning is unchanged. It follows that anyone who subscribes to a purely referential, or denotational, theory of lexical meaning will say that there has been no change in the meaning of the word 'dog'. And this is what Kripke and Putnam, and their followers, say. Those who draw a distinction between denotation and sense in the way that we have drawn it in this chapter can say that, although the denotation of 'dog' has not changed, its sense has: it is no longer related to 'animal' (and other lexemes) in the vocabulary of English as it was previously.

Fanciful examples of the kind that I have just presented may seem, at first sight, to be too far-fetched for serious consideration. But there are plenty of test-cases of a less fanciful kind on record which have been debated by semanticists over the years. Did the English lexeme 'whale' change its meaning when it was dis-covered that the whale is not a fish, but a mammal? Did the word 'atom' change its meaning when the atom was split? Does the noun 'sunrise', or the verb 'rise' used of the sun, mean something different now from what it (and its translation-equivalents in other languages) used to mean in pre-Copernican times (and still means for some people)? We shall have occasion to return to questions of this kind from time to time in later chapters. Such questions have been raised here because the discussion of natural kinds by philosophers has been of such importance in linguistic semantics in recent years.

The discussion of natural kinds has been of particular importance when it has also included, or has been combined with, the discussion of what have come to be called **prototypes** (which will be dealt with in the following section). The main philosophical thrust of the discussion of natural kinds is to cast doubt on what might be referred to as the classical view of definition in terms of the specification of the necessary and sufficient conditions for class-membership. As we shall see later, it has also had the effect of rehabilitating, or updating and rendering more plausible, a particular version of ostensive definition.

Before we take up the question of semantic prototypes, in the following section, it should be pointed out that the term 'natural kind', and my presentation of the topic so far, is misleading in one respect. In view of the traditional associations of the term 'natural kind' and its philosophical underpinnings in current discussion, words denoting natural kinds in the traditional sense might be thought to differ semantically from words denoting what I will call **cultural kinds**, like 'dirt' or 'chair'. There is no reason to believe that they do. We have prototypes of the one as we have prototypes of the other and we give the same kind of open-ended definitions combining both phenomenal and functional criteria. In fact, natural kinds in the traditional sense are often combined and divided by languages, in just the way that structuralists have suggested, sometimes arbitrarily, but often for culturally explicable reasons. For example, 'fruit' and 'vegetable' each cover several different kinds, and in their most common, everyday, sense are fuzzy and indeterminate. In so far as their denotation is clear in their prototypical, nuclear or focal, sense the principal criterion which serves to classify a particular natural kind as being either a fruit or a vegetable is culinary: whether it is eaten, in English-speaking communities, as part of a main meal with meat or fish; whether it is used to make soup; and so on. The truth of the matter seems to be that the cultural and the natural are so intimately associated in the vocabularies of human languages that it is often impossible to say, in most cases, that the one is more basic than the other, in either of the two senses of 'basic' discussed in the preceding section.

This fact emerges very clearly from research that has been carried out on a wide variety of languages, in selected areas of the vocabulary, by anthropologists, psychologists and linguists. Much of this research has been inspired, in recent years, by the important and seminal work on the vocabulary of colour by Berlin and Kay (1969). Other areas of vocabulary that have been investigated from the same point of view include those of shape, botanical and biological nomenclature, and cooking. In general reviews of this work it is customary for authors to emphasize the cross-cultural validity of certain focal categories. It is no less important, however, to insist upon the fact that there is also a good deal of culture-dependent variation across languages. What I said about the meaning of 'fruit' and 'vegetable' in the previous paragraph is typical of all lexical fields, including those of colour and shape. For example, the fact that 'red' and 'white' are used to distinguish two broad categories of wine is something that cannot be accounted for in terms of the focal meanings of these words. It is a culturally established convention, and one that must be learned as one learns to use 'red' and 'white' in a range of characteristic situations and characteristic collocations.

It must also be emphasized that what has been said in this section about the meaning of lexemes which denote natural (and cultural) kinds applies not only to lexemes denoting entities and substances in the physical world, but also to abstract terms and to expressions denoting mythical or imaginary entities and substances. In short, there is no reason to believe that there is anything special, from the point of view of linguistic semantics, about those words whose focal meaning is determined by the properties of the physical world and by the perceptual mechanisms of human beings.

3.4 SEMANTIC PROTOTYPES

It was pointed out in the preceding section that most speakers of English would have difficulty in specifying the defining characteristics of the natural kind denoted by the word 'dog'; that the denotation of 'dog' is, like that of other words denoting natural (and cultural) kinds, somewhat fuzzy and indeterminate; and that when it is important to decide whether an individual entity (or a particular class of entities) is a member (or subclass) of the natural kind in question – e.g., in a court of law or for scientific purposes – the decision is commonly entrusted to experts. But even experts – including lexicographers – often disagree among themselves or find it difficult, in the last resort, to decide non-arbitrarily whether something does or does not fall within the denotation of a so-called natural-kind expression. The denotation (if not the sense) of natural-kind expressions, it has been argued, is inherently indeterminate.

But, if this is so, how is it that speakers of a language seem to use such natural-kind expressions as 'dog' for the most part successfully and without difficulty? One answer to this question is that they only rarely find themselves operating in the fuzzy or indeterminate area of a word's meaning. Speakers of a language normally operate with what have come to be called **prototypes** (or stereotypes); and usually what they want to refer to conforms to the prototype. For example, the prototype for 'dog' might be rather like the Longman definition, which was contrasted with the Collins definition in section 3.2: "a common four-legged flesh-eating animal, especially any of the many varieties used by man as a companion or for hunting, working, guarding, etc.". I have now quoted the definition in full; and it will be observed that the additional part of the definition, running from "especially" to "etc.", indicates that there are several varieties of dogs and that some of these fall within the **nuclear extension** or **focal extension** of 'dog' (that is, they are more typical subclasses of the class than other, non-nuclear or non-focal, varieties are). As for the varieties, most native speakers of English could, no doubt, name a few, and dog-fanciers a lot more: spaniels, terriers, poodles, etc. When it is said that someone knows the meaning of 'dog', it is implied that they have just this kind of knowledge. As I pointed out earlier, the Longman definition unlike the Collins definition ("domesticated canine mammal") does not claim to be synonymous with what it defines. But this is not necessarily a flaw. Sometimes the descriptive meaning of a lexeme can be explained by means of a more or less synonymous paraphrase; in other cases, it can be best conveyed by means of an admittedly imperfect and open-ended definition of the prototype.

The notion of semantic prototypes that has just been explained originated in psycholinguistics and can be related historically to psychological research on the way cognitive categories are learned by infants and children in the course of their development into adults. It has long been clear, of course, that cognitive development proceeds simultaneously and in step with the acquisition of language and that the two developmental processes are not only temporally, but also, at least to some degree, causally connected. The exact nature of this causal connexion, or interdependence, between linguistic and cognitive development is not so clear. As we have seen, on one interpretation of what was referred to earlier as the Sapir–Whorf hypothesis, it is language that is seen as determining thought (3.3); according to the more traditional view of what causes what, it is the structure and operation of the mind that determines the grammatical and semantic structure of languages. Any linguistic theory that is based on the traditional view of the direction of causation between the mind and language I will here refer to, broadly, as **cognitivism**.

Cognitivism, which, as I have defined it, is an eminently traditional doctrine, has recently become very influential in linguistics, both in semantics and in grammar. Indeed, the terms 'cognitive grammar' and 'cognitive semantics' are now used quite widely in linguistics to refer to a variety of theories which have developed the basic principles of cognitivism in particular directions. And given the historical background that I have outlined in the previous paragraph, it is not surprising that the notion of semantic prototypes should have been developed, in the first instance, by cognitivists. It is important to realize, how-ever, that there is no necessary connexion between cognitivism and the notion of semantic prototypes. Cognitivism (which comes in various forms) does not carry with it a commitment to the use of the notion of semantic prototypes and, conversely, the use of semantic prototypes does not carry with it a commit-ment to cognitivism.

Since the notion of semantic prototypes is often coupled with that of natural kinds (and I have introduced it in this context in the preceding section) and the term 'natural kind' is historically associated with philosophical realism, there is a similar point to be made about cognitivism and realism. Cognitivists are often realists (in the philosophical sense of this term), but, in principle, they need not be: i.e., they may, but they need not, take the view that the structure of the world is essentially as it is perceived and categorized by the mind and that, since (according to the cognitivist) the grammatical and semantic structure of languages is determined by the categories of cognition, the grammatical and semantic structure of languages is determined, indirectly, by the structure of the world in terms of such ontolo-gical categories as natural kinds. Conversely, it is possible for someone to take the view (and many do) that what counts is not the ontological structure of the world as such, but representations of the world (independently of whether these representations are faithful representations or not).

In what follows, not only in this chapter, but throughout the whole book, I am adopting a naively realist view of the relation between language and the world. It is a view which is compat-ible with, but not dependent upon, various kinds of cognitivism and is presented throughout within the framework of what is sometimes called autonomous linguistics. It is also compatible with (though not logically dependent on) the assumption, which has long been accepted (though, as we have seen, it was challenged by what I call *tabula rasa* empiricists), that both lin-guistic and cognitive development are controlled by innate, genetically transmitted mechanisms.

As we have seen, the notion of semantic prototypes was invoked initially, in lexical semantics, in the definition of words denoting natural kinds, such as 'dog', 'tiger' or 'lemon'. But, as we have also seen in this chapter, there is no reason to say that the meaning of natural-kind words differs qualitatively from the meaning of words denoting cultural kinds. And the notion of semantic prototypes has been applied by linguists, not only to nouns denoting cultural kinds (such as 'bachelor', 'cup', or 'chair'), but to various subclasses of verbs and adjectives, including colour-terms.

The effect of the adoption of the notion of semantic prototypes in lexical semantics has been the rejection by many linguists of what is sometimes referred to as the checklist theory of definition. According to this theory, which derives from the classical, Aristotelian, notion of essential and accidental properties, every member of a class – and, more especially, every member of a natural kind – must possess (in equal measure) all those properties which, being individually necessary and jointly sufficient, constitute the intension of the class and subclass (the genus and the species) to which it belongs. These properties, in contrast with an entity's accidental properties, are essential in that they constitute its essence (or nature). Moreover, for each such property, the entity in question either has it or does not have it; there is no indeterminacy; and there is no question of more or less. Hence, the term 'checklist': to decide whether something does or does not fall within the scope of a definition – whether something is or is not a dog, a fish, a lemon, etc. – one checks the list of defining properties for the class to which it is thought to belong; and the question whether it does or does not belong to the class is always, at least in principle, decidable.

For further discussion of the implications of replacing the classical theory of lexical definition with a theory based on the notion of semantic prototypes, reference should be made to the works cited in the 'Suggestions for further reading' (several of these works contain a wealth of examples from several languages and from many different areas of the vocabulary). What has been said here about the so-called checklist theory of lexical meaning will be of particular relevance to componential analysis, which is dealt with in the following chapter. But it should be clear that traditional lexicographical practice has been strongly influenced by the classical, or Aristotelian, theory of definition in terms of the essential properties of things.

Rejection of the traditional view of lexical definition has also led many linguists to reject the no less traditional distinction between a dictionary and an encyclopaedia: to put it in psychological terms, between two kinds of knowledge, linguistic and non-linguistic. It is easy enough to draw this distinction in the abstract, especially in psychological terms. One can say that knowing the meaning of a word is a part of linguistic competence (in the Chomskyan sense of 'competence': see section 1.4) and is stored in the brain, in what is commonly referred to in the current literature of psycholinguistics as the mental lexicon, whereas non-linguistic, encyclopaedic, knowledge is stored elsewhere in the brain, may be qualitatively different as knowledge, and, unlike linguistic knowledge, may vary from individual to individual. The problem is that, although a certain amount of progress has been made by psycholinguists in the study of the mental lexicon in recent years, it is still by no means clear whether linguistic knowledge is qualitatively different from other kinds of knowledge (or belief) and stored, neurophysiologically, in another part of the brain.

As to other ways of drawing a distinction between a dictionary and an encyclopaedia that have been proposed in lexical semantics, they too must be treated with caution. Everything that has been said so far in Part 2 of this book tends to support the view that one's knowledge of language and one's knowledge of the world (including the culture in which the language operates) are interdependent. We can draw a distinction, as far as descriptive meaning is concerned, between sense and denotation. We can also say, legitimately, that the former is more definitely linguistic in that it is wholly language-internal, whereas the latter relates the language to the world. In doing so, we can accept that the lexical linkage of languages to the world, at least for some kinds of words, may very well involve knowledge (or belief) about the world. If we are guided by lexicographical practice, rather than simply by linguistic or psycholinguistic theory, we shall certainly take this view. As we have seen in our discussion of typical dictionary definitions for the natural-kind noun 'dog', it is not only dictionaries that are explicitly described as encyclopaedic which supply what might be described as encyclopaedic information about what such words (prototypically) denote. It may be added that many conventional reference dictionaries provide for such words pictures of what they (prototypically) denote (as well as definitions which, as was noted above, derive historically from the classical theory of definition); and that those who consult dictionaries of this kind usually find the pictures helpful, if not essential. Theories of lexical meaning that invoke the notion of natural (and cultural) kinds, and more especially those that also invoke the notion of prototypes, can be seen as providing philosophical and psycholinguistic support for this part of traditional lexicographical practice.

In what follows, we shall leave on one side the question whether the distinction between linguistic and non-linguistic (encyclopaedic) meaning is viable (as far as the denotation of all words that have denotation is concerned). We shall concentrate instead on the way in which the language-internal part of lexical meaning has been handled in recent linguistic semantics: we shall concentrate on sense, rather than denotation; on word-to-word, rather than word-to-world relations.

CHAPTER 4

The structural approach

4.0 INTRODUCTION

As we saw in the last chapter, words cannot be defined independently of other words that are (semantically) related to them and delimit their sense. Looked at from a semantic point of view, the lexical structure of a language – the structure of its vocabulary – can be regarded as a network of **sense-relations**: it is like a web in which each strand is one such relation and each knot in the web is a different lexeme.

The key-terms here are 'structure' and 'relation', each of which, in the present context, presupposes and defines the other. It is the word 'structure' (via the corresponding adjective 'structural') that has provided the label – 'structuralism' – which distinguishes modern from pre-modern linguistics. There have been, and are, many schools of structural linguistics; and some of them, until recently, have not been very much concerned with semantics. Nowadays, however, structural semantics (and more especially structural lexical semantics) is as well established everywhere as structural phonology and structural morphology long have been. But what is structural semantics? That is the question we take up in the following section.

We shall then move on to discuss two approaches to the task of describing the semantic structure of the vocabularies of languages in a precise and systematic way: **componential analysis** and the use of **meaning-postulates**. Reference will also be made, though briefly, to the theory of **semantic fields** (or **lexical fields**). Particular attention will be given to componential analysis, because this has figured prominently in the recent literature of lexical semantics. As we shall see, it is no longer as widely supported by linguists as it was a decade or so ago, at least in what one might think of as its classical formulation. The reasons why this is so will be explained in the central sections of this chapter. It will also be shown that what are usually presented as three different approaches to the description of lexical meaning – componential analysis, the use of meaning postulates and the theory of semantic fields – are not in principle incompatible.

In our discussion of lexical structure in this chapter, we shall make use of a few simple notions borrowed from modern logic. These notions will be useful for the treatment of sentence-meaning and utterance-meaning in Parts 3 and 4. Indeed, in the course of the present chapter it will become evident that the formalization of lexical structure in terms of the truth and falsity of propositions presupposes a satisfactory account of the way in which propositions are expresssed in natural languages. We cannot give such an account, even in outline, without discussing the propositional content of sentences. As we shall see in Part 3, propositional content is one part of sentence-meaning. Although we are still dealing with lexical meaning in this, the final chapter of Part 2, we are therefore looking ahead to the integration of lexical meaning and sentence-meaning. In doing so, we are tacitly addressing one of the questions posed in Part 1: which is logically and methodologically prior to the other, the meaning of words or the meaning of sentences? The answer, as far as sense and propositional content is concerned, is that they are interdependent, neither of them being logically or methodologically prior to the other.

4.1 STRUCTURAL SEMANTICS

Structuralism, as we saw in the preceding chapter, is opposed to atomism (3.3). As such, it is a very general movement, or attitude, in twentieth-century thought, which has influenced many academic disciplines. It has been especially influential in the social sciences and in linguistics, semiotics and literary criticism (and in various interdisciplinary combinations of two or all three of these). The brief account of structural semantics that is given here is restricted to what might be described, more fully, as structuralist linguistic semantics: i.e., to those approaches to linguistic semantics (and, as we shall see, there are several) that are based on the principles of structuralism. It should be noted, however, that structural semantics, in this sense, overlaps with other kinds of structural, or structuralist, semantics: most notably, in the post-Saussurean tradition, with parts of semiotic and literary semantics. Here, as elsewhere, there is a certain artificiality in drawing the disciplinary boundaries too sharply.

The definition that I have given of structural semantics, though deliberately restricted to linguistic semantics, is nevertheless broader than the definition that many would give it and covers many approaches to linguistic semantics that are not generally labelled as 'structural semantics' in the literature. First of all, for historical reasons the label 'structural semantics' is usually limited to lexical semantics. With historical hindsight one can see that this limitation is, to say the least, paradoxical. One of the most basic and most general principles of structural linguistics is that languages are integrated systems, the component subsystems (or levels) of which – grammatical, lexical and phonological – are interdependent. It follows that one cannot sensibly discuss the structure of a language's vocabulary (or lexicon) without explicitly or implicitly taking account of its grammatical structure. This principle, together with other, more specific, structuralist principles, was tacitly introduced (without further development) in Chapter 1 of this book, when I explained the Saussurean distinction between 'langue' and 'langage' (including 'parole') and, despite the organization of the work into separate parts, will be respected throughout.

The main reason why the term 'structural semantics' has generally been restricted to lexical semantics is that in the earlier part of this century the term 'semantics' (in linguistics) was similarly restricted. This does not mean, however, that earlier generations of linguists were not concerned with what we now recognize as non-lexical, and more especially grammatical, semantics. On the contrary, traditional grammar – both syntax and morphology, but particularly the former – was very definitely and explicitly based on semantic considerations: on the study of what is being handled in this book under the rubric of 'sentence-meaning'. But the meaning of grammatical categories and constructions had been dealt with, traditionally, under 'syntax', 'inflection' and 'word-formation' (nowadays called 'derivation'). Structuralism did not have as widespread or as early an effect on the study of meaning, either lexical or non-lexical, as it did on the study of form (phonology and morphology). Once this effect came to be discernible (from the 1930s), structural semantics should have been seen for what it was: lexical semantics within the framework of structural linguistics. Some, but not all, schools of structural linguistics saw it in this way. And after the Second World War all the major schools of linguistics proclaimed their adherence to what I have identified above as the principal tenet of structuralism.

We now come to a second historical reason why the term 'structural semantics' has a much narrower coverage in the literature, even today, than it should have and – more to the point – why the structural approach to semantics, identified as such, is still not as well represented as it should be in most textbooks of linguistics. By the time that the term 'structural semantics' came to be widely used in Europe (especially in Continental Europe) in the 1950s, the more general term 'structural linguistics' had become closely associated in the United States with the particularly restricted and in many ways highly untypical version of structuralism known as Bloomfieldian or post-Bloomfieldian linguistics. One of the distinguishing (and controversial) features of this version of structural linguistics was its comparative lack of interest in semantics. Another was its rejection of the distinction between the language-system and either the use of the system (behaviour) or the products of the use of the system (utterances). The rehabilitation of semantics in what one may think of as mainstream American linguistics did not come about until the mid-1960s, in the classical period of Chomskyan generative grammar, and, when this happened, as we shall see in Part 3, it was sentence-meaning rather than lexical meaning that was of particular concern to generative grammarians, on the one hand, and to formal semanticists, on the other.

Although the Bloomfieldian (or post-Bloomfieldian) school of linguistics was comparatively uninterested in, and in certain instances dismissive of, semantics, there was another tradition in the United States, strongly represented among anthropological linguists in the 1950s, which stemmed from Edward Sapir, rather than Leonard Bloomfield, and was by no means uninterested in semantics. In other respects also, this tradition was much closer in spirit to European structuralism. Sapir was mentioned above in connexion with what is commonly referred to as the Sapir–Whorf hypothesis: the hypothesis that every language is, as it were, a law unto itself; that each language has its own unique structure of grammatical and lexical categories, and creates its own conceptual reality by imposing this particular categorial structure upon the world of sensation and experience (3.3). When I mentioned the Sapir–Whorf hypothesis earlier, I noted that there was no necessary connexion between this kind of linguistic relativism (or anti-universalism) and the essential principles of structuralism. Not only is this so, but it is arguable that Sapir himself was not committed to a strongly relativistic version of the Sapir–Whorf hypothesis. Many of his followers were certainly not so committed. Indeed, they were responsible for promoting in the United States a particular kind of structuralist lexical semantics, componential analysis, one of the features of which was that it operated with a set of atomic components of lexical meaning that were assumed to be universal. As we shall see in Part 3, this was subsequently incorporated in the so-called standard theory of generative grammar in the mid-1960s.

As there are many schools of structural linguistics, so there are many schools of structural semantics (lexical and non-lexical). Not all of these will be dealt with, or even referred to, in this book. For reasons that will be explained in the following sections, we shall be concentrating on the approach to lexical semantics that has just been mentioned: componential analysis. This is not a distinguishable school of semantics, but rather a method of analysis which (with variations which will be pointed out later) is common to several such schools.

At first sight, componential analysis, which is based on a kind of atomism, might seem to be incompatible with structuralism. But this is not necessarily so. What really counts is whether the atoms of meaning into which the meanings of words are analysed, or factorized, are thought of as being logically and epistemologically independent of one another (in the way that logical atomists like Russell thought the meanings of words were logically and epistemologically independent: 3.2). Some practitioners of componential analysis take this view; others do not. But both groups will tend to emphasize the fact that all the words in the same semantic field are definable in terms of the structural relations that they contract with one another, and they will see componential analysis as a means of describing these relations. It is this emphasis on languages as relational structures which constitutes the essence of structuralism in linguistics. What this means as far as lexical meaning is concerned will be explained in the following sections.

As we shall see, looked at from this point of view, componential analysis in lexical semantics is, as it were, doubly structuralist (in the same way that distinctive-feature analysis in phonology is also doubly structuralist). It defines the meaning of words, simultaneously, in terms of the external, interlexical, relational structures – the semantic fields – in which semantically related and interdefinable words, or word-meanings, function as units and also in terms of the internal, intralexical and as it were molecular, relational structures in which what I am here calling the atoms of word-meaning function as units.

4.2 COMPONENTIAL ANALYSIS

One way of formalizing, or making absolutely precise, the sense-relations that hold among lexemes is by means of **componential analysis**. As the name implies, this involves the analysis of the sense of a lexeme into its component parts. It has a long history in philosophical discussions of languages. But it is only recently that it has been employed at all extensively by linguists.

An alternative term for componential analysis is **lexical decomposition**.

Let us begin with a much used example. The words 'boy', 'girl', 'man' and 'woman' all denote human beings. We can therefore extract from the sense of each of them the common factor "human": i.e., the sense of the English word 'human'. (Throughout this section, the notational distinction between single and double quotation-marks is especially important: see 1.5.) Similarly, we can extract from "boy" and "man" the common factor "male", and from "girl" and "woman", the common factor "female". As for "man" and "woman", they can be said to have as one of their factors the **sense-component** "adult", in contrast with "boy" and "girl", which lack "adult" (or, alternatively, contain "non-adult"). The sense of each of the four words can thus be represented as the product of three factors:

(1) "man"   = "human" × "male" × "adult"
(2) "woman" = "human" × "female" × "adult"
(3) "boy"   = "human" × "male" × "non-adult"
(4) "girl"   = "human" × "female" × "non-adult"

I have deliberately used the multiplication-sign to emphasize the fact that these are intended to be taken as mathematically precise equations, to which the terms 'product' and 'factor' apply exactly as they do in, say, $30 = 2 \times 3 \times 5$. So far so good. Whether the equations we set up are empirically correct is another matter. We shall come to this presently.

Actually, sense-components are not generally represented by linguists in the way that I have introduced them. Instead of saying that "man" is the product of "human", "male" and "adult", it is more usual to identify its factors as HUMAN, MALE and ADULT. This is not simply a matter of typographical preference. By convention, small capitals are employed to refer to the allegedly universal sense-components out of which the senses of expressions in particular natural languages are constructed. Much of the attraction of componential analysis derives from the possibility of identifying such universal sense-components in the lexical structure of different languages. They are frequently described as basic atomic concepts – in the sense of 'basic' that is dominant in the philosophical tradition (which, as was noted in Chapter 3, does not necessarily correspond with other senses of 'basic').

What then, is the relation between HUMAN and "human", between MALE and "male", and so on? This is a theoretically important question. It cannot be assumed without argument that MALE necessarily equals, or is equivalent with, "male": that the allegedly universal sense-component MALE is identical with "male" (the sense of the English word 'male'). And yet it is only on this assumption (in default of the provision of more explicit rules of interpretation) that the decomposition of "man" into MALE, ADULT and HUMAN can be interpreted as saying anything about the sense-relations that hold among the English words 'man', 'male', 'human' and 'adult'. We shall, therefore, make the assumption. This leaves open the obvious question: why should English, or any other natural language, have privileged status as a metalanguage for the semantic analysis of all languages?

We can now develop the formalization a little further. First of all, we can abstract the negative component from "non-adult" and replace it with the **negation-operator**, as this is defined in standard propositional logic: '$\sim$'. Alternatively, and in effect equivalently, we can distinguish a positive and a negative value of the two-valued variable $+/-$ADULT (plus-or-minus ADULT), whose two values are $+$ADULT and $-$ADULT. Linguists working within the framework of Chomskyan generative grammar have normally made use of this second type of notation. We now have as a basic, presumably atomic, component ADULT, together with its complementary $-$ADULT. If MALE and FEMALE are also complementary, we can take one of them as basic and form the other from it by means of the same negation-operator.

But which of them is more basic than the other, either in nature or in culture? The question is of considerable theoretical interest if we are seriously concerned with establishing an inventory of universal sense-components. It is in principle conceivable that there is no universally valid answer. What is fairly clear, however, is that, as far as the vocabulary of English is concerned, it is normally MALE that one wants to treat as being more general and thus, in one sense, more basic. Feminists might argue, and perhaps rightly, that this fact is culturally explicable. At any rate, there are culturally explicable exceptions: 'nurse', 'secretary', etc., among words that (normally) denote human beings; 'goose', 'duck', and in certain respects 'cow', among words denoting domesticated animals. As for HUMAN, this is in contrast with a whole set of what from one point of view are equally basic components: let us call them CANINE, FELINE, BOVINE, etc. They are equally basic in that they can be thought of as denoting the complex defining properties of natural kinds (see 3.3).

Earlier, I used the multiplication-sign to symbolize the operation by means of which components are combined. Let me now substitute for this the propositional connective of **conjunction**: '&'. We can then rewrite the analysis of "man", "woman", "boy", "girl" as:

(1a) "man"   = HUMAN & MALE & ADULT
(2a) "woman" = HUMAN & ∼MALE & ADULT
(3a) "boy"   = HUMAN & MALE & ∼ADULT
(4a) "girl"   = HUMAN & ∼MALE & ∼ADULT

And to this we may add:

(5) "child"   = HUMAN & ∼ADULT

in order to make clear the difference between the absence of a component and its negation. The absence of ∼MALE from the representation of the sense of 'child' differentiates "child" from "girl". As for 'horse', 'stallion', 'mare', 'foal', 'sheep', 'ram', 'ewe', 'lamb', 'bull', 'cow', 'calf' – these, and many other sets of words, can be analysed in the same way by substituting EQUINE, OVINE, BOVINE, etc., as the case may be, for HUMAN.

The only logical operations utilized so far are negation and conjunction. And, in using symbols for propositional operators, '∼' and '&', and attaching them directly, not to propositions, but to what logicians would call predicates, I have taken for granted a good deal of additional formal apparatus. Some of this will be introduced later. The formalization that I have employed is not the only possible one. I might equally have used, at this point, the terminology and notation of elementary **set-theory**. Everything said so far about the compositional nature of lexical meaning could be expressed in terms of sets and their complements and of the intersection of sets. For example, "boy" = HUMAN & MALE & ~ADULT can be construed as telling us that any individual element that falls within the extension of the word 'boy' is contained in the intersection of three sets H, M and ~A, where H is the extension of 'human' (whose intension is HUMAN = "human"), M is the extension of 'male' and ~A is the complement of the extension of 'adult'. This is illustrated graphically by means of so-called Venn diagrams in Figure 4.1.

There are several reasons for introducing these elementary notions of set-theory at this point. First, they are implicit, though rarely made explicit, in more informal presentations of componential analysis. Second, they are well understood and have been precisely formulated in modern mathematical logic; and as we shall see in Part 3, they play an important role in the most influential systems of formal semantics. Finally, they enable us to give a very precise interpretation to the term 'product' when we say that the sense of a lexeme is the product of its components, or factors.

Let me develop this third point in greater detail. I will begin by replacing the term 'product' with the more technical term 'compositional function', which is now widely used in formal

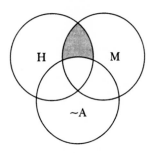

Figure 4.1 The shaded portion represents the intersection of H, M and ~A

semantics. To say that the sense of a lexeme (or one of its senses) is a **compositional function** of its sense-components is to imply that its value is fully determined by (i) the value of the components and (ii) the definition of the operations by means of which they are combined. To say that the sense of a lexeme is a **set-theoretic** function of its sense-components is to say that it is a compositional function of a particularly simple kind.

The notion of **compositionality**, as we shall see in Part 3, is absolutely central in modern formal semantics. So too is the mathematical sense of the term 'function'. All those who have mastered the rudiments of elementary set-theory at school (or indeed of simple arithmetic and algebra considered from a sufficiently general point of view) will be familiar with the principle of compositionality and with the mathematical concept of a compositional function already, though they may never have met the actual terms 'compositionality' and 'function' until now. It should be clear, for example, that a simple algebraic expression such as $y = 2x + 4$ satisfies the definition of 'compositional function' given above in that the numerical value of y is fully determined by whatever numerical value is assigned to x (within a specified range), on the one hand, and by the arithmetical operations of addition and multiplication, on the other.

The lexemes used so far to illustrate the principles of componential analysis can all be seen as property-denoting words. They are comparable with what logicians call **one-place predicates**: expressions which have one place to be filled, as it were, in order for them to be used in a well-formed proposition. For example, if 'John' is associated with the one-place predicate 'boy' (by means of what is traditionally called the copula: in English, the verb 'be', in the appropriate tense) and if the semantically empty indefinite article *a* is added before the form *boy* (so that 'boy' in the composite form *a boy* is the complement of the verb 'be'), the result is a simple declarative sentence which can be used to express the proposition "John is a boy". (For simplicity, I have omitted many details that will be taken up later.) Other words, notably transitive verbs (e.g., 'hit', 'kill'), most prepositions, and nouns such as 'father', 'mother', etc. are two-place relational predicates: they denote the relations that hold between the two entities referred to by the expressions that fill the two places (or alternatively, as in the case of 'father', 'mother', etc., the set of entities that can be referred to by the set of expressions that fill one of the places). This means that their decomposition must take account of the directionality of the relations. For example,

(6) "father" = PARENT & MALE

is inadequate in that it does not make explicit the fact that fatherhood is a two-place (or two-term) relation or represent its directionality. It may be expanded by adding **variables** in the appropriate places:

(7) "father" = (x,y) PARENT & (x) MALE,

which expresses the fact that parenthood (and therefore fatherhood) is a relation with two places filled (x,y) and that (in all cases of fatherhood – on the assumption that the variables are taken to be universally quantified) x is the parent of y and x is male. This not only makes clear the directionality of the relation (in the relative order of the variables x and y). It also tells us that it is the sex of x, not of y, that is relevant.

There are other complications. Most important of all is the necessity of introducing in the representation of the sense of certain lexemes a hierarchical structure which reflects the syntactic structure of the propositional content of sentences. For example, "give" is more or less plausibly analysed as one two-place structure (y,z) HAVE, embedded within another two-place structure $(x,*)$ CAUSE, where the asterisk indicates the place in which it is to be embedded:

(8) $(x, (y,z)$ HAVE$)$ CAUSE.

This may be read as meaning (the question of tense being left on one side) "x causes y to have z". And "kill" can be analysed, similarly, as a one-place structure embedded within the same causative two-place structure:

(9) $(x, (y)$ DIE$)$ CAUSE,

which may be read as meaning "*x* causes *y* to die". Representations of this kind presuppose a much more powerful system of formalization than the set-theoretic operations sufficient, in principle, for the examples used earlier in this section. Nevertheless, there is no doubt that the compositionality of more complex examples such as "give" and "kill" can be formalized. Various alternative proposals have been made in recent years, notably by linguists working within the framework of various kinds of generative grammar.

4.3 THE EMPIRICAL BASIS FOR COMPONENTIAL ANALYSIS

To say that componential analysis can be formalized is a quite different matter from saying that it is theoretically interesting or in conformity with the facts as they present themselves to us in real life. Theoretical motivation and empirical validity raise questions of a different order from those relating to formalization. The theoretical motivation for componential analysis is clear enough. It provides linguists, in principle, with a systematic and economical means of representing the sense-relations that hold among lexemes in particular languages and, on the assumption that the components are universal, across languages. But much of this theoretical motivation is undermined when one looks more carefully at particular analyses. First of all, there is the problem of deciding which of the two senses of 'basic' discussed in the previous chapter should determine the selection of the putative atomic universal components. There is no reason to believe that what is basic in the sense of being maximally general is also basic in the day-to-day thinking of most users of a language. Moreover, it can be demonstrated that, if one always extracts those components which can be identified in the largest number of lexemes, one will frequently end up with a less economical and less systematic analysis for particular lexemes than would be the case if one analysed each lexeme on its own terms.

As for the empirical validity of componential analysis, it is not difficult to show that this is more apparent than real. For example, the analysis of "boy", "girl" and "child" (i.e., of the sense of the English words 'boy', 'girl' and 'child') given in the preceding section tells us that all boys and girls are children. But this is not true: the proposition expressed by saying:

(10) *John is a boy and Jane is a girl*

does not imply the proposition expressed by saying

(11) *John and Jane are children*

(in the relevant, non-relational, sense of 'child'). And there is no point in arguing that this is a matter of the use, rather than the meaning, of 'child', or alternatively of the non-literal meaning or of some aspect of meaning other than sense. The English expressions 'male child' and 'female child' are not descriptively synonymous with 'boy' and 'girl'. At the very least, therefore, something must be added to the analysis to capture this fact. And what about the analysis of the sense of 'boy' and 'girl' in relation to that of 'man' and 'woman'? Even here not-ADULT creates difficulty. First of all, neither the proposition "That boy is now an adult" nor "That girl is now an adult" (unlike "That child is now an adult") appear to be in any way anomalous. How then, in this case, does the hypothetical universal sense-component ADULT relate to "adult" (the sense of the English word 'adult')? This question needs to be answered.

Second, there is the fact that, in most contexts, 'girl' and 'woman' are not used as contradictories, whereas 'boy' and 'man', though they may not be contradictories in the strict sense, are certainly more sharply opposed to one another semantically than 'girl' and 'woman' are. Finally, none of the more obvious and relatively objective biological or cultural criteria of adulthood – sexual maturity, legal majority, economic and social independence, etc. – is relevant, except in certain contexts, to the use, descriptively, of 'man' rather than 'boy' or of 'woman' rather than 'girl'. Needless to say, these difficulties are compounded when we start comparing the analysis of 'child' with that of 'lamb' or 'foal' – not to mention that of 'boy' and 'girl' with that of 'colt' and 'filly'.

Similarly, it can be argued that, although HUMAN is an essential component of "man" and "woman", it is not an essential component of "boy", and possibly not of "girl". The male offspring of the gods (e.g., Cupid) are regularly described as boys (and their female offspring, in the appropriate circumstances, as maidens); but they do not grow up to be men, and they are not said to be human. And, once again, it is unreasonable to say that, in cases like this, 'boy' or 'girl' is being used non-literally. We must be careful not to import our own metaphysical prejudices into the analysis of the vocabularies of natural languages. And we must not make the distinction between literal and non-literal meaning dependent upon them.

If componential analysis is defective both theoretically and empirically, why have I devoted so much space to it? Partly, because it has figured prominently in recent works on semantics and has guided a good deal of undoubtedly valuable research. Partly, also, because there is another way of looking at componential analysis which makes it less obviously defective. This is to take it, not as a technique for the representation of all of the sense (and nothing but the sense) of lexemes, but as a way of formalizing that part of their **prototypical**, nuclear or focal, sense which they share with other lexemes. For example, there is no doubt that 'boy' is used prototypically of human beings and furthermore that, in so far as we understand it when it is used descriptively of Cupid, we do so because we understand it, first of all, in relation to human beings. So HUMAN is criterial for the focal meaning of 'boy' and serves also, analogically, in non-focal uses. But it is not part of its intension: i.e., of the property which defines the class whose members it denotes. Most of the allegedly universal components that have been proposed are of this kind.

Componential analysis is no longer defended by linguists, on theoretical grounds, as enthusiastically as it was by many a few years ago. Some of the reasons for this change of heart on the part of many, though by no means all, linguists have to do with more general issues pertaining to any allegedly exhaustive and determinate analysis of the sense of lexemes. Others relate specifically to componential analysis as such. As I have suggested in the account of componential analysis that has been given here, it is perhaps empirically indefensible in what might be called its standard or classical version, especially if this is coupled with assumptions of universality. At the same time, it has been of considerable historical importance and is still quite widely accepted. In the following sections, we shall see that, far from being in conflict with other approaches to structural semantics, it is, at least in principle, fully compatible with them. In particular, it is compatible, not only with the appeal to prototypes, but also, as will be explained presently, with the use of what are called meaning-postulates.

4.4 ENTAILMENT AND POSSIBLE WORLDS

Entailment plays an important role in all theories of meaning, and a more central role in some than in others. Take the following two propositions, which I have labelled p and q (for reasons that will be explained immediately):

(12) "Achilles killed Hector" (p)
(13) "Hector died" (q)

Here the first proposition, p, necessarily implies, or **entails**, the second proposition, q: if it is the case that Achilles killed Hector, then it is necessarily the case that Hector died. In logical terminology, entailment is a relation that holds between p and q – where p and q are variables standing for propositions – such that, if the truth of q necessarily follows from the truth of p (and the falsity of q necessarily follows from the falsity of p), then p entails q. The key term here is 'necessarily'.

It should be noted, first of all, that entailment has been defined as a relation between **propositions**. This is important. Some authors talk of entailments as holding between sentences. In doing so, they are using the term 'sentence' either loosely or in a very special sense. Others, for reasons that we need not go into here, define entailment as a relation between statements. But this usage, too, rests upon a specialized definition of 'statement', which conflicts in several respects with its everyday sense in English and can lead to confusion. I will discuss the relation between sentences and propositions in Part 3, and the nature of statements, as well as that of questions, commands etc., in Part 4. At this point, I would simply draw readers' attention to the fact that here (as indeed earlier) I have tacitly extended my use of double quotation-marks to cover propositions. A proposition, as we shall see later, is one part of the meaning of the utterance in which it is expressed.

There is no standard symbolization of the relation of entailment. I will use a double-shafted arrow. Thus

(14) $p \Rightarrow q$

will mean "p entails q". The logical relation thus symbolized can be defined, in modal logic, in terms of implication and necessity. We need not go into the formalism. But we do need to discuss the notion of necessity itself. Propositions may be either necessarily or contingently true (or false). A **necessarily** true (or false) proposition is one that is true (or false) in all possible circumstances: or, as the seventeenth-century German philosopher, Gottfried Leibniz (1646–1716) put it, **in all possible worlds**. For example, the propositions

(15) "Snow is white"

and

(16) "Rabbits are human"

might well be necessarily true and necessarily false, respectively. A **contingently** true (or false) proposition, on the other hand, is one whose truth-value might have been, or might be, different in other circumstances (in other possible worlds). For example,

(17) "Napoleon was defeated at Waterloo"

is contingent in the required sense. We can envisage a possible world, or a possible state of the world, of which it is not true. This intuitively comprehensible notion of **possible worlds** (satirized, incidentally, in its theological development by Leibniz, in Voltaire's *Candide*) has been formalized in various ways in modern modal logic. For logical purposes, a possible world may be identified with the set of propositions that truly describe it. It is under this interpretation of 'world' that one talks of propositions being true in, rather than of, a world. It will be noted that I have used both ways of talking about worlds in this paragraph. For the present, I will draw no distinctions between these two ways of talking. It may be helpful, however, if one thinks of the world in which propositions are true (or false) as the inner, mental or cognitive, world and the world of which the propositions are true as the outer (i.e., extramental) world which is **represented** by the inner world.

This is straightforward enough as far as it goes. Problems emerge as soon as one looks at the notion of necessity more closely. We may begin by considering two kinds of necessary truths recognized by philosophers: analytic and logical. (These are not always clearly distinguished in linguistic semantics.) The notion of analytic truth (in the modern sense of 'analytic') derives from the work of the great eighteenth-century German philosopher Immanuel Kant (1724–1804). According to Kant, a proposition (traditionally represented as the combination of a subject and a predicate) is **analytically** true if the meaning of the subject is contained in that of the predicate and can be revealed by analysis. For example, granted that "female" (the meaning of 'female') or alternatively FEMALE (a universal sense-component which is identical with or includes "female") is included in "girl", the truth of

(18) "All girls are female"

can be demonstrated by the analysis of the subject-expression, 'all girls', and more especially of the lexeme 'girl'. The sense of 'girl' (i.e., "girl") can be analysed, or decomposed, into "human" × "female" × "non-adult": see (4) in section 4.2. So the proposition we are discussing is equivalent to

(19) "All human, female, non-adults are female",

in which the predicate "female" is patently contained in the subject. One can see immediately both the original motivation for the use of the term 'analytic' and the relevance, to this topic, of the technique of componential analysis. Nowadays, it is more common to reformulate the definition of analyticity in more general terms: an analytically true (or **analytic**) proposition is one which is necessarily true by virtue of its meaning – one which can be shown to be true by (semantic) analysis. This is the formulation that we shall adopt.

Any proposition that is not analytic is, by definition, **synthetic**. Therefore, all contingent propositions, such as

(20) "Napoleon was defeated at Waterloo",

are synthetic. (And, here again, I take the opportunity of reminding readers that (20) is a proposition only if the referring expressions in it, notably 'Napoleon' and 'Waterloo', are fixed in their reference.) It does not follow, however, that all synthetic propositions are contingent. This point is important and has been much discussed by philosophers. We shall not need to deal with it here. It suffices that, as linguists, we are aware that a case can be made for the (rationalist) view (rejected by many empiricist philosophers) that there are some synthetic necessary truths which are known to be true *a priori*: i.e., prior to, or independently of, experience.

We come now to the question of logical truth. A **logically** true (or false) proposition is one whose truth-value is determined solely by the **logical form** of the proposition: e.g.,

(21) "Every person who is female is female".

What is meant by 'logical form' is, in part, controversial. Even more controversial is the relation between the logical form of propositions and the structure of natural-language sentences. But for present purposes it may be assumed that 'logical form' is satisfactorily defined in standard systems of logic and that, in straightforward cases at least, we have an intuitive understanding of it. It may be assumed, for example, that

(22) "All female persons are female",
(23) "All red books are red",

etc. are recognized intuitively as logical truths. They would certainly be so classified, by virtue of their form (i.e., their structure), in all standard systems of logic. As I have said earlier, logical truths constitute one of two kinds of necessary truths.

Moreover, if logical form is held to be a part of the meaning of propositions, logical truths are a subclass of analytic truths. All this follows by definition. It has been argued that all analytic truths are also logical truths; but this is highly controversial and cannot be taken for granted. It has also been argued, or simply assumed without argument, that the only necessary truths are logical truths. In my view, there are very good reasons for recognizing different kinds, not only of non-logical necessity, but also of non-analytic necessity.

Linguists have often used the term 'necessarily', and even 'entailment', rather loosely. In so far as they are concerned with the semantic structure of natural languages, it is not necessarily true propositions as such that should be of interest to them, but analytically true propositions (including logical truths). Similarly, if entailment is defined as above, it is not entailment in its entirety that is, or should be, of central concern, but rather what might be called semantic, or analytic, entailment. Generally speaking, this is what linguists have in mind when they invoke the notion of entailment. Henceforth I will use the term 'entailment' in this narrower sense. It is of course possible to argue that all necessary truths are analytic, as I indicated earlier. On the face of it, however, this does not seem to be so.

First of all, there are propositions which, if true, are true by virtue of natural, or physical, necessity: i.e., by virtue of the laws of nature. The qualification, "if true", is important. We must never confuse the **epistemological status** of a proposition with its **truth-value**. There is a difference between a proposition's being true (or false) and a proposition's being held to be true. Propositions do not change their truth-value; their epistemological status, on the other hand, is subject to revision in the light of new information, changes in the scientific or cultural frame of reference which determines a society's generally accepted ontological assumptions, etc. (We have already noted the importance of allowing for such changes in our discussion of the Putnam–Kripke view of natural-kind expressions: see 3.3.) A proposition which is true by virtue of **natural necessity** might be:

(24) "All human beings are mortal".

Arguably this proposition, if true, is true by virtue of biological necessity (which, according to current conceptions, is a particular kind of natural necessity). And yet it is surely not analytic. The meaning of 'human' would not suddenly change (nor would the meaning of 'mortal') if it were discovered, contrary to popular belief and so far well-established scientific hypotheses, that some human beings are immortal or could be made so by regular and repeated surgical intervention.

Once we have seen the distinction between natural necessity and necessity by virtue of meaning in a fairly obvious case such as the one just mentioned, it is easier to appreciate that many examples of entailment which figure in the recent literature are dubious, to say the least. What about (25), for instance?

(25) "Jackie is pregnant" ⇒ "Jackie is female".

At first sight, one might be inclined to say that (25) is true by virtue of the meaning of 'pregnant' and 'female'. A moment's reflection, however, will show that we are not dealing with a valid example of semantic entailment. Let us suppose that advances in surgical and immunological techniques made it possible to transplant into a man a foetus-bearing womb (and to do everything else that the hypothesis requires) and then to deliver the child by Caesarean section. One can think of several variations on this theme, all of which, simply by being conceptually coherent, cast doubt upon the view that "female" is part of the meaning of 'pregnant'. But we do not have to speculate about the details. It suffices that we are able to discuss rationally the possibility of a man being pregnant and argue about the personal and social consequences. If we impose upon 'possible world' the same restrictions as we have imposed upon 'entailment', we can say that there are possible worlds in which "x is pregnant" does not entail "x is female" (where "x" is a variable which stands for any appropriate expression). After all, as Leibniz might have said, things could have been different in some world other than the best of all possible worlds, which God, in his wisdom, has actualized (and which, in ways yet to be revealed to theologians and scientists, he may change, for example by making it possible for men and women to share the onerous responsibility of child-bearing).

As we have recognized cultural kinds, in addition to natural kinds, so we might recognize cultural necessity, in addition to natural necessity. For example, it is arguably a matter of cultural necessity (in our culture), that marriage should be viewed as a symmetrical relation between two persons of different sex. This being so, provided that we are using English to talk about a culture in which the same conditions hold true (in relation to cohabitation, social and economic roles, etc.), we could say that "*x is married to y*" necessarily implies "*y* is married to *x*"; that the conjunction of "*x* is male" and "*x* is married to *y*" necessarily implies "*y* is female", etc. This is obviously different from natural necessity. Furthermore, it is easy to envisage other cultures (or subcultures in our own culture) in which homosexual unions (involving cohabitation, etc.) come to be, not only accepted, but regulated by law and religion on the same footing as heterosexual unions. One can envisage, without much difficulty, trilateral unions in which each member is correctly described, regardless of his or her biological sex, as the wife of one and the husband of the other. Or again, we can easily imagine amendments to our own divorce laws such that it becomes possible for one's partner's marital status to be changed without consequential and reciprocal changes in the status of the other. In such circumstances "*x* is married to *y*" would no longer necessarily imply "*y* is married to *x*". Would the meaning of 'married' have changed? It is at least arguable that it would not.

The consideration of possibilities such as this makes us realize that semantic entailment is by no means as clear-cut as it is often held to be. We do not have to go all the way with such philosophers as Quine (1953) in their criticism of the analytic/synthetic distinction. But we must certainly agree with him when he says that the distinction, as far as natural languages are concerned, is not sharp. I will not press the point further. But I would encourage the reader to look critically at what are alleged to be entailments in recent works in theoretical semantics. Many of them are certainly not entailments, and others are of doubtful status with respect to analyticity. And many sentences that are cited in textbooks of linguistics as examples of grammatical, but meaningless or semantically ill-formed, sentences, such as

(26) 'My uncle is pregnant again',

are, not only fully meaningful, but usable to assert what might be a true proposition in some possible world. We shall return to this question in the following chapter.

4.5 SENSE-RELATIONS AND MEANING-POSTULATES

In Chapter 3, a distinction was drawn between denotation and sense, and sense was defined in terms of **sense-relations**. Some sense-relations were exemplified, but without discussion. None of them, apart from descriptive synonymy, has yet been named or defined. For a more detailed account of various sense-relations, reference may be made to other publications. I will give the briefest possible outline here. My principal concern in the present context is to show how sense-relations of various kinds can be formalized.

Sense-relations are of two kinds: **substitutional** and **combinatorial** (or, in the Saussurean terms more familiar to linguists, **paradigmatic** and **syntagmatic**). Substitutional relations are those which hold between intersubstitutable members of the same grammatical category; combinatorial relations hold typically, though not necessarily, between expressions of different grammatical categories (e.g., between nouns and adjectives, between verbs and adverbs, etc.), which can be put together in grammatically well-formed combinations (or constructions). For example, a substitutional relation (of a particular kind) holds between the nouns 'bachelor' and 'spinster', whereas the relation that holds between the adjective 'unmarried' and the nouns 'man' and 'woman' is combinatorial. The lexically composite expressions 'unmarried man' and 'unmarried woman' are not only grammatically well-formed, but by virtue of what I will call the **congruity** of the sense of the adjective with the sense of both of the nouns they are also **collocationally** acceptable: that is, they can occur together in the same construction. It is intuitively obvious, on the basis of these and other examples, that a more specific, lexically and grammatically simpler, expression may be more or less descriptively equivalent to a lexically composite expression in which two (or several) more general expressions are combined. For example, 'foal' may be descriptively equivalent to 'baby horse'.

I shall have little to say here about combinatorial sense-relations, since they bring us into the area of grammatical meaning and sentence-semantics. It is important to note that certain lexemes are so highly restricted with respect to collocational acceptability that it is impossible to predict their combinatorial relations on the basis of an independent characterization of their sense. Classic examples from English are the adjectives 'rancid' and 'addled'. It is clearly an important part of knowing their sense to know that 'rancid' combines, or **collocates**, with 'butter', and 'addled' with 'egg' (and, metaphorically, with 'brain'). The view taken here is that the sense of any lexeme, whether it is highly restricted with respect to collocational acceptability or not, includes both its combinatorial and substitutional relations.

Only two kinds of substitutional relations of sense will be dealt with in detail here: hyponymy and incompatibility. They are both definable in terms of entailment.

The relation of **hyponymy** is exemplified by such pairs of expressions as 'dog' and 'animal', of which the former is a hyponym of the latter: the sense of 'dog' includes that of 'animal'. Entailment, as we saw in the previous section, is a relation that holds between propositions. However, provided that we keep this fact in mind, it is convenient to be able to say, in a kind of shorthand, that one word or phrase entails another, just as it may be convenient to be able to say, also in a kind of shorthand, that one sentence entails another. Adopting this kind of shorthand we can say one expression, f, is a hyponym of another expression, g, if and only if f entails g: i.e.,

(27) $f \Rightarrow g$.

For example, 'dog' entails 'animal'. Given a proposition p containing "dog", the substitution of "animal" for "dog" in p will yield another proposition q which is entailed by p. Thus:

(28) "I saw a dog" (p)

entails

(29) "I saw an animal" (q).

In this case no syntactic adjustments need to be made. We still have to relate propositions to utterances (and propositional content to sentences). If this can be done, the statement that 'dog' is a hyponym of 'animal' can be given a precise formal interpretation. All this will be of concern to us later. But what is the status of $f \Rightarrow g$ from a formal point of view?

It is best construed as what some logicians, following Carnap (1956), call a **meaning-postulate**. Generally speaking, the use of meaning-postulates has been seen by linguists as an alternative to componential analysis. Looked at from this point of view, the advantage of meaning-postulates over classical or standard versions of componential analysis is that they do not presuppose the exhaustive decomposition of the sense of a lexeme into an integral number of universal sense-components. They can be defined for lexemes as such, without making any assumptions about atomic concepts or universality, and they can be used to give a deliberately incomplete account of the sense of a lexeme. From an empirical point of view these are very considerable advantages. It is, after all, a matter of dispute whether it is possible, even in principle, to give a complete analysis of the sense of all lexemes in the vocabularies of natural languages. As I have emphasized, on several occasions, it is, to say the least, arguable that the sense of some natural-language lexemes is to a greater or less degree fuzzy and indeterminate.

Of course, the validity of any particular meaning-postulate, such as

(30) 'dog' $\Rightarrow$ 'animal'

for English, will depend upon whether the alleged entailment is in fact analytic. In this connexion, it is worth noting the possibility of ordering the meaning-postulates associated with a particular lexeme hierarchically in terms of their degree of analyticity. For example,

(31) 'bachelor' ⇒ 'unmarried'

(in the relevant sense of the word 'bachelor') seems to be more highly, or more definitely, analytic than

(32) 'bachelor' ⇒ 'adult'

and perhaps also than

(33) 'bachelor' ⇒ 'man'.

Let us suppose, for example, that child-marriages were legalized and became a matter of everyday occurrence in some English-speaking society. One would presumably not hesitate to use the word 'bachelor' of an unmarried child in such circumstances. And, arguably, there would have been no change in the sense of 'bachelor'. It is far more difficult to envisage comparable circumstances in which 'bachelor' ⇒ 'unmarried' is invalidated without some other associated change in the sense of either 'bachelor' or 'unmarried'. Regardless of the empirical status of the particular example, it is clear, therefore, that speakers of a language may regard some entailments of a word as more central or more determinate than other entailments of the same word.

Hierarchically ordered meaning-postulates can be used to capture the indeterminacy of the boundary between the analytic and the synthetic. I have made this point in relation to hyponymy, but it holds for all the sense-relations that can be formalized in terms of meaning-postulates. Before we continue, it is now worth noting that descriptive synonymy may be defined in terms of symmetrical hyponymy. Although the term 'hyponymy' is customarily used for an asymmetrical relation of entailment (i.e., where f entails g, but g does not entail f: 'dog' ⇒ 'animal' is true, whereas 'animal ⇒ 'dog' is false), there is nothing in the formal definition of hyponymy which makes this essential. Using a double-headed, double-shafted arrow to symbolize symmetrical entailment, we can say that

(34) $f \Leftrightarrow g$

establishes the descriptive synonymy of f and g (e.g., 'puppy' $\Leftrightarrow$ 'baby dog'). It can be readily proved that the definition of descriptive synonymy in terms of symmetrical entailment is equivalent to the following: two expressions are descriptively synonymous if and only if they have the same entailments.

The second kind of substitutional sense-relation to be mentioned here is **incompatibility**, which is definable in terms of entailment and negation:

(35) $f \Rightarrow \sim g$ and $g \Rightarrow \sim f$.

For example, 'red' and 'blue' are defined to be incompatible in this way: if something is (wholly) red it is necessarily not (even partly) blue, and conversely. A special case of incompatibility is **complementarity**, which holds within two-member lexical sets, where, in addition to (35), the following conditions are also satisfied:

(36) $\sim f \Rightarrow g$ and $\sim g \Rightarrow f$.

For example, not only does (i) 'married' entail the negation of 'unmarried' and (ii) 'unmarried' entail the negation of 'married', but (iii) the negation of 'married' entails 'unmarried' and (iv) the negation of 'unmarried' entails 'married'. Complementarity is often treated as a kind of antonymy ("oppositeness of meaning").

But **antonymy** in the narrowest sense – polar antonymy – differs from complementarity in virtue of **gradability** (in terms of more or less). This means that the conjunction of two negated antonyms is not contradictory. For example, 'good' and 'bad' are polar antonyms and "x is neither good nor bad" is perfectly acceptable, even though "x is not good" might be held to imply "x is bad" (in some looser sense of 'imply') in many contexts. When they are graded in an explicitly comparative construction ("x is better than y"), the following holds:

(37) $f^+ (x,y) \Rightarrow g^+ (y, x)$,

where the superscript plus-sign is a non-standard, but convenient, way of symbolizing "more". For example, if f is 'good' and g is 'bad', then f^+ and g^+ symbolize the selection of the forms *better* and *worse* ("more good" and "more bad"). If we substitute expressions referring to particular individuals for x and y, we see that, for example, "John is better than Peter" entails and is entailed by "Peter is worse than John".

In fact, expressions with the meanings "more good" and "more bad" are **two-place converses**. They are like corresponding active and passive verb-expressions ('kill' : 'be killed'), and also like such pairs of lexemes as 'husband' : 'wife' (due allowance being made in both cases for the associated grammatical adjustments). The verbs 'buy' and 'sell' exemplify the class of **three-place (lexical) converses**:

(38) 'buy' $(x, y, z) \Rightarrow$ 'sell' (z, y, x).

For example, "Mary (x) bought the car (y) from Paul (z)" entails, and is entailed by, "Paul (z) sold the car (y) to Mary (x)". Obviously, what I have here called syntactic adjustments (to avoid the more specific implications of the term 'transformation' in linguistics) need to be precisely specified. Provided that this is done and that we can give a satisfactory account of the relation between sentences, propositions and utterances, we can account formally for sets of entailments such as

(39) "John killed Peter" $\Rightarrow$ "Peter was killed by John",
(40) "Mary is John's wife" $\Rightarrow$ "John is Mary's husband",
(41) "John bought a car from Peter" $\Rightarrow$ "Peter sold a car to John",

and so on.

This is a big proviso! Before we address ourselves to it in Parts 3 and 4, it is worth emphasizing the fact that in this chapter we have been concerned solely with the descriptive meaning of expressions. Moreover, we have limited ourselves to a brief consideration of only the most important of the relations that hold, by virtue of sense, in the vocabularies of natural languages. My main concern has been to give the reader some idea of what is involved in the formalization of lexical structure and to outline two notions that linguists have invoked in this connexion in recent years: sense-relations and meaning-postulates. There is perhaps no reason, in principle, why the non-descriptive meaning of lexemes should not also be formalizable. But so far at least formal semantics has taken the same limited view of lexical structure as we have done here.

PART 3

Sentence-meaning

CHAPTER 5

Meaningful and meaningless sentences

5.0 INTRODUCTION

In the last three chapters we have been concerned with lexical semantics: i.e., with the meaning of lexemes. We now move on, in Part 3, to a consideration of the meaning of sentences.

The distinction between sentences and utterances was introduced in Chapter 1 (see 1.6). The need for drawing this distinction is reinforced by the discussion of grammaticality, acceptability and meaningfulness in the following section (5.1). But our main concern in this short, and relatively non-technical, chapter is the meaningfulness of sentences. Granted that some sentences are meaningful and others meaningless, what grounds do we have for drawing a theoretical distinction between these two classes of sentences? Is it a sharp distinction? Is there only one kind of meaningfulness?

What may be described as truth-based theories of the meaning of sentences have been particularly influential in modern times, initially in philosophical semantics, later in linguistic semantics. Two of these were mentioned in Chapter 1: the verificationist theory and the truth-conditional theory (1.7). According to the former, sentences are meaningful if (and only if) they have a determinate truth-value. In formulating the verificationist theory of meaning (or meaningfulness) in this way, I am temporarily neglecting to draw a distinction (as many verificationists did) not only between sentences and utterances, but also between propositions and propositional content, on the one hand, and between truth-values and truth-conditions, on the other. The reasons for drawing these distinctions (which were tacitly drawn in the slightly different formulation of the verificationist theory that was given in Chapter 1) will be explained below.

As we shall see, the verificationist theory, as such, in the form in which it was originally put forward (in the context of logical positivism), has been abandoned by most, if not all, philosophers of language. I should make it clear, therefore, that my principal aim in this chapter is not to give an account of the verificationist theory of meaning for its own sake, but rather for its historical significance in preparing the way for the truth-conditional theory of meaning, which was also mentioned in Chapter 1 and which is central in all modern versions of formal semantics. In my view, it is much easier to understand the truth-conditional theory of meaning and to see both its strengths and its weaknesses if one knows something about its predecessor, the verificationist theory, and the philosophical context in which verificationism arose. That there is a connexion between meaning and truth (as there is a connexion between truth and reality) is almost self-evident and has long been taken for granted by philosophers. In this chapter, we take our first steps towards seeing how this intuitive connexion between meaning and truth has been explicated and exploited in modern linguistic semantics.

5.1 GRAMMATICALITY, ACCEPTABILITY AND MEANINGFULNESS

As was noted in an earlier chapter, some utterances, actual or potential, are both grammatical and meaningful; others are ungrammatical and meaningless; and yet others, though fully grammatical and perhaps also meaningful, are, for various reasons, unacceptable (1.6).

To say that an utterance (more precisely, an utterance-type) is unacceptable is to imply that it is unutterable (more precisely, that one of its tokens is unutterable) in all normal contexts other than those involving metalinguistic reference to them.

Many such utterances are unacceptable for socio-cultural reasons. For example, there might be a taboo, in a certain

English-speaking society, upon the use of the verb 'die', rather than some euphemism such as 'pass away', in respect of members of the speaker's or hearer's immediate family. Thus, the fully grammatical and meaningful utterance

(1)   *His father died last night*

might be fully acceptable, but not the equally grammatical and (in one sense of 'meaningful') equally meaningful utterance

(2)   *My father died last night.*

Or again, in some cultures, it might be unacceptable for a social inferior to address a social superior with a second-person pronoun (meaning "you"), whereas it would be perfectly acceptable for a superior to address an inferior or an equal with the pronoun in question: this is the case (though the sociolinguistic conditions are often more complex than I have indicated here) in many cultures. It follows, that the same utterance with, arguably, the same meaning would be acceptable in some contexts but not in others. There are many such culture-dependent dimensions of acceptability. Some of them, as we shall see later, are encoded in the grammar and the vocabulary of particular languages. For this reason and others, one must be sceptical about the validity of the general principle, which is often taken for granted by semanticists, that whatever can be said in one language can be said in another. At the very least one must be sensitive to the different senses in which one can interpret the phrase 'can be said' (or 'can be uttered'). I will come back to this point in Part 4.

Somewhat different are those dimensions of acceptability which have to do with rationality and logical coherence. For example,

(3)   *I believe that it happened because it is impossible*

might be regarded as unacceptable from this point of view. Indeed, if uttered, (3) might well provoke the response:

(4)   *That doesn't make sense*

(though it is paradoxical, rather than being devoid of meaning or contradictory). What makes (3) unacceptable, in most contexts, is the fact that the speaker appears to be calling attention to his or her own irrationality; and this is an odd thing to do in most normal circumstances. However, even such utterances may be fully acceptable in certain contexts. In any event, one should not too readily concede, as some semanticists would, either that the sentence in question is uninterpretable or meaningless or, alternatively, that the proposition it expresses is necessarily false.

More generally (if I may now invoke the distinction between sentences and utterances), one should not take too restrictive a view of the meaningfulness of uncontextualized (or decontextualized) sentences: the semantic acceptability, or interpretability, of sentences is not something that can be decided independently of the context in which they might or might not be uttered.

5.2 THE MEANINGFULNESS OF SENTENCES

Sentences are, by definition, grammatically well-formed. There is no such thing, therefore, as an ungrammatical sentence. Sentences however may be either meaningful (semantically well-formed) or meaningless (semantically ill-formed). Utterances, in contrast with sentences, may be either grammatical or ungrammatical. Many of the utterances which are produced in normal everyday circumstances are ungrammatical in various respects. Some of these are interpretable without difficulty in the context in which they occur. Indeed, they might well be regarded by most of those who are competent in the language in question as fully acceptable. As we saw in Chapter 1, grammaticality must not be identified with acceptability; and, as we saw in the preceding section of this chapter, acceptability must not be identified with meaningfulness. But what do we mean by 'meaningfulness'?

In the preceding section we were careful to relate the notion of acceptability to utterances. At this point we will restrict our attention to what would generally be regarded as sentences and we will continue to operate with the assumption that the sentences of a language are readily identifiable as such by those who are competent in it, and more especially by its native speakers. As we shall see in due course, this assumption must be qualified. The distinction between grammatical and semantic well-formedness is not as sharp as, for the moment, we are taking it to be. Nevertheless, to say that the distinction between grammatical and semantic well-formedness – and consequently between grammar and semantics – is not clear-cut in all instances is not to say that it is never clear-cut at all.

There are many utterances whose unacceptability is quite definitely a matter of grammar, rather than of semantics. For example,

(5) *I want that he come*

is definitely ungrammatical in Standard English in contrast with

(6) *I want him to come.*

If (5) were produced by a foreigner, it would probably be construed, and therefore understood, as an incorrect version of (6). There is nothing in what appears to be the intended meaning of (5) which makes it ungrammatical. And many languages, including French, would translate (6) into something which is grammatically comparable with (5).

If someone, having uttered (5), not only refused the proffered correction, but insisted that it meant something different from the corrected version, we should simply have to tell them that, as far as Standard English is concerned, they are wrong. We can classify their utterance, unhesitatingly, as ungrammatical.

There are other, actual or potential, utterances which we can classify, no less readily, as grammatical, but meaningless. Among them, we can list, with their authors, such famous examples as

(7) *Colourless green ideas sleep furiously* (Noam Chomsky)
(8) *Quadruplicity drinks procrastination* (Bertrand Russell)
(9) *Thursday is in bed with Friday* (Gilbert Ryle).

Of course, none of these is uninterpretable, if it is appropriately contextualized and the meaning of one or more of its component expressions is extended beyond its normal, or literal, lexical meaning by means of such traditionally recognized rhetorical principles as **metaphor**, **metonymy** or **synecdoche**. The fact that this can be done – and indeed has been done on several occasions to considerable effect – merely proves the point that is being made here. As far as (9) is concerned, it is of course readily and immediately interpreted, both literally and metaphorically, if 'Thursday' and 'Friday' are construed as referring to persons (as in G. K. Chesterton's *The Man Who Was Thursday* and Daniel Defoe's *Robinson Crusoe*). Indeed, a moment's reflection will show that there is a euphemistic interpretation which is half-way between the fully literal and the definitely metaphorical. In order to assign an interpretation to (7)–(9), one does not identify, and tacitly correct, some general rule or principle which governs the grammatical structure of English, as we did in the case of (5); one tries to make sense of what, at first sight, does not of itself make sense on a literal, face-value, interpretation of the expressions which it contains.

We shall need to look later at the question of literal interpretation (see Chapter 9). All that needs to be said here is that (7)–(9) are grammatically well-formed and that, despite their grammaticality, they are literally meaningless. Any generative grammar of English will therefore generate, or admit as grammatically well-formed, not of course the utterances (7)–(9), but the sentences which correspond to them and from which (as will be explained in Chapter 8) they can be derived:

(7a) 'Colourless green ideas sleep furiously'
(8a) 'Quadruplicity drinks procrastination'
(9a) 'Thursday is in bed with Friday'.

The reader is reminded at this point that here, as throughout this book, utterances (in the sense of utterance-inscriptions or stretches of text) are represented in italics, whereas sentences, like other expressions, are represented by means of their citation-form enclosed in single quotation-marks.

To be contrasted with (7a)–(9a) are

(7b) **Green ideas sleeps furiously,*
(8b) **Drinks quadruplicity procrastination,*

(9b) *Thursday am on bed when Friday.*

In (7b)–(9b) the asterisk indicates grammatical ill-formedness. (7b) breaks the grammatical rule of agreement between the subject and the verb in English; (8b) is ungrammatical (in present-day English), not only as a declarative sentence, but also as an interrogative sentence, because it breaks the rules of word-order; and (9b), like (7b), breaks the rule of subject–predicate agreement and, additionally, uses a count noun without a determiner (*on bed*, which, in contrast with *in bed*, is not a grammatical idiom) and uses a conjunction in a position which syntactically requires a preposition (*when*, unlike *since*, cannot fulfil both functions).

It might seem pointless, at this stage, to distinguish notationally, as I have done, between sentences and utterances, but the reasons for doing so will be made clear in Part 3. As we shall see, sentences are expressions which may have several forms, including context-dependent elliptical forms.

It is also worth emphasizing that a distinction is being drawn here, implicitly, between ungrammatical strings of forms, such as (7b)–(9b), on the one hand, and non-grammatical gibberish, on the other, such as

(10) *On when am Thursday furiously bed,*

which cannot be said to violate any specific grammatical rules of English. This distinction is not generally drawn in generative grammar, because generative grammars, as formalized originally by Chomsky, partition strings of forms into two complementary subsets: A, the set of all grammatically well-formed strings (which are then identified with the sentences of the language in question), and B, its complement, the set of strings which by virtue of not being grammatical are defined to be ungrammatical. Strings of recognizably English word-forms, such as (10), which are neither grammatical nor ungrammatical, are not only not grammatical: they are, as it were, not even trying to be grammatical, and the question whether they are grammatically well-formed or ill-formed does not arise. More to the point, in the present connexion, they do not make sense and cannot be made to make sense by any kind of adjustment or correction. They are perhaps meaningless or nonsensical in the everyday use of the words 'meaningless' and 'nonsensical', but they are perhaps not rightly described as semantically ill-formed. The expressions 'well-formed' and 'ill-formed' first came into linguistics as part of the terminology of generative grammar: as they are commonly employed, they imply conformity to a set, or system, of precisely formulated rules or principles. As we shall see later, so-called formal semantics takes the view that, as there are rules (or principles) of grammatical well-formedness, so also there are rules (or principles) of semantic well-formedness. Whether this is or is not the case is a question that we can postpone until later. Here I am concerned to emphasize, first, that meaningfulness, or semantic well-formedness (if we use that term and, for the present at least, accept what it implies), is readily distinguishable, in clear cases, from grammaticality, and, second, that not every utterance which is judged to be unacceptable on the grounds that it does not make sense is properly regarded as semantically ill-formed.

But if the intuitive notion of making sense is not a reliable guide, what are the criteria which lead us to decide that an utterance, actual or potential, is semantically well-formed or ill-formed? We shall address this question in the following section.

5.3 CORRIGIBILITY AND TRANSLATABILITY

As we have seen, semantic well-formedness must be distinguished from grammatical well-formedness (grammaticality): both of them are included within, or overlap with, acceptability, as semantic ill-formedness and grammatical ill-formedness are included within, or overlap with, unacceptability. But – to repeat the question that was posed at the end of the preceding section – what are the criteria other than the intuitive notion of making sense which lead us to decide that an utterance is or is not semantically well-formed?

One of the criteria that was invoked earlier in connexion with grammaticality is what we may now label the criterion of **corrigibility** (5.2). Whereas

(5) *I want that he come*

can be corrected – by some speakers to

(6) *I want him to come*

and by others perhaps to

(6a) *I want for him to come*

 – without any change in what is assumed to be the intended meaning, Chomsky's classic example,

(7) *Colourless green ideas sleep furiously*

cannot. In those instances in which the distinction between grammatical and semantic unacceptability can be most clearly drawn, the former are corrigible and the latter are not.

Other kinds of unacceptability, some of which at first sight seem to be a matter of meaning, also fall within the scope of the notion of corrigibility. For example,

(2) *My father died last night*

might be corrected to, say,

(2a) *My father passed away last night*

in a language-community (of the kind referred to in section 5.1) in which the use of 'die' is prohibited with expressions referring to members of one's own family. But the unacceptability of (2) in such circumstances, is not such that we would say that it does not make sense. Its unacceptability is a matter of social, rather than descriptive, meaning. (And there are independent reasons for saying that, though corrigible, it is fully grammatical.)

In other instances, as we shall see later, the situation is less clear-cut. But, interestingly enough, the criterion of corrigibility and incorrigibility is still relevant in that it shows the pre-theoretically indeterminate cases to be genuinely indeterminate.

Another criterion that is sometimes mentioned by linguists is **translatability**. This rests on the view that semantic, but not grammatical, distinctions can be matched across languages. However, as we shall see later, it is not clear that what is semantically unacceptable in some languages is semantically unacceptable in all languages. The criterion of translatability can supplement, but it does not supplant, our main criterion, that of corrigibility.

We turn now to a discussion of a famous and influential philosophical criterion of meaningfulness: verifiability.

5.4 VERIFIABILITY AND VERIFICATIONISM

The verificationist theory of meaning – verificationism, for short – was mentioned in Chapter 1. As its name suggests, it has to do with truth. It was originally associated with the philosophical movement known as logical positivism, initiated by members of the Vienna Circle in the period immediately preceding the Second World War. Although logical positivism, and with it verificationism, is all but dead, it has been of enormous importance in the development of modern philosophical semantics. On the one hand, many of its proponents – notably Rudolf Carnap and Hans Reichenbach – were active in the construction of systems for the analysis of language which have led, more or less directly, to the methods of modern formal semantics. On the other, the very excesses and defects of logical positivism forced its opponents, including Wittgenstein in his later work and the so-called ordinary-language philosophers, to make explicit some of their own assumptions about meaning. As Ryle (1951: 250) has said of verificationism: "It has helped to reveal the important fact that we talk sense in lots of different ways".

We shall not pursue Ryle's point at this stage. Instead, I will take one version of the famous **verifiability principle** and, in the next few sections, use this to introduce the notion of truth-conditions and other notions that will be of use to us later. The principle may be stated, initially and for our purposes, as follows: "A sentence is factually significant to a given person if, and only if, he knows how to verify the proposition which it purports to express" (Ayer, 1946: 35). This formulation by A. J. Ayer, it will be noted, does not say that the meaning of sentences (or alternatively of propositions) is their method of verification. It simply provides a criterion of one particular kind of meaning – factual significance; it does not define meaning as such.

Even so, it raises a number of problems. The logical positivists wanted to say that all verification is ultimately a matter of observation. Yet, as Karl Popper has pointed out, universal statements of the kind that scientists tend to make cannot, in principle, be verified, though they may be falsified, by means of observation. For example, the statement that all swans are white can be falsified, by observing just a single instance of a black swan, but it can never be proved to be true on the basis of empirical investigation. Popper's point that falsifiability, rather than verifiability, is the hallmark of scientific hypotheses is now widely accepted (though it has its critics and requires to be formulated more carefully than it has been here).

5.5 PROPOSITIONS AND PROPOSITIONAL CONTENT

Ayer's formulation of the verifiability criterion draws upon (though it does not explain) the distinction between sentences and **propositions**. The nature of propositions is philosophically controversial. But those philosophers who accept that propositions differ, on the one hand, from sentences and, on the other, from statements, questions, commands, etc., will usually say that propositions

(i) are either true or false;
(ii) may be known, believed or doubted;
(iii) may be asserted, denied or queried;
(iv) are held constant under translation from one language to another.

There are difficulties, as we shall see later, about reconciling all four of these different criteria: (ii) and (iii) seem to be in conflict as far as some natural languages are concerned; and (iv) makes dubious assumptions about intertranslatability.

However, granted that propositions are defined to be the bearers of a determinate and unchanging truth-value, it is quite clear that they must be distinguished from sentences. For the same sentence can be used on one occasion to say what is true and on another to say what is false. And it is worth noting, in this connexion, that even sentences such as

(11) 'Napoleon was defeated at Waterloo in 1815'

can be used to assert a variety of true and false propositions. There are certain natural languages in which personal names and place-names are in one-to-one correspondence with their bearers. But neither English nor French is among them. In English the relation between a proper name and the set of entities or places which each bear that name is completely arbitrary. (The situation in French is slightly different, in that in France there are certain legal restrictions relating to the choice and assignment of personal names.) If 'Napoleon' happens to be the name of my dog and I am referring to my dog when I utter the above sentence, the proposition that I have asserted is presumably false.

Nor should it be thought that I have gratuitously or facetiously introduced the qualification 'presumably' here. I have done so in order to remind readers of the very important point that here, as always, whenever one says that something is or is not true, one is making certain background assumptions that others may not share. For example, I have tacitly ruled out the possibility that Napoleon Bonaparte may have been reincarnated as my dog. And there are indefinitely many such ontological assumptions – often loosely and inaccurately referred to as world-knowledge – which have a bearing upon the interpretation of sentences such as (11) on particular occasions of utterance. There is nothing in the structure of English which commits us to the denial of unfashionable or eccentric ontological assumptions.

But to return to the main theme. Philosophers and linguists frequently make the point that sentences containing definite descriptions (for example, 'the wooden door'), or, more obviously, personal pronouns ('I', 'you', etc.), demonstrative pronouns ('this', 'that') or demonstrative adverbs of place and time ('here', 'there', 'now', 'then') can be used to assert, deny or query indefinitely many true or false propositions. All too often they fail to add that this is also the case for sentences containing proper names and dates. The vast majority of sentences in the most familiar natural languages can be used, on particular occasions of utterance, to assert, to query or to deny indefinitely many propositions, each of which has a constant truth-value which is independent of that of each of the others that may be expressed by uttering the same sentence.

But what exactly is the relationship between sentences and propositions? This is a difficult question; and the answer that one will give to it depends in part upon one's theory of meaning. It suffices for present purposes to note that certain assumptions must be made, whether tacitly or explicitly, by anyone who says of sentences that they express propositions. Ayer, it will be noted, is more circumspect, in the quotation given above. He talks of sentences as **purporting** to express propositions; and it is easy to see why. The purport of a document is the meaning that it conveys by virtue of its appearance, or face-value, and standard assumptions about the interpretation of the author's intentions. Sentences of whatever kind may be uttered, in various circumstances, without there being any question of the assertion or denial of a proposition. For instance, if I am asked to provide someone with an example of an English sentence in the past tense, I might comply with their request by uttering (11). It is quite clear that, in the circumstances envisaged, the sentence that I have uttered is not to be construed as referring to or saying anything about anyone (or anything). Indeed, in one sense of the verb 'say' I have not said anything. For this and other reasons, we cannot say that sentences as such express propositions. What we can do, however, is to interpret the phrase, 'purport to express a proposition' in terms of the notion of characteristic use, as explained in Chapter 1. And this is what will be done throughout the next three chapters. We shall assume that all declarative sentences belong to the class of sentences whose members are used, characteristically, to make statements (that is, to assert or deny particular propositions) and that they have this potential for use encoded in their grammatical structure as part of their purport or **face-value**; that all interrogative sentences have encoded in their grammatical structure their potential for querying particular propositions; and so on.

Under this interpretation of the notion of purport, or face-value, we can temporarily and provisionally exclude from consideration not only a variety of metalinguistic uses of sentences and expressions, but also what will be identified in Part 4 as their **performative** and **indirect** uses.

Sentence-meaning is intrinsically connected with utterance-meaning, but can be distinguished from it by virtue of the distinction between the characteristic use of a sentence (which need not be its most frequent or psychologically most salient use) and its use on particular occasions. I have emphasized the notion of the **use** of sentences at this point because the so-called use theory of meaning, associated with Wittgenstein, Austin, and others, developed out of and in reaction to verificationism. What I want to do in this book is to throw a bridge between a restricted version of the meaning-as-use theory and the truth-conditional theory of descriptive meaning, which also developed historically out of verificationism. It is essential to the fulfilment of this purpose that what is said here about the purport, or face-value, of a sentence and what is said in Part 4 about the intrinsic connexion between sentence-meaning and utterance-meaning should be properly understood.

It is also important that a distinction should be drawn between the propositions expressed by a sentence on particular occasions of utterance and its propositional content. I will come to this presently. Strictly speaking, as we shall see, it is not propositions that sentences purport to express, but propositional content. Provided that this is understood, together with the point made earlier about the purported, or face-value, use of sentences, no confusion will arise if, occasionally and for brevity's sake, we say, as most authors do, that sentences express propositions.

5.6 NON-FACTUAL SIGNIFICANCE AND EMOTIVISM

There is one final point that may be made in connexion with Ayer's statement: "A sentence is factually significant to a given person if, and only if, he knows how to verify the proposition that it purports to express." This has to do with factual significance. It was by means of the verifiability principle that the logical positivists wanted to proscribe as meaningless, or nonsensical, sentences which purport to express metaphysical and theological propositions such as, let us say:

(12) 'Everything must have a cause'

or

(13) 'God is good'.

But it was soon realized that the principle of verifiability also ruled out (or, at least, did not obviously allow as meaningful) what many of them held to be the philosophically more respectable sentences which purport to express propositions of ethics and aesthetics, such as:

(14) 'Cannibalism is wrong'

or

(15) 'Monet was a better painter than Manet'.

One way round this problem was to say that, although such sentences as (14) and (15) are not factually significant, they have another kind of meaning: an emotive, or expressive, meaning.

Emotivism – the thesis that in making what purport to be factual statements in ethics and aesthetics one is not saying anything that is true or false, but giving vent to one's feelings – has now, like logical positivism itself, been abandoned by most of those who once professed it. In its day, it had the beneficial effect of obliging philosophers to look more closely at the logical status of different kinds of both meaningful and meaningless utterances. It is this that Ryle had in mind when he said, in the quotation given earlier, that the verification principle helped philosophers to see that there are different ways in which an utterance can be significant, or meaningful, and different ways in which it can be nonsensical. One important product of this insight into the diversity of meaning, as we shall see in Part 4, was Austin's theory of speech acts.

5.7 TRUTH-CONDITIONS

The truth-conditional theory of meaning, like verificationism, one of its historical antecedents, comes in several slightly different versions. What they have in common is their acceptance of the following thesis: to give an account of the meaning of a sentence is to specify the conditions under which it would be true or false of the situation, or state of the world, that it purports to describe. Alternatively, it is said that to know the meaning of a sentence is to know the conditions under which it (or the statement made by uttering it) would be true or false. Neither of these formulations is very precise as it stands, and they are not necessarily equivalent. For example, neither of them actually identifies the meaning of a sentence with its truth-conditions; and the second leaves open the question of what precisely is meant by knowing the truth-conditions of a sentence. We shall return to such questions in the following chapter.

For the present it suffices to draw readers' attention to the difference between the **truth-value** of a proposition and the **truth-conditions** of a sentence. To take a simple example:

(16) 'John Smith is unmarried'

purports to express a set of propositions, each of which has a particular truth-value according to whether whoever is being referred to by 'John Smith', on particular occasions of utterance, is unmarried (at the time of the utterance). We do not need to know who (or what) is being referred to on all or any of the occasions of the utterance of the sentence 'John Smith is unmarried' or whether the person being referred to (on the assumption that it is a person) is unmarried in order to know what **conditions** the world must satisfy for the proposition "John Smith is unmarried" to be true. In cases like this at least, we know how we might verify (or falsify) empirically any one of the propositions that a sentence purports to express.

Also, independently of any empirical investigation relating to a given John Smith's marital status, we can argue, on the basis of our knowledge of English, whether

(17) 'John Smith is not married'

or even

(18) 'John Smith is a bachelor'

has the same truth-conditions as (16). If (and only if) they have the same truth-conditions, we will say that they have the same **propositional content**. And a moment's reflection will tell us that (18) differs truth-conditionally from both of the others. Not every unmarried individual is a bachelor. For example, unmarried women are not bachelors (and, to reiterate a point made earlier, there is nothing in the structure of English that prevents a woman from bearing the name 'John Smith': we have only to think of the well-known women novelists George Eliot and George Sand). Or again, a child with the name 'John Smith' – or a racehorse, or a yacht, or indeed any entity whatsoever that is not only not married, but also not marriageable, and can be appropriately referred to with the name 'John Smith' – will fulfil the truth-conditions of (17), but not of (18). The situation with respect to (16) and (17) is less clear-cut. It is arguable (though not all native speakers will take this view) that an individual cannot be unmarried unless he or she (or it) could in principle have been married: i.e., is (or has been) marriageable. Those who take this view might say that sentences such as

(19) 'That racehorse is unmarried'

and

(20) 'That square-rigged schooner is unmarried'

are meaningless: that they do not make sense. Others might say that (19) and (20), though odd, are tautologous (and therefore meaningful) because each of the propositions that they could be used to express is analytic (and therefore true: see 5.8). Others, again, might wish to draw a potentially relevant distinction between (19) and (20); they might argue that the former is less obviously, or less definitely, **categorially incongruous** (and therefore less obviously meaningless) than the latter, in that it is quite easy to conceive of a culture in which racehorses (but not ships, on the assumption that they are indeed, by natural necessity, inanimate and incapable of mating and reproduction) are brought within the scope of the same laws as human beings with respect to cohabitation, the legitimacy of their offspring, etc.

As we saw earlier (and it is a point that will be emphasized throughout this book), if we are seriously concerned about both the theoretical and the empirical foundations of linguistic semantics, we must not dismiss as facetious or irrelevant the deliberate manipulation of a particular society's normal ontological assumptions when it comes to the testing of native speakers' (including one's own) intuitive judgements of meaningfulness or semantic equivalence. In this section we are concerned with truth-conditional equivalence as an important, if not the sole, component of the semantic equivalence of sentences. The principle of truth-conditional equivalence holds independently of the facts of the matter in particular instances:

(21)   Sentences have the same propositional content if and only if they have the same truth-conditions.

Readers are now invited to put to the test their understanding of the principle of truth-conditional equivalence, as formulated in (21), by trying to falsify the statement that (16a) and (17a) have the same propositional content:

(16a) 'That man is unmarried'

and

(17a) 'That man is not married'.

(These two sentences differ from (16) and (17), it will be noted, in that I have substituted the phrase 'that man' for the proper name 'John Smith'.) Are there any circumstances – in the actual world as we know it – under which it can be said truly (and properly) of the same fully adult (and therefore, let us assume, marriageable) male person, x, that x is both not married and not unmarried? Are there circumstances in which x could be truly and properly said to be both married and unmarried?

In this chapter, I have deliberately emphasized the historical connexion between verificationism and truth-conditional semantics. Most authors nowadays would not have done this on the grounds that verificationism as a philosophical doctrine is all but obsolete. But all the points made above about verificationism are relevant, in my view, to a proper understanding of truth-conditional semantics; and we shall draw upon them later. They could have been made in respect of truth-conditional semantics without mentioning logical positivism and verifiability. But there is much in present-day formal semantics which derives from its positivist origins.

In any case, it is important to realize that when it comes to the construction of a truth-conditional theory of meaning for natural languages, verifiability (or falsifiability) continues to present problems, not just of practice, but also of principle. It will not do to dismiss these problems on the grounds that verificationism itself has failed. As we have seen several times already, it is unreasonable to expect that competent speakers of a language should always be able to decide whether two expressions are necessarily true of the same classes of entities or not. If the truth-conditional theory of semantics is so formulated that it rules out what seems to be a genuine indeterminacy in the semantic structure of natural languages, it may be rejected without more ado. But, as we shall see in due course, it need not be formulated in this way.

5.8 TAUTOLOGIES AND CONTRADICTIONS

Two kinds of propositions that are of particular concern to logicians and semanticists are **tautologies** (in a technical sense of 'tautology') and **contradictions**. The former, as traditionally defined, are propositions which are necessarily true by virtue of their **logical form**. An example would be

(22) "Either it is raining or it is not raining".

Contradictions, on the other hand, are propositions that are necessarily false by virtue of their logical form. For example:

(23) "It is raining and it is not raining".

What is meant by 'logical form' in this context varies somewhat according to which system of logic we are operating with. But the above propositions would be shown to be tautologous and contradictory, respectively, in standard propositional logic by the definition of **negation** ("not"), **conjunction** ("both ... and"), and **disjunction** ("either ... or ...").

It will be noted that I am using double quotation-marks at this point, because we are not concerned with English sentences as such, but rather with their propositional content or with the propositions which they purport to express. (This use of double quotation-marks has been established in earlier chapters and is consistent with the general convention whereby expressions are distinguished notationally from their meanings.) It is important to emphasize once again that propositions, not sentences, are the bearers of truth and falsity.

Obviously, in construing "It is raining and it is not raining" as contradictory we have to make certain assumptions about the time and place being referred to: in particular, we must assume that we are not referring to different times and/or different places in the two constituent simpler propositions. "It is raining in Manchester and it is not raining in Timbuktu" is not contradictory. One might think that nothing but pedantry is involved in making points like this explicit. But, as we shall see later, there are important theoretical reasons for keeping such seemingly trivial points in mind.

Provided that we do keep the point that has just been made in mind and draw the distinction between sentences and propositions when it needs to be drawn, we can extend the application of the terms 'tautology' and 'contradiction' to sentences in a natural way. We can say of the sentences

(24) 'Either it is raining or it is not (raining)'

and

(25) 'It is raining and it is not (raining)'

that, taken at face-value, they are tautologous and contradictory, respectively. (By taking them at face-value, I mean interpreting them in terms of their purported propositional content and on the assumption that they are being used characteristically: see 5.5.) One of the principal tasks of semantic theory is to show how and why competent speakers of a language will recognize that some sentences are tautologous and others contradictory (unless there are good reasons in context for construing them otherwise than at their face value).

Logical truths, or tautologies, are a subclass of **analytic** truths: that is, propositions whose truth is determined wholly by their meaning (cf. Chapter 4). However, linguists commonly extend the terms 'tautology' and 'contradiction' to cover, not only those propositions (and sentences) whose truth or falsity is determined by logical form as this is traditionally conceived, but all kinds of analytically true or false propositions (and sentences). Thus, they would say that

(26) 'This bachelor is unmarried'

is a tautologous sentence, and

(27) 'This bachelor is married'

is a contradictory sentence, in that the first purports to express a tautology and the second a contradiction (on the assumption that 'bachelor' is taken in the relevant sense). We shall follow this practice.

Tautologies and, especially, contradictions are sometimes classified as being semantically anomalous. Taken at face-value, they are uninformative: they cannot be used to tell someone facts which they did not previously know or could not deduce themselves on the basis of their knowledge of the language and the ability to draw valid inferences from what they already know. And yet, whatever 'semantically anomalous' or 'meaningless' means in relation to tautologies and contradictions, it cannot mean "devoid of sense" (if 'sense' means "propositional content"). For tautologies and contradictions, as we have just seen, are by definition necessarily true and necessarily false respectively; and this implies that contradictory sentences, no less than tautologous sentences, must have determinable truth-conditions. The former are false and the latter true, as Leibniz put it, **in all possible worlds** (4.4). We can argue on both theoretical and empirical grounds about the range of data that is, or should be, covered by the terms 'tautology' and 'contradiction' (that is to say, about the coverage of the term 'analytic'). But we canot without inconsistency abandon the principle that analytically true and analytically false sentences are meaningful in the sense of having a truth-conditionally explicable propositional content.

CHAPTER 6

Sentence-meaning and propositional content

6.0 INTRODUCTION

This chapter is pivotal in the structure of the book. It is also one of the longest, and there is a distinct change of gear. We shall be making full use of logical notions and discussing in greater detail than we have done so far the basic concepts of modern formal, truth-conditional, semantics, which, as we saw in the preceding chapter, were first developed within logic and the philosophy of language and were subsequently extended to linguistics.

There is nothing new or revolutionary about the influence of logic on linguistics (and vice versa). Grammatical theory and logic have been closely associated for centuries. Indeed, much of the terminology of traditional grammar – 'subject', 'predicate', 'mood', etc. – is also part of the logician's stock in trade. But does this use of the same terminology reflect any more than a purely historical, and accidental, association between the two disciplines? Does the grammatical structure of a sentence correspond directly to the logical form of the proposition it expresses? More generally, is there nothing more to the meaning of a sentence than its propositional content? These are the principal questions that we shall be addressing in the present chapter.

Our general conclusion will be that there are certain aspects of sentence-meaning that cannot be adequately represented by standard propositional logic. In coming to this conclusion, however, we shall also see that our understanding of the way meaning is encoded in sentences has been greatly increased in recent years by the attempt to describe precisely the interaction between the logical form of propositions and the grammatical structure of sentences (and clauses).

Some parts of this chapter may seem somewhat technical to those who are not acquainted with modern formal logic. But none of the concepts that we shall be invoking is inherently difficult to understand. And it is only by looking at some of the points where propositional logic fails to give a full account of sentence-meaning that we can begin to appreciate both the achievements and the limitations of modern truth-conditional semantics.

6.1 THEMATIC MEANING

Sentences have the same propositional content if and only if they have the same truth-conditions. This is the principle which was established in the preceding chapter; and we shall stick to it throughout. We shall also continue to identify the propositional content of a sentence with its sense and, for present purposes, with its descriptive meaning.

One part of the meaning of sentences – as sentences are commonly defined – that is definitely not part of their propositional content is **thematic meaning**. For example, the following sentences, which differ in thematic meaning, all have the same truth-conditions, and therefore the same propositional content:

(1) 'I have not read this book',
(2) 'This book I have not read',
(3) 'It is this book (that) I have not read',
(4) 'This book has not been read by me'.

So too do the following:

(5) 'A man is standing under the apple-tree',
(6) 'There is a man standing under the apple-tree'.

This kind of meaning is called thematic because it is determined by the way speakers present what they are talking about (the **theme** of their utterance) in relation to particular contextual presuppositions. (This is the only sense in which the terms 'theme' and 'thematic' are employed in this book. Regrettably, there are other, less traditional, conflicting senses now current in the literature, which can lead to confusion.) Frequently, but not always, what the speaker presents as thematic is also **given** elsewhere in the context and can be taken for granted as being known to the addressees or readily identifiable by them.

Actually, it is by no means clear that (1)–(4), on the one hand, or (5)–(6), on the other, are different sentences. An alternative view would be that some or all of the following,

(1a) *I have not read this book,*
(2a) *This book I have not read,*
(3a) *It is this book (that) I have not read,*
(4a) *This book has not been read by me,*

are different forms of the same sentence, whose citation-form – the stylistically and contextually unmarked, or neutral, form – is (1a). That (2a) and (4a), if not (2a) and (1a), are traditionally regarded as forms of different sentences is perhaps no more than a consequence of the fact that Greek and Latin, much more clearly than English, had inflectionally distinct active and passive forms of the verb. As for (3a), this too would be traditionally regarded as a form of a distinct sentence, because, superficially at least, it is composed of two clauses. Similarly for

(5a) *A man is standing under the apple-tree,*

by comparison with

(6a) *There is a man standing under the apple-tree:*

(6a) is composed, at least superficially, of two clauses and is therefore composite, rather than simple. The distinction between simple and composite sentences is something we shall look at in the following section.

For our purposes, the most important point to be noted here is that the question whether (1a)–(4a) are forms of the same sentence or of two or more different sentences is not a matter of fact to be settled by observation or intuition, but a matter of theoretical decision. There are perhaps good reasons for saying that (1a) and (2a) are forms of different sentences (although a traditionally minded grammarian might take the contrary view): word-order plays a crucial structural role in the grammar of English. There are other languages, however, in which it does not. Much current syntactic theory, for reasons that we need not go into here, is typologically biased in that it makes it axiomatic that no two utterances that differ at all in word-order (more precisely, in the sequential order of their constituent forms, simple or composite) can be forms of the same sentence. This axiom is often built into the formalization of generative grammars (as it was in Chomsky's original formalization of transformational-generative grammar) by defining the sentence as a string of forms. From time to time, in this chapter and elsewhere in the present book, this point will be of importance. Obviously, if one took the view that (1a)–(4a) are all forms of the same sentence, whose citation-form is (1a), one would say that thematic meaning (in this case at least) is not a part of sentence-meaning. This view is not to be rejected out of hand.

It might be argued, then, that the difference between, say, (1a) and (2a) has nothing to do with the grammatical or semantic structure of the sentence of which they are alternative forms, but rather with the utterance of the same sentence in one contextually determined word-order or another. Issues of this kind will occupy us in Part 4, when we look more closely at what is involved in the utterance of a sentence. For the moment, it suffices to note that the kind of question with which we have been concerned in this section is usually begged, rather than properly addressed, in current works in linguistic semantics. Thematic meaning is primarily, if not wholly, a matter of utterance-meaning. Just how much, if any, is also to be regarded as a part of sentence-meaning is debatable. But it cannot be properly debated unless and until those involved in the debate say exactly what their criteria are for sentence-identity.

It should also be noted that, as we have seen earlier (1.3), it is somewhat unrealistic to discuss what we are now calling thematic meaning without mentioning stress and intonation. Much the same communicative effect can be achieved by putting heavy stress on *this book* in (1a) as can be achieved by uttering (2a). Moreover, when (2a) is uttered, it will not only have a non-neutral word-order, in contrast with (1a), but also a non-neutral intonation-contour. There is no general consensus among linguists as to how much of this thematically significant variation in the prosodic structure of utterances is to be accounted for in terms of sentence-structure.

One point, however, is clear. It is part of one's linguistic competence to be able to control and interpret variations of word-order and grammatical structure of the kind that are exemplified in the sentences cited above. It is also part of one's linguistic competence to be able to control and interpret differences of stress and intonation that are functionally comparable with such variations of word-order and grammatical structure. We cannot, therefore, hold simultaneously to the following two principles:

   (i)   linguistic competence is restricted to the knowledge of sentence-structure;
  (ii) all aspects of sentence-meaning are truth-conditional.

If we want to maintain (i), we must accept a much broader conception of sentence-structure than is traditional and, in doing so, abandon (ii). Alternatively, if we wish to defend (ii), we must either accept a much narrower conception of sentence-structure than is traditional or define thematic meaning to be something other than meaning. The view taken in this book is that there is no good reason to subscribe to either of the two principles.

6.2 SIMPLE AND COMPOSITE SENTENCES

A **simple** sentence, in traditional grammar, is a sentence that contains only one clause. What I am calling **composite** sentences – there is no generally accepted term for non-simple sentences – fall into two classes: **compound** and **complex**. The former may be analysed, at their highest level of structure, into two or more co-ordinate clauses; the latter into a main clause (which may be simple or composite) and at least one subordinate clause. Although these traditional distinctions are not without their problems, we can use them satisfactorily enough in our general discussion of the propositional content of sentences.

Roughly comparable with the distinction between simple and what I will call composite sentences is the distinction drawn in logic between simple and composite propositions. (What I am calling composite propositions are usually referred to as complex, and occasionally as compound. However, it seems preferable in the present context to standardize the grammatical and the logical terminology as far as possible. 'Composite' has the further advantage that it is transparently related both to 'compositional' and to 'component'.) But no distinction can be drawn (in standard first-order propositional logic) among different kinds of composite propositions that matches, in any significant way, the grammatical distinction between compound and complex sentences. For example,

(7)   'If he passed his driving test, I am a Dutchman'

is complex, whereas

(8)   'Either he did not pass his driving test or I am a Dutchman'

is compound.

The propositions expressed by the above two sentences are normally formalized in the propositional calculus by means of **implication** and **disjunction**, respectively:

(9)   "p implies q",

on the one hand, and

(10)   "either not-p or q",

on the other. At first sight, these two composite propositions (9) and (10) look as if they might differ semantically, but, as they are standardly interpreted by logicians, they do not. They have exactly the same truth-conditions. Granted that "p implies q" and "either not-p or q" correctly formalize the range of propositions that can be asserted by uttering our sample complex and compound sentences, (7) and (8), it follows that the sentences in question must have the same propositional content. And yet one might hesitate to say that, as sentences, they have the same meaning.

Even more striking are such examples as the following:

(11) 'He was poor and he was honest'
(12) 'He was poor but he was honest'
(13) 'Although he was poor, he was honest'.

Most people would probably say that all three sentences differ in meaning, but that the second, which is compound, is closer in meaning to the third, a complex sentence, than it is to the first, which is another compound sentence. Once again, however, the composite propositions expressed by these sentences are normally held to be semantically equivalent. If there is any difference of sentence-meaning in (11)–(13), then (on the standard view of propositional content), it is not a matter of propositional content. (The question why logicians normally treat the composite propositions expressed by (11)–(13) as equivalent will be taken up in section 6.3.)

There is much more that would need to be said in a fuller discussion of the relation between the grammatical structure of composite sentences and the logical form of composite propositions. For example, one would need to consider more generally the relevance to the propositional content of sentences of the traditional grammatical distinction between co-ordination and subordination (upon which the more particular distinction between compound and complex sentences is based). Rightly or wrongly, standard analyses of the logical form of the composite propositions expressed by uttering natural-language sentences take no account of this. Similarly, one would need to consider whether, and if so how, the traditional classification of subordinate clauses as nominal, adjectival, adverbial, etc., should be reflected in the formalization of the propositional content of complex sentences. This too is something that is not taken into account, except partially and indirectly, in standard formal-semantic analyses of natural-language sentences.

What is commonly referred to in the literature of linguistic formal semantics as the **rule-to-rule hypothesis** rests on the assumption that, generally speaking, there is congruence between grammatical structure and logical form (see 7.2). If this assumption is valid, it is to be anticipated that further developments in the application of the notions of formal semantics to

the analysis of the propositional content of the sentences of natural languages will exploit some of these traditional notions
about the grammatical structure of composite sentences. Some
of them appear to be relevant, at least intuitively, to the semantic analysis of sentences. However, there is as yet no consensus
among linguists whether, and if so how, they should be represented formally in purely syntactic terms.

As we shall see, in connexion with the principle of compositionality in Chapter 7, formal semantics always presupposes
and operates in conjunction with a particular syntactic model.
We shall be looking at two historically important approaches to
the formalization of sentence-meaning which sought to give
effect to this principle in quite different ways. One of them, the
Katz–Fodor theory, originated in linguistics and used the
Chomskyan model of transformational-generative grammar (in
its so-called standard version); the other, Montague semantics,
originated in formal logic and used a very different, less powerful, but logically (and in certain respects semantically) more
elegant and more perspicuous, model of syntactic analysis (categorial grammar). In the last twenty-five years or so, these two
different models of syntactic analysis have been further refined
and modified, and other models have been developed which
seek to combine the theoretical and descriptive strengths of
both (without, ideally, the weaknesses of either). These developments have been motivated by both empirical and theoretical
considerations. Not only has a much wider range of relevant
data been investigated, but there has also been a conscious
attempt by linguists, as there was not in an earlier period, to get
the best fit – to achieve the highest degree of congruence –
between grammatical and semantic structure in their descriptions of natural languages.

Throughout this book I have deliberately adopted the conceptual framework and, as far as possible, the terminology of traditional grammar. Students who are familiar with modern
syntactic theory should have no difficulty in making the necessary terminological adjustments and, if they have some knowledge of the more recent developments to which I have just been
referring, they will see the force of the comments about syntactic

and semantic congruence. Students who do not have this familiarity with modern syntactic theory, however, are in no way disadvantaged. Everything that follows in Chapter 6 is intended to be comprehensible (and has at times been deliberately simplified for the purpose) on the basis of a fairly non-technical knowledge of traditional grammatical concepts. One or two of the relevant concepts drawn from modern generative grammar will be introduced and explained in Chapter 7, where something more will also be said about compositionality, grammatical and semantic congruence, and the rule-to-rule hypothesis.

In this section, we have been considering the relation between the grammatical structure of composite (i.e., compound and complex) sentences and the logical form of composite propositions. In doing so, we have adopted the traditional view of the distinction between clauses and sentences, according to which a composite sentence is composed of more than one clause and a simple sentence is composed of, and may be identified with, a single clause. We have also tacitly taken the view, for which there is some support both in traditional grammar and modern linguistic theory, that sentences are more basic than clauses, in that (i) there is no distinction to be drawn between clauses and sentences as far as simple sentences are concerned and (ii) the clauses of composite sentences can be derived from simple sentences by **embedding** them (or some transform of them) in complex sentences or **conjoining** them (or some transform of them) in compound sentences. (The terms 'embedding', 'conjoining' and 'transform' are drawn from the terminology of Chomskyan transformational-generative grammar, which will be referred to again in Chapter 7, but the concepts with which they are associated are traditional enough and have their place in many different models of grammatical structure.) According to an alternative view of the relation between sentences and clauses (as we shall see in section 6.6), it is the clause, rather than the sentence, that is the more basic structural unit and the one that corresponds most closely to the proposition. Everything that has been said in this section and in the following sections could be reformulated in terms of this alternative view; and, from time to time, I will remind readers that this is so by using the phrase 'sentence (or clause)' in place of 'sentence' and, when we come to section 6.6, 'sentence-type (or clause-type)' in place of 'sentence-type'.

In conclusion, it may also be useful to make explicit the fact that, in this section and throughout this book, the term 'logical form' is being used with reference solely to the structure of propositions (and propositional content): the term 'form', in this context, is in fact synonymous with 'structure'. The reason for making this point is that the term 'logical form' is used in certain modern theories of syntax for an underlying level of grammatical structure (roughly comparable with what was called the deep structure of sentences in the so-called standard model of transformational grammar: see 7.3). The two senses of the term are of course connected; but they must not be confused.

6.3 TRUTH-FUNCTIONALITY (1): CONJUNCTION AND DISJUNCTION

As we saw in the preceding section, under standard logical assumptions the composite propositions expressed by sentences such as (11)–(12) are held to be semantically equivalent. This is because the operations whereby composite propositions are formed out of simple propositions are, by definition, **truth-functional**.

What this means is that the truth-value of a composite proposition is fully determined by – is a **function** of (in the specialized mathematical sense of 'function' explained in Chapter 4) – the truth-values of its component propositions and the specified effect of each operation. The four operations that are of concern to us are conjunction, disjunction, negation and implication.

Conjunction (&) creates a composite proposition (p & q: "p-and-q"), which is true if, and only if, both p and q are true. **Disjunction** (∨), mentioned earlier, creates a composite proposition (p ∨ q: "either-p-or-q") which is true, if, and only if, either p is true or q is true (or both are true). **Negation** (∼) creates a composite proposition (∼p) out of a simple proposition (p); and ∼p is defined to be true when p is false and false when p is true.

Implication (→) creates a composite proposition (*p* → *q*: "*p*-implies-*q*") which is true if, and only if: (i) both *p* and *q* are true, (ii) both *p* and *q* are false, or (iii) *p* is false and *q* is true.

The question which we now have to address is whether the operations associated with the formation of composite sentences in natural languages are similarly truth-functional. In this section we shall restrict our attention to compound sentences formed by means of the operation of conjunctive and disjunctive co-ordination. Sentences which are commonly held to exemplify implication and negation will be dealt with in subsequent sections.

At first sight, the logical definition of conjunction and its application to the semantic analysis of compound sentences in natural languages might seem to be straightforward enough. We have already noted, however, that there seems to be a difference of meaning between such sentences as (11) and (12) – a difference which can be associated with the English forms *and* and *but* (and with grammatically and semantically comparable forms in other languages). Let us now look more closely at what I will call clausal *and*-co-ordination: the co-ordination of clauses by means of *and*. This is the most neutral kind of conjunctive co-ordination in English; and its closest equivalent in the propositional calculus is undoubtedly logical conjunction (&). Even *and*-co-ordination, however, is problematical from the point of view of truth-functionality.

Very often there is felt to be some kind of temporal or causal link between the situations described by the component propositions, such that the ordering of the clauses expressing these propositions is semantically significant. For example

(14) 'John arrived late and missed the train'

and

(15) 'John missed the train and arrived late'

would normally be used in different circumstances. To make the point briefly, but loosely: *and* here appears to mean "and then" or "and therefore". Obviously, if *and* does have this meaning, it is not equivalent to the connective for propositional conjunction, &. For *p* & *q* has the same truth-values as *q* & *p*.

But does *and* – more precisely, the co-ordination of clauses in sequence by means of *and* – actually have the meaning "and then" or "and therefore"? An alternative view is that "then" or "therefore" is not part of the propositional content, but something that is merely implied (in a broad sense of 'implied') by our general tendency to adhere to the communicative norms of relevance and orderliness. Those who hold this view would argue that, in normal circumstances and in default of contextual information to the contrary, we can reasonably infer from the utterance of the sentence 'John arrived late and missed the train' that John's late arrival was the cause of his missing the train even though there is nothing in the actual meaning of the sentence that gives us this information – because we can assume that the speaker is not misleading us by deliberately and gratuitously flouting the ground-rules, or maxims, of normal communicative behaviour.

It is, of course, possible to think of circumstances in which (14) and (15) could be uttered to assert two otherwise unconnected facts. But these circumstances must be rather special and will generally be clear from the context of utterance. Let us grant, therefore, that in what we may think of as more normal or more usual contexts of utterance anyone uttering either (14) or (15) would be implying, if not actually expressing, the fact that there was some kind of causal connexion between John's late arrival and his missing the train.

This argument has been used by adherents of truth-conditional semantics. We shall come back to this in Chapter 9 in our discussion of Grice's notion of **conversational implicature**. At this point, however, it is worth noting that, however persuasive the arguments might be in the case of the English form *and*, they cannot be assumed to hold for all natural languages. It so happens that English has compound, as well as complex, sentences and what can be plausibly seen as a neutral co-ordinating conjunction. Many familiar European languages are like English in this respect, but not all languages are.

The arguments in favour of a truth-functional analysis of composite sentences in English are rather less persuasive when they are used in support of the thesis that sentences containing *but* or *although* have the same meaning as sentences containing *and*, as in (12) and (13) mentioned earlier. If we concede the truth-functionality of what I have called the most neutral kind of conjunctive co-ordination involving the use of *and*, we must also allow that speakers may utter sentences such as (11) in several prosodically different forms which also differ in meaning. For example, they may superimpose upon their utterance of what is in itself a grammatically and lexically neutral compound sentence such as (11) a prosodic contour (comprising stress and intonation) which indicates their own feelings about the propositions expressed and the connexion between them. That is to say, it is possible to say (11a) *He was poor and he was honest*, (11a) being one of the forms – an utterance-inscription – which results from the utterance of (11), in such a way that, in asserting the conjunction of the two propositions, p & q, speakers simultaneously reveal their surprise that both p & q should be true. In such circumstances, they might equally well have uttered, not a form of (11), but of (12) or even of (13), each with the appropriate prosodic contour. There would be no difference in the composite proposition which they assert, and no readily identifiable difference in the degree or nature of the feeling that they indicate. Nevertheless, the two sentences differ in meaning, since *but*, unlike *and*, is never a purely neutral marker of the conjunction of propositional content.

Similar problems arise, in certain languages, in connexion with disjunction. For example, in Latin there are two ways of translating English *either-or* sentences. One can use the particles ... *vel* ... *vel* ... or alternatively the particles ...*aut* ...*aut* ... . It has been suggested, at times, that the difference between these two alternatives is that the *vel*-construction is used for **inclusive** disjunction and the *aut*-construction for **exclusive** disjunction.

An inclusive disjunction, $p \lor q$, is true, not only if either p or q is true and the other is false, but also if both p and q are true. An exclusive disjunction, on the other hand, is true only if either p is true and q false or q is true and p false: it excludes the possibility of both p and q being true. For example, the following regulation might, in principle, be interpreted either inclusively or exclusively:

(16) *Students who do not arrive in time or have not completed all their assignments will be refused admission to the examination.*

If it is interpreted inclusively (which is clearly the most likely interpretation in a case like this), this would mean that students who fail to fulfil both conditions, in addition to students who fail to fulfil only one of the conditions, will be refused admission; if it were interpreted exclusively, this would mean that students failing to fulfil only one of the conditions would be refused admission, but not necessarily students who fail to fulfil both conditions. In other cases, an exclusive interpretation is more likely: e.g.,

(17) *For the main course you may have meat or fish.*

Usually, when logicians use the term 'disjunction', without qualification, they mean inclusive disjunction.

To return, then, to the Latin example. In fact, it does not seem to be the case, except perhaps in the specialized usage of logicians, that *vel* is used for inclusive and *aut* for exclusive disjunction. What is true, however, is that the *aut*-construction is stronger or more expressive than the *vel*-construction, in much the same way that *but*-conjunction is stronger and more expressive than *and*-conjunction in English. It is difficult to be more precise than this without attributing to *aut*, in contrast with *vel*, several distinct meanings.

Perhaps the best way of explaining what is meant by 'stronger and more expressive' in this context is to say that the nearest equivalent to the *aut*-construction in (spoken) English is (*either*) ... *or* ... with heavy stress on the disjunctive particles. Much the same effect is achieved in French by adding *bien* to the otherwise neutral disjunctive particles (*ou*) ... *ou* ..., and in Russian similarly by adding *zhe*. In some contexts, stronger or more expressive disjunction will indeed be understood to be exclusive in the logician's sense; in others, however, it will indicate that, in the speaker's opinion, the alternatives p and q are the only propositions worth considering and will dramatize, or emphasize, the necessity of opting for one or the other. The distinction between inclusive and exclusive disjunction can be accounted for truth-functionally; the distinction between neutral and stronger, or more expressive, disjunction cannot.

6.4 TRUTH-FUNCTIONALITY (2): IMPLICATION

Implication (more precisely, what logicians call **material implication**) is usually rendered into English by means of a conditional sentence: for example,

(18) 'If Ann has passed her driving test, her parents have bought her a Porsche'.

As was mentioned in section 6.2, the composite proposition $p \rightarrow q$ ("p-implies-q") is true, by definition, not only when both p and q have the same truth-value (i.e., when both are true or both are false), but also when p is false and q is true. (It follows that $p \rightarrow q$ is false only when p is true and q is false.) So the proposition expressed by (18) – if it has the logical form of "p implies q" – is true not only (i) if Ann has passed her driving test and her parents have bought her a Porsche (p & q), but also (ii) if she has not passed her driving test and/but her parents have bought her a Porsche ($\sim p$ & q), and (iii) Ann has not passed her driving test and her parents have not bought her a Porsche ($\sim p$ & $\sim p$). Most people find (ii), if not (iii), paradoxical. Indeed, the fact that any false proposition (materially) implies every true proposition is commonly referred to as one of the **paradoxes of implication**.

A second point is that (in standard propositional logic) the truth-value of "p implies q", like that of "p and q", is totally independent of any causal connexion between the situations described by each of the component propositions. For example, the proposition expressed by

(19) 'If Lady Godiva had blue eyes, Ann's parents have bought her a Porsche'

would be true (independently of the colour of Lady Godiva's eyes) if the parents of the person referred to by 'Ann' and 'she' (in the form *her*), on some occasion of the utterance of the sentence, have indeed bought her a Porsche. Once again, most people find this paradoxical. More generally, they find it paradoxical that the truth-functionality of an implication is unaffected by the absence of any kind of causal connexion between the situations referred to in the two component propositions, *p* and *q*. Of course, it is always possible to devise a more or less plausible connexion for any two clauses in any conditional sentence and thereby eliminate the apparent paradox; and the full importance of this fact will emerge in our treatment of the notion of **relevance** in Chapter 9. For example, the Porsche might have been a prize for knowing or discovering the colour of Lady Godiva's eyes. But what if we do not seek to eliminate the so-called paradoxes of implication in this way?

One of the conditional sentences cited earlier, which is here repeated,

(7) 'If he passed his driving test, I am a Dutchman',

is interesting (but highly untypical) from this point of view. As it would normally be used (by non-Dutchmen), it depends for its effect upon the known falsity of *q* ("I am a Dutchman") and the presumed absence of any causal link between the situations described by *p* (in this case "He passed his driving test") and *q*. Under these circumstances, we might well be prepared to say that the composite proposition $(p \rightarrow q)$ expressed by the sentence as a whole is equivalent to the one expressed by 'Either he did not pass his driving test or I am a Dutchman' $(\sim p \lor q)$, and that it is true if both *p* and *q* are false. But this is surely because the utterance of this sentence is rhetorically equivalent to the denial of *q* in a context in which the denial of *p* is non-informative. In other words, the speaker can trade on the hearer's knowledge that the speaker is not a Dutchman and the hearer's consequential ability to infer the falsity of *p* ("He passed his driving test") from the truth of the presumably informative composite proposition "*p* implies *q*". The speaker can be all the more certain that the hearer will draw the correct inference in a case like this because the proposition "I am a Dutchman" has been conventionalized in some English-speaking societies for this very purpose. However, any sufficiently preposterous or self-evidently false proposition will serve the same rhetorical purpose ("If he has got a degree in linguistics, I am the Queen of Sheba", etc.). We do indeed make rhetorical, or as many would say these days pragmatic, use of at least a subclass of conditional sentences in the way that I have just illustrated.

In this section, we have been dealing with what logicians call material implication. There are other kinds of implication recognized in current linguistic semantics (and pragmatics), two of which may be mentioned here: **entailment** and **implicature**. The former, sometimes called strict implication, was introduced in section 4.4 in association with the notion of possible worlds: as we saw there, a proposition p entails a proposition q if, when p is true, q also is necessarily (and not just contingently) true (i.e., it is true in all possible worlds). The notion of entailment plays a major role in formal semantics: it is by no means restricted to the purpose for which it was introduced earlier (for the definition of sense-relations between lexemes). Implicature, by contrast, is a looser kind of implication, closer to what is often meant by 'implication' in everyday, non-technical, usage: a proposition p is said to **implicate** (rather than to imply) a proposition q if the truth of q can be reasonably inferred from p in the context in which p is asserted or is otherwise known or assumed to be true. The important point to note for the moment is that implicature is context-dependent and therefore, in terms of the theoretical framework adopted in this book, is a matter of utterance-meaning. It will be dealt with in Part 4.

6.5 TRUTH-FUNCTIONALITY (3): NEGATION

As we saw in section 6.2, negation (symbolized by '$\sim$') is regarded by logicians as an operation which forms a composite proposition ($\sim p$) out of a simple proposition (p). As far as standard, two-valued, propositional logic is concerned, the truth-functional definition of negation is straightforward: whenever p is true, $\sim p$ is false and whenever p is false, $\sim p$ is true. It is further allowed that negation should be **recursive**, so that the negation of $\sim p$, yields $\sim \sim p$, which is equivalent to p (two negatives make a positive), the negation of $\sim \sim p$ yields $\sim \sim \sim p$, which is equivalent to $\sim p$, and so on. How does the standard logical account of negation relate to the meaning and use of negative sentences in natural languages? More particularly, how much of the meaning of negative constructions is part of the propositional content of sentences?

There are various ways in which negative sentences are constructed in natural languages. Only rarely, however, is there any reason to say that a negative sentence is grammatically composite by contrast with the corresponding positive, or affirmative, sentence. Generally speaking, corresponding sentences of opposite **polarity** have the same clause-structure, and what we can identify most easily with propositional negation applies within clauses and does not extend to whole sentences. Indeed, in many languages (including Finnish and Irish) the negative polarity of a clause (like its mood or its tense) is marked not by means of a separate particle like the English *not*, but by special forms of the verb, or predicate. Hence the traditional maxim: negation of the predicate is equivalent to negation of the proposition.

But there is one kind of predicate-negation which is clearly not equivalent to the negation of the whole proposition. This may be exemplified by

(20) 'John is unfriendly',

which, unlike

(21) 'John is not friendly',

expresses a proposition that is not just the **contradictory** of the proposition expressed by

(22) 'John is friendly',

but its **contrary**. "John is unfriendly" is not simply the negation of "John is friendly": it implies "John is hostile". (In standard logical terminology, one proposition is the contradictory of another if it is impossible for both of them to be true and both false. One proposition is the contrary of another if both cannot be true, though they may both be false.) It is quite possible for John to be neither friendly nor unfriendly.

In fact, 'John is not friendly' is often used in everyday conversation as if it had the same sense as 'John is unfriendly'. (We are not concerned, in this context, with spoken utterances of (21) in which the forms *not* and *friendly* are, as it were, hyphenated prosodically. In such utterances, *not friendly* is obviously to be interpreted as the form *unfriendly* would be.) There are three ways of handling this fact. The first, which is excluded by the formulation I have just used, is to say that there are two distinct sentences represented in written English by 'John is not friendly' and that they are distinguished, at least optionally, in spoken English by means of rhythm and intonation. But rhythm and the fine differences of intonation that are involved in cases such as this are universally excluded by linguists from what they consider to be part of the prosodic structure of sentences. The second way is to say that there is one sentence, and that it is structurally ambiguous. But there are no other, independently motivated, reasons for adopting this view. The third way is to draw upon the distinction between sentence-meaning and utterance-meaning and to say that 'John is not friendly' is a single unambiguous sentence which can be uttered in a particular way, and perhaps also in identifiable contexts, with more or less the same communicative effect as the utterance of 'John is unfriendly'. It is the third of the three analyses that is adopted here.

It is also possible to have negated nominal expressions occurring as clause-constituents. For example,

(23) 'Non-students pay the full entrance-fee'

expresses a proposition which differs from, and does not entail (though it may, in context, implicate) the proposition expressed by

(24) 'Students do not pay the full entrance-fee'.

Nominal negation of this kind ('non-students'), like predicative negation ('do not pay'), has an effect on the propositional content of the clause in which it occurs and is in principle truth-functional; but it cannot be readily formalized in standard propositional logic.

To be contrasted with nominal negation of the kind exemplified by 'non-students' above is the use of negative indefinite pronouns such as 'no-one' or 'nothing' or the semantically comparable nominals introduced with the adjectival 'no' (e.g., 'no man': cf. French 'aucun homme', German 'kein Mensch', etc.). It is obvious, upon reflection, that

(25) 'No-one telephoned'

expresses a proposition which contradicts the proposition expressed by

(26) 'Someone telephoned',

whereas

(27) 'Someone did not telephone',

which looks as if it is the negative sentence that most directly corresponds to (26), can be conjoined with (27) to express the non-contradictory composite proposition,

(28) "Someone telephoned and someone did not telephone".

Most logicians and linguists have taken the view, until recently at least, that the propositions expressed by (25), (26) and (27) differ in logical form from the propositions expressed by, say,

(29) 'John telephoned'

and

(29a) 'John did not telephone'.

Standard logical analyses of the propositional content of (25), (26) and (27) all make use of the **existential quantifier** with or without negation, as the case may be, and handle the semantic difference between (25) and (27) in terms of the relative order of the quantifier and the negation operator. The most notable difference between the negative sentences (25) and (29a), from this point of view, is that the latter (when it is used to make a statement) is associated with a particular kind of **existential presupposition**: that is, it conveys the speaker's presupposition that there exists some entity that may be appropriately referred to with the expression 'John'. There is no existential presupposition associated with the use of 'nobody', 'nothing', etc. The standard analysis of (25) correctly accounts for its difference, in this respect, from (29a). But it does so at the price of discounting their apparent grammatical parallelism.

Consideration of sentences such as those listed above within a more comprehensive discussion of negation in English and other languages raises further problems. How are positive sentences containing 'some' (or 'someone', 'somewhere', etc.) related grammatically and semantically to corresponding negative sentences containing 'any' (or 'anyone', 'anywhere', etc.)? (What is the relation, for example, between 'He saw someone' and 'He did not see anyone'?) And how are they related to corresponding negative sentences containing 'some'? (Does 'He saw no-one' mean exactly the same as 'He did not see anyone'?) Problems like this, involving the complex interaction of negation, the use of determiners, quantifiers and indefinite pronouns (and adjectives), etc., have been extensively treated by linguists in recent years. In some cases, the facts themselves are in dispute, especially when it comes to alleged differences of meaning which cannot be accounted for truth-functionally. But it is very difficult to handle even the undisputed cases of propositional negation in a theoretically unified framework within which grammatical structure and logical form can be put into correspondence simply and systematically.

Negation is an operation that applies to a single expression. But the expression in question can be simple or composite. In $\sim p$, the expression to which the operator applies – the expression that is in its **scope** – is simple, whereas in $\sim (p \ \& \ q)$ it is composite. Everything within the matching left and right brackets that immediately follow the negation-operator is in its scope: in default of such brackets the negation-operator is taken to apply to the smallest expression on its right. There is therefore a significant difference between $\sim (p \ \& \ q)$ and $\sim p \ \& \ q$: between, say,

(30) "Mary was not (both) well-and-cheerful"

and

(31) "Mary was (both) not-well and cheerful"

(if I may informally indicate the difference by means of hyphens).

It is easy to see that there are other such differences of scope in respect of propositional negation in natural languages. For example, the English sentences

(32) 'John did not kiss Mary because she was his sister'

can be construed in two ways: as

(33) "It was because she was his sister that John did not kiss Mary"

or, alternatively, as

(34) "It was not because she was his sister that John kissed Mary".

Under interpretation (33), the sentence in question is taken to be one in which negation applies only to the propositional content of the main clause ("John kissed Mary"); under interpretation (34), it is a sentence in which negation applies either to the content of the subordinate clause ("because she was his sister") or (and this is perhaps the preferred analysis) to the composite proposition "John kissed Mary because she was his sister". Of course, the difference between (33) and (34) is not correctly formalized in terms of the truth-functional difference between $\sim p$ & q and $\sim (p$ & $q)$. As we have seen, the propositional calculus cannot draw the distinction between conjunction and causal subordination. Nevertheless, it is intuitively clear that the difference between (33) and (34) is, in principle, formalizable in terms of the scope of propositional negation. There are many such examples.

The scope of negation is also relevant in modal logic, which extends the propositional calculus by means of the logical operators of necessity (N) and possibility (M). The proposition

(35) "It is not necessary that p" $(\sim Np)$.

differs truth-functionally from

(36) "It is necessary that not $\sim p$" ($N \sim p$).

For example,

(37) "The sky is not necessarily blue"

differs in truth-value from

(38) "Necessarily, the sky is not blue".

As we shall see in Part 4, at least some of what can be identified as modality in natural languages can be ascribed to the propositional content of sentences. In such cases, there is some degree of correspondence between the scope of negation and grammatical structure. For example, the utterance

(39) *He may not come*

can be construed, syntactically, in two ways (and thus put into correspondence with two different sentences), according to whether the negative particle *not* has **narrower** or **wider scope** than the modal verb 'may':

(40) "It is possible that he will not come" ($M \sim p$),

in contrast with

(41) "It is not possible/allowed that he will come" ($\sim Mp$).

What cannot be formalized, even in modal logic, is the difference between the assertion of a negative proposition ("I say that it is not raining") and the denial of a positive proposition ("I deny that it is raining"); or again, the difference between the assertion of a positive proposition ("I say that it is raining") and the denial of a negative proposition ("I deny that it is not raining"). Here, too, we have differences that can be accounted for in terms of the scope of negation. Moreover, they are differences that are reflected, at least partly, in the syntactic and prosodic structure of sentences in many languages. But assertion and denial are not, and cannot be, constituents of propositions or propositional content; they are different kinds of communicative acts. In so far as the difference between assertion and denial, and between other kinds of communicative acts, is systematically encoded in what was earlier referred to as the face-value of sentences, it is yet another part of the meaning of sentences that is not part of their propositional content.

6.6 SENTENCE-TYPE, CLAUSE-TYPE AND MOOD

It is by now common enough for linguists to draw a terminological distinction between declarative sentences and statements, between interrogative sentences and questions, between imperative sentences and commands, between optative sentences and wishes, between exclamative sentences and exclamations. It is far less common for them to point out that, in traditional usage, there is a crucial difference between 'declarative', 'interrogative' and 'exclamative', on the one hand, and 'imperative' or 'optative', on the other. The former set of terms subclassify sentences according to what is often called **sentence-type**. (This is a quite different sense of the term 'type' from the sense in which 'type' is opposed to 'token'. As we shall see in Part 4, within the conceptual and terminological framework adopted in this book, the type/token distinction does not apply to sentences, since, unlike utterances, they are not forms.) The terms 'imperative' and 'optative', however, go traditionally with 'indicative', 'subjunctive', 'dubitative', 'evidential', etc., and subclassify sentences (or clauses) according to **mood**. Some terms, notably 'conditional', are used traditionally both of sentence-type and mood: this point, in respect of the term 'conditional', will be picked up presently, since conditional propositions have long been of particular concern in logical semantics.

At this point, I should remind the reader that, although we are operating throughout this book with two fundamental distinctions, the distinction between lexical meaning (or word-meaning) and sentence-meaning, on the one hand, and the distinction between sentence-meaning and utterance-meaning, on the other, it is arguable that it is clauses, rather than sentences, that correspond most closely to propositions and also that they are more basic grammatically (cf. 6.2). In what follows, I will, for simplicity, use the terms 'sentence' and 'sentence-type', where some grammarians might prefer to use 'clause' and 'clause-type'. My principal reason for continuing to operate, primarily, with 'sentence' and 'sentence-type' is that these are the terms that are most commonly used in formal semantics (where, furthermore, a clear distinction is not always drawn between sentences and propositions). Nothing of substance is affected by this purely terminological decision, since everything that is said in Parts 3 and 4 of this book could be reformulated without difficulty in terms of clause and clause-types. (When it comes to the detailed integration of semantics and syntax within a particular theoretical framework, the selection of sentences or clauses as basic, and in what sense of 'basic', does of course make a difference. But at the level of generality at which we are operating in this introductory work this is something we need not be concerned with.) In order to make explicit the possibility of adopting an alternative view, I have included 'clause-type' in the section heading, and I have occasionally added the terms 'clause' and 'clause-type' in brackets.

There is a connexion between sentence-type (or clause-type) and mood. But type and mood are partly independent dimensions of the grammatical structure of sentences (and clauses), and it is important not to confuse them. In particular, it is important not to confuse or to conflate 'declarative' with 'indicative', as philosophers and even linguists do at times. A sentence cannot be simultaneously interrogative and declarative; but in many languages it can be both interrogative and indicative (as these terms are traditionally understood): i.e., it can be interrogative in sentence-type and contain, as its sole or principal clause, one that is indicative in mood. But it can also be, in some languages if not in English, both interrogative and subjunctive. For example, the Latin sentence

(42) 'Quid faceret?',

which is in the imperfect subjunctive, differs grammatically and semantically from

(43) 'Quid faciebat?',

which is in the imperfect indicative. Both (42) and (43) can be translated into English according to context in various ways: e.g., as

(42a) 'What was he/she to do?'

or

(43a) 'What was he/she doing?'.

It is important to realize that the semantic difference between (42) and (43) in Latin is exactly parallel with the difference between

(42b) 'Quid faciam?' ('What am I do to?')

and

(43b) 'Quid facio?' ('What am I doing?'),

in which the verbs are in the present tense subjunctive and indicative, respectively, and the subject is in the first person. Sentences such as (42) and (42b) can also be analysed as having the same propositional content as (43) and (43b) respectively, but as combining with this a non-propositional – truth-conditionally unanalysable – expressive, and more particularly **subjective**, component of meaning (see 10.6). The English translations of (42) and (42b) which I have given above are potentially misleading in that they do not grammaticalize this subjective component of utterances by means of the category of mood in a one-clause sentence, and they encourage the semanticist to look for a non-subjective analysis involving the embedding of the propositional content of one clause within that of another. Modern English, in most dialects, makes very little use of the distinction between the indicative and the subjunctive even in subordinate clauses.

Just as, in some languages, a sentence can be both interrogative and non-indicative, so too there are languages in which a sentence can be declarative without being indicative. Indeed, there are languages (notably, members of the American-Indian Siouan family) in which there are various kinds of non-indicative declarative sentences, but no indicative sentences at all. Speakers of such languages, when they use a sentence to make a statement cannot but encode in the verbal component of their utterance, by the choice of one grammatical mood rather than another, some subjective qualification of their commitment to the truth of the proposition they express or some other indication of what may be referred to later as its **epistemic status**. (What is meant by 'epistemic' and 'subjective qualification' will be explained in sections 8.4 and 10.5.) In so far as the sentences in question are members of a class (a sentence-type) which is associated, characteristically, with making statements, they are declarative. But none of the subclasses is indicative (in mood), because none of the moods in these languages is associated with the neutral (objective or non-subjective) expression of propositional content (in the making of statements, the asking of questions, or whatever). The indicative, in those languages which have such a mood, is traditionally regarded as the mood of factuality. Obviously, one can not only assert or deny, but also query, presuppose, or even simply consider (in soliloquy or thought), the factuality of a proposition.

An indicative sentence (or clause) is by definition a sentence (or clause) in the indicative mood, as an imperative, subjunctive or optative sentence (or clause) is a sentence (or clause) in the imperative, subjunctive or optative mood, in those languages which have any or all of these moods. Mood, as a grammatical category of the sentence (or clause), is frequently encoded inflectionally, throughout the languages of the world (as it is in Latin and Greek and the other Indo-European languages), in the grammatically distinct – more precisely, morphosyntactically distinct – forms of the verb in the sentence (or clause) of which the verb is the head. It is for this reason that mood is often defined, in traditional grammars, as a category of the verb. But this association of mood with verbal inflection is, in principle, contingent. As we shall see later, mood is best defined as that category which results (in those languages which have it) from the grammaticalization of **subjective modality** and other kinds of expressive meaning, including some part of what is nowadays commonly referred to as illocutionary force (8.3). Much of this, in English, is encoded in the modal verbs, which

have taken over many of the functions of the Old English subjunctive as part of a process which has been going on for centuries and has made Modern English, in this respect as in others,
morphologically more analytic (or periphrastic) and less synthetic (or inflecting). A similar long-term process has been taking place in other Germanic languages and in the Romance
languages, though most of these still have a somewhat richer system of verbal inflections than Modern English. One of the consequences of this, as we shall see, is that it is much easier to
objectify and propositionalize the inherently expressive and subjective, non-propositional, components of the meaning of utterances in English than it is in many other languages.

The point that I have been making here about the need to distinguish sentence-type from mood is of more than purely terminological interest. As we shall see in Part 4, this distinction can
be seen as supporting a tripartite analysis of the logical structure
of both sentences and utterances in preference to the bipartite,
or even unitary, analysis favoured by many logicians and formal
semanticists. Terminology is, in any case, especially important
in this area of semantics, since it helps us to keep apart, not only
sentence-type and mood (which are frequently confused even
by linguists), but also form and function.

As was mentioned earlier, some terms, such as 'conditional',
are traditionally used to label one of the moods in certain
languages (e.g., in French or Italian), as well as being used
more generally to label sentences (typically complex, but in
some cases compound or paratactic) which are used, characteristically, to express composite propositions, or implications (see
6.4). Whenever one employs such terms, one must be careful
not to confuse either the formal with the functional or the narrower with the broader formal category. To take the French or
Italian so-called conditional mood, for example: on the one
hand, it does not occur in all conditional sentences, but only in
that subclass of conditional sentences which are used characteristically to express counterfactual conditional propositions (and
it occurs in the main clause, rather than the subordinate, conditional, clause); and, on the other, it has other functions in addition to its use in conditional sentences. One of these uses, which

is of particular interest in the context of a discussion of the need to distinguish form from function and sentence-type (or clause-type) from mood, is in declarative sentences to express a particular kind of subjective epistemic modality, comparable with that expressed by what is called the **evidential** mood in the many languages throughout the world that have such a mood (e.g., in addition to the Siouan family referred to above, Turkish and Bulgarian).

Much the same point that I have made about the term 'conditional' can also be made about 'subjunctive' and 'optative', which are sometimes used in philosophical and logical semantics, in contrast with 'indicative', with reference to function rather than form or to sentence-type rather than mood. Having made this point, in the remaining sections of this chapter I will let the term 'declarative sentence' (abbreviated as 'declarative') stand for 'indicative declarative sentence'. This is how it is usually interpreted in recent work in linguistic semantics. The important thing to remember is that in many languages there are also various kinds of non-indicative declarative sentences.

We must now return briefly to the question of prosodic structure. In this section (and throughout this book), we have opted for the view that the classification of sentences (and clauses) by type is wholly a matter of their grammatical structure, in both the written and the spoken language. It has already been noted, however, that, in normal conversation, spoken utterances, in all languages, are **punctuated** and **modulated** – i.e., invested with various kinds of subjective, non-propositional, meaning – by superimposing upon the string of forms of which they are composed a particular prosodic contour (see 1.3). In speech, the grammatical structure and the prosodic structure of utterances are generally complementary and mutually supportive, but, as we shall see presently, they may also be in apparent conflict. For example, a declarative sentence may be uttered **ironically** to express a proposition that contradicts the proposition which, taken at face-value, it purports to express (e.g., *That's a clever thing to do!*); an interrogative sentence may be uttered to make, indirectly, a statement of the kind that is traditionally (and somewhat misleadingly) referred to as a *rhetorical question* (e.g., *Who could possibly think that such negotiations would bring lasting peace to the region!*).

We shall look at some of these apparent conflicts between sentence-meaning and utterance-meaning in Part 4. The point being made here is the more general one, that in speech the prosodic (and paralinguistic) structure of the utterance would normally resolve the apparent conflict or contradiction. The fact that we have excluded prosodic structure from sentence-structure (and that we have therefore drawn a distinction between sentence-meaning and utterance-meaning, for both the written and the spoken language, where it has been drawn) is well motivated from a methodological point of view. It does not follow that in drawing the distinction in this way and at this point, we are providing a realistic analysis of the production and interpretation of utterances.

Having established the distinction between sentence-types (and clause-types) and mood and having noted that not all declarative sentences (or clauses) are in the indicative mood (in all languages that have such a mood), we shall now move on to consider the relation between interrogatives and declaratives.

6.7 THE MEANING OF INTERROGATIVE AND DECLARATIVE SENTENCES

It is generally recognized that sentences other than declaratives present problems for truth-conditional theories of sentence-meaning. In this section, we shall be concerned with one class of non-declaratives, namely interrogatives, and shall be comparing them semantically with declaratives. In the following section we shall look at two other classes of non-declarative sentences, drawing upon the points made here and introducing others. The general conclusion towards which we are proceeding is that not even declarative sentences are fully analysable semantically in terms of a standard truth-conditional theory of meaning.

In English, as in many other languages, there are two grammatically distinct subclasses of interrogative sentences, which can be put into correspondence (by means of the notion of characteristic use and face-value meaning) with two subclasses of questions: yes-no **questions** and what I will call **x-questions**. We shall restrict our attention initially to what may be referred to, derivatively, as *yes–no* interrogatives, such as

(44)   'Is the door open?'.

This is systematically related, in terms of its grammatical and lexical structure, to the declarative sentence

(45)   'The door is open'.

And the systematic grammatical and lexical relation between the two would seem to reflect a no less systematic semantic relation. But what is the nature of this semantic relation? Intuitively, it would seem that they share much, if not all, of their propositional content, but differ with respect to the totality of their sentence-meaning.

There are several ways of assigning truth-conditions to (44), such that both the similarity and difference between its meaning and that of (45) are systematically accounted for. One is to say that it has the same meaning as

(46)   'I ask whether the door is open'.

But this is readily shown to be unsatisfactory. First of all, it seems clear that the meaning of (44) is independent of its being used to ask a question. For example, there is nothing illogical or contradictory about the utterance

(47)   *Is the door open? – that is a question which I refuse to ask.*

And yet there should be if (44) and (46) have the same meaning.

Secondly, if we adopt this approach, we are presumably committed to the view that the meaning of the grammatically complex sentence (46) is simpler than the meaning of the grammatically simple sentence (44). This is in itself counter-intuitive; and it is in conflict with the principle of compositionality (which was mentioned in Chapter 4 and will be discussed with reference to sentence-meaning in section 7.2). But, to make matters worse, we also have to reckon with the fact that the subordinate clause which operates as the complement, or direct object, of the verb 'ask' in (46), is generally regarded as being grammatically comparable with the *that*-clause which operates as the complement of the verb 'say' in

(48) 'I say that the door is open',

the former, *whether the door is open*, being related to, and perhaps derived from, (44) in exactly the same way as the latter, *that the door is open*, is related to (45). But it is generally agreed that the truth-conditions of (48) are clearly different from the truth conditions of (45). And there is no good reason to challenge this consensus, especially as (i) English is, in this respect, by no means untypical of languages which grammaticalize the distinction between so-called **direct-discourse** and **indirect-discourse** constructions and (ii) there are many languages which do not have indirect-discourse constructions but few, if any, that do not have direct-discourse constructions. It is clearly unsatisfactory to treat indirect-discourse constructions as more basic and grammatically simpler than direct-discourse constructions.

A third, and conclusive, reason for rejecting the view that (44) and (46) – and (45) and (48) – are truth-conditionally equivalent is that acceptance of this view presupposes that we have a satisfactory and independently motivated truth-conditional analysis of (46) – and of (48). But, as we shall see in Chapter 8, it is only when (46) and (48) are given a special performative interpretation (and have a particular aspectual meaning) that they can be said to be semantically equivalent to (44) and (45), respectively. The performative analysis of sentences (in contrast with the performative analysis of some or all kinds of utterances), though favoured by several of the so-called generative semanticists in the early 1970s, has now been universally rejected on both grammatical and semantic grounds. Another way of accounting for the meaning of interrogative sentences such as (44) within the framework of truth-conditional semantics is by identifying it, semantically, with the set of declaratives, including 'The door is open', that may be used correctly or acceptably to answer it when it is uttered to ask a question. This approach to the semantic analysis of interrogatives has been adopted, and developed with great subtlety, in much recent work in formal semantics. All that needs to be said about it here is that, whatever its advantages from a purely logical point of view, it is hardly the approach that would be chosen by someone working in linguistic semantics who was not determined, for metatheoretical reasons, to force the whole of sentence-meaning into a truth-conditional straitjacket.

Much more attractive is the view taken by Gottlob Frege, the German scholar whose seminal work on the philosophy of language in the late nineteenth century has been of central importance in the formalization of semantics. According to Frege, and his present-day followers, the meaning of 'Is the door open?' is composed of both a propositional and a non-propositional component. The propositional component, "The door is open", it shares with 'The door is open'; the non-propositional component is that part of its meaning by virtue of which it is used, characteristically, for questions rather than statements. But 'The door is open' also has a non-propositional component, namely that part of its meaning which makes it appropriate for uttering statements. Frege's formulation was slightly different from the one that I have just given, partly because he did not distinguish between sentences and utterances – or indeed, at times, between sentences, clauses and propositions ('Satz' in German covers all three). But my formulation preserves the substance of Frege's and adjusts it, terminologically and conceptually, to the broader notion of meaning adopted in this book.

Frege's view, which does not require us to assign truth-conditions to non-declaratives, saves the appearances. For the appearances, across a large sample of the world's languages, certainly suggest that the meaning of corresponding open declaratives and interrogatives of the kind exemplified by 'The door is open' and 'Is the door open?' respectively can be factorized into two parts. Generally speaking, in languages in which there is a clearly identifiable distinction between declaratives and interrogatives, the latter differ from the former in one of three ways: by a difference of word-order, by the occurrence of a special interrogative particle, or by morphological variation in the verb. It is sometimes said that there is another way of distinguishing declaratives and interrogatives: by means of intonation.

On the view taken here and made explicit above, however, this kind of intonational difference, which in many languages distinguishes questions from statements, should be attributed, not to the structure of sentences, but to the process and products of utterance. This means that there are languages (e.g., Italian, Spanish, Modern Greek — to name but a few of the more familiar European languages) in which there is no difference, at the sentence-level, between declaratives and *yes—no* interrogatives. The difference between statements and *yes—no* questions is normally marked prosodically in speech and by punctuation in writing.

Sentences that are grammatically neutral with respect to the distinction between declaratives and interrogatives (but can be used appropriately in the utterance of either statements or questions) are the only sentences whose meaning may be exhausted by their propositional content. (Whether even such sentences, in Italian, Spanish, Modern Greek, etc., can be said to be wholly devoid of non-propositional meaning depends on the way the grammatical categories of tense and mood are handled semantically: see 10.3, 10.5.) Sentences whose grammatical structure marks them as either declarative or interrogative have as the non-propositional component of their meaning an indication of their potential for use, characteristically, with one communicative function rather than another: that of making statements, on the one hand, or of asking questions, on the other. And in many languages the grammatical structure of such sentences is often readily analysable into a propositional and a non-propositional part. As we shall see in Chapter 7, several versions of transformational grammar, including the earliest version developed by Chomsky (1957) and subsequently adopted (with modifications) by Katz and Postal (1964), have exploited this fact.

So far we have discussed only neutral, or unmarked, *yes—no* interrogatives: i.e., interrogatives which do not encode, grammatically or lexically, the speaker's presuppositions or expectations with respect to the addressee's response. Non-neutral, or marked, interrogatives differ from neutral interrogatives in that they do encode such information. For example, so-called tag-interrogatives – more precisely, reversed-polarity tag-interrogatives – in English, such as

(49) 'The door is open, isn't it?'

and

(50) 'The door isn't open, is it?'

encode the speaker's expectation that the question will be answered in the affirmative or the negative, respectively: i.e., that, when these sentences are used with their characteristic function of presenting a proposition to an addressee and asking him or her to assign a truth-value to the proposition presented, by using these marked, non-neutral, constructions speakers (a) indicate (whether sincerely or not) what they themselves consider the truth-value to be and (b) in the tag explicitly seek the addressee's agreement or confirmation. Thus (49) would be used, characteristically, to present the proposition "The door is open" as one to which the speaker is disposed to assign the value true and (50) would be used, characteristically, to present the same proposition ("The door is open") as one to which the speaker is disposed to assign the value false or, alternatively, to present the corresponding negative proposition ("The door is not open") as one to which he or she is disposed to assign the value true. Many languages (including Latin) have distinct marked, or non-neutral, *yes–no* interrogatives, which are semantically, if not grammatically, comparable with (49) and (50).

Let us now turn to *x*-interrogatives. In English these contain one of a set of interrogative forms, adjectives, pronouns or adverbs, including *who/whom*, *what*, *which*, *when*, *where* and *how*. (Since all of these, except *how*, in their written form begin with *wh*-, the sentences that contain them are often referred to as **wh-sentences**. And the terms '*wh*-sentence' and '*wh*-question' are often extended to the description of languages other than English.)

The reason for calling such sentences *x*-interrogatives is almost self-evident. Looked at from the point of view of their logical structure, they can be thought of as sentences which contain a restricted variable (x) in their propositional component, for which, when such sentences are used to ask a question, the addressee is invited to supply a value falling within the range of the variable. For example, 'who' in the form *who* or *whom* restricts the value of x to persons (of which the prototypical exemplars are human beings). Thus

(51) 'Who has been eating my porridge?',

when used to ask a question, solicits from the addressee an answer which will identify the person who has been eating the speaker's porridge, by supplying as the value of x an appropriate referring expression, such as 'Goldilocks', or 'the little bear from next door', or 'the person who left these footprints on the path', or 'whoever it was who saw us going out this morning'. As always, reference is context-dependent: it is determined, first of all, by the speaker's general ontological beliefs and assumptions and, then, by his or her more specific background beliefs and assumptions relevant to the particular context of utterance and often acquired in the course of the particular conversation to which the utterance contributes and of which it constitutes a part. So too, and for the same reasons, is the range of the restricted variable in the propositional content of x-questions.

But what is the propositional content of (51)? It is intuitively clear that the x-interrogative (51) is closely related semantically to

(52) 'Someone has been eating my porridge',

which differs from (51) formally in that it has the indefinite pronoun 'someone', rather than the interrogative pronoun 'who' in subject position. Looked at from a logical point of view, 'someone' can be thought of as a **free** (or unbound) restricted variable whose range is the same as that of the interrogative pronoun 'who'. To say that it is a restricted variable, as we have noted above, is to say that it does not range over all the entities in the universe of discourse, but over a (proper) subset of these: in the present case, entities that are (more precisely, are assumed or presumed to be) persons – entities that belong to the class $\{x: x$ is a person$\}$. To say that a variable is free is to say that it is not bound – its reference is not fixed within its range – either by a logical operator (such as the universal or existential quantifier) or otherwise. In standard systems of logic, formulae which contain free variables are not regarded as propositions, but as propositional functions: they are converted into propositions either by **binding** the variables they contain or by substituting for them constants, whose reference is fixed (within any given universe of discourse).

The logical distinction between bound and free variables and its correlates in natural languages have been of immense importance recently, not only in logical and linguistic semantics, but also in grammatical theory. This is why it has been explained here, where its applicability is especially easy to appreciate. We shall be exploiting it later, as we shall also be exploiting the difference between propositions and propositional functions in our discussion of reference (10.1).

But we have still not established the nature of the semantic relation between (51) and (52). It is obviously not the same as that which holds between (44) and (45), since (52) has its own *yes–no* interrogative. In fact, it has two:

(53a) 'Has someone been eating my porridge?'
(53b) 'Has anyone been eating my porridge?'.

What difference there is, semantically, between (53a) and (53b) is difficult to determine: the *some/any* distinction which exists in English is notoriously controversial and will not be dealt with in this book. In any case, it is not directly relevant to the point at issue. For present purposes, let us simply agree that (53b) is the normal *yes–no* interrogative which corresponds with (52) – when (52) is also being used normally – in the same way that (44) corresponds with (45). It follows that (53b) has the same propositional content as (52). But so too, apparently, has (51).

The difference between (53b) and (51) – more generally, between *yes–no* interrogatives and *x*-interrogatives – has to do with the **scope** of the interrogativity that is encoded in them and with what are commonly referred to as the **presuppositions** of the questions that the two subclasses of interrogatives are (characteristically) used for. In (53b), as in (44), the whole of the propositional content is within the scope of the interrogativity; and, if either of these sentences is used to ask a question (unless there is some contextual, or in speech prosodic, limitation of scope), it will be the proposition expressed by the corresponding declarative (uttered as a straightforward, un-qualified, statement) that is queried. And in uttering (53b) or (44), in these circumstances, the speaker gives no indication of his or her presuppositions as to the truth or falsity of the proposition expressed. In (51), in contrast, it is only part of the propositional content that is within the scope of the interrogativity. In uttering (51) to ask a question, in normal circumstances, the speaker takes for granted, or presupposes, the truth of the proposition that would be expressed by the utterance of (52) in the same context and, by using the pro-noun 'who' in what might be referred to as the x-position, focuses upon the identity of the person referred to by 'someone'.

Many different kinds of presupposition have been recognized by logicians and linguists; and it is not clear how they relate to one another and to different kinds of implication. We shall return to this question in Part 4. What has been said here about presupposition (and scope) is relatively informal and theory-neutral. It also applies to the full range of x-interrogatives that is found in English (and in other languages), not only pronom-inal, but also adjectival and adverbial.

At this point, it is important to note that formally and to some extent functionally there are overlaps and parallels in many languages, not only between x-interrogatives and declaratives containing indefinite pronouns, adjectives and adverbs, but also between x-interrogatives and declaratives containing demonstrative and relative pronouns, adjectives and adverbs. It must also be added that in many, if not most, of the lan-guages of the world, it is impossible to identify all of these as grammatically and semantically distinct constructions. We must be careful, therefore, not to assume that every natural language grammaticalizes differences and equivalences of sentence-meaning in exactly the same way.

In this section we have concentrated upon the meaning of interrogative sentences in relation to that of declarative sen-tences. We have seen that, not only interrogatives (as one subclass of non-declaratives), but also declaratives, grammaticalize a non-propositional component of meaning, which expresses their characteristic use (as does that of interrogatives and other non-declaratives) and combines this with their propositional content and, in certain languages more obviously than in English, with yet another component of sentence-meaning expressed by mood. We have also noted that, although it is presumably possible to make statements and to ask questions in all languages (though not necessarily statements and questions that are purely neutral, or unmarked, in terms of modality), there are languages which do not grammaticalize the distinction between declaratives and interrogatives.

Interrogativity has been dealt with here as a property of sentences which is distinct from, but may combine with, mood (indicative, subjunctive, etc.) in those languages that have such a grammatical category. This is certainly the way it should be dealt with in the grammatical and semantic analysis of the Indo-European languages and many other languages throughout the world. In other languages, however, interrogativity may well be grammaticalized in one of the moods. Whether, and to what degree, this is the case is difficult to establish.

One reason for this difficulty is that it is hard to draw a functional distinction (unless the language itself clearly grammaticalizes or lexicalizes the distinction) between asking a question and expressing doubt. There are several American-Indian languages (including Menomini, Serrano and Hidatsa) which have what is traditionally called a **dubitative** mood; and the use of the term 'dubitative' implies that grammarians describing these languages have decided that the characteristic, if not the sole, function of the mood so labelled is that of expressing the speaker's doubt. But if speakers express doubt as to the truth of a particular proposition, in conversation rather than in soliloquy, they may well be understood in context (and expect to be understood) to be inviting the addressee to resolve their doubt for them: i.e., to be asking (and not merely posing) a question.

Conversely, of course, a sentence whose characteristic function is deemed to be that of asking questions – and which is for that reason said to be interrogative (either in sentence-type or in mood) – may also be used for the expression of doubt without the intention of soliciting from the addressee the resolution of that doubt (or any other kind of response). English lexicalizes the expression of doubt in the verb 'wonder' (in one of its senses), which is commonly used either (a) as a verb of report with an indirect-discourse complement or (b) parenthetically with a first-person subject in a clause which is adjoined (paratactically rather than syntactically) to an interrogative sentence. These two possibilities are exemplified by

(54) 'x wondered whether the door was open'
(55) 'Is the door open, I wonder?',

respectively. An utterance of (55) by *x* might be subsequently reported to *y* by uttering (54) as a statement. But so too might be an utterance of the interrogative sentence 'Is the door open?' without the parenthetical clause 'I wonder', if *y* had reason to believe, in context (and this might be made clear prosodically or paralinguistically), that *x* was simply expressing doubt and not asking a question.

To be compared with both (54) and (55) is the declarative

(56) 'I wonder whether the door is open'.

This is syntactically parallel with (54) and can of course be used to make a statement. Much more frequently, however, such sentences are used, like (55), either directly to express doubt or indirectly to ask a question. According to whether an utterance of (56) is interpreted in one way or the other, it will be reported with (54) or

(57) 'x asked whether the door was open'.

Similarly, if *y* has reason to believe that *x*, in uttering (55), is indirectly asking a question rather than simply expressing doubt, it will be appropriate for *y* to report this by saying (57).

The upshot of this discussion – which could be extended by introducing into it direct-discourse constructions for comparison with both (55) and (56) – is that interrogativity and dubitativity are closely related and, in default of any information, in the context of utterance, as to whether the speaker expects a response or not, may be ultimately indistinguishable. It is not surprising, therefore, to discover, first, that some languages do not grammaticalize the difference between them and, second, that, when they are grammaticalized, grammarians will argue as to whether it is interrogativity or dubitativity that is characteristically expressed by the utterance of sentences of a particular type or in a particular mood. It is perhaps only when semantic distinctions are lexicalized, rather than grammaticalized, that what is expressed is explicit enough for such arguments to be settled empirically. This point, as we shall see, applies in the analysis of imperatives and other non-declaratives, as well as in the analysis of interrogative and dubitative sentences (or indeed of non-indicative declaratives).

6.8 OTHER KINDS OF NON-DECLARATIVES: IMPERATIVES, EXCLAMATIVES, VOLITIVES, ETC.

In this section we shall be concerned primarily with imperative and exclamative sentences (and clauses), which are the other principal classes of non-declaratives, in addition to interrogatives, that are distinguished grammatically in English. We shall also look briefly at volitives and at one or two other classes of non-declaratives which are found in other languages.

Imperative and exclamative sentences are different from declaratives and interrogatives, and from one another, in several respects. But the same general point can be made about them as was made, in the preceding section, about declaratives and interrogatives: in addition to their propositional content, they also encode and grammaticalize (in those languages in which the relevant distinctions are indeed grammaticalized) some kind of non-propositional component of sentence-meaning. As declarative sentences grammaticalize their characteristic use for making statements and interrogative sentences grammaticalize their characteristic use for asking (or posing) questions, so imperative sentences grammaticalize their characteristic use for issuing commands, requests, entreaties, etc., and exclamative sentences their characteristic use for uttering what are traditionally called exclamations. Let us begin with exclamative sentences.

In English, and many other languages, there is a structural similarity between exclamative sentences and dependent interrogative clauses. For example,

(58) 'How tall he is'

has the same structure, at least superficially, as the subordinate clause in

(59) 'I wonder how tall he is'.

Functionally, however, there is a clear difference between exclamatives of the kind exemplified by 'How tall he is' and interrogatives. In fact, exclamatives of this kind are best seen, semantically, as a subclass of expressive declaratives, in which the non-propositional part of what distinguishes the meaning of 'How tall he is' from the meaning of

(60) 'He is very tall'

is grammaticalized, rather than being expressed, in utterance, by a particular prosodic contour. It is because it is grammaticalized and is correlated with systematic restrictions on polarity, the use of modal verbs, etc., that 'How tall he is' is rightly regarded by grammarians as an exemplar of a distinct sentence-type. It is, of course, important not to confuse exclamatives with exclamations. Sentences of all types may be uttered with that particular expressive modulation which is conveyed in the spoken language by stress and intonation, and in the written languages by means of the exclamation-mark. Exclamation is something very different from making statements, issuing commands and requests, and asking (or posing) questions. Let us now turn to imperatives.

Imperative sentences (and clauses), it will be recalled, are sentences (and clauses) in the imperative mood, which in many languages is in contrast with other moods, such as indicative, subjunctive, optative or dubitative (6.6). English, as we have also noted, has a relatively poor system of moods by comparison with many, and perhaps most, of the world's languages.

Imperative sentences, in English and other languages, cannot be put into correspondence with declarative (indicative) sentences as readily as can interrogative (indicative) sentences of the kind that were discussed in the preceding section, such as (44) and (45), which are here repeated and renumbered as (61) and (62), respectively.

(61) 'Is the door open?'
(62) 'The door is open'.

The reason for this is that mood is not independent of **tense** and **aspect**. Whereas (61) obviously has the same propositional content as (62) it is not obvious that

(63) 'Open the door!'

has the same propositional content as the declarative sentence

(64) 'You open the door',

if (a) tense is held to be a part of the propositional content of a sentence and (b) what is traditionally regarded as the tense of (64) is given its most usual interpretation.

As far as condition (b) is concerned, it should be noted that, as the term 'tense' is traditionally used in the description of English, the grammatical category of tense is not clearly distinguished from that of aspect. As we shall see later, in many languages aspect is more important than tense (as tense is nowadays defined by linguists) and, in contrast with tense, what it expresses is definitely part of the propositional content of sentences (10.4). The major aspectual distinction grammaticalized in English is **progressive** (e.g. '*x* is/was opening the door') versus **non-progressive** (e.g., '*x* opens/opened the door'). For present purposes, aspect is important in that 'open' belongs to a particular **aspectual class** of verbs – the majority in English – which do not normally occur in the simple (non-progressive) present tense with straightforward present-time reference. Moreover, from a semantic point of view it might be argued that the time-reference of a request or command made by uttering (63) is made implicitly, rather than explicitly, in the act of requesting or commanding; that (unless it is made explicit by means of a temporal adverb or adverbial) its reference is to the future, immediate or less immediate as the case may be; and that the sentence itself is tenseless. In support of this view is the fact that in many languages in which tense is encoded inflectionally the imperative is clearly unmarked for tense. As to the inherently future reference of commands and requests (in normal circumstances), it is to be noted that, even if their temporal reference is made explicit by means of the word 'now' or the phrase 'at this very moment', it must be to a point or period of time that is later, if only infinitesimally, than the time of utterance. From this point of view it is interesting to consider a structurally ambiguous utterance such as

(65) *I am telling you to open the door now,*

in contrast with the non-ambiguous utterances,

(66) *I am now telling you to open the door*

and

(67) *I am now telling you to open the door now.*

Two points may be made in relation to this example. First, (65) can have the meaning of either (66) or (67). Second, in (67) the reference of 'now' differs according to whether it locates the act of telling or the anticipated act of opening the door in time.

There is the further point that the grammatical categories of mood and tense are undoubtedly interdependent in all languages that have both. And mood, whose function is usually if not always non-propositional, is far more common throughout the languages of the world than tense. Only a minority of the world's languages have tense as a grammatical category; and many of the functions of tense in those languages that have it are quite definitely non-propositional. I will come back to this point in Part 4.

Condition (a) is even more important, and more controversial. From the point of view of classical logic, propositions are eternally true or false, and therefore of their very nature tenseless. It is when propositions are treated as objects of mental acts or attitudes, on the one hand, or of such communicative acts as assertion and denial, on the other, that one is tempted to introduce tense into propositions themselves, anchoring them to the moment at which the mental or communicative act is performed. We shall not be able to deal with the problem of reconciling these two different views of propositions in the present book. It should be noted, however, that it is a problem that is all too often ignored in general treatments of tense, not only by linguists, but also by logicians. Since natural languages differ considerably as to how they grammaticalize and lexicalize indirect discourse, it is possible that different analyses are appropriate for different kinds of languages.

In fact, standard tense-logic, so called, is demonstrably inadequate for the analysis of tense as it actually operates in those natural languages that have it. But richer and more powerful systems of tense-logic are now being developed by formal semanticists; and it may well be that these will prove to be more suitable for the semantic analysis of tense in natural languages than currently available systems are. Whether they can successfully integrate the propositional (and purely temporal) and the non-propositional (modal and subjective) functions of tense is as yet uncertain.

But let us now return to imperative sentences without considering any further the question of tense. Imperative sentences constitute a subclass of sentences that are used, characteristically, to issue what are nowadays commonly called **directives** (commands, requests, prohibitions, etc.). For example, (63) might be used by x to order or request y (or in the appropriate context to grant y permission) to perform a particular action. The effect of y's compliance with this order or request would be to bring about a state of affairs, or situation, in which the door, having been closed, is now open: i.e., to bring about a change in the world, in consequence of which the truth-conditions, not just of (62), but, more specifically, of

(68) 'y has opened the door'

and the truth-conditionally equivalent passive sentence

(69) 'The door has been opened by y,

are satisfied. It follows that, although imperative sentences, as such, may not have truth-conditions, they can be put into systematic correspondence with declarative sentences that do. This being so, it is clearly possible in principle to bring imperative sentences within the scope of truth-conditional semantics; and various attempts have been made to do this. The question remains, however, as to what exactly is the propositional content of an imperative sentence.

If we adopt the methodological principle of saving the appearances for those languages in which there is a systematic and morphologically transparent relation between imperative and indicative sentences, we can say that, not only the imperative, but also the indicative, operates semantically upon the propositional content. This means that we can then say of (63) that it does indeed have the same propositional content as the declarative sentence (64) – but only when (64) is used to refer to a point rather than a period of time. Such uses of present-tense, non-progressive, sentences with verbs of the same aspectual class as 'open', though unusual in making straightforward descriptive statements, are quite normal in English, in the appropriate contexts, as we shall see when we look at so-called performative utterances in Part 4.

What has just been said about tense holds true of many natural-language phenomena. It is not difficult to demonstrate the inadequacy of current treatments of natural languages within the framework of standard propositional logic. Much of this chapter has been devoted to just that task. But my purpose throughout has been constructive. We learn more from a demonstrably inadequate, but precisely formulated, theory than we do from one that is so vaguely expressed that we do not even see its inadequacy. Let us bear this point in mind as we move on to consider some of the recent work in formal semantics.

CHAPTER 7

The formalization of sentence-meaning

7.0 INTRODUCTION

This chapter follows on from the preceding one and looks at two historically important and highly influential theories of sentence-meaning which, since the mid-1960s, have been associated with the attempt to formalize the semantic structure of languages within the framework of Chomskyan and non-Chomskyan generative grammar.

The first is the Katz–Fodor theory of meaning, which originated in association with what we may now think of as the classical version of Chomsky's theory of transformational-generative grammar. The second theory is a particular version of possible-worlds semantics, initiated also in the late 1960s by Richard Montague, and, having been further developed by his followers, is now widely recognized as one of the most promising approaches to the truly formidable task of accounting for the propositional content of sentences in a mathematically precise and elegant manner.

The treatment of both theories is very selective and almost completely non-technical. I have been more concerned to explain some of the basic concepts than to introduce any of the formalism. At the same time, it must be emphasized that modern formal semantics is a technical subject, which cannot be understood without also understanding the mathematical concepts and notation that are a part of it. This chapter should definitely be read in conjunction with the more specialized introductions to formal semantics mentioned in the 'Suggestions for further reading'. Students who have mastered the concepts that are explained below should be able to tackle these other works and, equally important, to contextualize them within the framework of a broader approach to linguistic semantics than is customarily adopted by formal semanticists.

There is a sense in which the Katz–Fodor theory is now out-dated, as also in much of its detail is the so-called standard theory of transformational grammar. But, as I explain below, taken together, both theories are historically important, in that they introduced linguists to the principle of compositionality, as this is understood in formal semantics. Each of them is widely referred to in textbooks and is still taught in linguistics courses (if only as a foundation upon which to build). In my view, a good knowledge of each is indispensable for anyone who wishes to understand the more recent developments in linguistic seman-tics. They can also be used, as I use them here, with the more spe-cific purpose of introducing students of linguistics to formal semantics.

In the last twenty years or so considerable progress has been made in the formalization of the semantic structure of natural languages. However, as we shall see in the later sections of this chapter, it is so far only a relatively small part of linguistic mean-ing that has been brought within the scope of formal semantics.

We begin the chapter by considering the relation between for-mal semantics and linguistic semantics, as the latter has been defined in Chapter 1; and we end with a (non-technical) discus-sion of some of the underlying philosophical concepts upon which formal semantics is based. These are generally taken for granted, rather than explained, in more technical works.

7.1 FORMAL SEMANTICS AND LINGUISTIC SEMANTICS

The term 'formal semantics' can be given several different inter-pretations. Originally, it meant "the semantic analysis of formal systems (or formal languages)" – a formal system, or formal language, being one that has been deliberately constructed by logicians, computer scientists, etc. for philosophical or practical purposes. More recently, the term has been applied to the analysis of meaning in natural languages, but usually with a number of restrictions, tacit or explicit, which derive from its philosophical and logical origins.

In this book, we are not concerned with formal semantics for its own sake, but only in so far as it is actually or potentially applicable to the analysis of natural languages. I will now introduce the term 'formal linguistic semantics' to refer to that part, or branch, of linguistic semantics which draws upon the methods and concepts of formal semantics for the analysis of the semantic structure of natural languages. In doing so, I am deliberately avoiding commitment, one way or the other, on the question whether natural languages are fundamentally different, semantically, from non-natural (i.e., artificial or constructed) languages. Some twenty years ago, Richard Montague, whose own theory of formal semantics we shall be looking at in a later section, gave it as his opinion that there is "no important theoretical difference between natural languages and the artificial languages of logicians" and that it is "possible to comprehend the syntax and semantics of both kinds of languages within a single natural and mathematically precise theory". Whether Montague was right or wrong about this is still unclear. Indeed, given his failure to say exactly what he meant by 'important theoretical difference', it is not obvious that he was making, or intended to make, any kind of empirically confirmable claim about the semantic (and syntactic) structure of natural languages. He was declaring an attitude and, as it turned out, initiating a highly productive, but deliberately restricted, programme of research.

Formal linguistic semantics is generally associated with a restricted view of sentence-meaning: the view that sentence-meaning is exhausted by propositional content and is truth-conditionally explicable. As we have seen in Chapter 6, there are – or would appear to be – various kinds of meaning encoded in the lexical or grammatical structure of sentences which are not readily accounted for in terms of their propositional content. Two reactions are open to theorists and practitioners of formal linguistic semantics in the face of this difficulty, if they accept, as most of them do, that it is a genuine difficulty. One reaction is to say that what we have identified as a part of sentence-meaning is not in fact encoded in sentences as such, but is the product of the interaction between the meaning, properly so called, of the sentence itself and something else: contextual assumptions and expectations, non-linguistic (encyclopaedic) knowledge, conversational implicatures, etc., and should be handled as a matter of pragmatics rather than semantics. The second reaction is to accept that it is indeed a part of sentence-meaning and to attempt to provide a truth-conditional account of the phenomena by extending the formalism and relaxing some of the restrictions associated with what one may now think of as classical versions of formal semantics. Both attitudes are represented among formal semanticists who have been concerned with the analysis of linguistic meaning in recent years.

I have made it clear, in the preceding chapter, that, in my view, formal linguistic semantics has failed, so far, to account satisfactorily for such phenomena as tense, mood and sentence-type and has not been sufficiently respectful of the principle of saving the appearances. I cannot emphasize too strongly, therefore, that, in my view, this failure does not invalidate completely the attempts that have been made to deal with these and other phenomena. The failure of a precise, but inadequate, account often points the way to the construction of an equally precise, but more comprehensive, theory of the same phenomena. And even when it does not do this, it may throw some light, obliquely and by reflection, upon the data that it does not fully illuminate. Many examples of this can be cited. To take but one: so far, no fully satisfactory account of the meaning of the English words 'some' and 'any' (and their congeners: 'someone', 'anyone', 'something', 'anything', etc.) has been provided within the framework of formal linguistic semantics. Nevertheless, our understanding of the range of potentially relevant factors which determine the selection of one or the other has been greatly increased by the numerous attempts that have been made to handle the data truth-conditionally. Those who doubt that this is so are invited to compare the treatment of 'any' and 'some' in older and more recent pedagogical grammars of English, not to mention scholarly articles on the topic. They will see immediately that the more recent accounts are eminently more satisfactory.

What follows is a deliberately simplified treatment of some of the principal concepts of formal semantics that have been widely invoked by linguists in the analysis of the propositional content of the sentences of natural languages. No account is taken, in this chapter, of anything other than what is uncontroversially a part of the propositional content of sentences in English. It will be clear, however, from what was said in Chapter 6, that natural languages vary considerably as to what they encode in the grammatical and lexical structure of sentences and that, according to the view adopted in this book, much of sentence-meaning, in many natural languages including English, is non-propositional.

Whether formal linguistic semantics can ever cover, or be co-extensive with, the whole of linguistic semantics is an open question. Formal linguistic semantics, in its present state of development, is certainly a long way from being co-extensive with linguistic semantics, either theoretically or empirically. But progress is being made, and it is conceivable that, in due course, far more of the insights and findings of non-formal linguistic semantics, traditional and modern, will be successfully formalized (probably by relaxing the restriction of sentence-meaning to what is truth-conditionally explicable). In this connexion, it is worth noting that, as there is a distinction to be drawn between linguistic theory (in the traditional sense of 'theory' in which theories are not necessarily formalized) and theoretical linguistics (as the term 'theoretical linguistics' is nowadays used: i.e., to refer to such parts of linguistic theory as have been formalized, or mathematicized), so there is a distinction to be drawn between semantic theory and theoretical, or formal, semantics. In recent years, each has drawn upon and, in turn, influenced the other; and this process of mutual influence will no doubt continue.

7.2 COMPOSITIONALITY, GRAMMATICAL AND SEMANTIC ISOMORPHISM, AND SAVING THE APPEARANCES

The principle of **compositionality** has been mentioned already in connexion with the sense of words and phrases. Commonly described as **Frege's principle**, it is more frequently discussed with reference to sentence-meaning. This is why I have left a fuller treatment of it for this chapter. It is central to formal semantics in all its developments. As it is usually formulated, it runs as follows (with 'composite' substituted for 'complex' or 'compound'): the meaning of a composite expression is a function of the meanings of its component expressions. Three of the terms used here deserve attention; 'meaning', 'expression' and 'function'. I will comment upon each of them in turn and then explain, first, why the principle of compositionality is so important and, second, to what degree it is, or appears to be, valid.

(i) 'Meaning', as we have seen, can be given various interpretations. If we restrict it to descriptive meaning, or propositional content, we can still draw a distinction between sense and denotation (see 3.1). Frege's own distinction between sense and reference (drawn originally in German with the terms 'Sinn' and 'Bedeutung') is roughly comparable, and is accepted in broad outline, if not in detail, by most formal semanticists. (Frege, like many formal semanticists, did not distinguish between the denotation of an expression and its reference on particular occasions of utterance: see section 3.1. I will pick up this point in relation to the principle of compositionality presently.) I will take the principle of compositionality to apply primarily to sense. But it may be assumed to apply also to denotation; and, as we shall see in a later section, many formal semanticists have defined sense in terms of a prior notion of denotation.

(ii) The term 'expression' is usually left undefined when it is used by linguists. But it is normally taken to include sentences and any of their syntactically identifiable constituents. I have given reasons earlier for distinguishing expressions from forms, as far as words and phrases are concerned. More controversially perhaps, in also including sentences among the expressions of a language, I have allowed that a sentence, like words and phrases, may have, not only several meanings, but also several forms. I will now assume that there is an identifiable subpart of every sentence that is the bearer of its propositional content, and that this also is an expression to which the principle of compositionality applies. For example, if we take the view that corresponding interrogative and declarative sentences have the same propositional content, we shall say that what they share is an expression (which of itself is neither declarative nor interrogative). Some logicians who have taken this view (as did Frege) have called the expression in which the propositional content is encoded the **sentence-radical**; but this term has not won more general acceptance, and there is no widely used alternative. I will employ instead the term **sentence-kernel**, or **kernel**, which has occasionally been used in linguistics, for grammatical, rather than semantic, analysis. (Indeed, the use that I am making of this term is very close to the use that Chomsky made of the term 'kernel-string' in the earliest version of transformational-generative grammar formalized by him.) The kernel of a sentence (or clause), then, is an expression, which has a form (not necessarily pronounceable) and whose meaning is (or includes) its propositional content.

(iii) The term 'function' is being employed in its mathematical sense; i.e., to refer to a rule, formula or operation which assigns a single **value** to each member of the set of entities in its **domain**. (It thus establishes either a many-one-to-one or one-to-one correspondence between the members of the domain, D, and the set of values, V: it **maps** D either into or on to V.) For example, in standard algebras there is an arithmetical function, normally written $y = x^2$, which for any numerical value of x yields a single and determinate numerical value for x^2 and thus determines the value of y. Similarly, in the propositional calculus there is a function which for each value of the propositional variables in every well-formed expression maps that expression into the two-member domain {True, False}, or, alternatively and equivalently, {1, 0}. As we saw earlier, this is what is meant by saying that composite propositions are truth-functional. I have now spelled this out in more detail and deliberately introduced, with some redundancy, several of the technical terms that are commonly employed in formal semantics. We shall not go, unnecessarily, into the technical details of formal semantics, but the limited amount of terminology introduced here will be useful later, and it will give readers with a knowledge of elementary set-theory some indication of the mathematical framework within which standard versions of formal semantics operate.

But what is the relevance of the notion of compositionality, formalized mathematically, to the semantic analysis of natural-language expressions? First of all, it should be noted that competence in a particular language includes (or supports) the ability to interpret, not only lexically simple expressions, but indefinitely many lexically composite expressions, of the language. Since it is impossible for anyone to have learned the sense of every composite expression in the way that one, presumably, learns the sense of lexemes, formal semanticists argue that there must be some function which determines the sense of composite expressions on the basis of the sense of lexemes. Second, it is reasonable to assume that the sense of a composite expression is a function, not only of the sense of its component lexemes, but also of its grammatical structure. We have made this assumption throughout; and it can be tested empirically in a sufficient number of instances for us to accept it as valid. What is needed, then, in the ideal, is a precisely formulated procedure for the syntactic composition of all the well-formed lexically composite expressions in a language, coupled with a procedure for determining the semantic effect, if any, of each process or stage of syntactic composition. This is what formal semantics seeks to provide.

Formal linguistic semantics, as such, is not committed to any particular theory of syntax. Nor does it say anything in advance about the closeness of the correspondence between grammatical and semantic structure in natural languages. There is a wide range of options on each of these issues. That there is some degree of correspondence, or isomorphism, between grammatical and semantic structure is intuitively obvious and can be demonstrated, in particular instances, by appealing to various kinds of grammatical ambiguity. For example, the ambiguity of such classic examples as:

(1) *old men and women*

is plausibly accounted for by saying that its two interpretations

(2) "men who are old and women"

and

(3) "old men and old women"

reflect a difference of grammatical structure which matches semantic structure. Under one interpretation, represented in (2), 'old' is first combined with 'men' (by a rule of adjectival modification) and, then, the resultant composite expression 'old men' is combined with 'women' (by means of the co-ordinating conjunction *and*), so that semantically, as well as grammatically, 'old' applies to 'men', but not to 'women': i.e., 'men', but not 'women', is both grammatically and semantically within the **scope** of 'old'. (We have already met the notion of scope in relation to negation and interrogativity: see 6.5, 6.7.) Under the other interpretation, (3), the grammatical rules can be thought of as having operated in the reverse order, so that 'old' applies to the composite expression 'men and women': i.e., the whole phrase 'old men and women' is grammatically and semantically within the scope of 'old'. Grammatical ambiguity of this kind – so-called immediate-constituent or phrase-structure ambiguity – can be handled in many different, but in this respect descriptively equivalent, systems of grammatical analysis; and it is relatively easy to match the grammatical rules of adjectival modification and phrasal co-ordination (however they are formalized) with rules of semantic interpretation.

The question is whether the degree of correspondence, or isomorphism, between grammatical and semantic structure is always as high as this. Many formal semanticists have assumed that it is and have used the so-called **rule-to-rule hypothesis** to guide their research. This may be formulated, for our purposes, non-technically as follows: (i) every rule of the grammar (and more particularly every syntactic rule) can be associated with a semantic rule which assigns an interpretation to the composite expression which is formed by the grammatical rule in question; and (ii) there are no semantically vacuous grammatical rules. The problem is that it is not usually as clear as it is in the case of (1) that correspondence between grammatical and semantic structure in natural languages is a matter of theory-neutral and empirically determinable fact. Those scholars who subscribe to the so-called rule-to-rule hypothesis are subscribing to a particularly strong version of the principle of compositionality.

To be compared with the rule-to-rule hypothesis, which can be seen as a methodological principle adopted by certain formal semanticists to guide them in their research, is the traditional methodological principle of saving the appearances – being duly respectful of the phenomena – which I have invoked on several occasions. A classic case of violating the principle of saving the appearances was Russell's (1905) analysis of the propositional content of grammatically simple (one-clause) sentences containing noun-phrases introduced by the definite article, such as

(4) 'The King of France is bald',

whose logical form, under Russell's analysis, turned out to be a composite (three-clause) structure, for two of whose (conjoined) component propositional structures (one containing the existential quantifier and the other the operator of identity) there is no syntactic support. One of the things about Montague's work that attracted linguists was that it brought the logical form of (the propositional content of) many such sentences of English and other natural languages into closer correspondence with their apparent syntactic structure.

In the account of formal linguistic semantics that is given in this chapter, I will begin by considering two of the best-known approaches to the problem of determining the compositional function (whatever it is) which assigns sense to the lexically composite expressions of natural languages. I will do so at a very general level, and I will restrict my treatment to what is uncontroversially a matter of propositional content. The two approaches to be considered in the following sections of this chapter are the Katz–Fodor approach and what might be described as classical Montague grammar. I have added a section on possible worlds. The purpose of this is twofold. In the context in which it occurs, it is intended primarily to provide rather more background, philosophical and linguistic, than is usually given in textbook treatments of formal semantics for the particular notion of intensionality that has been developed by Montague and his followers. But it will also serve the more general purpose of raising two questions which have been much discussed (and left unresolved) in the past and have been begged, rather than answered, in much recent work in linguistic semantics, both formal and non-formal: (1) Do all natural languages have the same semantic structure? (2) Do all natural languages have the same descriptive and expressive power? Formal semantics may not be able to provide an answer to either of these two questions, but it has clarified some of the issues.

7.3 DEEP STRUCTURE AND SEMANTIC REPRESENTATIONS

What I will refer to as the Katz–Fodor theory of sentence-meaning is not generally described as a theory of formal semantics, but I will treat it as such. It originated with a paper by J. J. Katz and J. A. Fodor, 'The structure of a semantic theory', first published in 1963. The theory itself was subsequently modified in various ways, notably by Katz, and has given rise to a number of alternatives, which I will not deal with here. Indeed, I will not even attempt to give a full account of the Katz–Fodor theory in any of its versions. I will concentrate upon the following four notions, which have been of historical importance, and are of continuing relevance: **deep structure**, **semantic representations**, **projection-rules** and **selection-restrictions**. In this section we shall be concerned with the first two of these four notions, which are of more general import than the other two and, though they may now be obsolete in their original form, have their correlates in several present-day theories of formal semantics.

The Katz–Fodor theory is formalized within the framework of Chomskyan generative grammar. It was the first such theory of semantics to be proposed, and it played an important part in the development of the so-called standard theory of transformational-generative grammar, which Chomsky outlined in *Aspects* (1965). I will treat it as an integral part of the *Aspects* theory, even though, as it was first presented in 1963, it was associated with a slightly modified version of the earlier, *Syntactic Structures* (1957), model of transformational-generative grammar.

Looked at from a more general, historical, point of view, the Katz–Fodor theory can be seen as the first linguistically sophisticated attempt to give effect to the principle of compositionality. Traditional grammarians had for centuries emphasized the interdependence of syntax and semantics. Many of them had pointed out that the meaning of a sentence was determined partly by the meaning of the words it contained and partly by its syntactic structure. But they had not sought to make this point precise in relation to a generative theory of syntax – for the simple reason that generative grammar itself is of very recent origin.

As I have said, I will discuss the Katz–Fodor theory, not in its original formulation, but (in what may now be thought of as its classical version) as it was presented in the period immediately following upon the publication of Chomsky's *Aspects*. The main consequence, as far as this book is concerned, is that we shall be operating with a particular notion of **deep structure**, which has now been abandoned by almost all linguists, including Chomsky. The arguments for and against the classical notion of deep structure, which divided the more orthodox Chomskyan transformationalists from the so-called generative semanticists in the late 1960s and early 1970s, are interesting and important. Some of the theoretical issues that were hotly discussed at the time have now been resolved. I will not go into them here.

One advantage of operating with the classical notion of deep structure, in a book of this kind, is that it is more familiar to non-specialists than any of the alternatives. Another is that it is simple to grasp and has been widely influential. What will be said about projection-rules and selection-restrictions in the following section is not materially affected by the adoption of one view of deep structure rather than another, or indeed by the abandonment of the notion of deep structure altogether. It is also worth emphasizing that, even if the classical notion of deep structure can no longer be justified on purely syntactic grounds, something like it, which (borrowing and adapting a *Syntactic Structures* term) I am calling the **sentence-kernel**, might well be justifiable on partly syntactic (or morphosyntactic) and partly semantic grounds (see section 7.2). The significance of this point will be explained as we proceed.

According to the standard theory of transformational grammar, every sentence has two distinct levels of syntactic structure, linked by rules of a particular kind called **transformations**. These two levels are **deep structure** and **surface structure**. They differ formally in that they are generated by rules of a different kind. For our purposes the crucial point is that deep structure is more intimately connected with sentence-meaning than surface structure is. Surface structure, on the other hand, is more intimately connected with the way the sentence is pronounced. Omitting all but the bare essentials, we can represent the relation between syntax, semantics and phonology, diagrammatically, as in Figure 7.1.

With reference to this diagram, we can see that the grammar (in the broadest sense of the term) comprises four sets of rules, which, operating as an integrated system, puts a set of **phonological representations** (PR) into correspondence with a set of **semantic representations** (SR). What has just been said is often expressed, loosely and non-technically, by saying that the grammar is a system of rules which relates sound and meaning. But it is important to realize that this is indeed a very loose way of making the point; and, as experience has shown, it has led to a good deal of confusion among students and non-specialists. This point is worth developing in some detail.

Sound is external to the language-system, and independent of it; sound is the physical medium in which language-utterances (as products of the use of the language-system) are, normally or naturally, realized (and externalized) in speech; considered from a psycholinguistic (and neuropsychological) point of view, phonological representations can be thought of as part of the competence which underlies speech; spoken forms can, however, be transcribed into another medium as written forms, and conversely; the central and essential part of a language – its grammar and associated lexicon – is therefore, in principle, independent of its phonological system. Meaning, on the other hand, is not a medium (physical or non-physical) in which a language is realized. One can argue about the psychological or ontological status of meaning; one can argue as to whether the notion that meaning exists, or can exist, independently of the existence of language-systems (or, more generally, of semiotic systems, including languages) is justifiable; but whatever view we take on such questions, there can be no doubt that the relation between meaning and the language which encodes it is different from the relation between sound and the language which can be realized in it. Neither the use of

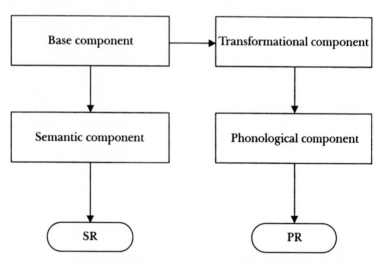

Figure 7.1 The standard theory of transformational grammar. The deep structure of a sentence is the output of the base component and the input to both the transformational component and the semantic component; the surface structure of a sentence is the output of the transformational component and the input to the phonological component. 'PR' stands for 'phonological representation' and 'SR' for 'semantic representation'.

the term 'representation' in both semantics and phonology nor the input–output symmetry of the left-hand and right-hand sides of the diagram in Figure 7.1 should be allowed to obscure this difference.

So much, then, for phonological representations and, for the moment, semantic representations. The base component, it should be noted, contains, not only the non-transformational, **categorial**, rules of syntax, for the language in question, but also its **lexicon**, or dictionary. And the lexicon provides for each lexeme in the language all the syntactic, semantic and phonological information that is necessary to distinguish that lexeme from others and to account for its occurrence in well-formed sentences. The base component, then, generates a set of deep structures, and the transformational component converts each of these into one or more surface structures.

I said earlier that deep structure is more intimately connected with meaning, and surface structure with pronunciation. Figure 7.1 makes this point clear by means of the arrows which link the several components of the grammar. All the information required by the semantic component is supplied by the base, and therefore is present in the deep structure of sentences; all the information required by the phonological component is present in the surface structures that result from the operation of transformational rules. As far as the relation between syntax and semantics is concerned, Figure 7.1 expresses the famous principle that **transformations do not affect meaning**; there is no arrow leading from the transformational to the semantic component.

This principle is intuitively appealing, provided that 'meaning' is interpreted as referring to propositional content: it is less so, if (i) sentence-meaning is held to include thematic meaning and what is encoded in difference of mood and sentence-type and (ii) corresponding sentences which differ grammatically in thematic structure, mood or sentence-type are held to be transformationally related and to share the same deep structure (see Chapter 6). The principle that transformations do not affect meaning implies that any two, or more, sentences that have the same deep structure will necessarily have the same meaning.

For example, corresponding active and passive sentences (which differ in thematic structure), such as

(5) 'The dog bit the postman'

and

(6) 'The postman was bitten by the dog',

have often been analysed as having the same deep structure: see Figure 7.2. (This is not how Chomsky treated them in *Aspects*, but for present purposes that is irrelevant.) Most such pairs of active and passive sentences (apart from sentences containing what a logician would describe as the natural-language equivalents of quantifiers) are truth-conditionally equivalent, and therefore have the same propositional content. Arguably, however, they differ in thematic meaning, in much the same way that 'I have not read this book', 'This book I have not read', etc. differ from one another in thematic meaning: see Chapter

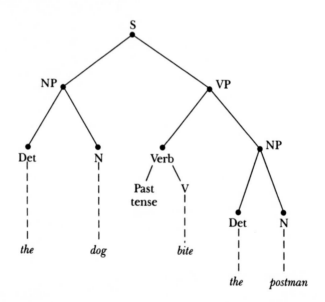

Figure 7.2 Simplified representation of the deep structure of 'The dog bit the postman' and of 'The postman was bitten by the dog'.

6, examples (1)–(4) and (5)–(6). For syntactic reasons that do not concern us here, sets of sentences such as 'I have not read this book', 'This book I have not read', etc. are given the same deep structure in the standard theory, whereas corresponding active and passive sentences are not. But this fact is irrelevant in the context of the present account. So too is the fact that much of the discussion by linguists of the relation between syntax and semantics has been confused, until recently, by the failure to distinguish propositional content from other kinds of sentence-meaning. The point that is of concern to us is that some sentences will have the same deep structure, though they differ quite strikingly in surface structure, and that all such sentences must be shown to have the same propositional content. This effect is achieved, simply and elegantly, by organizing the grammar in such a way that the rules of the semantic component operate solely upon deep structures.

7.4 PROJECTION-RULES AND SELECTION-RESTRICTIONS

We now come to the notions of projection-rules and selection-restrictions as these were formalized by Katz and Fodor (1963) within the framework of Chomskyan transformational-generative grammar.

In the Katz–Fodor theory the rules of the semantic component are usually called **projection-rules**. In the present context, they may be identified with what are more generally referred to nowadays as **semantic rules**. They serve two purposes: (i) they distinguish meaningful from meaningless sentences; and (ii) they assign to every meaningful sentence a formal specification of its meaning or meanings. I will deal with each of these two purposes separately.

We have already seen that the distinction between meaningful and meaningless sentences is not as clear-cut as it might appear at first sight (see 5.2). And I have pointed out that, in the past, generative grammarians have tended to take too restricted a view of the semantic well-formedness of sentences. In this section we are concerned with the formalization of semantic ill-formedness (meaninglessness), on the assumption that, even though it may not be as widespread as is commonly supposed, it does in fact exist. Our assumption, more precisely, is that in English and in other natural languages, there are some grammatically well-formed, but semantically ill-formed, sentences (though not as many as linguists tended to assume in the classical period of Chomskyan transformational-generative grammar).

The Katz–Fodor mechanism for handling semantic ill-formedness is that of **selection-restrictions**. These are associated with particular lexemes and are therefore listed, in what we may think of as dictionary entries, in the lexicon. They tell us, in effect, which pairs of lexemes can combine with one another meaningfully in various grammatical constructions. For example, they might say that the adjective 'buxom' can modify nouns such as 'girl', 'woman', 'lass', etc., but not 'boy', 'man', 'lad', etc., that the verb 'sleep' can take as its subject nouns such as 'boy', 'girl', 'cat', etc. (or, rather noun-phrases, with such nouns as their principal constituent), but not such nouns as 'idea' or 'quadruplicity'; and so on. If the selection-restrictions are violated, the projection-rules will fail to operate. Consequently, they will fail to assign to the semantically ill-formed sentence a formal specification of its meaning – thereby marking the sentence as meaningless and (provided that this information is preserved in the output) indicating in what way the sentence is semantically ill-formed.

A further task of the selection-restrictions, operating in conjunction with the projection-rules, is to block certain interpretations as semantically anomalous, while allowing other interpretations of the same phrases and sentences as semantically acceptable. For example, in some dialects or registers of English, the word 'housewife' is polysemous: in one of the senses ("housewife$_1$") it denotes a woman who keeps house; in another ("housewife$_2$") it denotes a pocket sewing-kit. Many phrases in which 'housewife' is modified by an adjective ('good housewife', 'beautiful housewife', etc.) will be correspondingly ambiguous. But 'buxom housewife', presumably, will not, since "housewife$_2$", unlike "housewife$_1$", cannot combine with the meaning of 'buxom'. In general, then, the selection-restrictions will tend to cut down the number of interpretations assigned to lexically composite expressions. In fact, the failure to assign any interpretations at all to a sentence, referred to in the previous paragraph, can be seen as the limiting case of this process. The rules select from the meanings of an expression those, and only those, which are compatible with the (sentence-internal) context in which it occurs.

The Katz–Fodor theory of sentence-meaning is formulated within the framework of componential analysis (see 4.2). For example, instead of listing, in the lexical entry for 'buxom', all the other lexemes with which it can or cannot combine, the theory will identify them by means of one or more of their sense-components. It might say (in an appropriate formal notation) that 'buxom' cannot be combined, in semantically well-formed expressions, with any noun that does not have as part of its meaning the sense-components HUMAN and, let us assume, FEMALE. As we have seen, componential analysis runs into quite serious problems, if it is pushed beyond the prototypical, or focal, meaning of expressions. It is for this reason that most of the textbook examples used by linguists to illustrate the operation of Katz–Fodor selection-restrictions are empirically suspect. But we are not concerned, at this point, with the validity of componential analysis. Nor is it necessary to take up once again the problem of drawing a distinction between contradiction and semantic ill-formedness. My purpose has been simply to explain what selection-restrictions are and how they are formalized in the Katz–Fodor theory.

It is important, however, to say something here about **categorial incongruity**, which was mentioned at the end of Chapter 5; and what I have to say will be relevant to other theories of formal semantics. The term 'categorial incongruity' is intended to refer to a particular kind of semantic incompatibility which, in particular languages, is intimately associated with grammatical, more precisely syntactic, ill-formedness. It may be introduced by means of the following examples:

(7) 'My friend existed a whole new village'

and

(8) 'My friend frightened that it was raining'.

Arguably, although I have represented them as sentences, each of them is both grammatically and semantically ill-formed. Their ungrammaticality can be readily accounted for by saying that 'exist' is an intransitive verb (and therefore cannot take an object) and that 'frighten', unlike 'think', 'say', etc., cannot occur with a *that*-clause as its object. (Such examples are handled by Chomsky in *Aspects* in terms of what he calls strict subcategorization.) The fact that they do not make sense – that they have no propositional content – can be explained by saying that it is inherent in the meaning of 'exist' that it cannot take an object, and that it is inherent in the meaning of 'frighten' that it cannot take as its object an expression referring to such abstract entities as facts or propositions. But which, if either, of these two explanations – syntactic or semantic – is correct?

The question is wrongly formulated. It makes unjustified assumptions about the separability of syntax and semantics and ignores the fact that, although natural languages vary considerably as to what they grammaticalize (or lexicalize), there is, in all natural languages, some degree of congruence between semantic (or ontological) categories and certain grammatical categories, such as the major parts of speech, gender, number, or tense. Whether one accounts for categorial incongruity by means of the syntactic rules of the base component or alternatively by means of the blocking, or filtering, mechanism of the projection-rules is, of itself, a technical issue of no empirical import. What is important is that, whatever treatment is adopted, the details of the formalization should distinguish cases of categorial incongruity from (a) cases of contradiction and from (b) what are more generally handled in terms of selection-restrictions.

Contradictory propositions are meaningful, but necessarily false. Expressions whose putative semantic ill-formedness results from the violation of selection-restrictions can often be given a perfectly satisfactory interpretation if one is prepared to make not very radical adjustments to one's assumptions about the nature of the world. Categorially incongruous expressions are meaningless and they cannot be interpreted by making such minor ontological adjustments. (A classic Chomskyan example of a sentence containing a mixture of contradictory and categorially incongruous expressions is 'Colourless green ideas sleep furiously': see 5.3). These boundaries may be difficult to draw in respect of particular examples. But the differences are clear enough in a sufficient number of cases for the distinctions themselves to be established.

Let us now return to the Katz–Fodor projection-rules. We have seen how they distinguish meaningful sentences from at least one class of meaningless, or allegedly meaningless, sentences. They also have to assign to every semantically well-formed sentence a formal specification of its meaning or meanings. Such specifications of sentence-meaning are described as **semantic representations**.

It follows from what has been said so far that a sentence will have exactly as many semantic representations as it has meanings (the limiting case being that of meaningless sentences, to which the projection-rules will assign no semantic representation at all). It also follows that sentences with the same deep structure will have the same semantic representation. The converse, however, does not follow; in the standard theory of transformational-generative grammar, sentences that differ in deep structure may nevertheless have the same meaning. This is a consequence of the existence of synonymous, but lexically distinct, expressions (see 2.3) and of the way in which lexicalization is handled in the standard theory. We may simply note that this is so, without going into the details.

But what precisely are semantic representations? And how are they constructed by the projection-rules? These two questions are, of course, interdependent (by virtue of the principle of compositionality). A semantic representation is a collection, or amalgamation, of sense-components. But it is not merely an unstructured set of such components. As we saw in section 4.3, it is not generally possible to formalize the meaning of individual lexemes compositionally in set-theoretic terms. It is even more obviously the case that sentence-meaning cannot be formalized in this way. If a semantic representation were nothing more than a set of sense-components (or semantic markers, in Katz–Fodor terminology), any two sentences containing exactly the same lexemes would be assigned the same semantic representation. For example, not only

(5) 'The dog bit the postman'

and

(6) 'The postman was bitten by the dog',

but also (5) and

(9) 'The postman bit the dog'

(and each of indefinitely many pairs of sentences like them), would be assigned the same semantic representation as one another. This is patently incorrect. What is required is some formalization of semantic representations that will preserve the semantically relevant syntactic distinctions of deep structure.

It is probably fair to say that in the years that have passed since the publication of 'The structure of a semantic theory' by Katz and Fodor little real progress has been made along these lines. The formalization has been complicated by the introduction of a variety of technical devices. But no general solution has been found to the problem of deciding exactly how many projection-rules are needed and how they differ formally one from another. And most linguists who are interested in either generative grammar or formal semantics are now working within a quite different theoretical framework.

One reason why this is so, apart from developments in Chomskyan and post-Chomskyan generative grammar since the mid-1970s, is that the whole concept of semantic representations has been strongly criticized, on two grounds, by logicians and philosophers.

First of all, they have pointed out that Katz–Fodor semantic representations make use of what is in effect a formal language and that the vocabulary-units of this language (conventionally written in small capitals, as in Chapter 4) stand in need of interpretation, just as much as do the natural languages whose semantic structure the formal language interprets. This objection may be countered, more or less plausibly, by saying that the formal language in question is the allegedly universal language of thought, which we all know by virtue of being human and which therefore does not need to be interpreted by relating its lexemes to entities, properties and relations in the outside world.

The second challenge to the notion of semantic representations comes from those who argue that they are unnecessary; that everything done satisfactorily by means of semantic representations can be done no less satisfactorily without them – by means of rules of inference operating in conjunction with meaning-postulates. This approach has the advantage that it avoids many of the difficulties, empirical and theoretical, associated with componential analysis.

7.5 MONTAGUE GRAMMAR

What is commonly referred to as Montague grammar is a particular approach to the analysis of natural languages initiated by the American logician Richard Montague in the late 1960s. During the 1970s, it was adopted by many linguists, who saw it (as did Montague himself) as a semantically more attractive alternative to Chomskyan transformational-generative grammar. (Montague himself died when still quite young, in 1971, and did little more than lay the foundations of what linguists inspired by his ideas called 'Montague grammar'.) In this context, 'grammar' is to be understood as covering both syntax and semantics.

Some of the differences between Montague grammar and the Katz–Fodor theory are a matter of historical accident. Montague's work is more firmly rooted in logical semantics than the Katz–Fodor theory is and gives proportionately less consideration to many topics that have been at the forefront of linguists' attention. In fact, 'grammar' for Montague included only part of what the standard theory of generative grammar sets out to cover. There is nothing in Montague's own work about phonological representation or inflection. The Katz–Fodor theory, on the other hand, finds its place (as Figure 7.1 in section 7.3 indicates) within a more comprehensive theory of the structure of languages, in which semantics and phonology (and indirectly inflection) are on equal terms. Linguists who have adopted Montague grammar have seen it as being integrated, in one way or another, with an equally comprehensive generative, though not necessarily Chomskyan, theory of the structure of natural languages, covering not only syntax (and morphology), but also phonology. Having said this, however, I must repeat one of the points made in section 7.3: phonology, unlike semantics, is only contingently associated with grammar (and, more particularly, syntax) in natural languages. The fact that Montague, like most logical semanticists, showed little interest in phonology (and morphology) is, therefore, neither surprising nor reprehensible.

More to the point is the status of transformational rules, on the one hand, and of componential analysis, or lexical decomposition, on the other. Montague himself did not make use of transformational rules. There were at least three reasons for this. First, the syntactic rules that he used in what we may think of as the base component of his grammar are more powerful than Chomskyan phrase-structure rules. Second, he was not particularly concerned to block the generation of syntactically ill-formed strings of words, as long as they could be characterized as ill-formed by the rules of semantic interpretation. Third, he had a preference for bringing the semantic analysis of sentences into as close a correspondence as possible with what transformationalists would describe as their surface structure. There is therefore no such thing as deep structure in Montague's own system. But this is not inherent in Montague grammar as such; and, during the 1970s, a number of linguists made proposals for the addition of a transformational component to the system. At the same time, it must also be noted, as we shall see, that the role of transformational rules was successively reduced in Chomskyan transformational-generative grammar in what we now think of as the post-classical period. By the end of the 1970s, if not earlier, the view that Montague took of the relation between syntax and semantics no longer seemed as eccentric and as badly motivated to generative grammarians as it may have done initially. And there are now, in any case, many different, more or less Chomskyan, systems of generative grammar, other than Chomsky's own system (which has been continually modified over the years and is now strikingly different from the standard, or classical, *Aspects* system). No one of these enjoys supremacy; and no linguist, these days, could sensibly think that formal semanticists have a straight choice between two, and only two, rival systems of linguistic analysis and description, when it comes to the integration of semantics and syntax.

As for componential analysis (or lexical decomposition), much the same remarks can be made here too. Montague grammar as such is not incompatible, in principle, with the decomposition, or factorization, of lexical meaning into sense-components. Indeed, some linguists have made proposals for the incorporation of rules for lexical decomposition within the general framework of Montague grammar. But, once again, as I have mentioned in the previous section and in Chapter 4, componential analysis is not as widely accepted by linguists now as it was in the 1960s and early 1970s.

The comparison of Chomskyan generative grammar with Montague grammar is complicated by the fact that, as I have said, some of the differences between them derive from purely historical circumstances. Most earlier presentations of Montague grammar were highly technical and took for granted a considerable degree of mathematical expertise and some background in formal logic. The situation has improved recently in that there are now good textbook presentations that are designed specifically for students of linguistic semantics. As for textbook accounts of Chomskyan generative grammar (of which there are many), most of these, whether technical or non-technical, fail to draw the distinction between what is essential to it and what is contingent and subject to change. They also fail to distinguish between generative grammar, as such, and generativism or what is commonly referred to nowadays as the generative enterprise.

Montague grammar is of its nature a very technical subject (just as Chomskyan generative grammar is). It would be foolish to encourage the belief that any real understanding of the details can be achieved unless one has a considerable facility in mathematical logic. However, it is not the details that are of interest to us here. My purpose is simply to explain, non-technically, some of the most important features of Montague grammar, in so far as they are relevant to the formalization of sentence-meaning and are currently exploited in linguistic semantics. In doing so, I will concentrate upon such features as may be expected to have an enduring influence, independently of current or future developments in linguistics and logic, and in the philosophy and psychology of language.

Montague semantics – the semantic part, or module, of a Montague grammar – is resolutely truth-conditional. Its applicability is restricted, in principle, to the propositional content of its sentences. Just how big a restriction this is judged to be will, of course, depend upon one's evaluation of the points made in the preceding chapter. Most of the advocates of Montague semantics have no doubt been committed, until recently at least, to the view that the whole of sentence-meaning is explicable, ultimately, in terms of propositional content. It has long been recognized, however, as was noted in the preceding chapter, that non-declarative sentences, on the one hand, and non-indicative sentences, on the other, are problematical from this point of view. Various attempts have been made to handle such sentences within the framework of Montague grammar. But so far none of these has won universal acceptance, and all of them would seem to be vulnerable to the criticisms directed against the truth-conditional analysis of non-declarative and non-indicative sentences in Chapter 6. In what follows we shall be concerned solely with propositional content.

Unlike certain other truth-conditional theories, Montague semantics operates, not with a concept of absolute truth, but with a particular notion of relative truth: **truth-under-an-interpretation** or, alternatively, in the technical terminology of model theory, **truth-in-a-model**. (I will say something presently about the sense in which the initially puzzling term 'model' is being employed here.) What model theory does in effect (though it is not usually explained in this way) is to formalize the distinction that is drawn in this book between propositions and propositional content. As used by Montague and his followers (who were in turn drawing upon the work of Carnap and others), it does this by drawing upon the distinction between **extension** and **intension** and relating this to a particular notion of **possible worlds**, which originated (as we saw in section 4.4) with Leibniz. Model theory is by no means restricted to the use that is made of it by Montague: it is much more general than that. But for the moment we can limit the discussion to Montague's version of model theory, since this is so far the one most familiar to linguists.

The traditional distinction between extension and intension has been exploited in a variety of ways in modern logic and formal semantics, so that the term 'intensional' (not to be confused with its homophone 'intentional') has a quite bewildering range of historically interconnected uses. We shall be concerned only with those uses that are of immediate relevance. We may begin (following Carnap) by identifying Frege's distinction between reference ('Bedeutung') and sense ('Sinn') with the distinction between extension and intension. (We should note that, as was mentioned earlier, Frege's word for reference – which he did not distinguish from denotation, as he did not distinguish sentences from either utterances or propositions – is the ordinary German word for meaning.) It is generally agreed nowadays that sense, rather than reference, is what is encoded in the sentences of natural languages, and this is what the German word 'Bedeutung' would normally be used for. We can now go on to apply the extension/intension distinction to the analysis of sentence-meaning, saying that the sense, or intension, of a sentence is its propositional content, whereas its reference, or extension, is its truth-value (on particular occasions of utterance). Most people at first find it strange that Frege, and following him many, though not all, formal semanticists, should have taken sentences (or propositions) to refer to truth or falsity, rather than to the situations that they purport to describe. But this view of the matter has certain formal advantages with respect to compositionality.

The next step is to invoke the notion of possible worlds. As we saw earlier, necessarily true (or false) propositions are propositions that are true (or false) **in all possible worlds**. The notion has also been applied, in an intuitively plausible way, in the definition of descriptive synonymy, as follows: expressions are descriptively synonymous if, and only if, they have the same extension in all possible worlds. Since expressions are descriptively synonymous if, and only if, they have the same sense (which we have identified with their intension), it follows that the intension of an expression is either its extension in all possible worlds or some function which determines its extension in all possible worlds. The second of these alternatives is the one that is adopted in Montague grammar. The intension of an expression is defined to be a function from possible worlds to extensions. But what does this mean?

The answer that I will give to this question is somewhat different from the answer that is given in standard accounts of formal semantics, but it is an answer that is faithful to the spirit of Montague semantics and philosophically defensible. My deliberately non-technical explanation of the basic notions of Montague's version of model-theoretic possible-worlds semantics is couched as far as possible in terms of the notions and distinctions that have been explained and adopted in earlier chapters.

7.6 POSSIBLE WORLDS

Leibniz introduced the notion of possible worlds for primarily theological purposes, arguing that God, being omniscient (and beneficent), would necessarily actualize the best of all possible worlds and, though omnipotent, was none the less subject in his creativity to the constraints of logic: he could create, or actualize, only logically possible worlds. As exploited by modern logicians, the notion of possible worlds has, of course, been stripped of its theological associations, and it has been converted into a highly technical, purely secular and in itself non-metaphysical, concept. But some knowledge of its philosophical and theological origins may be helpful (especially when it comes to the use that is made of the notion of possible worlds in epistemic and deontic logic). Hence this brief philosophical interlude.

Every natural language, let us assume, provides those who are competent in it with (a) the means of identifying the world that is actual at the time of speaking – the **extensional** world – and distinguishing it from past and future worlds, and (b) the means of referring to individual entities and sets of entities, on the one hand, and to substances, on the other, in whatever world has been identified. We may refer to whatever means is used to identify temporally distinct worlds (tense, adverbs of time, etc.) as an **index** – more precisely, a temporal index – to the world in question. I shall have more to say about this in Chapter 10: here I will simply draw readers' attention to the connexion between the term 'index', as I have just used it, and 'indexicality'. An alternative to 'index', in this sense, is 'point of reference': possible worlds are identified from a particular point of reference.

Granted that one can identify the world that is explicitly or implicitly identified, how does one know what is being referred to by the expression that is used, when a sentence is uttered? For example, how does one know what 'those cows' refers to in the utterance of

(10) 'Those cows are pedigree Guernseys'?

The traditional answer, as we have seen, is that one knows the concept "cow" and that this, being the **intension** (or sense) of 'cow', determines its **extension**. (One also needs to be able to interpret the demonstrative pronoun 'that' and the grammatical category of plurality. But let us here assume – and it is a not inconsiderable assumption – that the meaning of 'that' and plurality, not to mention the grammatical category of tense, can be satisfactorily handled in model-theoretic terms.) Concepts are often explained in terms of pictures or images, as in certain versions of the ideational theory of meaning (see 1.7). But we can now think of them more generally, as **functions** (in the mathematical sense): that is, as rules, or operations, which assign a unique value to the members of their **domain**. It is as if we had a book of rules for all the expressions in the language (the rules being their intensions) and that we were able to identify the extension of any given expression in any particular world (the domain of the function) by looking up the rule (or function) and applying it to the world. This rule, then, is a function from possible worlds to an extension: it **picks out** from the world that is its domain the set of entities that are being referred to; and this set is the value of the function. At this point, it should be noted that everything that has been said here, more or less loosely and semi-technically, can be fully formalized within the framework of set-theory.

But speakers of a language do not have, and in principle cannot have, a list of rules in their heads for all the expressions in a language. Apart from any other psychological considerations that would render this hypothesis implausible, there is the fact, mentioned in an earlier section of this chapter, that some, and perhaps all, natural languages contain infinitely many expressions. And competent speakers of such languages are able, by virtue of their competence, grammatical and semantic, to produce and interpret any arbitrarily selected member of these infinite sets of expressions. Clearly, as Chomsky argued forcefully when he laid the foundations of generative grammar, the human brain does not, and being physical cannot, have infinite capacity for the storage of language-systems (and the processing of the products of their use in performance). What is required, then, is yet another function (or set of functions), which determines the intension of composite expressions on the basis of the intension of basic expressions (lexemes) and of the syntactic rules (the rules of composition) which generate them.

All I have done so far, of course, is to reformulate Frege's principle of compositionality within an intensional framework, as Montague's predecessors, such as Rudolf Carnap, had done in the 1940s. As I said earlier, I have been taking the principle of compositionality to apply primarily to sense and denotation, and only derivatively to reference. Reference is mediated in this respect by denotation and context – in a way that is in part explained, informally, in later chapters. Most formal semanticists do not draw a clear distinction between reference and denotation. (Nor, of course, did Frege.) It is arguable, however, that the distinction was implicitly drawn by Montague, partly by means of his indices – which can be seen as relativizing the identification of particular referents to a particular context of utterance – and partly by the syntactic and semantic properties which he associated with the special entity-category (e) which he introduced into one of the systems of grammar with which he operated in his analysis of quantifiers. But, in saying this, I am perhaps going beyond the evidence. And Montague's followers, in any case, have only recently begun to make explicit and to exploit more fully this feature of Montague grammar.

Let us return, therefore, to what is historically beyond dispute. This is that Montague sought to establish a much closer correspondence between syntax and semantics than was formalized in the standard theory of transformational-generative grammar of the mid-to-late 1960s. He achieved this, in so far as he was successful, by adopting a particular kind of **categorial grammar** and by putting the categories of syntax (roughly comparable with the major categories and subcategories of traditional grammar: noun-phrases, nouns, predicates, intransitive verbs, transitive verbs, adverbs, etc.) into one-to-one correspondence with intensional categories.

Categorial grammar as such does not concern us directly in this book. All that needs to be said about it here is that it is a particularly elegant kind of grammar, which derives all the other syntactic categories from the basic categories of name and proposition, or noun-phrase and sentence. (In the particularly interesting version of categorial grammar to which I alluded above, names and other kinds of noun-phrases are not basic, but derived, categories, formed out of the entity-category and nouns.) The term 'categorial' reflects its philosophical origins. Categorial grammar in itself is no more closely associated with one kind of ontological framework than it is with another. It does rest, however, upon the principle of **categorial congruity**, the violation of which results in categorial incongruity, which was mentioned earlier (and this is why I used the term 'categorial' in this connexion): the principle of syntactic and semantic congruity, or interdependence, with respect to the rules of composition. This notion of congruity (in Latin, 'congruitas') is eminently traditional (and played an important part in medieval logic and grammatical theory). It can perhaps be seen as the antecedent of the present-day formal semanticist's rule-to-rule hypothesis.

So far, I have restricted the discussion to possible worlds that differ from the actual world only in that they have been actualized in the past or will be actualized in the future: i.e., worlds, or states of the world, that are only temporally distinguished one from another and succeed, or replace, one another on a single time-line. But there is no need to maintain this restriction. Indeed, the real pay-off from the formalization of possible worlds by Montague and others comes from the fact that it enables one to handle, in a logically respectable way, statements about worlds which may never be actualized: the worlds of one's dreams, hopes and fears; the worlds of science-fiction, drama, and make-believe. It does so by allowing the index by which different worlds are identified to be composite and to include non-temporal, as well as temporal, components. I will come back to this point, in connexion with the notion of epistemic modality, in Chapter 10. At this stage, it will be sufficient to note that Montague grammar was more successful than earlier formal systems constructed by logicians for the semantic analysis of some of the features of natural languages. It was more successful in the sense that it provided a more perspicuous analysis of the phenomena than standard logical analyses which had held sway until then: in short, it was more respectful of the principle of saving the appearances (see 7.2).

In particular, Montague grammar could handle, in an intuitively satisfying way, a range of well-known problems in philosophical semantics. One of these derives from the fact that in certain so-called **intensional** (or referentially **opaque**) contexts the substitution of expressions with the same extension affects truth-conditionality: i.e., **Leibniz's Law** (of intersubstitutability *salva veritate*) does not hold. For example,

(11) 'I wanted to meet the first woman Prime Minister of Great Britain'

and

(12) 'I wanted to meet Margaret Thatcher'

have different truth-conditions, if 'the first woman prime minister of Great Britain' is given an intensional interpretation: i.e.,
if, to make the point loosely, the speaker wanted to meet whoever happened to be the first woman prime minister of Great
Britain and did not care, and might not have known, who that
was. Verbs such as 'want', as well as 'believe', 'hope', etc., are
commonly referred to either as intensional verbs (or predicates)
or verbs of propositional attitude. For historical reasons, the
extensional (or non-intensional) and the intensional interpretations of sentences such as (11) are often referred to by logicians
and formal semanticists as *de re* and *de dicto* interpretations,
respectively.

Another problem which standard, non-intensional, formal
semantics has difficulty in handling derives from the fact that
many natural-language expressions do not denote anything
that actually exists in the (real) world and yet are obviously not
synonymous. For example, 'unicorn' and 'centaur', let us
assume, do not denote anything – or to put it in terms of set-
theory, denote the empty set (the set with no members) – in the
world as we know it: i.e., there are no entities in the real world
such that they would be truly described as unicorns or centaurs.
Granted, these may not be problems which, of themselves,
cause non-philosophers to lose sleep. But they are all connected
with the more general problem of formulating, as precisely as
possible, the principles whereby speakers are able to assign interpretations to expressions according to the context in which they
are used and to identify the referents of referring expressions.

In what has been said about possible worlds so far in this section, we have for simplicity adopted a psychological point of
view: I have talked as if it is the aim of formal semantics to construct models of the mental representations that human beings
have of the external world. Looked at from this point of view, a
proposition is true or false of the actual or non-actual world
that it represents according to whether it is **in correspondence
with** that world or not. This is a perfectly legitimate way of talking about formal semantics, and it is one that is favoured by

many psychologists, linguists and computer scientists interested in artificial intelligence. But it is not the one that is customarily adopted by logicians and philosophers. There are, in fact, several philosophically different ways in which the term 'possible world' can be interpreted.

Indeed, in the elementary exposition which I have given here of Montague's system of possible-worlds model-theoretic semantics, I have not been absolutely consistent in my own use of the term 'possible world'. (I have also been deliberately inconsistent, and somewhat vague, in my use of the term 'model'.) Just now I have talked of propositions as being true or false **of** the world that they represent; elsewhere I have said that propositions are true or false **in** a world, tautologies being true, and contradictions false, in all possible worlds. It is perhaps more in line with everyday conceptions and with traditional usage to say that propositions represent, or describe, a world, rather than that they are, in some sense, in it. However, many philosophers and logicians have adopted the second way of talking. Without going further into this question, I will simply note that some formal semanticists have explicitly defined a possible world to be a set of propositions, while others have said that a proposition is the set of worlds in which, or of which, it is true. For purely logical purposes it makes little difference which of these views we adopt, though the choice between them may be motivated by broader philosophical considerations.

It would be impossible, and inappropriate in a book of this kind, to go into the philosophical ramifications of the adoption of one view of possible worlds, and propositions, rather than another. Nor is it necessary as far as the applicability of formal semantics to the analysis of natural languages is concerned, to resolve such thorny philosophical issues as the reality of the external world; the ontological or psychological status of propositions, semantic representations, etc.; or the validity of the notion of truth-by-correspondence. In conclusion, however, I should like to emphasize that model-theoretic, or indexical, semantics provides one, at least in principle, with the means of formalizing many of the phenomena found in natural languages that were not satisfactorily formalized in earlier systems of formal semantics. For example, it enables one to formalize various relations of **accessibility** holding between different possible worlds. To take just one aspect of this: there is an intuitively clear sense in which, in the everyday use of language, we normally operate with the assumption that the past, but not the future, is accessible to us. And this assumption is built into the structure of the system of tenses and moods in many, if not all, languages. Indexical semantics can handle phenomena of this kind. More generally, it allows us to formalize the fact that speakers are constrained by certain kinds of accessibility in their selection, or construction, of the possible worlds that they refer to and in the way that they refer to them; and also of the fact that they necessarily refer to the world that they are describing from the viewpoint of the world that they are in. These two facts, as we shall see in Chapter 10, are crucial for any proper treatment of indexicality and modality in natural languages. We now turn to a consideration of utterance-meaning and, in so doing, move from semantics in the narrower sense to what many refer to these days as pragmatics.

PART 4

Utterance-meaning

CHAPTER 8

Speech acts and illocutionary force

8.0 INTRODUCTION

So far we have not exploited to any significant degree the terminological distinction between 'sentence' and 'utterance' that
was introduced in Chapter 1. Nor have we exploited the associated distinctions between Saussure's 'langue' and 'parole' and
Chomsky's 'competence' and 'performance', which, as we saw
in Chapter 1, need to be reformulated, as non-equivalent
dichotomies within the system–process–product trichotomy, if
we are to avoid the confusion that exists in the account that is
given of these technical distinctions in most textbooks.

Much of the work that has been done in formal semantics (in
so far as it has been applied to the analysis of natural languages)
has been based on the view that languages are sets of sentences
and that sentences are used primarily, if not exclusively, to
make descriptive statements. Typically, therefore, no distinction
is drawn in formal semantics between sentence-meaning and
propositional (i.e., descriptive) content. This is clearly a very
limited view of what a language is and (as we saw in Chapter 6)
of sentence-meaning. It is a view that has been much criticized.

One of the most influential critics in recent years was the
Oxford philosopher, J. L. Austin (1911–60), whose ideas have
been much discussed, not only by philosophers, but also by linguists (and representatives of many other disciplines). In this
chapter, we use Austin's theory of so-called speech acts as a

departure-point for the analysis of utterance-meaning that follows in Chapters 9 and 10.

8.1 UTTERANCES

The term 'utterance', as was pointed out in Chapter 1, is ambiguous as between a process-sense and a product-sense (1.6). ('Process' is here being used as a term which is broader than 'action' or 'activity': an action is a process controlled by an agent; an act is a unit of action or activity.) The term 'utterance' can be used to refer either to the process (or activity) of uttering or to the products of that process (or activity). Utterances in the first of these two senses are commonly referred to nowadays as **speech acts**; utterances in the second sense may be referred to – in a specialized sense of the term – as **inscriptions**. (The term 'inscription', which was introduced in Chapter 1, is not widely used by linguists. It must not be interpreted as being more appropriate to the written than it is to the spoken language.) It is one of my principal aims in this chapter to clarify the relation between speech acts and inscriptions and, in doing so, to develop in more detail the distinction between sentence-meaning and utterance-meaning. I will operate, as far as possible, with the terms and concepts which derive from the work of J. L. Austin and are now widely employed in linguistics and related disciplines. But I shall need to add one or two distinctions of my own, in order to make more precise than Austin and his followers have done the rather complex relation that holds between speech acts and sentences. I will also introduce into the discussion points which are given less emphasis in what may be referred to as the Anglo-American tradition than they are in the typically French tradition which stems from the work of Emile Benveniste (1966, 1974).

The term 'speech act' is somewhat misleading. First of all, it might seem to be synonymous with 'act of utterance', rather than to denote – as it does (in the sense in which it tends to be used by linguists) – some particular part of the production of utterances. Second, it throws too much emphasis on that part of the production of utterances which results in their inscription in the physical medium of sound. However, since 'speech act' is now widely employed, in linguistics and philosophy, in the technical sense that Austin and more particularly J. R. Searle (1969) gave to it, I will make no attempt to replace it with another more appropriate term. It must be emphasized, however, that (i) 'speech act' is being used throughout in a highly specialized sense and (ii) like 'utterance', on the one hand, and 'inscription' or 'text', on the other, is intended to cover the production of both written and spoken language. Everything that is said in this chapter (and throughout this book) is intended to be consistent with what was said in Chapter 1 about competence and performance, on the one hand, and about the language-system, the use of the language-system, and the products of the use of the language-system, on the other, and to be neutral with respect to a number of differences which divide one school of linguistics from another at the present time. For example, it is neutral between generativist and non-generativist approaches to the analysis of language and languages, between cognitivism and anti-cognitivism, between functionalism and anti-functionalism, and between formalism and anti-formalism. More positively, my presentation of what has come to be called the theory of speech acts is intended to give more of the relevant philosophical background than is usually given in textbook accounts for linguists.

Austin himself never presented a fully developed theory of speech acts. The nearest he came to doing so was in the William James lectures, which were delivered at Harvard in 1955 and published, after his death, as *How to Do Things With Words* (1962). He had been lecturing on the same topic for some years previously in Oxford and had delivered papers relating to it as early as 1940, but did not leave behind him a fully revised and publishable manuscript of his William James lectures. It is hardly surprising, therefore, that there is no agreed and definitive version of his theory of speech acts. Indeed, it is not clear that Austin was even trying to construct a theory of speech acts, in the sense in which the term 'theory' is interpreted by many of those who have taken up his ideas. He belonged to the so-called ordinary-language school of philosophy, whose members tended to be suspicious of formalization and the drawing of sharp distinctions.

Austin's main purpose, originally at least, was to challenge what he regarded as the descriptive fallacy: the view that the only philosophically interesting function of language was that of making true or false statements. More specifically, he was attacking the verificationist thesis, associated with logical positivism: the thesis that sentences are meaningful only if they express verifiable, or falsifiable, propositions. We have already looked at verificationism in connexion with the notion of truth-conditionality (see 5.4). As we have seen, when Austin first concerned himself with the question, the verificationists had already had to face the objection that their criterion of meaningfulness had the effect of ruling out, not only the so-called pseudo-statements of theology and metaphysics, but also those of ethics and aesthetics. One response to this objection, it will be recalled, was to concede that sentences such as

(1) 'Cannibalism is wrong'

or

(2) 'Monet is a better painter than Manet'

cannot be used to make descriptive statements, but only emotively: i.e., to express one's feelings (see 5.5).

Another was to say that, although such sentences can be used to make true or false statements, what speakers are describing when they make such statements are their own or someone else's attitudes, rather than objective reality. What Austin did in his relatively early papers was to criticize the second of these alternatives. He subsequently pointed out that many more of our everyday utterances are pseudo-statements than either the verificationists or their opponents had realized. For example, according to Austin, if one utters the sentence

(3) 'I promise to pay you £5',

with the purpose of making a promise (and of communicating to one's addressee the fact that one is making a promise), one is not saying something, true or false, about one's state of mind, but committing oneself to a particular course of action.

This, in brief, is the philosophical context in which Austin first put forward his now famous distinction between **constative** and **performative** utterances. A constative utterance is, by definition, a statement-making utterance. (Austin prefers 'constative' to 'descriptive', because, in his view, not all true or false statements are descriptions. For simplicity of exposition in the present context, the two terms may be treated as equivalent.) Performative utterances, in contrast, are those in the production of which the speaker, or writer, performs an act of doing rather than saying.

This distinction between saying and doing (reflected in the title of Austin's Oxford lectures, 'Words and deeds') was eventually abandoned. However, the distinction between constative and non-constative utterances, as such, was not abandoned. It is simply that, in the latest version that we have of Austin's own work, constative utterances are presented as just one class of performatives. Similarly, saying – in the statement-making, or assertive, sense of the verb 'say': the sense in which one says that something is or is not the case – is seen as a particular kind of doing. And, as we shall see, Austin goes into the question of saying and doing in considerable detail. In fact, this is what Austin's theory of speech acts, in so far as it is a theory, is all about. It is a theory of pragmatics (in the etymological sense of 'pragmatics': "the study of action, or doing").

Moreover (although Austin did not develop the implications of this viewpoint), it is a theory of social pragmatics: a theory of saying as doing within the framework of social institutions and conventions taken for granted and accepted by the doers (or actors). This aspect of Austin's theory has not always been given the emphasis that it deserves.

A second distinction which Austin draws is between **explicit** and **primary** performatives. This distinction applies, in principle, to both constative and non-constative utterances. For the present, it suffices to say that an explicit performative is one in which the utterance-inscription contains an expression which denotes or otherwise makes explicit the kind of act that is being performed. This definition will need to be refined in several respects. As it stands, it is perhaps broader than Austin intended, and yet narrower than it ought to be. But it certainly covers all the examples that Austin and his followers have used to illustrate the class of explicit performatives. In particular, it covers non-constative utterances of sentences such as (3). Such sentences contain a so-called performative verb, and it is the occurrence of this verb, 'promise', together with the fact that it has a first-person subject and is in the simple present indicative form, which makes explicit the nature of the speech act that is being performed when the sentence is uttered in order to make a promise.

Of course, one can make a promise without doing so by uttering an explicit performative. For example, one can make a promise by uttering the sentence

(4) 'I will pay you £5'.

In this case, one will have produced what Austin refers to as a primary (i.e., non-explicit) performative. This is non-explicit, in terms of the definition given above, in that there is no expression in the utterance-inscription itself (*I'll pay you £5*) which makes explicit the fact that it is to be taken as a promise rather than a prediction or a statement.

This will serve as a sufficient, though informal and rather imprecise, account of what Austin had in mind when he drew his distinction between explicit and primary performatives. It will be noted that it is utterances, not sentences, that are classified as being constative or non-constative, and as being either explicitly performative or not. When linguists use the term 'performative sentence' they are usually referring to sentences such as 'I promise to pay you £5', which contain a so-called performative verb and are commonly uttered as explicitly non-constative utterances.

As will be clear from what was said about declarative and non-declarative sentences in Chapter 6, example (4) is a declarative sentence because it belongs to a class of sentences typical members of which are used **characteristically** to make statements. It was emphasized at that point that this does not imply that each member or any particular subclass of that class is used normally or even commonly for that purpose. Even if (3) were never used for making statements, but only for making promises, it would still be a declarative sentence by virtue of its grammatical structure. And (3) can, of course, be used (in contemporary Standard English) for making statements of various kinds. There should be no need to labour this point here. But it must be borne in mind throughout this chapter.

In what follows I will make use of several of Austin's terms. But I will not always give to them exactly the same interpretation as he gave them. In some instances, Austin's own interpretation is far from clear; in others, it is clear enough, but controversial. There is the further problem that Austin's view of the distinction between sentences and utterances was very different from the one that I have adopted in this book. I will therefore reinterpret Austin's theory of speech acts in the light of this distinction.

8.2 LOCUTIONARY ACTS

To perform what Austin called a locutionary act is to produce an utterance (i.e., an utterance-inscription) with a particular form and a more or less determinate meaning.

Many of the utterances that we produce in everyday conversation – i.e., most of the products of our locutionary acts – are ungrammatical; some are grammatical, but elliptical (e.g., *Been here long?*, *Nice weather for the time of year*, etc.); some are neither grammatical nor ungrammatical; yet others, of course, are both ungrammatical and unacceptable – resulting from so-called performance errors: inattention, lapses of memory or malfunctioning of one kind or another in the actual production of language-signals.

Since we are deliberately restricting our attention, for the time being, to utterances that are grammatically well-formed and non-elliptical, we can temporarily ignore much of the complexity that a fuller discussion of locutionary acts would require. In particular, we can temporarily assume that to perform a locutionary act is necessarily to utter a sentence. However, it is important at this point to note that two people can utter the same sentence without necessarily saying the same thing, and they can say the same thing without necessarily uttering the same sentence.

In fact, there are various ways in which one can interpret the everyday expression 'say the same thing'. Austin's theory of speech acts can be seen as addressing itself to this issue and as (partially) explicating the several senses of the verb 'say' in which saying is doing. Let us begin by noting that the following sentence is ambiguous, according to whether the verb 'say' is taken as meaning "assert" or "utter":

(5) 'John and Mary said the same thing'.

Under one interpretation, it has much the same truth-conditions, and therefore the same propositional content, as

(6) 'John and Mary asserted the same proposition'.

Under the other, it may be paraphrased, in the technical metalanguage that we have been building up, as

(7) 'John and Mary produced the same utterance-inscription'.

It is also worth noting that, although the word 'thing' would not normally be regarded as ambiguous, there is a striking and theoretically important difference between one class of things and another. Propositions, as we have seen, are abstract entities of a particular kind. Utterance-inscriptions, on the other hand, have physical properties, which are identifiable by means of one or more of the senses: hearing, sight, touch, etc.

It is clear from what has been said in earlier chapters that it is possible to assert the same proposition by uttering different sentences. This point may now be developed further. First of all, the same proposition may be asserted (let us assume) by uttering sentences of different languages: e.g.,

(8) 'It is raining' (English),
(9) 'Il pleut' (French),
(10) 'Es regnet' (German).

Second, it may be asserted by uttering two sentences of the same language with the same propositional content, such as corresponding actives and passives: e.g.,

(11) 'The dog bit the postman'

and

(12) 'The postman was bitten by the dog'.

Conversely, as we saw in Chapter 7, one can assert different propositions by uttering the same sentence in different contexts and by assigning different values to the referring expressions that it contains. For example,

(13) 'My friend is waiting for me'

expresses indefinitely many propositions according to the value assigned to 'my friend' and 'I' and the time that is being referred to by the tense of the verb. We have noted, then, that there is an important distinction to be drawn between the utterance of sentences and the assertion of propositions.

There is also a distinction to be drawn between the utterance of sentences and the production of utterance-inscriptions. This can be shown by means of a few simple examples. Let us suppose that John says

(14) *I'll meet you at the bank*

and Mary says

(15) *I'll meet you at the bank*.

Or, again, let us suppose that they both say

(16) *Flying planes can be dangerous*.

We can readily agree that in one sense of 'say', in each instance, they have said the same thing: they have produced the same utterance-inscription. More precisely (as we shall see presently), they have produced tokens of the same utterance-type. Let us also agree that what they have uttered is, in each case, a sentence. But have they both uttered the same sentence?

It is important to realize that we cannot answer this question without knowing not only what forms have been uttered, but also of what expressions they are forms. If *bank* in John's utterance is a form of 'bank₁' (meaning "financial institution") and *bank* in Mary's is a form of 'bank₂' (meaning "sloping side of a river"), they have uttered different sentences. Similarly, if *flying* in John's utterance is a form of the intransitive verb 'fly' (so that 'flying planes' means roughly "planes which are flying") and *flying* in Mary's is a form of the corresponding transitive verb 'fly' (so that 'flying planes' means roughly "to fly planes"), they have once again uttered different sentences. Regrettably, there is a good deal of confusion in the literature relating to the point that has just been made, deriving from the fact that sentences were originally defined (untraditionally) by generative grammarians as strings of forms which may or may not have the same grammatical structure. Here and throughout, I have adopted a more traditional view of sentences.

The fact that one can produce the same utterance-inscription without having uttered the same sentence is obscured in a good deal of recent work in semantics and pragmatics by the looseness with which the terms 'sentence' and 'utterance' are employed. It is arguable that Austin, too, fell victim to the failure to draw a sufficiently sharp distinction between sentences and utterances. But he was certainly aware of the point that has just been illustrated; and he had a more sophisticated understanding of the complexity of the relation between sentences and utterances than many of his followers appear to have. For the analysis that he himself gives of locutionary acts, unclear though it is in certain respects and technically defective in others, certainly depends upon his recognition of the fact that phonetically identical utterances can differ in terms of their constituent expressions and their grammatical structure.

This leads us to an additional point: phonetic identity is not a necessary condition of the identity of utterances. If we ask Mary to repeat John's utterance of (14), we do not expect her to mimic his voice-quality or to reproduce such paralinguistic features as rhythm and tempo. We do not even expect her to imitate John's accent, though it might differ strikingly from her own. For example, if John is a working-class Londoner with a Cockney accent and Mary is an upper-class lady from New England, they will pronounce *I'll meet you at the bank* and almost every other potential utterance of English in characteristically different ways. And yet in many cases, if not all, pairs of phonetically distinct utterance-inscriptions will be identified by native speakers as **tokens** of the same **type**.

This shows that phonetic identity is not a necessary condition of the type/token identity of utterance-inscriptions. It also illustrates the point that the type/token identity of utterances is, up to a point, theory-independent: it can be established in particular instances without reference to one theory of language-structure rather than another. But theory-independence, in this sense, breaks down in respect of the intonation-contour of utterances. It simply is not clear, in everyday life, whether two intonationally distinct pronunciations of *I'll meet you at the bank* would count as tokens of the same type. In both cases there is room for debate as to whether stress and intonation are relevant or not. For simplicity of exposition, however, I will here take the view that for two people to produce the same utterance-inscriptions, it is sufficient for them to utter what they and others will recognize as the same string of forms, regardless of the intonation-contour and stress-pattern that are superimposed upon it. And I will take the same view as far as sentences are concerned.

For example, if John says

((17) *It's raining*

with falling intonation and a neutral stress-pattern, whereas Mary says

(18) *It's raining*

with emphatic stress and rising intonation on the form *raining*, I will declare them, not only to have produced the same utterance-inscription, but also to have uttered the same sentence:

(19) 'It is raining'.

I also count the contraction of *it is* to *it's*, and all similar phenomena, as irrelevant to the type/token identity of utterance-inscriptions. This is not so much a matter of fact as of theoretical and methodological decision. Many linguists would disagree, on theoretical grounds, with the view that I have taken here. But few linguists, so far, have given serious attention to the question; and much of what appears to be genuine disagreement might turn out to be purely terminological.

We can now split the performance of a locutionary act into two logically independent parts: (i) the production of an inscription in some appropriate physical medium; and (ii) the construction of such and such a sentence. They are logically independent, because the same inscription can be associated with two or more quite different sentences and, conversely, the same sentence can be associated with two or more quite different inscriptions. Using Austin's terms, we can say that a locutionary act is the product of (i) a **phonic** act of producing an inscription (in the phonic medium of sound); and (ii) a **phatic** act of constructing a particular sentence in a particular language. The first of these two acts is, of course, dependent upon the use of one medium rather than another. The production of utterances in some non-phonic medium – notably when one is writing, rather than speaking – will involve non-phonic acts of one kind or another. As I said earlier, the term 'speech act' should not be interpreted as applying only to the production of spoken utterances. The same goes for the term 'locutionary act'.

We have not yet finished with the analysis of locutionary acts; we still have to reckon with the fact that sentences are uttered in particular contexts and that part of the meaning of the resultant utterance-inscription derives from the context in which it is produced. This is notably the case in respect of the reference of the referring expressions that it contains; and reference, as we have seen in Part 3, is part of utterance-meaning, not sentence-meaning. The third component of the locutionary act, which includes the assignment of reference and may be described more generally as contextualization, is what Austin calls the **rhetic** act.

I will make no further use of Austin's terms 'phonic', 'phatic' and 'rhetic'. They are not widely employed in the literature; and I have, in any case, given them a somewhat different interpretation from the one that Austin himself did. What is important is the tripartite analysis itself, which depends, as we have seen, partly on the distinction between language and medium and partly on the distinction between sentences and utterance-inscriptions.

It may be worth adding, in view of the fairly general confusion and misunderstanding that exists in this respect, that the distinction between sentences and utterance-inscriptions is not simply a distinction between types and tokens. This follows from the fact that two utterance-inscriptions produced on different occasions can be identified as tokens of the same type without knowing what sentences have been uttered. Moreover, as I have emphasized in this section, tokens of the same utterance-inscription can result from the utterance of different sentences; and, conversely, tokens of different utterance-inscriptions can be produced by uttering one and the same sentence on different occasions. This point is crucial for any theory of language-structure that operates with a more or less traditional notion of the sentence. Anyone who adopts a traditional view of the sentence (as we are doing in this book) will want to be able to say, for example, that tokens of

(20) *I have*,

whether spoken or written, result from the utterance of indefinitely many sentences. They will want to say that (20) is an elliptical form of any one of a set of sentences, including

(21) 'I have done the washing up'
(22) 'I have been to California'
(23) 'I have (got) a personal computer'.

Conversely, they may also want to be able to say (as I will), that a sentence such as

(24) 'I have done the washing up'

can be uttered not only as

(25) *I have done the washing up,*

but also as

(26) *I have done it*
(27) *I have*
(28) *Me*

(with some appropriate prosodic contour, if these utterances are inscribed in the phonic medium). As we shall see in Chapter 9, the analysis of locutionary acts outlined in this section enables us to make statements like these in a way that is both theoretically and empirically satisfying. But, now that I have explained in some detail what is involved in the performance of a locutionary act, we can look at what is generally regarded as Austin's most original contribution to the study of meaning: his development of the notion of illocutionary force.

8.3 ILLOCUTIONARY FORCE

Saying is doing. But there are distinguishable senses of the verb 'say'. In one sense, it means, roughly, "utter" or, more technically, "perform a locutionary act". As we have just seen, saying in this sense of the verb involves three different kinds of doing:

   (i) the act of producing an inscription;
  (ii) the act of composing a sentence;
 (iii) the act of contextualizing that sentence.

To utter a sentence, in all normal communicative contexts, is to perform a complex act in which these three kinds of doing are integrated and have as their product some identifiable and meaningful language-signal: an utterance-inscription. It does not follow, of course, from what has just been said that these three acts are psychologically or physiologically distinct in the actual production of utterances. So far, at this level, relatively little is known by psychologists about the details of utterance. The analysis presented here is intended to be neutral with respect to particular approaches to psycholinguistics and phonetics.

There is yet another sense of 'say' in which, as I have already pointed out, it is possible for two people to say the same thing without performing the same locutionary act and without uttering the same sentence. They can say that something is, or is not, the case: that is, they can assert the same proposition. For example, let us suppose that John says (or writes)

(29) *Peter is mad*

and Mary, on some other occasion, says (or writes)

(30) *Your brother is mad.*

Let us further suppose that 'Peter' and 'your brother' refer to the same person and that 'mad' is being used with the same sense (rather than on one occasion with the meaning "insane" and on the other with the meaning "angry"). Provided that they have indeed asserted a proposition, John and Mary will have asserted the same proposition, and will therefore have said the same thing in this other sense of 'say'. But, in saying, respectively, *Peter is mad* and *Your brother is mad*, they will not necessarily have made an assertion.

To make an assertion, or statement, is not to perform a locutionary act of one kind rather than another; it is to perform a locutionary act whose product – an utterance-token – has one kind of **illocutionary force**, rather than another. According to Austin, as we have seen, the constative or descriptive function of a language is only one of its functions. We also use languages to ask questions, issue commands and make promises; to threaten, insult and cajole; and, of course, to do all those things for which Austin originally employed the term 'performative' – to baptize a child into the Christian faith, to plight one's troth, to sentence a convicted criminal, and so on. In short, there are many different language-functions and correspondingly many different kinds of illocutionary force.

But how many? One way of tackling this question is to ask how many verbs in a particular language can be used in explicitly performative utterances in the same way that 'promise', for example, can be used non-constatively in the utterance of (3) of section 8.1 above, repeated here as:

(31) 'I promise to pay you £5'.

There are hundreds, if not thousands, of such verbs in English. Some of them are more or less synonymous: e.g., 'implore' and 'beseech'. Others, though obviously not synonymous, can be seen intuitively as falling into classes with common characteristics. For example, 'promise' and 'undertake' are semantically related in that, when they are used in explicitly performative utterances, their use commits the speaker to a particular course of action. All such verbs, and therefore the particular kinds of illocutionary force which they serve to make explicit, may be grouped together as members of one class. Similarly for other sets of semantically related performative verbs: e.g., 'order', 'command', 'request', etc., all of which have the common property that, when they are used in explicitly performative utterances, their use expresses the speaker's will that some other person, usually the addressee, should carry out a particular course of action. Such utterances (orders, commands, requests, etc.) are commonly referred to collectively nowadays as **directives**.

Austin himself provided the outlines of one classificatory scheme of this kind at the very end of *How to Do Things With Words*. Other such schemes, differing to a greater or less extent from Austin's, have since been put forward by his followers. The very fact that alternative more or less plausible classifications are possible constitutes a problem. How do we decide between one classification and another? There is no reason to suppose that the set of performative verbs in English or in any other language will give lexical recognition to every possible kind of illocutionary force. There is still less reason to suppose that there must be some uniquely correct analysis of such verbs, applicable to all cultures and to all languages. Indeed, the vast majority of performative verbs in English and other languages are obviously culture-dependent. For example, the meaning and use of the verb 'swear', in so far as it differs from that of 'promise' and 'undertake', on the one hand, or 'covenant', 'contract' and 'guarantee', on the other, depends upon the culturally established institution of the taking of oaths.

Moreover, it is now clear that it is wrong to attach particular importance to performative verbs. Admittedly, they had a special status in Austin's original formulation of the distinction between constative and performative utterances. But this was because at that time he was mainly concerned to challenge the descriptive fallacy. Looked at from this point of view, sentences such as

(32) 'I promise to pay you £5'

were obviously of greater theoretical interest than sentences such as

(33) 'I will pay you £5'.

In terms of the later, more general, notion of illocutionary force which he developed in *How to Do Things With Words*, we have no grounds for confining our attention to declarative sentences containing performative verbs.

It is also worth noting at this point that the definition of 'explicit performative' which I gave earlier in this chapter ("one in which the utterance-inscription contains an expression which denotes or otherwise makes explicit the kind of act that is being performed") makes no reference to performative verbs as such. For example, the expression 'by Heaven' might be used by members of a particular group of English speakers as an equally explicit alternative to the use of the verb 'swear', in order to indicate that they are taking an oath. In which case, in the appropriate circumstances,

(34) *By Heaven, I'll pay you £5*

would count as an explicit performative: 'by Heaven' would make explicit, though it does not denote, the illocutionary force of the utterance. It is but a short step to the recognition of the further possibility that speakers should be able to make explicit the illocutionary force of this utterance, not by using a particular expression, but by using a particular modal particle, a particular grammatical mood or, even, a particular intonation-pattern. I will come back to this.

For various reasons, then, there seems to be little point in drawing up comprehensive and allegedly universal schemes for the analysis of illocutionary force based on the existence of a particular set of performative verbs in particular languages. There is perhaps even less point in trying to establish a watertight classification of all possible speech acts in terms of the necessary and sufficient conditions that they must satisfy in order for them to count as instances of one class rather than another. Most speech acts, as I have said, are culture-specific in that they depend upon the legal, religious or ethical conventions and practices institutionalized in particular societies. If the society is one, like our own, with firmly established principles for deciding at law whether something is or is not, let us say, a breach of contract, it may be relatively easy to propose necessary and sufficient conditions constitutive of speech acts of this particular kind. But we are deluding ourselves if we think that all speech acts are regulated, in this way, in the societies in which they operate. Even the act of promising, which looks as if it might be readily definable in terms of the conditions that regulate it, turns out to be problematical from this point of view. It certainly cannot be assumed without argument that promising, in the sense in which we understand the verb 'promise', is an illocutionary act (i.e., a locutionary act with a particular illocutionary force) that can be performed with all languages and in all cultures. And yet assumptions of this kind are commonly made in some of the more specialized work in the theory of speech acts.

Although most speech acts are culture-specific, there are others that are widely, and perhaps correctly, assumed to be universal. They include making **statements** (or **assertions**), asking **questions** and issuing **directives**. It has been argued, on philosophical grounds, that these three classes of illocutionary acts are not only universal, but basic – in two senses of 'basic': first, that no human society could exist in which acts of this kind have no role to play; second, that many, if not all, culture-specific illocutionary acts can be seen as belonging to a more specialized subclass of one of the three basic classes. For example, as I mentioned earlier, swearing on oath that something is so is obviously a culture-specific act. But swearing that something is so is also one way of making a strong statement; and statement-making, it is argued, is basic and universal.

I will not go into the question of the relation between basic and non-basic speech-acts. However, I would emphasize one point: even if the allegedly basic acts of making statements, asking questions and issuing directives are universal, they too are regulated, in all societies, by more or less culture-specific institutions, practices and beliefs. One recognizable dimension of cultural variation, in this respect, is that of politeness. It is impolite, in all societies, to speak out of turn: that is, to speak when the social role that one is playing does not grant authority and precedence or, alternatively, when the rules that govern **turn-taking** in that society do not grant one the authority to speak at that point. It is also impolite, in some societies, to be too assertive in the exercise of one's locutionary and illocutionary authority. For example, it might be considered impolite, in certain circumstances, to make a straightforward unqualified assertion or to issue a blunt and unqualified command. The origin and more or less conventionalized used of various kinds of **indirect speech-acts** can be explained in such terms as these, as, for example, in English, where *Would you pass the sugar?* (originating as a question and commonly so punctuated in its written form) is used in preference to *Pass the sugar* (a direct command).

Politeness, however, is but one of the dimensions of cultural variation that regulate the use of the allegedly basic speech-acts. Furthermore, though it has a certain cross-cultural validity and under a sufficiently general interpretation of 'politeness' may be universal, it does not manifest itself in the same way in all societies. One must be careful, therefore, not to assume that generalizations made on the basis of one's experience of one kind of society will be valid in respect of all human societies. This point should be borne in mind in all that follows. For the discussion and exemplification of the part played by politeness and other factors in the regulation of language-behaviour in different cultures, reference may be made to recent work in sociolinguistics and pragmatics.

8.4 STATEMENTS, QUESTIONS AND DIRECTIVES

We are assuming that all languages provide their users with the means of making statements, asking questions and issuing directives: i.e., of producing utterances with these kinds of illocutionary force. It does not follow from this assumption, however, that all languages will grammaticalize these differences of illocutionary force. As we saw in Chapter 6, it is quite possible for sentences to exist which are neutral in sentence-type or mood: sentences (or clauses) which are neither declarative nor interrogative, on the one hand, and are not indicative, subjunctive or imperative, on the other.

Nevertheless, it may well be clear enough what illocutionary act is being performed when one of these sentences is uttered. This may be clear not only from the context in which it occurs, but also from the prosodic structure that is superimposed upon the resultant utterance-inscription. For example, if English had no interrogative sentence, so that

(35) 'The door is open'

was not declarative, but neutral in sentence-type, it would be possible to utter this sentence (as *The door is open*) with, let us say, a falling intonation-contour to make a statement and rising intonation-contour to ask a question. This point was made earlier. It may now be generalized in terms of the more detailed account of the process of uttering sentences which is being outlined in this chapter.

But it was also asserted earlier that many languages, including English, do in fact grammaticalize distinctions of sentence-type and mood: and furthermore that there is an essential connexion between sentence-type and mood, on the one hand, and what we are now calling illocutionary force, on the other. What is the nature of this connexion? And how do statements, questions and directives differ from one another semantically? I will do no more than provide a partial answer from a particular point of view.

To make a statement is to express a proposition and simultaneously to express a particular attitude towards it. I will call this attitude, for reasons which will be clearer when we look at the notion of modality, **epistemic commitment**. (The term 'epistemic', which comes from a Greek word meaning "knowledge", is used by logicians to refer to that branch of modal logic that deals with knowledge and related matters.) Anyone who states a certain proposition is committed to it, not in the sense that they must in fact know or believe it to be true, but in the sense that their subsequent statements – and anything that can be legitimately inferred from their accompanying and subsequent behaviour – must be consistent with the belief that it is true. Hence the unacceptability or paradoxical character of

(36) *It is raining but I don't believe it*

(construed as a statement). In making any such statement the speaker is guilty of a breach of epistemic commitment.

When one asks a neutral (i.e., epistemically unbiased) question, one expresses a proposition and simultaneously expresses one's attitude of non-commitment with respect to its truth-value. But there is more to it than this. As was noted in Chapter 6, *Is the door open? – that is a question which I refuse to ask* is a perfectly acceptable utterance. In this case a question is **posed**, but not asked. To ask a question then is not merely to express the propositional attitude of non-commitment – that is, to pose the proposition as a question – but also, in so doing, to indicate to one's addressee – prosodically, paralinguistically or otherwise – that one desires them to resolve one's uncertainty by assigning a truth-value to the proposition in question. It follows, for this and other reasons, that questions are not, of their nature, a subclass of directives (as several authors have suggested).

What then of commands, requests and other kinds of directives? These differ from statements and ordinary (i.e., neutral) questions in that they involve a different kind of commitment on the part of the speaker: **deontic commitment**. (The term 'deontic' comes from a Greek work relating to the imposition of obligations. Like 'epistemic', it is borrowed from modal logic.) In issuing a directive speakers commit themselves not to the truth, or factuality, of some proposition, but to the necessity of some course of action. To make the same point in more traditional terms: they express, not their belief that something is so, but their will that something be so.

In making a request (rather than issuing a command or an order), speakers express their will that something should be so, but they also explicitly concede to the addressee the right of non-compliance. Requests are in this respect like non-neutral, so-called leading or conducive, questions – questions such as

(37) *The door is open, isn't it?*,

in the utterance of which speakers express their own tentative or provisional commitment to the truth-value of the proposition "The door is open" but simultaneously concede to the addressee the right to reject it (see 6.7). Another way of making the point is to say that in conducive questions and requests the speakers express their commitment to the "it-is-so" or "so-be-it" component of the utterance and invite the addressee to do the same.

The analysis of statements, questions, commands and requests that has been presented in outline here suggests that their illocutionary force can be factorized, in each case, into two components: a component of commitment ("I say so") or non-commitment, on the one hand, and what might be referred to as a **modal** component of factuality ("it is so") versus desirability ("so be it"), on the other. I have used the term 'modal' in this connexion (instead of introducing some more specialized terminology) for two reasons. First, the distinction between factuality and various kinds of non-factuality falls within the scope of what logicians have traditionally referred to as modality: I have prepared the way for the treatment of modality that will be given later by deliberately introducing the terms 'epistemic' and 'deontic' (10.5). Second, such distinctions are commonly grammaticalized in languages in the category of **mood**. It is important to realize, however, that mood in natural languages may also grammaticalize different kinds or degrees of commitment.

The grammatical category of mood must not be confused with what some logicians refer to as the mood of a proposition, which rests upon the objectification of the essentially subjective component of commitment. This is only part of what is covered by the grammatical category of mood, which, as we shall see in Chapter 10, always expresses subjectivity. If a language has a grammatical mood which is used distinctively and characteristically for the purpose of expressing the speaker's unqualified epistemic commitment, that mood is traditionally described as the **indicative**. Similarly, if a language has a grammatical mood which is used distinctively and characteristically for the purpose of imposing one's will on others for the purpose of issuing directives, that mood is traditionally described as the **imperative**.

As we shall also see in Chapter 10, there are various ways in which the speakers can qualify their epistemic or deontic commitment. All natural languages provide their users with the prosodic and paralinguistic resources which enable them to do this in speech. Some, but by no means all, natural languages grammaticalize different kinds and different degrees of commitment in the category of mood; and some languages lexicalize or semi-lexicalize them by means of modal adverbs and particles.

All this will be taken up later in connexion with the notion of subjectivity. I have mentioned it here, without detailed development or exemplification, in order to show how a fairly traditional view of mood can be reformulated within the framework of the theory of speech acts developed by Austin and his followers. As we have seen in this chapter, Austin began by identifying explicit performatives as a rather special class of utterances, in the production of which the speaker is doing something, rather than saying something, by means of language. He later came to realize that all saying is doing and that all kinds of saying – including the production of statements, questions and directives – are regulated by the central concepts of authority and commitment.

Austin himself recognized the social basis of these concepts, even though he did not go into this aspect of the matter in detail; and at this point he makes contact, though not explicitly, on the one hand with the later Wittgenstein and, on the other, as we shall see in the next chapter, with Grice. He might just as well have emphasized the personal, or expressive, character of the concepts of authority and commitment. This is what is done in the traditional grammarian's accounts of mood, couched in terms of the speaker's judgement and will. Here, as elsewhere, not only in the use of language, but in all communicative behaviour, the expressive merges with the social and is ultimately indistinguishable from it.

Indeed, as some philosophers, anthropologists and social psychologists have argued, there is an important distinction to be drawn, in this connexion, between persons and individuals, in that it is persons rather than individuals that one is, or should be, concerned with in the discussion of communication. It has also been argued that the person (or the self) is a social product – the product of socialization – and that socialization is a process in which the acquisition and use of a particular language in a particular culture plays a vital part. This point also will be picked up in connexion with the notion of subjectivity (10.6).

One final point must now be made. The theory of speech acts is sometimes advocated, or criticized, as if it were an alternative to truth-conditional semantics. It should be clear from earlier chapters of this book that the two theories are, in principle, complementary. Truth-conditional semantics, as it is currently applied to natural languages, is a theory of the propositional content of sentences; speech-act theory – if we grant that it is or aspires to be a theory – deals with the illocutionary force of utterances. There has been much discussion by linguists and philosophers of the question whether Austin was right or wrong when he said that utterances such as *I promise to pay you £5*, when used to make a promise, are neither true nor false, but either efficacious (or felicitous) or not. I have said nothing about this controversy here, because in my view it is of no consequence whether we resolve the issue one way or the other; and how we resolve it depends not so much on the facts of the matter as on the theoretical and philosophical framework within which we are operating. The most important point, for our purposes, is that the illocutionary force of ordinary descriptive statements, such as *It is raining*, cannot be accounted for satisfactorily within the framework of truth-conditional semantics. Austin is at one with Frege in making this point. I judge it to be incontrovertible.

CHAPTER 9

Text and discourse; context and co-text

9.0 INTRODUCTION

We have been operating with the assumption that utterance-meaning is crucially dependent on context. So far, however, I have made no attempt to say what context is or how it determines the meaning of utterances and controls our understanding of them. Nor have I said anything in detail about spoken and written text: I have, however, made it clear in previous chapters that speech must be distinguished from writing (and the products of speech from the products of writing), even though, in the technical metalanguage of semantics that we have been building up throughout the book, 'utterance' and 'text' are being applied to the products of both speech and writing.

In this chapter, we shall be dealing with both text (and discourse) and context (and co-text). As we shall see, text and context are complementary: each presupposes the other. Texts are constituents of the contexts in which they are produced; and contexts are created, and continually transformed and refashioned, by the texts that speakers and writers produce in particular situations. It is clear that even sentence-sized utterances, of the kind we considered in the preceding chapter, are interpreted on the basis of a good deal of contextual information, most of which is implicit.

We shall begin by recognizing explicitly that the term 'sentence' is commonly used by linguists (and also by non-linguists) in two senses, one of which is, to put it loosely, more abstract than the other. It is the more abstract sense of 'sentence' that is relevant when linguists talk about a grammar as generating the sentences of a language and when semanticists draw a distinction, as I have been doing, between sentence-meaning and utterance-meaning. Relatively few linguists use the technical terms 'system-sentence' and 'text-sentence' that I introduce below. Most of those who draw a distinction between sentence-meaning and utterance-meaning do, however, acknowledge the importance of distinguishing between the more abstract and the more concrete sense of 'sentence'. They would also recognize that the relation between these two senses has to be made explicit on the basis of a satisfactory theoretical account of the role of context in the production and interpretation of utterances. As we shall see, linguists who are engaged in the construction of such a theoretical account (whether they call themselves semanticists or pragmaticists) have drawn heavily on Paul Grice's notion of **implicatures**.

9.1 TEXT-SENTENCES

Before we can talk sensibly about the relation between text and context, we must look again at the status of sentences.

It was pointed out, in the previous chapter, that many of our everyday utterances are grammatically incomplete or elliptical. Some of them are ready-made locutions of fixed form: *Good heavens!*, *Least said, soonest mended*, etc. I shall have no more to say about these. I mention them merely to indicate that, in all languages, there are such expressions, finite in number and in some cases of more or less determinate grammatical structure, whose form and meaning cannot be accounted for, synchronically, in terms of the utterance of sentences. They must of course be accounted for in the description of the grammatical and semantic structure of particular languages. But they do not raise problems different in kind from those which arise in the analysis of the infinite set of potential utterance-inscriptions, any one of which can, in principle, result from the utterance of sentences. Only a finite, and relatively small, subset of this infinite set of potential utterances is ever actualized in the day-to-day use of a language. But, as generative grammarians have rightly insisted in recent years, linguistic theory cannot be restricted to the analysis of a finite set of actual utterance-inscriptions, however large and representative of (the products of the use of) a language that set might be. In insisting upon this point (which is generally accepted by formal semanticists whether or not they subscribe to the principles of generative grammar as these are currently formulated within linguistics), generative grammarians were merely reasserting something which had been taken for granted, over the centuries, by theorists and practitioners of traditional grammar. What is new and exciting in generative grammar (as also in formal semantics) is the attempt to give full effect to the principle of compositionality in accounting for the grammatical structure (and meaning) of the sentences of natural languages. However, there has been a good deal of confusion, both in generative grammar (and formal semantics) and in traditional grammar about the relation between sentences and utterances. Our first task in this section is to clear up this confusion. It is the infinite set of potential utterance-inscriptions with which we are mainly concerned here.

Paradoxical though it may appear, the product of the utterance of a sentence is not necessarily a sentence. The apparent paradox disappears immediately if we draw a distinction between a more abstract and a more concrete sense of 'sentence'. Sentences in the more abstract sense are theoretical constructs, which are postulated by linguists, in order to account for the acknowledged grammaticality of certain potential utterances and the ungrammaticality of others. They may or may not have some kind of psychological validity in the production and interpretation of utterances (i.e., utterance-inscriptions), but they certainly do not occur as the inscribed, and transcribable, products of utterances. I will refer to sentences in this more abstract sense of the term as **system-sentences**; they are what are generated by the grammatical rules in a generative grammarian's model of some **language-system** (operating upon a vocabulary, or lexicon, which is part of the same language-system). But the term 'sentence' is also used both traditionally and in modern linguistics (as also in everyday non-technical discourse) in a more concrete sense.

So, let me now introduce the term **text-sentence** for this more concrete sense of 'sentence' — the sense in which sentences are a subclass of utterance-inscriptions and, as such, may occur (in some languages at least) as whole texts or as segments of text. This will allow us to say that the utterance of a particular system-sentence, such as

(1) 'I have not seen Mary',

will result, in some contexts, in the production of a text-sentence, such as

(2) *I have not seen Mary*

(with or without the contraction of *have not* to *haven't*, and with some contextually appropriate prosodic structure). This may look like the multiplication of theoretical entities beyond necessity. But there is a very considerable pay-off.

I have said that the utterance of a sentence is not necessarily a sentence. This is readily illustrated with reference to the utterance of 'I have not seen Mary'. Let us suppose that we are faced with the following text, either written or spoken:

(3) *Have you seen Mary? I haven't. Peter hasn't either. She is never here when she should be.*

It comprises four segments, or **text-units**, only the first and (possibly) the fourth of which would normally be described as complete sentences. The second and third are what would be traditionally regarded as elliptical **sentence-fragments**. And yet, in this context, *I haven't* is just as much the product of the utterance of the system-sentence (1) as is the text-sentence (2) in other contexts. (This is empirically demonstrable by asking informants, as teachers of traditional grammar in school would ask their pupils, to make *I haven't* into a full sentence.) And its propositional content cannot be identified unless we are able to identify the sentence that has been uttered in the performance of the locutionary act of which *I haven't*, in this context, is the product. The same goes, of course, for *Peter hasn't either* with respect to 'Peter has not seen Mary' (and perhaps also for *She* *is never here when she should be* with respect to 'Mary is never here when she should be here').

It is important to realize that, although I have introduced a certain amount of technical terminology to handle the requisite theoretical distinctions, the distinctions themselves are real enough in our everyday experience of the use of language. We have no difficulty in deciding that *I haven't* has the propositional content of 'I have not seen Mary' in one context, of 'I have not been to Switzerland' in another, of 'I have not got any money' in yet a third, and so on. In fact, out of context *I haven't* is infinitely ambiguous. In context, *I haven't* loses it ambiguity only in so far as it is possible to say which of the infinitely many sentences of English (with the appropriate grammatical structure) has been uttered.

I will continue to use the term 'sentence' in both senses, relying upon the notational distinction between single quotation-marks and italics to make clear what kind of units I am referring to. Most linguists, as I have said, do not draw a clear conceptual distinction between system-sentences and text-sentences; the fact they they do not introduces a good deal of confusion into the discussion of the relation between sentence-generating grammars and the production (and interpretation) of texts. Arguably, it has also vitiated much of the work done in text-linguistics from the point of view of generative grammar. This will be evident from what follows. The sense in which texts are generated (i.e., produced) in particular situations is different from the sense in which sentences (i.e., system-sentences) are generated as abstract, mathematical, objects by the rules of a generative grammar.

9.2 WHAT IS A TEXT? AND WHAT IS TEXT?

Considered from the viewpoint of semantics (and pragmatics), text and context are complementary: each presupposes the other. I will come to context presently. But what is a text and what is text? As we shall see, these are two distinct (but related) questions. Let us start with the former: what is a text?

One answer that is often given is that a text is a sequence of sentences. As it stands, this is clearly unsatisfactory – if 'sentence' means, as it must in this context, "text-sentence". True, there are some texts that would satisfy the definition, notably texts of a more formal character. But the vast majority of everyday colloquial texts are made up of a mixture of sentences, sentence-fragments and ready-made locutions. However, this defect in the definition of 'text' that has just been given is only one aspect of a more serious deficiency: its failure to make explicit the fact that the units of which a text is composed, whether they are sentences or not, are not simply strung together in sequence, but must be connected in some contextually appropriate way. The text as a whole must exhibit the related, but distinguishable, properties of **cohesion** and **coherence**.

Roughly speaking, the distinction between cohesion and coherence has to do with the difference between form and content; and some such distinction, however it is drawn by different schools of linguists, is both intuitively attractive and theoretically justifiable. To return to our sample text, (3): that the products of the utterance of 'I have not seen Mary' should have the form *I haven't*, rather than *I have not seen Mary*, is a matter of **cohesion**. So too is the use of *either* in *Peter hasn't either* and the use of the pronoun 'she', rather than 'Mary' in the first clause of *She is never here when she should be*. Cohesion is destroyed if the first three text-units are put in a different order, such as:

(4) *Peter hasn't either. I haven't. Have you seen Mary?*

It is also destroyed if we replace each of the text-units with the corresponding full text-sentence.

(5) *Have you seen Mary? I haven't seen Mary. Peter hasn't seen Mary (either). Mary is never here when she should be here.*

It is evident that (5) does not have the same kind of **connectedness** that (3) had. For this reason it is less easy, though not impossible, to take the sequence as a text, rather than as a string of unconnected (or disconnected) utterances. Ellipsis and the use of pronouns, as well as the use of particular connecting particles and conjunctions (*therefore*, *so*, etc.) commonly serve to create and sustain that kind of connectedness to which the term 'cohesion' is applied. Languages differ considerably with respect to the degree to which they permit or oblige their users to connect text-units in sequence by means of explicit indications of cohesion.

The other kind of connectedness – **coherence** – is a matter of content, rather than form. In default of any contextual indication to the contrary, what is being said in any one text-unit is assumed to be **relevant** to what has just been said in the immediately preceding text-units. For example, in (3) the propositional content of the fourth text-unit

(6) *She is never here when she should be*

will normally be taken to be relevant to that of the preceding three. In particular, 'she' will be understood to refer to Mary (by virtue of the kind of cohesion that is called **anaphora**) and the general statement that the speaker is making about Mary will be understood as a comment upon her absence at that time, rather than as the expression of some totally unconnected passing thought. Similarly, if one heard or read the following sequence of two text-sentences,

(7) *The whole family went to town last Saturday. Veronica bought a dress, while John kept the children occupied in the toy-shop,*

one would normally assume that Veronica was one of the family, and presumably the mother; that she bought the dress in town; and that the toy-shop was also in town. None of these propositions has been explicitly formulated, still less asserted; and any one of them might be contradicted, in specific contexts of utterance, by other propositions that are part of the speaker's and hearer's background beliefs and assumptions. We shall return to the question of coherence and relevance later in the chapter. Meanwhile, there are three points to be mentioned here and given due emphasis.

First, as we have already noted, the question "What is a text?" differs from the more general question "What is text?". What are commonly referred to as texts, whether written or spoken, are deliberately composed by their authors as discrete wholes with determinate beginnings and ends. And, like (3) and (7), they are more or less readily divisible into text-units, some of which (though not all) can be classified as (text-)sentences. Moreover, longer texts, such as novels or plays, can usually be divided hierarchically into larger and smaller whole units (chapters and paragraphs, or acts, scenes and speeches), each of which is internally cohesive and coherent and can be analysed into smaller, sequentially ordered, units: chapters into sequences of paragraphs, paragraphs into sequences of (text-)sentences, and so on. Most of the text that we produce in our day-to-day use of language is not organized in this way.

The second point to be noted is that, as I am using the term 'text', individual text-sentences, sentence-fragments and fixed locutions all count as units of text in relation to their context of utterance, regardless of whether they are embedded in larger stretches of text or not.

Finally, it must be emphasized that the account that I gave of speech acts in the previous chapter is intended to cover in principle all aspects of the production of text. Speech-act theorists have been concerned primarily with the production of text-sentences (without drawing the distinction that I have drawn between text-sentences and system-sentences). But the utterance of a sentence, in practice, always involves its **contextualization** – the process of making the product of utterance both cohesive and coherent in relation to its context. As I have said, text and context are complementary. What then is context? And how does it relate to utterance-meaning? We shall begin by discussing the relation between context and utterance-meaning.

9.3 UTTERANCE-MEANING AND CONTEXT

Context determines utterance-meaning at three distinguishable levels in the analysis of text or discourse. First, it will usually, if not always, make clear what sentence has been uttered – if a sentence has indeed been uttered. Second, it will usually make clear what proposition has been expressed – if a proposition has been expressed. Third, it will usually make clear that the proposition in question has been expressed with one kind of illocutionary force rather than another. In all three respects, context is relevant to the determination of what is said, in the several senses of 'say' that were identified in the preceding chapter.

But utterance-meaning goes beyond what is actually said: it also includes what is implied (or presupposed). And context is highly relevant to this part of the meaning of utterances. In this section, we shall restrict our attention to what is said: to the locutionary and illocutionary aspects of utterance-meaning. We shall rely initially upon an intuitive everyday notion of what context is. That context may tell us what sentence has been uttered is obvious from our discussion of locutionary acts. As we saw, tokens of the same utterance-type can result from the utterance, on different occasions, of different sentences. In such cases, the utterance-inscription itself will usually be either grammatically or lexically ambiguous (or both). For example,

(8)   *They passed the port at midnight*

is lexically ambiguous. However, it would normally be clear in a given context which of the two homonyms, 'port$_1$' ("harbour") or 'port$_2$' ("kind of fortified wine"), is being used – and also which sense of the polysemous verb 'pass' is intended. Polysemy, unlike homonymy, does not give us grounds for distinguishing one sentence from another (on a traditional view of sentences). But it may none the less give rise to lexical ambiguity. In collocation with 'port$_2$', the most salient sense of 'pass', in most contexts, is undoubtedly the one in which it means "hand from one to another". But it is easy to see that in an appropriate context 'pass' meaning "go past" can be collocated with 'port$_2$' just as readily as it can be collocated, in other contexts, with 'port$_1$'.

We do not know what propositional content is being expressed unless we know what sentence is being uttered. Moreover, if the sentence contains one or more polysemous expressions, we do not know in what sense they are being used. Context, therefore, is a factor in the determination of the propositional content of particular tokens of utterance-inscriptions on different occasions of utterance. Usually, we operate with contextual information below the level of consciousness in our interpretation of every-day utterances. Most of the ambiguities, whether lexical or grammatical, therefore pass unnoticed. For example, the phrase 'the vintage port' would normally be interpreted as referring to wine, and 'the busy port' as referring to a harbour. From time to time, however, we are made aware of such ambiguities, precisely because our contextual beliefs and assumptions differ from those of our interlocutors. We may then either fail to understand what they are saying, hesitating between alternative interpretations, or misunderstand their utterances by taking them in the wrong sense. The second of these two possibilities is often exploited by humorists and comedians, who deliberately set up the context in such a way that their audience will unconsciously assign one interpretation to an utterance-inscription and then, in the so-called punch-line, suddenly reveal to them, more or less indirectly, that they have been led up the garden path.

In some cases there is no need to set up the context specially for the purpose. The out-of-context saliency of what is subsequently revealed to be what may be referred to as the garden-path interpretation will suffice. To take a rather hackneyed example: if

(9) *Three strong girls went for a tramp*

is followed, after a brief pause, with

(10) *The tramp died,*

the comedian will probably secure the desired effect, simply by virtue of the out-of-context saliency of the sense of 'go for a tramp' in which it falls, semantically and syntactically, with 'go for a walk', 'go for a ride', 'go for a swim', etc.

Both contextually determined and out-of-context saliency are, of course, exploited for more serious purposes in literature, where readers may well be expected to hold two or more interpretations in mind simultaneously and either to hesitate between them or to combine them in some way, in order to construct a richer composite interpretation. Ambiguity is commonly described by philosophers and linguists as if it were of its nature pathological – something which gets in the way of clarity and precision. This is a highly prejudiced and unbalanced view of

the matter. Not only is it frequently, and erroneously, associated
with the view that all sentences have precise and determinate
meanings; it is based on the equally erroneous assumption that
clarity and the avoidance of vagueness and equivocation are
always desirable, regardless of genre, style and context. Nothing
that is said about ambiguity in this section, or anywhere else in
this book, should be taken to imply that ambiguity is, or should
be, avoided in all contexts.

Let us now turn to the second of the two levels at which context determines utterance-meaning: let us take up the fact that
context can make clear, not only which sentence has been
uttered (and, in the case of polysemous sentences, with what
meaning), but also what proposition has been expressed. In
Part 3, I drew a distinction between 'proposition' and 'propositional content', and a corresponding distinction between 'reference' and 'referential range' (or 'referential potential'). I
pointed out that, whereas the propositional content of a sentence
and the referential range of its component expressions can be
established without appeal to the context of utterance, it is not
generally possible to establish what proposition is being
expressed, without knowing in what context the sentence is
uttered. We can now relate this point to the immediately preceding discussion of text and context.

As we have seen, *I haven't* can be put into correspondence, by
means of the notion of contextualization, with any one of an infinite set of sentences. In our sample text (3), it can be identified
as the product of the utterance of the sentence 'I have not seen
Mary', which contains two referential (i.e., potentially referring) expressions: 'I' and 'Mary'. What do they refer to?
Obviously, out of context there is no way of knowing. If we
make certain assumptions about the production of the text, we
can say that the speaker or writer – more generally, the locutionary agent – is referring to himself or herself by means of 'I'
and to some third person (i.e., to some person other than himself
or herself and his or her addressee) by means of 'Mary'. It is
worth noting, however, that we cannot be sure even of this simply on the basis of our knowledge of English. There are circumstances in which speakers may refer to someone other than

themselves by means of 'I' (notably when they are acting as interpreters); and there are circumstances in which one may refer to one's addressee by name, rather than by the pronoun 'you', so that 'Mary' could in principle be used to refer to the addressee. In any case, granted that the locutionary agent is referring to himself or herself with 'I' and to someone else with 'Mary' (and that a proposition is being expressed), we cannot say what proposition is being expressed and evaluate it for truth or falsity without knowing who the locutionary agent and Mary are.

We also need to know when the utterance was produced. The fact that the locutionary agent used the present-perfect form *haven't (seen)*, rather than *didn't (see)*, *hadn't (seen)*, *don't (see)* (or *can't (see)*), is relevant to the truth-value of the proposition that he or she expresses. (So too, incidentally, is the fact that in most contexts there will be a tacitly understood reference to the period of time of which the predicative expression 'have seen' is, or is not, true. For example, the speaker may have seen Mary on the previous day, or even a very short time before, and yet be held to have made a true statement in saying *I haven't.*) In the case of other utterances, we need to know, not only the time, but also the place of utterance, in order to establish what proposition has been expressed. For example, this is so in respect of the fourth text-unit in (3), which, unlike the second and third, happens to be a text-sentence, rather than an elliptical sentence-fragment:

(11) *She is never here when she should be*:

'here' normally refers to the place of utterance, so that the proposition "Mary is here" may be true in respect of one place at certain times and false of that place at other times. Questions of this kind will occupy us in Chapter 10. Let us merely note for the present that the vast majority of utterance-inscriptions in most languages are implicitly, if not explicitly, **indexical** or **deictic**, so that they express different propositions according to the context in which they are produced. This point has already been mentioned in connexion with the treatment of sentence-meaning in formal (linguistic) semantics in Chapter 7.

We come, finally, to the contextual determination of illocutionary force. As we saw in the preceding chapter, the same sentence may be uttered on different occasions with different kinds of illocutionary force. For example,

(12) 'I will give you £5'

may be uttered as a promise or as a prediction. Or again,

(13) 'Sit down'

may be uttered, in what is normally regarded as its most characteristic use, as a request or a command; it may also be used in order to grant the addressee permission to sit down. Frequently, but not always, the prosodic contour (i.e., the stress and intonation) will indicate to the addressee that the utterance has one kind of illocutionary force rather than another. But whether this is also indicated prosodically or not (in the case of spoken utterances), it will usually be clear, in context, what kind of illocutionary act has been performed. For example, it will usually be clear whether the speaker has the authority to order the addressee to sit down or to grant him or her permission to do so.

Indeed, much of our day-to-day language activity is so closely integrated with other kinds of social behaviour and activity that the occurrence of an utterance with a particular illocutionary force is often predictable from the socially identifiable situation in which it occurs. For example, we would not normally sit down in someone else's house or office without being invited to do so. On the other hand, in most situations – paying a call on a new neighbour, coming to see the bank-manager about an overdraft, etc., it will be evident to us and to our interlocutor that at a certain point in the conversation an invitation of this kind should be made. This being so, addressees do not have to calculate or determine the illocutionary force of *Sit down*, from first principles, in terms of the meaning of the sentence 'Sit down' and their assessment of the speaker's motivation for saying what he or she has said. The situation itself predisposes addressees to expect either this very utterance-inscription or another with the same illocutionary force (*Won't you sit down?*, *Why don't you take a seat?*, etc.). It is arguable that most so-called indirect speech-acts, of the kind that were mentioned in the preceding chapter, can be accounted for in this way. At any rate, there can be no doubt that, in many instances, the illocutionary force of an utterance is strongly determined by the context in which it occurs.

To recapitulate, then, context determines utterance-meaning at three distinguishable levels in the analysis of text. I have still not said what context is or how it is handled theoretically: we shall come to that presently. From what has been said in this section, however, it will be evident that the context of an utterance includes, not only the relevant **co-text** (i.e., the relevant surrounding text), but also the relevant features of the situation of utterance. As we shall see later, what is sometimes referred to as the **context of situation** can, and should, be defined in such a way that it subsumes everything in the co-text that bears upon the question of cohesion, coherence and relevance.

9.4 IMPLICATION AND CONVENTIONAL IMPLICATURES

There is an everyday meaning of the verb 'imply' in which we can, and usually do, imply by means of our utterances something other than what we actually say. For example, asked to give an opinion about a person's character, one might say

(14)   *He'd share his last crust of bread with you.*

Obviously, it has not actually been said of the person in question that he is both kind and generous. But one might reasonably be held to have implied this. Let us introduce a distinction, then, between what is actually said, or expressed, in an utterance-inscription and what is conveyed either by what is said or by the fact of saying what is said.

Much of the information that is **conveyed** from speaker to addressee in day-to-day conversation is implied, rather than asserted. In some cases, of course, it is not clear whether the speaker intends the addressee to draw a particular inference or not. And this opens the way for misunderstanding and misrepresentation, on the one hand, and for the subtle manipulation of the addressee's opinion, on the other. However, in what one may think of as the standard kind of situation, not only do addressees draw the inferences that speakers intend them to draw, but these inferences are such that the speakers themselves, if asked, would also subscribe to them. I have assumed that this is so in respect of (14). It is easy enough, however, to devise a situation of utterance in which the hearer would not draw the inference that the person referred to is kind and generous. It is equally easy to think of circumstances in which the speaker might insincerely and deceitfully intend the addressee to draw this inference.

In recent years, the notion of **implicature** has been introduced into the philosophy of language, and subsequently into linguistics, to bridge part of the gap between the standard logical notions of implication and entailment with which formal semantics operates, on the one hand, and the broader everyday notion of implication, on the other. According to Paul Grice in his 1967/8 William James Lectures (see Grice, 1975, 1989), there are two kinds of implicatures: **conventional** and **conversational**. The difference between them is that the former depend on something other than what is truth-conditional in the conventional use, or meaning, of particular forms and expressions, whereas the latter derive from a set of more general principles which regulate the proper conduct of conversation. Conversational implicatures will be discussed in the following section.

It has been argued, for example, that the difference between the forms *but* and *and* in English can be accounted for in terms of the notion of conventional implicature. Those who take this view, including Grice himself, would say that the following two sentences have the same propositional content:

(15) 'He is poor and he is honest',
(16) 'He is poor but he is honest'.

If they also identify sentence-meaning with propositional content, they would say that the two sentences have the same meaning. Most native speakers of English operating with an everyday notion of 'meaning' would probably disagree (see 6.3). The proponents of truth-conditional semantics can meet this challenge – if they accept that there is such a thing as conventional implicature – by attributing the apparent difference in meaning to the conventional implicature associated with the form *but*. They can say that the use of *but*, in contrast with *and*, indicates that the speaker feels that there is some kind of contrast between the conjoined propositions.

For example, on the assumption that the two sentences are being used to make a statement and 'he' refers to the same person in each of the conjoined clauses, in uttering (16) the speaker might be **implicating** (though not asserting) that it is unusual for someone to be both poor and honest. But would the implication, or implicature, be as determinate as this? Out of context there is no way of knowing exactly which of several propositions speakers are implicating. They might be indicating (whether voluntarily or not) that they are surprised, not that anyone should be both poor and honest, but that a man should be; or, alternatively, that anyone in this person's circumstances or this person in any circumstances should be. Indeed, they may not be indicating their own surprise at all, but merely their expectation that their interlocutor will be surprised. In fact, there is a whole range of further possibilities, most of which can be subsumed loosely under the notion of contrast. But it is remarkably difficult, in most cases, to say exactly what is being implicated by the use of *but* and impossible to do so without considering in some detail the actual context of utterance.

It is usually taken for granted by those who have discussed the notion of implicature that the difference between *and* and *but* cannot be part of the propositional content of the compound clauses in which they occur (and we tacitly accepted this view in section 6.3). But there are circumstances in which speakers can use *but* and *and* contrastively within the scope of the verb 'say', and even of the adjective 'true'. For example, they might claim at some point in the argument that their interlocutor is misrepresenting them:

(17) *I did not say that he was poor but honest, I said that he was poor and honest. And that's a very different thing. Personally, I don't find it surprising that anyone should be both. Let us recapitulate then. It is*

> true that he is poor and honest; it is not true − in my view at least −
> that he is poor but honest. We both subscribe to the truth of the
> proposition that he is poor and he is honest. We appear to disagree as
> to the truth of the proposition that he is poor but he is honest.

I have deliberately constructed this passage in such a way that
it starts with an everyday use of 'say' and ends with what is a
recognizably technical use of 'proposition'. There is little
doubt, I think, that it is more natural to use *but* and *and*
contrastively within the scope of the verb 'say' than within the
scope of 'proposition'. And yet the passage, as a whole, is surely
linguistically, if not philosophically or logically, acceptable;
and whether it is judged to be philosophically or logically
acceptable will, of course, depend on the adoption of particular
assumptions.

It is not difficult to find or construct similar examples in which
compound clauses containing *but* can be used after the verb
'say' in what appears to be, at least, the meaning of 'assert' (in
the logician's sense of 'assert'). This does not prove that *but* contributes something other than what *and* contributes to the propositional content of such clauses. What it does show, however, is
that the distinction between what is said and what is conventionally implicated is not always clear in the everyday use of the
verb 'say'. More important, it also shows how the lexical and
grammatical resources of a particular language can be **adapted**
and **exploited** to propositionalize what is not of its nature propositional. This point is of the greatest importance. It will be
taken up and given further exemplification in Chapter 10 with
particular reference to modality and subjectivity.

The only other example that Grice himself gave in his 1967/8
lectures to illustrate his notion of conventional implicature is
the use of *therefore*. Once we look at the full range of language-
use, however, rather than simply at more or less formal argumentation, as Grice does, we can extend the list of forms which
meet his criteria for conventional implicature very considerably.
Many of the connectives that serve to give cohesion to a text,
linking one text unit with another, fall within the scope of his
definition: *however, moreover, nevertheless and yet*, etc. So too do

modal particles such as *even, well,* or *just,* as in the following utterances:

(18) *Even Horace likes caviare,*
(19) *You may well be right,*
(20 *It was just one of those things.*

English, like French, has relatively few modal particles, in comparison with German, Russian and many other languages. But,
as examples (18)–(20) demonstrate, it does have some. Moreover, their meaningfulness and their conventionality is evident
from the fact that they can be mistranslated; and it is worth
noting that mistranslation is possible even where exact translation is not.

A second point to be made is that there seems to be no reason
to restrict the notion of conventional implicature to connectives
and particles. As we saw in Part 2, many fully lexical expressions
are descriptively synonymous, but differ in respect of their social
and expressive meaning. Most, if not all, of this difference
would seem to fall within the scope of Grice's definition of conventional implicature. That is to say, morphological and syntactic distinctions, as well as differences between lexemes and
particles, may be associated with what many semanticists, following Grice, would classify as conventional implicatures.

So, too, does much of the difference that is carried in
particular contexts by the choice of one form of an expression,
rather than another. For example, if the speaker says

(21) *Christ tells us to love our neighbour*

or

(22) *Christ has told us to love our neighbour*

rather than

(23) *Christ told us to love our neighbour,*

he or she can be held to have implicated that Christ's injunction
or exhortation had, and still retains, a certain authority and
validity. In fact, differences of tense and mood, not only in

English but in many languages, are commonly associated with differences of expressive meaning; and they are notoriously difficult to translate satisfactorily from one language to another. Even if we restrict ourselves to the medium-transferable, verbal part of utterances, we can see that a much broader range of lexical and grammatical resources than have been considered by Grice (and his followers) under the rubric of conventional implicature can be used by speakers to implicate conventionally something over and above what they actually say.

A third, and final, point is that, just as there is no reason to limit the applicability of the notion of conventional implicature to the use of a language in more or less formal argumentation, so there is no reason to limit it to propositional, or descriptive, meaning. I have already suggested that differences of social and expressive meaning among descriptively synonymous expressions (in so far as they are lexicalized in particular languages) can be brought within the scope of the notion of conventional implicature. But social and expressive meaning is conveyed at all levels of language-structure; and it is very heterogeneous. Few logicians or linguists would wish to push the notion of conventional implicature as far as I have done. Indeed, there are many who would deny that it has any validity at all. Some truth-conditionalists would argue that the alleged implicatures are either entailments or are implicatures of the kind that Grice called conversational, rather than conventional. Others have argued that the phenomena we have been discussing should be dealt with as cases of presupposition, but presupposition is also a somewhat controversial topic within the framework of truth-conditional semantics (and pragmatics).

For further discussion of (so-called) conventional implicature, students are referred to the more specialized works mentioned in the 'Suggestions for further reading'. In conclusion, it may be pointed out that those who have no prior theoretical commitment to an exclusively truth-conditional definition of 'meaning' can accept that all sorts of meaning are encoded – i.e., in Grice's terms, made conventional – in the grammatical and lexical (and phonological) structure of particular languages. Of course, this does not reduce the difficulty of deciding, in the case of individual utterances and more generally, exactly what meaning is encoded in the lexemes, particles and grammatical categories of particular languages.

9.5 CONVERSATIONAL IMPLICATURES

Grice's so-called conversational implicatures have aroused far more attention in linguistics than have his conventional implicatures. I say "so-called" because the ordinary sense of 'conversational' is much narrower than Grice's. We are concerned, not solely with conversations, but with all kinds of social interaction involving either spoken or written language.

The basic idea is that language-activity, most typically, is a kind of rational (and purposive) social interaction governed by the **principle of co-operation**. In what may now be regarded as his classic formulation of this principle, Grice recognized several kinds of co-operation which he grouped under the headings of **quantity**, **quality**, **relation** and **manner** (1975: 45–46). Each of these comprises a set of one or more subprinciples, formulated by Grice as prescriptive **maxims**, which participants normally obey, but may on occasion flout or violate.

Let us take first the subprinciple of **quantity**. This may be formulated as follows:

(24) Say as much as, and no more than, is required (in the present context and for present purposes).

Other formulations will be found in the literature, most of which (including Grice's) employ the expressions 'be [as] informative [as]' or 'make your contribution [as] informative [as]'. I have deliberately employed a slightly more general formulation, and one which explicitly mentions context. But (24) is faithful to the spirit of Grice's original and points the way to subsequent developments in what may be referred to as **neo-Gricean pragmatics**. For the present, however, (24) may be interpreted as being equivalent to

(24a) Give as much information as, and no more than, is
       required (in the present context and for present pur-
       poses).

Now, by appealing to (24) or (24a), we can account for the fact
that, if *x* asks (of *y*)

(25) *Have you done the washing-up and put everything away?*

and *y* replies

(26) *I have done the washing up,*

y may be held to have implied, in most contexts, that he or she
has not put everything away. This implication, or implicature,
derives from *y*'s presumably deliberate failure to say *Yes* or its
equivalent to the composite proposition which is expressed in
x's utterance and is put to *y* for acceptance or rejection. The simple proposition "I have done the washing-up" is less informative
than "I have done the washing-up and I have put everything
away". On the assumption that *y* is being duly co-operative
and is being sufficiently (but not excessively) informative, *x* can
reasonably infer that *y* is not able truthfully to assert "I have
put everything away".

   x's assumption (in default of any evidence to the contrary)
that *y* is being truthful depends upon *x*'s assumption that *y*,
being co-operative, is obeying the second subprinciple of **quality**:

(27) Tell the truth, and do not say anything for which you have
      insufficient evidence.

Once again, this formulation differs, in wording though not in
spirit, from Grice's original formulation. We shall come back to
the subprinciple of quality presently. Meanwhile, let us note
that truthfulness – i.e., telling the truth (and nothing but the
truth, though not necessarily the whole truth) – is closely allied
to sincerity (which has played an important role in the theory
of speech acts). It is also important to note that to tell the truth
is not the same as to say what is true (i.e., to assert a set of one
or more true propositions). One can say what is true whilst

believing it to be false or not knowing that it is true. One can also say what is true with the intention to deceive, saying what one says in such a context or in such a manner, that one knows or believes that the addressee will take it to be false. It is the volitional, or moral, concepts of truthfulness and sincerity which underpin Grice's view of communication. These are regulated, differently in different cultures and in different social contexts, not only by sufficiency of evidence, but also by a variety of social constraints, including those imposed by the accepted, culture-dependent, norms of **politeness**.

Grice's subprinciple of **relation** has associated with it the single maxim:

(28) Be relevant.

By appealing to (28), we can impose an interpretation on the following dialogue:

(29) *x*: *The clock is slow.*
(30) *y*: *There was a power cut this morning.*

In doing so, we assume that the propositional content of *y*'s statement bears some relation to that of *x*'s: in particular, that *y* is, or might be, supplying an explanation for what *x* asserts to be the case. Of course, our assumption that *y*'s utterance is relevant to *x*'s in this way depends not only upon our background knowledge about electric clocks, but also upon the further assumption that *y* shares this background knowledge and knows that the clock in question is, or might be, operated by electricity directly supplied from the mains. It is easy to see that such everyday conversational exchanges as the above may depend for their cohesion and coherence – for the property of connectedness in virtue of which we classify them readily enough as texts – upon a whole set of assumptions of this kind, specific to particular cultures and to particular groups.

The subprinciple of **manner** was explicated by Grice in terms of (at least) four maxims, as follows:

(31) Be perspicuous, by (i) avoiding obscurity of expression, (ii) avoiding ambiguity, (iii) being brief (avoiding unnecessary prolixity), and (iv) being orderly.

It will be seen immediately that there is likely to be a correlation, on the one hand, between being brief and giving no more information than is required, and, on the other, between being relevant and being orderly. The fact that there are, at least intuitively, such correlations suggests that Grice's four sub-principles can be modified and reduced in number. And this is what has happened in so-called neo-Gricean pragmatics. These later, more technical, developments are not dealt with in this book.

Much of the interest aroused by Grice's work on conversational implicatures derived from its explanatory potential in respect of a variety of phenomena that are troublesome from the viewpoint of formal semantics. These include metaphorical interpretation, (so-called) indirect speech-acts, anaphoric reference, and the assertion of tautologies and contradictions. Not all of these can be dealt with here. It will be helpful, however, to say something about the applicability of Grice's maxims of co-operative interaction by means of language, first of all, to the interpretation of metaphor and, then, to indirect speech-acts. This will set the context for some general comments on Grice's underlying assumptions and on the difference between implicature and other kinds of implication (and presupposition) which have been studied intensively by both linguists and logicians in the last twenty years or so. We will begin with **metaphor**.

We shall take as our example:

(32) 'John is a tiger',

which can be assigned both a literal and a metaphorical interpretation. Before considering how it might be interpreted metaphorically in the light of Grice's principles of co-operative interaction, we must note that the point made about the literal interpretation of sentences such as (7)–(9) in section 5.2 is also relevant here.

Twentieth-century linguists of a positivist bend of mind (including many generative grammarians) have often described sentences such as (32) as being either anomalous or contradictory. However, provided that it does not violate conditions of categorial congruity of such generality that it could not be interpreted, not only in the actual world, but in any possible world, sentence (32) is perfectly well-formed semantically. Moreover, the proposition that it purports to express is not necessarily false. First of all, there is nothing in the structure of English which prevents anyone from assigning the proper name 'John' to an animal, wild or domesticated (or even to an inanimate entity): this fact must always be borne in mind when English sentences containing proper names are under discussion, but it is not of primary concern here. More important is the fact that (32) can be given a non-contradictory literal interpretation, even if 'John' is being used to refer to a person.

Indeed, there are all sorts of, socio-culturally normal, everyday situations in which 'John is a tiger' might be uttered (with reference to a man or boy) to assert a true proposition. For instance, John might be playing the role of a tiger in a play about animals. Arguably, the proposition "John is a tiger" would then be true, under a literal interpretation of 'tiger' (and also, incidentally, of the verb 'be'). Granted, there are many philosophers who would challenge this, but in doing so they might simply be revealing their uncritical attachment to a positivist concept of literal meaning. I mention this kind of interpretation of the sentence in question in order to show that we may not need to adjust our ontological assumptions to any significant degree in the assignment of a literal interpretation to sentences which, at first sight, might look as if they cannot sustain one. Needless to say, if we abandon the ontological assumption that the same individual cannot be (simultaneously) both a human being and a tiger (in any possible world), we can immediately assign to (32) a whole range of alternative interpretations which are non-metaphorical and, arguably, non-contradictory. As we shall see later, the fact that this is so casts doubt on the sharpness of the distinction which is drawn by many authorities between conventional and conversational implicatures, on the one hand, and between implicature and other kinds of implication (including strict implication, or entailment), on the other. More generally, it casts doubt on what Quine referred to many years ago as one of the "two dogmas of modern empiricism":

the assumption that there is an absolutely sharp and unchallengeable distinction between the analytic and the synthetic. This was mentioned above in the discussion of entailment and possible worlds (4.4). It will be taken up again, later in this section, in connexion with the notion of the **defeasibility** or cancellability of normally unchallenged contextual assumptions. For the moment, however, it suffices to note that the notion of context-independent literal meaning with which many formal semanticists operate is tacitly associated with their own context-dependent, philosophically challengeable, ontological assumptions.

It is also worth noting at this point that there is no closer connexion between literal sense and truth-conditionality than there is between metaphorical sense and truth-conditionality. If a statement is made metaphorically by uttering the sentence 'John is a tiger', the proposition thereby expressed – whatever proposition it is – will have just as determinate a truth-value as a proposition such as "John is ferocious" or "John is aggressive". Granted, there may be some indeterminacy attaching to the process of metaphorical interpretation itself: it may not be clear to an addressee which of several metaphorical interpretations he or she should assign to the utterance. But this is comparable with the problem of deciding which of the several literal senses of a polysemous expression is the one intended; and it has nothing to do with truth-conditionality as such.

I am not saying, of course, that all metaphorical expressions are truth-conditionally determinate, but simply that they do not differ from non-metaphorical expressions in terms of a characteristically distinctive, context-dependent, indeterminacy. Many metaphorical statements will certainly be truth-conditionally indeterminate; and many will contain an expressive, or socio-expressive, component, which might be held to affect the determinacy of truth-value. But in this respect they are no different from non-metaphorical statements such as

(33) *Mary is beautiful*

or indeed

(34) *John is aggressive*

and

(35) *John is dynamic.*

Linguists who distinguish semantics from pragmatics by means of the criterion of truth-conditionality and ascribe the meta-phorical interpretation of utterances to pragmatics tend to miss this point.

How then do Grice's maxims of co-operative interaction apply to the process of metaphorical interpretation? The general answer is, not that they guide addressees in their search for one metaphorical interpretation rather than another, but that they motivate the search itself. They enable the addressee to **calcu-late** (or **compute**) the intended meaning of the utterance as a function of its literal meaning and of the context in which it is uttered. For example, hearing or reading *John is a tiger*, addres-sees might reason deductively as follows, saying to themselves as it were:

(36) *The speaker/writer cannot mean that literally. However, I have no grounds for believing that he/she is being unco-operative. His/her utterance has the form of a statement. Therefore, he/she must be try-ing to tell me something, which presumably makes sense to us both (in the light of our beliefs and assumptions about the world, etc.). He/she must also believe (if he/she is being co-operative) that I can work out the non-literal meaning for myself – presumably on the basis of the literal meaning (of the whole utterance-inscription or of one or more of its component expressions). One contextually accept-able way of using language to convey something other than what is actually said is by means of metaphor. Let me see whether I can inter-pret the utterance metaphorically.*

I have spelt this out in some detail (though I have omitted one or two steps in the reasoning) in order to emphasize the multiplicity of assumptions that go into Gricean explanations of metaphor and other phenomena.

Let me now make explicit a few of the points that are implicit in the above account of the way in which addressees are assumed to get from the literal interpretation of an utterance to some contextually **relevant** metaphorical interpretation. First, their assumption or inference that the utterance-inscription cannot have a literal interpretation does not depend upon its being semantically anomalous or contradictory: all that is required is that the literal sense should be contextually irrelevant (or improbable). Second, the whole process is subject to the constraints imposed by the participants' beliefs and assumptions (including their beliefs and assumptions about one another's beliefs and assumptions): all communication is subject to such constraints. Third, I have included as a separate step the addressee's recognition of the contextual appropriateness of metaphor: in certain contexts metaphor is more frequently used than in others. Indeed, there may well be occasions, determined by the socio-cultural situation or literary genre, when the use of metaphor is so common that the addressee can skip the earlier steps in the reasoning process outlined above and start with the assumption that a given statement is more likely to be meant metaphorically than literally.

As I have said, Grice's maxims, of themselves, do not resolve for the addressee the problem of deciding upon one metaphorical interpretation of 'John is a tiger' rather than another. But that is not their purpose. Grice's aim was to maintain, as strictly and as consistently as possible, the distinction between what is actually said and what is conveyed (over and above, or instead of, what is said) by the fact of saying it (and not saying something else) and, at the same time, to bridge this gap, at least in principle, by showing how the application of one or more of the maxims, by rational and co-operative addressees, to particular utterances in particular contexts of utterance, can enable them to calculate, or compute, the intended meaning. The context-dependent **calculability** (or computability) of conversational implicatures – their calculability being probabilistic, or heuristic, rather than algorithmic, or deterministic – is generally taken to be one of their defining properties. As we have seen, it is the maxim of relevance which is likely to play the major role in the metaphorical interpretation of such utterances as (32). And it will yield various results in various contexts of utterance.

The way in which Grice's maxims apply to the interpretation of **indirect speech-acts** is, at least in principle, straightforward enough. As we saw earlier, the very notion of performing one illocutionary act indirectly "by way of performing another" is theoretically controversial (8.3). Moreover, many of the text-book examples of so-called indirect speech-acts involve the use of conventionalized, quasi-formulaic, locutions whose meaning in utterances of this kind should be regarded, from the viewpoint of synchronic descriptive linguistics, as being encoded in the language-system. It may well be that the utterance of the inter-rogative sentence

(37) 'Do you mind if I smoke?'

with the allegedly indirect illocutionary force of a request is dia-chronically explicable in terms of the notion of conversational implicature. But it is highly implausible to suggest that present-day speakers of Standard English would interpret an utterance of (37) as a request only secondarily, after having first inter-preted it as an information-seeking question. We do not need to discuss this point further in the present context.

Let us consider instead the following imaginary, but I trust realistic, bit of dialogue:

(38) *x*: *I want to watch TV now.*
       y: *You have not put your toys away.*

x, we shall assume, is a young child; and *y* is the mother (or some other person with acknowledged authority and responsibility). Each of them has uttered a declarative sentence; but neither of them, presumably, intends thereby to augment the other's knowledge of the world by making a true statement; and neither of them interprets the other's utterance as being motivated, even incidentally, by this intention. Indeed, *y*'s statement (and let us grant that it is a statement), if true, tells *x* nothing of which *x* is not already, perhaps resentfully and petulantly, aware. Whether *x*'s utterance is correctly classified as a state-ment or a request (or both) is a question that need not concern us. What matters is that it is interpreted by *y*, in the context in which it is uttered, as a request for permission to watch television. Let us now assume that it is one of the rules of the household that x is not allowed to watch television unless and until x has put his or her toys away (or, more generally, has done a set of chores of which this is one). Given this assumption, our little bit of dialogue evidently manifests the properties of coherence and relevance. And x, being reminded of the rule and perceiving its relevance, may correctly interpret y's utterance as implicating a refusal to grant x's request.

What examples such as this demonstrate is that some, if not all, of what have been referred to in the literature as indirect speech-acts can be plausibly accounted for in terms of the more general and more powerful notion of Gricean implicatures. This being so, there are many authorities who would seek to do away with the notion of indirect speech-acts altogether; and there are some who would question whether there is any need for illocutionary force as a distinct and identifiable part of the meaning of utterances. Recent work in pragmatics has certainly given much more prominence to implicature than it has to that of either direct or indirect illocutionary force.

These more recent developments have not been (and will not be) discussed in the present book. To conclude this section, I will explain and comment briefly upon the logical properties of Grice's conversational implicatures which are generally held to distinguish them from other kinds of implication (or presupposition). The most important of these properties is what Grice referred to as their **defeasibility**. To say that implicatures are defeasible is to say that their validity is context-dependent and that in particular contexts they can be cancelled without contradiction or any other kind of anomaly. For example, the conjunction of two clauses by means of *and*, as in

(39) *John arrived late and missed the train,*

would normally implicate that there is a temporal and/or causal connexion between the situations described in the two conjoined clauses. As we saw in an earlier chapter, proponents of the view that *and*-conjunction in English is truth-functional have been

able to invoke the notion of implicature in support of this view
(6.3). On the assumption that anyone uttering (39) is being
duly respectful of the subprinciples of manner (being orderly)
and relation (being relevant), its utterance will conversationally
implicate – i.e., **licence the inference** – that John missed the
train because he arrived late (presumably at the station). The
fact that this causal connexion is merely implicated, and neither
expressed in what is said nor entailed (i.e., strictly implied) by
what is said, is demonstrated by its defeasibility in appropriate
contexts of utterance. For example, the implicature can be readily cancelled, without contradiction, by explicitly denying that
there is a causal connexion between John's late arrival and his
missing the train:

(40) *John arrived late and missed the train, but it was not because he
      arrived late that he missed the train [the train was delayed and did
      not leave until ten minutes after he got there. So, why did he miss the
      train? Maybe he did so deliberately].*

There is nothing anomalous about (40) either with or (in appropriate context) without the overtly explanatory portion of text
which I have added in square brackets. And, as we saw in the
preceding section, the use of *but*-conjunction to cancel the normal conversational implicature associated with *and*-conjunction
is explicable in Gricean terms, by appealing to the complementary notion of conventional implicature. The property of defeasibility distinguishes conversational implicature, not only from
entailment, but also from conventional implicature.

Many other kinds of what would usually be called implication
in the everyday sense of the term (*x didn't actually say that, but it's
what he/she implied*), but which do not fall within the scope of
'implication' as this is defined by logicians, have been more or
less plausibly accounted for by invoking Grice's notion of conversational implicature (see 6.3). These other kinds of so-called
implication include the very common tendency to interpret a
conditional as a biconditional: to interpret "if p, then q" as "if
and only if p, then q". For example, the utterance of

(41) *If Ann passes her driving text, her parents will buy her a Porsche*

would normally be held to imply that Ann's parents will not buy her a Porsche if she does not pass her driving text. But this is not actually said: it is conversationally implicated and is of course defeasible.

Of particular interest in this connexion are what have come to be called **scalar implicatures** involving quantifiers, such as 'some' and 'many', and numerals (as well as modal, evaluative adjectives and certain other classes of expressions). To exemplify:

(42)   *The Browns have two daughters*

will normally implicate that the Browns have only (i.e., no more than) two daughters (and in many contexts it will also implicate that they have no sons: *Have the Browns got any children?*). But the implicature is readily cancelled, in an appropriate context, by adding, for example,

(43)   *– in fact, they have three.*

Scalar implicatures of various kinds have been intensively discussed in the literature. They are mentioned here because they illustrate very clearly the property of defeasibility.

The second property generally held to distinguish conversational implicature from other kinds of implication is their **calculability**. This was mentioned above (and illustrated), in connexion with the interpretation of metaphorical utterances such as *John is a tiger*: see (32) and (36). As was emphasized at that point, the calculability (or computability) of conversational implicatures is heavily context-dependent and in many, if not all, contexts non-deterministic. Whether the implicatures are in fact calculated in actual contexts of utterance and, if so, whether they are calculated deductively and step by step, as suggested in (36) – these are questions which are currently the subject of debate and research among logicians and psychologists. Another issue, as yet unresolved, is whether the knowledge of information which is involved in the addressee's calculation of conversational implicatures (in so far as addressees calculate them) is always propositional.

A third property of conversational implicatures, according to Grice, is what he called **non-detachability**. This rests, at least initially, on a straightforward application of the non-technical, everyday, distinction between meaning and form. An implicature is non-detachable if it is inseparably attached to the meaning of an utterance and does not derive merely from its form. It follows from this formulation of what is meant by non-detachability that (as Grice himself realized) implicatures based on the subprinciple of manner will not necessarily be non-detachable: the manner in which something is said (in the relevant sense of 'manner' and of 'say') affects the form of what is said. Two synonymous utterances which differ in length, in grammatical complexity or in the technicality or obscurity of the words used may well give rise, for this very reason, to different implicatures. When they do, it will obviously not be possible to substitute the one for the other in the same context without changing the implicatures associated with them. In other instances, however, it should be possible to vary the form of an utterance (i.e., an utterance-inscription) and to hold constant its meaning (what is said) without thereby affecting what is implicated.

The putative non-detachability of conversational implicatures turns out to be highly problematical, even in the case of those which are not based on the subprinciple of manner. Apart from anything else, the question whether two expressions are synonymous (in any or all of their meaning) cannot be answered unless and until one has decided what constitutes synonymy. Many proponents of formal semantics will opt for the relatively narrow notion of descriptive synonymy, defined in terms of truth-conditional equivalence (see 2.3). Those who adopt a broader notion of synonymy might well argue that the apparent detachability of implicatures associated with two formally distinct, truth-conditionally equivalent, utterances is itself evidence for the view that the alleged implicatures are part of the linguistically encoded meaning of the utterances in question and that the utterances are not in fact synonymous.

Nor is the criterion of identity of form as straightforward as it might appear to be. Much of the textbook discussion of particular examples cites the examples in question in their written form, even when they are assumed to have been spoken. This means that potentially relevant prosodic (and paralinguistic) differences of form are not generally taken into account. One such class of examples is the following set of sentences:

(44) '*It is possible that p*'

in contrast with

(45) '*It is not impossible that p*'.

Discussion of such examples usually proceeds on the assumption that (45) is grammatically unambiguous. This is, however, a questionable assumption. On certain theories of the grammatical structure of English, (45) splits into at least two grammatically and semantically distinct subclasses, one of which manifests the phenomenon of sentence-negation (or clause-negation) and the other that of phrasal (or semi-lexical) negation; and this difference of grammatical structure is normally, if not always, reflected in spoken utterances by differences of stress, intonation and rhythm (see 6.5).

In conclusion, then, let me emphasize once again that many of the attempts made by linguists and philosophers to draw a sharp distinction between semantics and pragmatics founder on their failure to draw, and to apply consistently, a distinction between sentence-meaning and utterance-meaning and to say exactly what is and what is not encoded in the structure of sentences. All too often identity of orthographic form is tacitly assumed to be a sufficient condition of sentence-identity.

9.6 WHAT IS CONTEXT?

One of the points that emerges from our discussion of Grice's notion of conversational implicature in the previous section is the double role played by context. First of all, the utterance itself is embedded in what J. R. Firth and others have called a context of situation; and, as we saw in our discussion of metaphor, in order to decide whether a metaphorical interpretation is probable or not, one may need to know what the context of situation is. Second, having decided that information is being conveyed over and above the information contained in what has been said, the addressees have to infer what this additional information is on the basis of contextual information which they share with their interlocutors.

There has been a tendency, until recently, for linguists and philosophers to neglect the context of situation in their presentation of Grice's maxims. It is arguable that they have, for this reason, failed to bring out as clearly as they should have done the fact that language-behaviour is a culture-dependent activity. What constitutes sincerity and politeness may differ considerably from one society to another. Nor can we assume that rationality will manifest itself, in relation to the quality of information or its relevance, in the same way in all cultures. In fact, Grice's own presentation, and that of many of his followers, may well suffer from some degree of socio-cultural bias – a bias which is now being corrected by those working in conversational analysis and in what has come to be called the ethnography of speaking.

It is arguable that Grice's work also suffers from its philosophical bias in favour of descriptive, or propositional, meaning. This is revealed, not only in his acceptance of a truth-conditional theory of meaning, but also in his conception of context – in the second of its two roles referred to above. For him, and for many of those who have drawn upon his ideas, context is taken to be a set of propositions in relation to which new propositions can be evaluated for truth and added to the context (or rejected as untrue).

But much of the knowledge that is involved in the production and interpretation of utterance-inscriptions is practical, rather than propositional: it is a matter of knowing how to do something, not of knowing that something is the case. Of course, it is always possible (in certain languages at least) to describe practical knowledge as if it were propositional. For example, instead of saying that a speaker must be able to tell whether his or her interlocutor is of higher or lower social status, we can say that the speaker must know which, if either, of the following two propositions is true: "x is of higher status than y" and "x is of lower status than *y*" (where *x* and *y* stand for referring expressions which will identify the speaker and addressee respectively). However, the fact that we can formulate practical knowledge in propositional terms, does not mean that it is in fact propositional. A strong case can be made for the view (taken for granted throughout this work) that social and expressive information is non-propositional.

It would seem, therefore, that context in both of the roles identified earlier in this section is, to a considerable degree, non-propositional. One of the advantages of the theory of speech-acts that we looked at in the previous chapter is that, in Austin's formulation at least, it gives full recognition to the social basis of language. It is, as I said, a theory of social pragmatics (in the etymological sense of 'pragmatics'): a theory of a particular kind of social doing. Grice's notion of language-behaviour as co-operative interaction fits in well with this; and, as I mentioned at the end of the preceding section, it need not be coupled with the assumption that the norms, or maxims, that he formulated for one kind of discourse in one culture – one kind of **language-game**, as the later Wittgenstein would have put it – are universally valid.

No simple answer, then, can be given to the question "What is context?". For the limited purposes of this book, it suffices to emphasize the fact that, in the construction of a satisfactory theory of context, the linguist's account of the interpretation of utterances must of necessity draw upon, and will in turn contribute to, the theories and findings of the social sciences in general: notably of psychology, anthropology and sociology. For further discussion of the role of context (including co-text), as also for what has come to be called neo-Gricean pragmatics, students are referred to the 'Suggestions for further reading'. In this chapter we have concentrated on the basic concepts as they were originally developed.

CHAPTER 10

The subjectivity of utterance

10.0 INTRODUCTION

Having looked at the notion of context in detail in the preceding chapter, we can now return to the question of speech acts and locutionary agency. We shall begin with **reference** – the relation that holds between linguistic expressions and what they stand for in the world (or the universe of discourse) on particular occasions of utterance. We shall then take up a particular kind of reference, **deixis**, which depends crucially upon the time and place of utterance and upon the speaker's (more precisely, the locutionary agent's) and the addressee's roles in the utterance-act itself.

We shall then consider the grammatical categories of **tense** and **aspect**, neither of which is universal, but both of which, together or separately, are found in many unrelated languages throughout the world. As we shall see, tense, unlike aspect, is a referential (and more specifically deictic) category.

Another grammatical category that is closely connected with tense (and in some languages is found independently of tense) is **mood**. As the term 'mood' would suggest, there is a historical association between the grammatical category of mood, as this is traditionally defined, and what is referred to as modality in modern logic and formal semantics. There are, however, important differences between the way in which modality (and mood) are handled, typically, in present-day formal semantics and the way in which mood and modality have been described in traditional grammar. The account that I give of modality and mood in section 10.5 is intended to clarify the differences and to emphasize the continued validity of the more traditional view both of mood and of modality. I shall be drawing, once again, upon points made in Chapter 6.

In this final chapter I shall be dealing with topics that everyone would agree are crucial in the construction of a theory of natural-language meaning. But I shall be dealing with them from a point of view which is by no means universally accepted, especially in formal semantics. I shall be giving particular emphasis to what I am calling the **subjectivity of utterance**. What I mean by 'subjectivity' in this context was implicit in Chapters 8 and 9 and is made explicit in Chapter 10, especially in the concluding section.

10.1 REFERENCE

Reference, as we have seen at various points in this book, is a context-dependent aspect of utterance-meaning: it is a relation that holds between speakers (more generally, locutionary agents) and what they are talking about on particular occasions. The **referential range** of referring expressions is fixed by their meaning in the language (i.e., by their sense and denotation). But their actual reference depends upon a variety of contextual factors.

One cannot generally determine the reference of an expression, then, without regard to its context of utterance. What one can do within the restrictions of sentence-based semantics, is to establish the **intension** of the expression. As we saw in Chapter 7, standard model-theoretic semantics (of which Montague's system is a particular version) does in fact incorporate reference within sentence-meaning – by making the meaning of a sentence relative to an **index** (or point of reference), in which all the relevant contextual information is specified. But this does not affect the substance of what has been said here about reference as a part of utterance-meaning. Standard model-theoretic semantics operates with an untraditional notion of the sentence and, consequently, with a different notion of sentence-meaning; and, as we saw in Chapter 7, it adopts a particular definition of 'intension'. We shall not be concerned with these differences of definition and formalization in the present chapter. But we shall take up, at an intuitive and informal level, the notions of possible worlds and intensionality, which were introduced in Part 3 in connexion with Montague grammar.

Simple propositions are normally analysed by logicians into expressions of two kinds: names and predicates. Names serve to pick out – to **refer to** – entities (or sets of entities) in some possible world about which statements are being made; predicates serve to ascribe properties to single entities (or sets of entities) and to ascribe relations to ordered pairs, triples, etc. of entities (or sets). All this is formalized in standard predicate logic.

Names, in the everyday sense of the word 'name', are not the only kind of referring expressions. Moreover, from a semantic point of view, they are rather special, in that, of themselves and in languages such as English, they have no descriptive content. (The qualification "in languages such as English" is intended to indicate that natural languages may vary with respect to the way naming operates and is integrated with other cultural practices and customs. Philosophical discussions of proper names rarely mention this possibility or its theoretical significance.) For example, 'Napoleon' is arbitrarily associated with indefinitely many entities (persons, animals, ships, etc.) which in principle have nothing in common. True, one of these entities – or some concept, or intension, associated with him – is, for historical reasons, salient, in the cultures in which English is commonly used. (And some of the others have acquired their names as a consequence of this fact and of its actual or attributed significance in the light of the conventions that regulate the assignment of names in particular cultures.) This means that, in default of specific contextual information to the contrary, for most speakers of English the name 'Napoleon' will usually be taken to refer to this culturally salient entity. It also means that there will be a whole host of shared associations and connotations clustering around the name 'Napoleon', which go to make up what some philosophers refer to as the intension, or individual concept, "Napoleon". However, it does not mean that the name 'Napoleon' as such has any descriptive content or sense.

Apart from proper names, there are two main subclasses of referring expressions that are distinguishable, both syntactically and semantically, in English: noun-headed noun-phrases and pronouns. Actually, the traditional analysis of what I am calling **noun-headed noun-phrases** (e.g., 'the boy', 'those four old houses') can be challenged on both syntactic and semantic grounds. For simplicity, I will adopt the conventional view, according to which it is indeed the noun that is the head, or principal constituent, in such phrases: hence my term 'noun-headed'. It is also worth pointing out that I am here (and elsewhere in this book) using the term 'noun-phrase' (abbreviated as 'NP') in the sense in which it is now commonly used in linguistics. Noun-phrases, in this sense, are not necessarily composed of more than one word: i.e., they are not necessarily phrases in the traditional sense of the term 'phrase'.

In some languages, words denoting classes of entities can be employed to refer to individuals without any accompanying modifier (definite or indefinite article, demonstrative adjective, etc.): this is not the case in English, where nouns such as 'man' or 'tree' (**count nouns**) cannot be employed, without modification by means of a determiner ('the', 'that', etc.), a quantifier ('one', etc.) or some more complex expression, to refer to individuals. But languages vary considerably in this respect, and there are many differences of detail among languages which fall into one class (English, French, German, etc.) and languages which fall into another (Russian, Latin, etc.). I mention this fact because most of the discussion of referring expressions in general, and of noun-headed noun-phrases in particular, in the recent literature is skewed towards languages that behave, syntactically, more or less like English. My treatment of reference in this book is highly selective and, of necessity, uses examples from English. I must, therefore, emphasize the importance of bearing constantly in mind that English is only one of several thousand natural languages, many of which do things differently.

Noun-headed noun-phrases can be classified semantically in several ways. One subclass to which philosophers have devoted considerable attention is that of **definite descriptions**:

expressions which refer to some definite entity and identify it, in part, by means of the descriptive content of the expression. English examples include 'the man' and 'John's father'. As the term 'definite description' suggests, all such expressions may be factorized, semantically if not syntactically and lexically, into two components. One of these, as we have just noted, is descriptive (e.g., the word 'man' in 'the man'); the other is purely referential (e.g., the definite article 'the' in English). I shall come back to this purely referential component of definite descriptions in the following section. Here it will suffice to point out that the referential component is non-descriptive, in that it does not identify the entity that is being referred to by describing any of its context-independent properties.

The head-noun (e.g., 'man' in 'the man') in so-called definite descriptions will be more or less descriptive of the referent according to the specificity or generality of its sense. At the limit of generality in English is the word 'entity', which can be used to refer to physical and non-physical objects and is derived from a Latin word which was deliberately created by philosophers to have exactly the degree of generality that it does have. Since it is descriptively unrestricted, it can combine freely with any other modifying adjective, noun, relative clause, prepositional phrase, etc. But the vast majority of entity-denoting nouns in English are not like this. They fall into different **sortal categories** according to what are held to be the essential (or ontologically necessary) properties of the classes of entities that they denote. For example, 'thing' denotes a class of inanimate entities, concrete or abstract; 'person' denotes a subclass of animate entities of which human beings are the prototypical (though possibly not the sole) members. Similarly for verbs, adjectives, adverbs, etc: they too, like nouns, fall into more or less general categories according to the generality or specificity of their sense (and denotation). For example, 'exist' differs categorially from 'occur' (or 'happen'); 'think' differs (on more than one dimension or level of difference) from 'swim'; 'circular' differs from 'clever'; and so on. These differences of denotational category (or subcategory) – based on actual or assumed ontological differences of kind, quality, process, etc. (which may in part determine and in part be determined by the formal and substantive universals of human cognition) – are the source of what I have called categorial incongruity and have distinguished from contradiction (see section 7.4).

The two logically separable components of definite descriptions give rise to two different kinds of **presupposition**: existential and sortal (or categorial). For example, whoever uses the expression 'the woman' or 'the man', in what we may call, loosely, an ordinary context, is committed to the existential presupposition that the referent exists and the sortal presupposition that it is of a particular sort, or category: the category of persons. It is existential presupposition, however, that has been most extensively discussed in recent years by both philosophers and linguists. The reason is that the violation of an existential presupposition, unlike the violation of a sortal presupposition (e.g., *Quadruplicity drinks procrastination, Thursday is in bed with Friday*: see section 5.2), cannot be accounted for as being in any way anomalous within the framework of sentence-based semantics. To take the now famous example: there is nothing wrong with the sentence

(1) 'The (present) king of France is bald'.

It is in the utterance of this sentence (to make a statement) at a time when there is no king of France that the existential presupposition is violated.

We shall not go into the various controversies associated with the notion of existential presupposition. I will simply point out that, on the view of sentences, utterances and propositions taken in this book, anyone who deliberately violates an existential presupposition in using what purports to be a definite description fails to express any proposition at all. Looked at in this way, much of the recent discussion of presupposition by philosophically minded semanticists – important though it may appear to those who are committed to a strictly truth-conditional theory of meaning – is of secondary importance in linguistic semantics. But there are, none the less, one or two important points to be made in this connexion.

First, it is not just definite descriptions that involve existential presuppositions, but referring expressions of all kinds. Reference is intrinsically connected with existence; one cannot successfully refer to something that does not exist. One can, of course, successfully refer to imaginary, fictional and hypothetical entities; but in so doing, one presupposes that they exist in an imaginary, fictional or hypothetical world. Similarly, one can (and frequently does) refer to dead persons. One can refer to them in a past-tense sentence as existent in a world (or state of the world) which itself no longer exists (e.g., *Socrates was condemned to death in 399 BC for (allegedly) corrupting the young men of Athens*). More interestingly, one can refer to them as existent in the present world in literature or oral tradition (e.g., *Socrates tells us [in the works of Plato] that no-one does wrong knowingly or voluntarily*).

Second, the falsity of the descriptive content of a referring expression – whether it is a definite description or not – does not nullify the act of reference and render it void. One can successfully, but mistakenly, refer to someone or something by means of a description which, as it happens, is false. Let us suppose – to adopt and modify a now famous example – that x and y are at a cocktail party and that x notices some third person, z, holding in his hand a tumbler filled with a colourless liquid and also containing ice and lemon. In these circumstances x might successfully refer to z for the benefit of y by using the expression 'the man (over there) drinking gin and tonic'. We shall come back to the meaning of the bracketed 'over there' in the next section: here it is sufficient to note that, whether an expression of this kind is added to the definite description or not, in the circumstances envisaged there will commonly be some gesture or other signal drawing the addressee's attention to the referent. Let us now further suppose that, as a matter of fact, z's glass contains, not gin and tonic, but water (and even that z is not drinking it, but merely holding it for someone else). The fact that the descriptive content of 'the man drinking gin and tonic' is false does not mean that x has failed to refer to z. If y successfully identifies z as the intended referent, x has successfully referred to z. Indeed, x need not be mistaken about the facts in order to refer successfully (but falsely) to z. There are all sorts of everyday situations in which, out of politeness or for other reasons, we refer to people, animals or things by means of descriptions that we know or believe to be false. For example, x, who knows or believes that z is the offspring of an extramarital affair between y's wife and some third person (a fact of which y may or may not be ignorant), may none the less successfully refer to z with the phrase 'y's son' (or 'your son' when x is talking to y). In short, the actual truth or falsity of the descriptive content of a referring expression is not directly relevant to its success. Normal human interaction is governed by a set of culturally determined conventions, amongst which truthfulness is often very properly moderated by politeness. The Gricean maxim of quality ("say only what you believe to be true") does not operate in all contexts (see 9.5).

What I now want to emphasize is that definite descriptions – more obviously than proper names – are context-dependent. Their use as referring expressions cannot be satisfactorily accounted for solely within the framework of sentence-based truth-conditional semantics. When speakers employ a definite description, they indicate by means of the referential part of the expression that they are performing an act of reference, and, in doing so, they tacitly assure the addressee that the descriptive part of the expression will contain all the information that is required, in context, to identify the referent. Various qualifications and elaborations would need to be added in a fuller treatment. But this is the central point.

Definite descriptions are only one of many subclasses of noun-headed noun-phrases used as referring expressions. Another, of course, is that of indefinite descriptions (in certain contexts and used with what is called specific, though not definite, reference): 'a man', 'a certain girl', etc. A third, which has been the object of a good deal of discussion and research, is that of so-called quantified noun-phrases: 'all men', 'every girl', etc. All sorts of previously unsuspected problems have arisen in recent attempts to formalize the notion of reference and put it on a sound theoretical footing. Here I will mention just one such problem, since it is closely related to the principal concerns of this chapter and has been extensively discussed in philosophical semantics: the problem of **referential opacity**.

A referentially opaque context is one in which the substitution of one referring expression for another expression with the same reference does not necessarily hold constant the truth-conditions of the sentence in which the substitution is made. (I have stated the principle in respect of sentences and truth-conditions. With the necessary adjustments it can also be stated for utterances and truth-values.) I have already illustrated this phenomenon in section 7.6. I pointed out, it will be recalled, that

(2) 'I wanted to meet Margaret Thatcher'

and

(3) 'I wanted to meet the first woman Prime Minister of Great Britain'

do not necessarily have the same truth-conditions. There are two reasons why this is so. The first, of course, is that the proper name 'Margaret Thatcher' (like 'Napoleon' and most proper names in some, though not all, cultures) is not constant in its reference: therefore there are (presumably) many persons in Great Britain and elsewhere who currently bear this name to whom the descriptive content of 'the first woman Prime Minister of Great Britain' does not apply. The fact that the reference of almost all noun-phrases, including proper names, is context-dependent has been emphasized throughout this chapter. However, it is the second reason why (2) and (3) do not have the same truth-conditions which is of primary concern to us here. This is that 'the first woman Prime Minister of Great Britain' can be given either a straightforward **extensional** interpretation, in which it serves to identify a particular person (in the way that has been outlined in this section) or an **intensional** interpretation, in which – to make the point rather crudely and perhaps tendentiously for the moment – what counts is not the actual person that the locutionary agent has in mind, but some concept that fits the descriptive content of the expression.

This kind of intensionality is traditionally identified by means of the Latin phrase *de dicto* ("about what is said"), contrasted with *de re* ("about the thing"), which are widely employed nowadays in modal logic and logical semantics in the sense indicated here. We shall return to the question of intensionality, in relation to reference, in a later section. Here it is sufficient to note that such generally accepted *de re* / *de dicto* ambiguities of the kind illustrated here give us particularly cogent reasons for extending the theory of reference beyond the bounds of what I have loosely and inadequately called ordinary contexts. Indeed, it is arguable, as we shall see later, that there is much more intensionality involved in so-called ordinary contexts than is generally supposed. Throughout this section, however, I have been adopting a fairly conventional view of reference.

The third main class of referring expressions, in addition to names and noun-headed noun-phrases, is that of pronouns. Much of what has been said here about reference applies also to them. Since they are intrinsically connected with deixis and indexicality, I will deal with them in the next section.

10.2 INDEXICALITY AND DEIXIS

The third class of referring expressions mentioned, though not discussed, in the previous section is that of pronouns. Traditionally, pronouns are thought of as noun-substitutes (as the term 'pronoun' suggests). But most subclasses of pronouns (other than relative pronouns: 'who', 'which' and, in certain instances, 'that' in English) also have a quite different function, which arguably is more basic than that of standing for an antecedent noun or noun-phrase. This is their **indexical** or **deictic** function. (We have already met the terms 'indexicality' and 'deixis' in Chapter 9; and the term 'index' was used in a related sense, in the discussion of model-theoretic semantics, in Chapter 7. Indexicality and deixis will be dealt with from a much broader point of view in this section.) The only two subclasses of pronouns that will be mentioned here, however, are **personal pronouns**, on the one hand ('I', 'you', 'we', etc.) and **demonstrative pronouns**, on the other ('this', 'that'). But 'indexicality' and 'deixis' are commonly employed nowadays to cover a far wider range of phenomena, including demonstrative adverbs ('here', 'there'), the grammatical category of tense, and such lexical differences as are exemplified in English by the verbs 'come' versus 'go' or 'bring' versus 'take'.

The terms 'indexicality' and 'deixis', as we shall see, can both be explained, from an etymological point of view, on the basis of the notion of gestural reference. But they have entered linguistics and related disciplines at different times and by different routes. 'Indexicality' (or rather 'index' from which 'indexicality' derives) was introduced into logic and the philosophy of language via semiotics by the American philosopher C. S. Peirce (mentioned, in another connexion, in Chapter 2); it is only recently that it has come to be employed by linguists. 'Deixis' (and more especially the adjective 'deictic') has a much longer pedigree – going back, as it does, to the work of the ancient Greek grammarians; but it was made familiar to linguists and others, in the sense that it now bears, by the German psychologist K. Bühler (1879–1963). So far, there is no generally accepted and theoretically well-motivated distinction drawn between the two terms. But it would be in the spirit of the use that is currently made of them in philosophy, linguistics and psychology to think of indexicality as a particular kind of deixis: namely, as deixis in so far as it is relevant to the determination of the propositional meaning of utterances. I will tacitly adopt this view. However, I would emphasize that I am doing no more than codifying a historically explicable difference of usage. It so happens that the philosophical tradition in which 'indexicality' has been defined is one that takes a characteristically narrow view of meaning.

As I said earlier, the terms 'deixis' and 'index' both originate in the notion of **gestural reference**: that is, in the identification of the referent by means of some bodily gesture on the part of the speaker. ('Deixis' means "pointing" or "showing" in Greek; 'index' is the Latin word for the pointing-finger. Pointing with the hand or finger is a method of identification by bodily gesture, which may have a natural, biological, origin and is institutionalized with this function in many cultures.) Any referring expression which has the same logical properties as the bodily gesture in question is, by virtue of that fact, deictic. Personal and demonstrative pronouns, in their relevant uses, are the most obvious kinds of linguistic expressions that have such properties and are clearly deictic in terms of this etymological definition. For example, instead of saying *I am happy*, one could point to oneself and say *Happy*; instead of saying *That's beautiful*, one could point to a particular painting at an exhibition and say *Beautiful*. Of course, one could simultaneously point to the referent and use the appropriate deictic expression; and many deictic expressions are normally used, in fact, in association with some kind of gestural reference.

It is worth noting at this point that the philosophical notion of **ostensive definition** (as was made clear, though not in these terms, in Chapter 3) rests upon an understanding of gestural reference and deixis. Ostension is non-verbal, gestural, reference intended and, when successful, understood as fulfilling an essential role in the definition of linguistic expressions; and 'ostension' is simply a Latin-based word with much the same meaning, etymologically speaking, as 'deixis'.

Etymology may explain the source of the term 'deixis'; it cannot of course account fully for its current use. To do this we must invoke the notion of the **deictic context**, operating as an integral part of the context of utterance. Every act of utterance – every locutionary act – occurs in a spatio-temporal context whose centre, or **zero-point**, can be referred to as the here-and-now. But how do we identify the here-and-now on particular occasions of utterance? Clearly, there is no other way of defining the English demonstrative adverbs 'here' and 'now' (or comparable expressions in other languages) than by relating them either (i) to the place and time of utterance or (ii) to the time and place of a mental act of more or less conscious awareness or reflection. The former may be referred to as **locutionary deixis**; and the latter, for reasons which will become clear when we take up the discussion of subjectivity in the final section of this chapter, as **cognitive deixis**. (It is a philosophically and psychologically controversial question, which, if either, of these two kinds of deixis is more basic and how they are related to one another.) Defined in terms of locutionary deixis, 'here' refers to where the speaker is (at the moment of utterance) and 'now' refers to the moment of utterance (or to some period of time which contains the moment of utterance). The complementary demonstrative adverbs 'there' and 'then' are negatively defined in relation to 'here' and 'now': 'there' means "not-here" and 'then' means "not-now".

The deictic context, then, is centred upon the speaker's here-and-now: it is, in this respect, **egocentric**. The first-person pronoun, 'I' in English, refers (normally) to the actual speaker: i.e., to whoever is speaking at that moment. As the role of speaker — more generally, the role of the locutionary agent — passes from one person to another in the course of a conversation, so the zero-point of the deictic context will be switched back and forth, together with the reference of 'I' and 'here'. The reference of 'now' does not, of course, switch back and forth in the same way, since speaker and hearer normally operate with the same temporal frame of reference and with common assumptions about the passage of time. But 'now' is continuously re-defined, within this shared temporal frame of reference, by the act of utterance. So, too, of course, are past, present and future, which (in locutionary deixis) are defined, explicitly or implicitly, in relation to the now of utterance. We can think of the pronoun 'I' and the demonstrative adverbs 'here' and 'now' — and comparable expressions in other languages — as referring expressions which single out and identify the logically separable components of the spatio-temporal zero-point of the deictic context. In model-theoretic semantics, all three components (with or without others that will not be discussed here) are commonly included in the index, or point of reference. Each such index, as we have seen, distinguishes one possible world from its alternatives (see 7.6).

The way in which spatio-temporal deixis can tell us what proposition has been expressed (in the utterance of a particular sentence by a particular speaker at a particular time) has been illustrated in section 9.3. All that needs to be done here is to emphasize the general point that most utterances (i.e., utterance-inscriptions) in all languages are indexical or deictic, in that the truth-value of the propositions that they express is determined by the spatio-temporal dimensions of the deictic context.

If the utterance contains a personal pronoun, a demonstrative of any kind, a verb in the past, present or future tense, any one of a whole host of expressions such as 'yesterday', 'next year', 'abroad', or a verb such as 'come' or 'bring', the fact that it will express different propositions in different deictic contexts is obvious enough; and this fact is very properly noted and discussed in all contemporary textbooks of semantics.

But the spatio-temporal dimensions of the deictic context may be implicit in an utterance even when they are not made explicit either grammatically or lexically; and this fact is not always mentioned or, if mentioned, given the emphasis it deserves. Let us consider, for example, an utterance such as

(4) *It is raining.*

Unless there are contextual indications to the contrary (e.g., the speaker might be reporting the content of a long-distance telephone conversation), it will refer to the time and place of the act of utterance itself: it will be logically equivalent to (i.e., express the same proposition as)

(5) *It is raining here and now.*

English, of course, like many (but by no means all) languages, grammaticalizes the temporal dimension of the deictic context in its tense-system. If we were to translate *It is raining* into a language without tense (e.g., Chinese or Malay), there would be no explicit indication in the utterance-inscription itself of the fact that it refers to the present, rather than to the past or the future: both "now" and "here" (and not only "here" as in English) would be implicit.

Languages vary enormously with respect to the degree to which they grammaticalize or lexicalize spatio-temporal deixis. It is also important to realize that even languages that are superficially very similar (e.g., English, French, German) may differ considerably in many points of detail. For example, French 'ici' and 'là' do not have exactly the same meaning as 'here' and 'there'; German 'kommen' and 'bringen' do not exactly match 'come' and 'bring'. A good deal of research on spatio-temporal deixis has been carried out recently from several points of view, but so far on only a very limited number of the world's languages. The evidence currently available reinforces the view taken here: that its role in natural languages is all-pervasive. Theoretical semantics and pragmatics have made a start, as we have seen, with the formalization of deixis (or indexicality); but none of the systems developed so far is sufficiently general or sufficiently comprehensive to cope with the range and diversity of deictic information encoded in different natural languages.

Two distinctions must now be drawn. The first is between what I will call **pure** and **impure deixis**: between expressions whose meaning can be accounted for fully in terms of the notion of deixis and expressions whose meaning is partly deictic and partly non-deictic. For example, the first-person and second-person pronouns in English, 'I' and 'you', are purely deictic: they refer to the locutionary agent and the addressee without conveying any additional information about them. Similarly, the demonstrative adjectives and adverbs (in contrast with the demonstrative pronouns), 'this' versus 'that' and 'here' versus 'there', when they are used with spatio-temporal reference, are pure deictics: they identify the referent (an entity or a place) in relation to the location of the locutionary act and its participants. But the third-person singular pronouns – 'he', 'she' and 'it' – are impure deictics: they encode the distinctions of meaning which are traditionally associated with the terms 'masculine', 'feminine' and 'neuter'. Since these distinctions are based upon properties of the referent which have nothing to do with his, her or its spatio-temporal location or role in the locutionary act, they are clearly non-deictic. Impure (i.e., not fully) deictic expressions encode and combine both deictic and non-deictic information.

The terminologically non-standard distinction which I have just drawn between pure and impure deixis – there is no standard terminology – is very important and so far has not received the attention it deserves in semantic theory. Consider, for example,

(6) *What's that?*

in contrast with

(7) *What's that thing?*

The pronoun 'that' in (6), though not in all contexts, is a pure deictic. The noun-phrase 'that thing' in (7), on the other hand, is impurely deictic: it is composed of the purely deictic 'that' (here functioning as an adjective) and the noun 'thing' (which is in implicit contrast with such descriptively non-synonymous words as 'person' and 'animal' and encodes the speaker's categorial, or ontological, assumptions about the entity in question). To be compared with (6) and (7) in this respect are

(8) *Who's that?*

and

(9) *Who's that person?*

Once again, the pronoun 'that' (in (8)) is purely deictic and the noun-phrase 'that person' is impurely deictic. It will be noticed, however, that there is a categorial distinction in the interrogative pronouns 'who' and 'what' in English which encodes the difference between "person" and "thing". It follows that, as whole utterances, (6) and (7) are semantically equivalent; and so, in turn, are (8) and (9).

This apparently simple example illustrates not only the nature of the distinction which I am drawing between pure and impure deixis, but also the gaps and asymmetries which exist in the grammatical and lexical structure of natural languages and the problems which arise, in consequence, when one starts to take seriously the principle of compositionality in relation to the distinction between semantics and pragmatics.

We cannot go into such questions here. But students with a native or near-native command of English will get some sense of the complexity which lies behind or underneath even apparently simple examples such as (6)–(9) if they reflect upon the following facts:

(i)   There is a categorial gap between the interrogative pronouns and adjectives 'who' and 'what', such that one would not normally use either (6) or (8) to query the individual identity of an entity which is presupposed to be neither a person nor a thing, but an animal. There is no such gap between the personal pronouns: animals, like babies, can be referred to either with 'it' or, in the appropriate circumstances, with 'he' or 'she'.

(ii) Whereas (8) is non-ambiguous, (6) has both an individual (or entity-referring) and a sortal (or categorial) meaning: "What (or which) individual [thing] is that?" versus "What kind [of thing] is that?".

(iii) The utterance-inscriptions *What person is that?* and *What is that person?* are non-ambiguous, the former, like (8) and (9), having only an individual meaning and the latter only a sortal meaning; *What animal is that?* is in this respect ambiguous, but *What is that animal?* has only a sortal meaning.

Facts such as these, which any native speaker of English takes into account, for the most part unconsciously, in the production and interpretation of utterances, cannot be discounted by semanticists: they are part and parcel of one's linguistic competence.

Languages vary considerably with respect to the kind of non-deictic information which they combine with deictic information in the meaning of particular expressions. And it is important to note that the non-deictic part of the meaning of impure deictics may be either descriptive (or propositional) or socio-expressive. The latter is very commonly encoded in the meaning of pronouns: notably, and on a scale that is unparalleled in European languages, in Japanese, Korean, Javanese and many languages of South-East Asia. The so-called T/V distinction that is found in many European languages – 'tu' versus 'vous' in French, 'du' versus 'Sie' in German, 'tu' versus 'usted' in Spanish, etc. – which has been much discussed in the sociolinguistic and psycholinguistic literature, exemplifies the phenomenon on a relatively small scale and in respect only of the pronouns used to refer to the addressee. In all languages that have the T/V distinction, the non-deictic meaning that is associated with it is perhaps primarily social, being determined by social role or the relatively stable interpersonal relations that hold between speaker and addressee. But in some languages (e.g., Russian), the switch from the T-pronoun to the V-pronoun, or conversely, can also indicate the speaker's change of mood or attitude. This is but one example, however, of the tendency for social and expressive meaning to merge and to be, at times, inseparable. Hence the composite term 'socio-expressive'.

The second distinction (which is not to be confused with the distinction between pure and impure deixis) is between **primary** and **secondary deixis**. Primary deixis is of the kind that can be accounted for in terms of gestural reference within the framework of the deictic context, as this has been described above. Secondary deixis involves the displacement or reinterpretation of the spatio-temporal dimensions of the primary deictic context. This displacement or reinterpretation can be of several different kinds, and in some cases it can be appropriately called metaphorical. Here, I will give just one example. As primary deictics, the English demonstratives can be analysed in terms of the notion of spatio-temporal proximity to the deictic centre: 'this' and 'here' refer to entities and places that are located in the place that contains the speaker (or to points or periods of time that are located in the period of time that contains the moment of utterance) – this is what 'proximity' means when it is used, technically, in discussions of deixis. Of course, the boundaries of the place or time that contains the deictic centre can be shifted indefinitely far from the centre: 'here' can have the same reference as 'this room' or 'this galaxy', and 'now' the same reference as 'this moment' or 'this year'. There are complications of detail (and arguably the traditional term 'proximity' is misleading). But the principle is clear, in so far as it is relevant to the present example. Now, among the several uses of the demonstratives that can be analysed in terms of the notion of secondary deixis, there is a particular use of 'that' versus 'this' which is recognizably expressive, and whose expressivity can be identified as that of emotional or attitudinal dissociation (or distancing). For example, if speakers are holding something in the hand they will normally use 'this', rather than 'that', to refer to it (by virtue of its spatio-temporal proximity). If they say *What's that?* in such circumstances, their use of 'that' will be indicative of their dislike or aversion: they will be distancing themselves emotionally or attitudinally from whatever they are referring to.

This is but one example of one kind of secondary deixis. I have chosen it because it illustrates fairly clearly (and without the need for long preliminary explanation of unfamiliar linguistic material or additional technical distinctions) what I mean by the displacement or reinterpretation of a primarily spatio-temporal dimension of the deictic context. There is at least an intuitively evident connexion between physical and emotional proximity or remoteness.

As we shall see in section 10.5, secondary deixis of the kind that has been illustrated here is very close to subjective modality. Before turning to that and related topics, however, I should make it clear that the distinction that I have drawn here between primary and secondary deixis rests upon the standard view according to which deixis is to be defined, first and foremost, as a matter of spatio-temporal location in the context of utterance. The standard view of deixis is the one that is presented in all textbooks of linguistics, traditional and non-traditional, and in most specialized monographs and articles that deal with deixis. This is also the view which underpins treatments of deixis, or indexicality, in formal semantics. It is arguable, however, that the standard view of deixis derives from philosophically challengeable, empiricist, assumptions about the primacy of the physical world (and of locutionary, rather than cognitive, deixis). An alternative, and perhaps equally defensible, view is that the egocentricity of the deictic context is of its very nature cognitive in that it is rooted in the subjectivity of consciousness – in the sense in which subjectivity will be explained later (see 10.6). So far this alternative view has had little effect upon what may be regarded as mainstream linguistic semantics. But there are signs that the situation is changing in this respect.

It is impossible to discuss in an introductory book of this kind the full range of phenomena that fall within the scope of the term 'deixis' (as this term is used nowadays by linguists). But something should be said about the grammatical category of tense, which, as I mentioned earlier in this section, is found in many, but not all, natural languages. Tense will be dealt with in the following section.

10.3 THE GRAMMATICAL CATEGORY OF TENSE

The term 'tense' is one of the terms of traditional grammar that is widely used in its traditional sense by those who would claim no special expertise in linguistics. It is of course derived ultimately (via Old French) from the Latin word 'tempus', meaning "time".

One of the points made in the preceding section was that there are many natural languages which do not have tense. Many students, initially, find this difficult to accept. It is important to emphasize, therefore, that the fact that a language does not have tense does not mean that speakers of such languages (e.g., Chinese or Malay) cannot distinguish linguistically between present and past events or between present and future events. What it means is that such distinctions of deictic temporal reference are lexicalized, rather than grammaticalized. It is as if in English there were a grammatically correct tenseless sentence such as

(10) 'It be raining (now/yesterday/tomorrow)',

which could be used in place of

(10a) 'It is raining (now)'
(10b) 'It was raining (yesterday)'
(10c) 'It will be raining (tomorrow)',

to refer to the present, the past and the future as the case may be. In English, temporal deictic reference is both grammaticalized (as tense) and lexicalized (in a wide range of adverbs). Very often, however, the tense is redundant in that the context makes it clear whether the event being referred to took place in the past, is taking place in the present or will take place in the future. There is nothing odd, therefore, about a language without tense. Tenseless languages are not intrinsically less expressive or semantically poorer (provided that they have a sufficiently wide range of lexical expressions) than tensed languages. I should add, in passing, that it is of course possible to define the term 'tense' in such a way that it covers lexical expressions. But the traditional distinction between grammaticalization and lexicalization is not to be jettisoned lightly. The fact that the distinction is not sharp, so that, for example, the modal and auxiliary verbs of English or various classes of particles in English and other languages can be regarded as semi-grammatical (or semi-lexical), rather than as being fully grammatical or fully lexical, is irrelevant. In the standard usage of linguists (if not of philosophers and logicians), tense is by definition a matter of grammaticalization.

It is now generally accepted that tense involves, not just temporal reference as such, but **deictic** temporal reference: i.e., that it involves reference to a point or interval of time which is determined in relation to the moment of utterance. When it is being used with what is generally regarded as its basic meaning, the present tense (in any language that has a present tense) refers either to the moment of utterance itself (the temporal zero-point – the now of the here-and-now – of the deictic context) or, more commonly, to an interval, or period, which contains the moment of utterance. Traditional definitions of 'tense', upon which all standard dictionary definitions are based, are misleading or defective in that they do not make explicit the essentially deictic character of tense. Dictionary definitions of tense are usually defective in other respects also.

First of all, they tend to be typologically restricted in that they make tense a morphological (or, more especially, an inflectional) category of the verb. Now, it is empirically the case that in most morphologically synthetic, or inflecting, languages that do have tense the difference between one tense and another is marked by inflectional variation in the forms of the verb. This is the case, for example, in English: cf. *is/was, sing(s)/sang*. But not all languages are morphologically synthetic; and, even if a language is morphologically synthetic and furthermore has verbal inflection, there is no reason in principle why distinctions of tense must necessarily be expressed in inflectionally variant forms of the verb. They might be expressed by sentential (or clausal) particles which are no more closely associated grammatically with the verb than with any other part of speech in the clause (or sentence). In any case, independently of the way in which tense is expressed in languages of various morphological types, considered from a semantic point of view, tense (in tensed languages) is always a sentential (or clausal) category.

A second defect of most standard dictionary definitions derives from the assumption that all tense-systems in natural languages are three-term systems based on the grammaticalization of past, present and future. Given both the objective and the subjective directionality of time, in nature and as it is experienced by human beings, it is of course possible to define past, present and future universally in relation to the temporal zero-point (locutionary or cognitive) of the deictic context. It does not follow, however, that all languages with tense must necessarily have a past tense, a present tense and a future tense. There are in principle many different ways in which distinctions of deictic temporal reference might be grammaticalized. Most natural-language tense-systems are, in fact, basically dichotomous, rather than trichotomous.

The most common dichotomous tense-distinction in the languages of the world is past versus non-past. Less common by far (if it is properly described as a distinction of tense, rather than mood) is future versus non-future. Equally easy to define (by neglecting the directionality of time) are present versus non-present (cf. the lexicalization of this distinction in the deictic adverbs 'now' and 'then') or either proximate versus non-proximate or remote versus non-remote. None of these, unlike past versus non-past, is found as the basic distinction in a two-term tense-system in any well-studied natural language that has been fully and reliably described in the literature. Some of these distinctions may, however, be combined with others to form more complex two-level (or perhaps multi-level) tense-systems involving both **absolute** and **relative tense**.

The distinction between (so-called) absolute and relative tense that has just been invoked may be illustrated by comparing a simple past tense with what is traditionally called a pluperfect tense. Consider, for example, on the assumption that they are being used in a normal context of utterance (in order to make a straightforward statement of fact), the following two sentences:

(11) 'John's uncle died (last week)'

(12) 'John's uncle had died (the previous week)'.

The form *died* refers absolutely (in this sense of 'absolutely') to past time: i.e., to a point (or interval) of time that precedes the moment of utterance. The pluperfect (or past-perfect) form *had died* refers to a point or period of time that is past in relation to a contextually given time which, in this instance, is itself past in relation to the moment of utterance: in other words, the pluperfect (in certain of its uses) refers to a past-in-the-past. As this example shows, the terms 'absolute' and 'relative' are somewhat misleading, since so-called absolute tense is also relative, in that it is defined in relation to a point of reference. (Alternative terms are 'primary' and 'secondary': but these are in conflict with other relevant senses of 'primary' and 'secondary', including the sense in which I used them in the preceding section.) The difference between absolute and relative tense is perhaps best described as being one of degree. The relativity of so-called absolute tense is of degree 1; that of so-called relative tense is of degree 2.

Complex two-level tense-systems based on a variety of two-term distinctions of deictic temporality are common throughout the languages of the world. For example, there are many languages which grammaticalize the difference between the proximate and the non-proximate past and/or future (or, alternatively, between the remote and the non-remote past and/or future). All of these, in so far as they are indeed based (purely and primarily) on deictic temporality, can be readily formalized in one or other of the systems of tense-logic that have been developed in recent years. For example, using p to stand for the tenseless proposition "John's uncle die" (the reference of 'John's uncle' being fixed in context) and *Past* as the past-tense operator, we can satisfactorily formalize (11) and (12) respectively (provided that *Past* is itself given the appropriate definition):

(11a) *Past* (p)

and

(12a) *Past* (*Past* (p)).

As to the precise interpretation of (11a) and (12a), this will of course depend upon the way in which the tense-operators are defined in the particular system of tense-logic that is used for the formalization.

One way of interpreting tense-operators is by using them as indices to possible worlds (see 7.6). For example, (11a) can be seen as meaning that p is true in (or of) some possible world which is past in relation to (i.e., which has preceded) the world indexed by the cognitive or locutionary temporal zero-point (t_0 = "now"), and (12a) as meaning that p is true in (or of) some world which is past in relation to the world which is past in relation to the world indexed by t_0. Clearly, present-tense and future-tense operators (and, in principle, proximate-tense and remote-tense operators) can be defined in terms of deictic temporality and can be used similarly as indices to possible worlds. It is also clear that, from a theoretical point of view, there is no problem about constructing an indefinitely large number of complex multi-level tense-systems by combining a small number of tense-operators in a variety of ways and by allowing tense-operators to be combined with one another and with other propositional operators (of negation, modality, etc.) without limit.

But (11a) and (12a), interpreted in this way, do not satisfactorily represent the meaning of (11) and (12). As the adverbials in the brackets, 'last week' and 'the previous week', make clear, the simple past tense and the pluperfect tense have definite reference, at least in utterances of these sentences in contexts in which the reference of these adverbials is either explicit or implicit. The adverbials merely make explicit what otherwise would probably be implicit in the context of utterance. In this respect, (11) and (12) are typical of most, if not all, tensed sentences (or clauses) in English and other natural languages. As many grammarians have observed, tense is comparable, semantically, with the definite article or demonstrative pronouns and adverbs. Like them, it is basically deictic and definite, but, also like them, it may be anaphoric or may combine deixis with anaphora. The fact that this is so means that any system of tense-logic which treats natural-language tenses as being comparable with the existential quantifier ("There is some earlier/later world in which p is true") needs to be modified. In fact, it is well recognized by formal semanticists that current systems of tense-logic do not satisfactorily formalize even the purely temporal meaning of the most basic dichotomous or trichotomous tense-distinctions of natural languages.

Having said this, I must however go on to emphasize that this evident inadequacy of formal semantics (in its current state of development) does not imply that linguistic semantics has nothing to learn from recent and continuing attempts to bring the tense-systems of natural languages within its scope. This is a point I have been making throughout this book, and it is a point that I will make once again, with respect to the analysis of mood and modality, in the following section. There is no doubt that the notion of possible worlds, indexed for deictic temporal reference, is a powerful and intuitively attractive notion for the further development of linguistic semantics.

Standard definitions of tense usually fail to make explicit the fact that the reference of natural-language tenses, in contrast with that of the tense-operators of certain systems of tense-logic, is characteristically definite, rather than indefinite. They also fail to make explicit the further fact (although this is more obvious) that it is characteristically **incidental**. For example, in uttering (11) one would not normally be referring to some point of time in the past in order to say something about this point of time. The proposition expressed would not be a proposition about time in the sense that the tenseless proposition "John's uncle die" is a proposition about the contextually determined referent of the expression 'John's uncle'. It is possible in some natural languages, if not all, to refer directly to points or intervals of time and to make statements about them: it is even possible, arguably, to treat the events that occur at a particular time (e.g., the death of John's uncle) as properties of the time referred to. But it is not possible to do this, except in very special contexts, by means of tense. Non-incidental reference to time, whether deictic or non-deictic, involves the use of lexical expressions and, generally, also of more complex grammatical constructions. Looked at from the viewpoint of logical semantics, direct (non-incidental) reference to time (as also to space) requires that the language in which reference is made should be of a higher order than first-order formal languages such as the simple (unextended) predicate calculus. Many, if not all, natural languages are higher-order languages in this sense. But whether they are or are not has nothing to do with their being tensed or tenseless languages.

Tense may now be defined rather more fully than it was earlier in this section as the category which results from the grammaticalization of incidental (definite) deictic temporal reference. I have put 'definite' in brackets, since the question whether definiteness of reference is necessarily, rather than just typically, associated with tense is debatable. In other respects, however, the definition that I have just given is intended to be uncontroversial – uncontroversial, that is to say, as a definition of **pure** and **primary** tense (in the sense of 'pure' and 'primary' established in section 10.2).

The application of the definition in the description of particular languages is far from uncontroversial. As was mentioned at the end of the preceding section, there are those who would argue that the standard view of deixis, and more especially of tense, "derives from philosophically challengeable, empiricist, assumptions about the primacy of the physical world (and of locutionary, rather than cognitive, deixis)". There are alternative, non-standard, theories of tense which do not take temporality as such to be what is grammaticalized by tense. Such theories are to be taken seriously; but, since they are non-standard, they will not be discussed further in this book.

Granted that pure primary tense grammaticalizes temporality, there is still room for argument as to whether what are normally regarded as tenses in particular languages exhibit pure primary tense in all or any of their uses. Even in English, and more strikingly in many other languages, there are uses of the past tense and of the future tense that are modal, rather than temporal (for modality see 10.5). Indeed, as far as what is traditionally classified as the future tense in English is concerned, grammarians are nowadays divided on the issue whether it is basically – and purely and primarily – a tense (in terms of the standard definition of tense). Formally, of course, it differs from what is undoubtedly the major two-term tense-distinction in English: past versus non-past. What I am now calling the past versus non-past distinction is traditionally described as a distinction between past tense and present tense. But the term 'non-past' is formally (and perhaps also semantically) more appropriate. Whereas the past versus non-past distinction (or past-tense versus present-tense distinction) is marked inflectionally, the so-called future tense is formed periphrastically with 'will' and 'shall'. Morphologically and syntactically 'will' and 'shall' are comparable with the modal auxiliaries 'may', 'must' and 'can'. Arguably, they are also comparable with the modal auxiliaries semantically, in many of their uses, including their use as so-called future auxiliaries.

It is probably fair to say that contemporary linguistically sophisticated and authoritative accounts of the tense-system of Modern English are evenly divided on the question whether the so-called future tense (with 'will' and 'shall') is basically temporal or modal. The fact that there is this division of opinion is itself significant: it shows that, as is commonly the case, the question is not readily answered and may not be answerable in the terms in which it is formulated. But whatever view individual linguists take on this issue, they will all agree that there are many uses of the so-called future, in English and many other languages, that are clearly modal rather than temporal. They may also agree that reference to the future, in contrast with reference to the past or the present, is generally, if not always, tinged either with uncertainty or, alternatively, with expectancy and anticipation. Such attitudes are traditionally regarded as modal and, as we shall see in the following section, are frequently expressed by the grammatical category of mood. All that needs to be said in summary is that the distinction between temporality and modality, and therefore the distinction between tense and mood, is not always clear-cut in the description of particular languages and that this is especially so in the case of the so-called future tense. Mood and modality are dealt with in section 10.5. But before that, something must now be said about aspect, which, as we shall see, has not generally been distinguished from tense, until recently, in the grammatical analysis of many languages, including English.

10.4 THE GRAMMATICAL CATEGORY OF ASPECT

The term 'aspect', unlike 'tense', is not one that is widely used by non-specialists. By comparison, not only with 'tense', but also with 'mood' and many terms employed by grammarians, it is of comparatively recent (i.e., nineteenth-century) origin. It is only very recently indeed that it has been used in relation to languages other than Russian and other Slavonic languages. Traditionally, what is identified as aspect (in a wide variety of languages throughout the world) was subsumed under the term 'tense'. For example, the Latin, French or English forms *cantabat, chantait, was singing* were classified as forms of the imperfect; and the imperfect was described as one of a set of tenses which differed from language to language, but included such other so-called tenses as the simple past, the perfect, the present, the future and the future perfect. Many writers of standard reference grammars and many textbooks used in schools still employ those traditional terms and give them their traditional interpretation. In doing so, they contribute to, and perpetuate, what has been correctly described as a long-standing "terminological, and conceptual, confusion of tense and aspect" (Comrie, 1976 : 1).

The definition of aspect is, if anything, even more controversial than is that of tense. But some parts of the difference between tense and aspect are clear enough and nowadays undisputed. The first is that, whereas tense is a deictic category, aspect is not. The second is that what are traditionally referred to as separate tenses of the verb (such as the so-called imperfect of Latin, French or English) typically combine both tense and aspect. For example, *was singing* differs from *is singing* (deictically) in tense, but not in aspect; conversely, *was singing* differs from *sang* in aspect, but not in tense. That the aspectual identity between *was singing* and *is singing* is non-deictic should be intuitively obvious; and it is readily demonstrable, empirically, by paraphrase and other accepted techniques in the semanticist's armoury.

The same point that has just been made about the difference between *was singing* and *sang* can also be made about the difference between *cantabat* and *cantavit* in Latin or *chantait* and *chanta* in standard literary French, even though neither of the Latin or French forms is semantically equivalent to either of the English forms; *cantabat* and *cantavit* (in one of its two meanings), on the one hand, and *chantait* and *chanta*, on the other, differ in aspect, but not in tense. In contrast with English, however, there is no comparable present-tense aspectual distinction: the present-tense forms *cantat* and *chante* cover the whole range that is covered jointly by the aspectually distinct English forms *is singing* and *sings*. This is not untypical. There are many languages (with both tense and aspect) in which there are more past-tense than present-tense (or future tense) aspectual distinctions.

As I have said, the definition of aspect in general linguistic theory is controversial. One point of controversy is whether it is basically a temporal category or not. For simplicity of exposition, I will here assume that it is. In making this assumption, I am tacitly presenting an objectivist, rather than a subjectivist, account of aspect (in a sense of 'subjective' and 'subjectivity' that will be explained in later sections of this chapter). Subjectivist theories of aspect would emphasize the speaker's (or locutionary agent's) point of view, rather than what are assumed to be the objective temporal characteristics of the situation (state of affairs, event, process, etc.) that is described by the propositional content of the sentence that is uttered. Although I will not develop this point here, I should emphasize that, even if it is conceded that aspect is basically an objective, temporal, category, in all languages that have aspect there are many subjective uses of aspectually marked forms. Current accounts of aspect in formal semantics are defective in that they cannot handle such uses.

How, then, is aspect defined as an objective temporal category? It is impossible to give the same kind of answer to this question as to the question what is tense. For what it is worth, a general definition of aspect might run as follows: aspect is the category which results from the grammaticalization of the internal temporal constituency (or contour) of situations (actions, events, states, etc.). Unfortunately, there is no single word of everyday, non-technical English which covers "actions, events, states, etc.". Some authorities now use the word 'situation' (as I am doing) as a technical term for this purpose, making it clear that in this technical sense it denotes, not only states of affairs, but also momentary events, on the one hand, and activities and processes, on the other.

What the general definition of aspect that I have just given makes explicit is the fact that (like tense and mood) it is a grammatical, rather than a lexical, category. There are those who also use the term 'aspect' to refer to what we can agree are comparable aspectual differences among different subclasses of verbs and adjectives: but this broad, non-standard, usage of the term can lead to confusion and should be avoided.

Aspect, then, is a grammatical category. Unlike tense, however, it is intrinsically connected with the verb or, more generally, with the predicate. Whereas the meaning that is expressed by tense is arguably not part of the propositional meaning of sentences, there is no question but that the kind of meaning that is expressed by aspect (granted that aspect is basically an objective, temporal, category) is included within the propositional content of sentences (or clauses). Arguably, 'He is singing' and 'He was singing' have the same propositional content (and in appropriate contexts may express exactly the same proposition): under this analysis of their meaning, tense will be a sentential operator which indexes the proposition (deictically) to the world which it purports to describe. But 'He sings' and 'He is singing' are, not just semantically, but truth-conditionally, non-equivalent in any world they purport to describe. Looked at from a semantic point of view – and more particularly from the viewpoint of formal semantics – the difference between tense and aspect that I have just mentioned, coupled with the fact that the former is deictic and the latter non-deictic, is perhaps the most important difference that there is between these two grammatical categories.

Having emphasized the difference between aspect and tense in general linguistic theory, I must also emphasize the fact that in many natural languages there are verb-forms which are difficult to assign unhesitatingly and exclusively to one of the two categories rather than the other. I must also point out that aspect is far more common throughout the languages of the world than tense is and, as well as being combined with tense in many languages, is found in many other languages that lack tense.

Among the notions that are most commonly invoked in discussions of aspect are: duration, punctuality, completion, frequency and inception. It would be impossible in the space available to consider how these temporal properties are encoded in the grammatical systems of particular languages. For this, reference must be made to works listed in the Bibliography. However, I must mention, and comment briefly upon, the distinction between the so-called **perfective** and the **imperfective** aspects of Russian and other Slavonic languages. I will then use these comments as a peg upon which to hang one or two very general observations about the relation between semantics and ontology.

Although scholars disagree about the details, it is commonly accepted nowadays that the function of what is traditionally referred to as the perfective is to represent situations holistically – i.e., in their temporally unstructured completeness – rather than as being temporally extended or structured. This very general characterization of the function, or meaning, of the perfective is admittedly difficult to understand without lengthy commentary and exemplification. Such explanation and exemplification as may be required is now readily accessible in textbook treatments of aspect. The first point that I wish to make has to do with the term 'completeness', and more particularly with the fuller expression 'temporally unstructured completeness'. 'Completeness' must not be confused with 'completion'. Regrettably, this confusion is all too common and has been propagated in many standard textbooks. What is at issue here can be related to the ontological distinction (which is lexicalized in English though not in all languages) between events, on the one hand, and states, processes, activities, etc., on the other.

Events (in the ideal) are like mathematically defined points in that they have position, but (ideally) no magnitude: they occur (or take place) in time, but they are not temporally extended. It does not make sense to ask of an (ideal) event, defined in this way, as it makes sense to ask of a state or activity: "How long did it last?" or "How long did it take?". Of course, in the physical world, there are no ideal events: a flash of lightning or a rap on the door, and even the Big Bang itself, will have had, objectively, some extension in time (or space-time). But situations which, as a matter of fact, have temporal extension (i.e., duration) can be perceived, subjectively, as instantaneous (i.e., as events). Moreover (to come now to the heart of the matter), situations which are obviously and perceptibly durative can be represented as events: i.e., as situations whose temporal extension or internal temporal structure is irrelevant. The choice between the perfective and the imperfective aspect in Russian (and between variously named, but more or less equivalent, aspects in other languages) is in this sense subjective, even if the aspectual distinction itself is defined in terms of what appear to be the objective notions of temporal extension and instantaneity. Not only the definition of the terms 'perfective' and 'imperfective', but, as I have been emphasizing throughout this section, the semantic analysis of aspect in general is even more controversial than is that of tense. The point that I have just made about subjectivity in the aspectual representation of situations holds independently of the question whether one takes a subjectivist or an objectivist view of the definition of aspect.

It also holds more generally in respect of the relation between semantics and ontology. Throughout this book I have adopted the viewpoint of naive realism, according to which the ontological structure of the world is objectively independent both of perception and cognition and also of language. As we have dealt with particular topics, this view has been gradually elaborated (and to some degree modified); and a more technical metalanguage has been developed in order to formulate with greater precision than is possible in the everyday metalanguage the relations of reference and denotation that hold between language and the world.

According to the viewpoint adopted here, the world contains a number of first-order entities (with first-order properties) which fall into certain ontological categories (or natural kinds); it also contains aggregates of stuff or matter (with first-order properties), portions of which can be individuated, quantified, enumerated – and thus treated linguistically as entities – by using the lexical and grammatical resources of particular natural languages. All natural languages, it may be assumed, provide their users with the means of referring to first-order entities and expressing propositions which describe them in terms of their (first-order) properties, actual or ascribed, essential or contingent: such languages have the expressive power of first-order formal languages.

Whether all natural languages have the greater expressive power of various kinds of higher-order formal languages is a more controversial, and as yet an empirically unresolved, question. But some natural languages certainly do; and English, which, duly extended and regimented, we are currently using as our metalanguage, is one of them. It enables its users to reify, or hypostatize, the properties of first-order entities, the relations that obtain among them, and the processes, activities, and states of affairs (and other kinds of situations) in which they are involved. The lexical resources which English provides for this purpose include the second-order count nouns that I have employed in the preceding sentence, and throughout this section ('property', 'relation', 'process', 'situation', etc.), together with the appropriate verbs ('occur', 'take place', 'endure', etc.) and adjectives ('instantaneous', 'static'/'dynamic', 'durative', etc.), which enables us to treat them metalinguistically as entities and to categorize them ontologically.

The grammatical resources that English provides for this purpose include the quantifiers, determiners and classifiers that are used primarily for first-order reference: their use, secondarily, for second-order reference (with expressions such as 'the situation in which John found himself', 'the initial phase of this continuing process', etc.) is what justifies the employment, in this context, of the traditional philosophical terms 'reification' and 'hypostatization'. This kind of reification, or hypostatization, is consonant with, and may well be connected historically with, the development of particular languages for abstract philosophical or scientific discourse.

Independently, however, of the development of a special second-order vocabulary and the associated grammatical resources for this purpose in particular languages, there is another, related, phenomenon which is found in very many languages throughout the world and should be mentioned in this connexion. This is the modelling of the vocabulary and grammar of temporal reference and denotation on that of spatial reference and denotation. For example, in many languages the case-system or set of prepositions (or postpositions) will use the same case or preposition in the formation of both temporal and spatial expressions; and there is often, if not always, justification for saying that the temporal meaning has derived historically from the earlier spatial meaning. So widespread is this phenomenon that it has given rise to a general approach to the analysis of natural languages known as **localism**. The localist approach to case, as it is commonly explained, holds that temporal expressions are intrinsically more abstract than spatial expressions and that the modelling of temporal reference and denotation on spatial reference and denotation is part of the more general process of modelling the abstract upon the concrete.

Not surprisingly, there are localist theories of tense and aspect, which have been developed with reference to a wide range of languages. They are now given more prominence in readily accessible textbooks and monographs written in English than was the case until recently; and I will not go into them here. What I will do is emphasize the fact that, just as tense is semantically comparable with demonstratives and determiners, so aspect is semantically comparable with classifiers and quantifiers, and also with such properties as countability, which distinguishes first-order entities from first-order aggregates of stuff or matter. This parallelism is well recognized in traditional accounts of aspect. To make the point baldly: as space is to first-order (extensional) entities, so time is to second-order (extensional) entities, situations. In other words, situations are located in time, just as physical objects are located in space. At this level of generality, what I have just said may sound high-falutin and irrelevantly philosophical. Its relevance and specificity will be evident to anyone who looks at any of the detailed accounts of aspect in general or of the aspectual systems that are now available.

10.5 MODALITY, MODAL EXPRESSIONS AND MOOD

There is an obvious etymological connexion between the terms 'modality', 'modal' and 'mood'. Though obvious, it is historically quite complex; and all three terms have been given a variety of conflicting interpretations by linguists and logicians, both traditionally and in more recent work. Students should be aware that the term 'mood', in particular, has long been used in different, though ultimately related, senses by linguists and logicians. Since linguistic semantics has been strongly influenced by logical semantics in recent years, 'mood' is now frequently employed by linguists in the logician's sense of the word; and this can cause confusion. In this section, and throughout this book, I am using it solely and consistently in the sense in which it is used in traditional grammar: i.e., with reference to such grammatical categories as 'indicative', 'subjunctive' and 'imperative'. As was noted in Chapter 6, many if not all the functions of mood are non-propositional and beyond the scope of truth-conditional semantics; the grammatical categories of mood and tense are interdependent in all natural languages that have both categories; and mood is more widespread than tense throughout the languages of the world. Before taking up these points, I must say something about modality.

The only kind of **modality** recognized in traditional modal logic is that which has to do with the notions of necessity and possibility in so far as they relate to the truth (and falsity) of propositions: **aletheutic**, or **alethic**, **modality**. (Both 'aletheutic' and 'alethic' come, indirectly, from the Greek word for truth: 'aletheutic' is etymologically preferable, but 'alethic' is now widely used in the literature.) We have already looked at the question of the necessary truth and falsity of propositions on several occasions, and with particular reference to entailment and analyticity in Chapter 4. In section 6.5, we noted that the modal operators N and M (or $\Box$ and $\Diamond$), like the operator of negation in the propositional calculus, are truth-functional.

It may now be added that aletheutic necessity and possibility are interdefinable under negation: they are inverse opposites or (to use the more technical terminology of mathematical logic) **duals**. To adapt one of the examples used in section 6.5:

(13) "Necessarily, the sky is blue"

is logically equivalent to

(14) "It is not possible that the sky is not blue"

(i.e., $(Np = {\sim}M{\sim}p)$, or $(\Box p = {\sim}\Diamond{\sim}p)$);
and

(15) "Possibly, the sky is blue"

is logically equivalent to

(16) "It is not necessarily the case that the sky is not blue"

(i.e., $(Mp = {\sim}N{\sim}p)$ or $(\Diamond p = {\sim}\Box{\sim}p)$).
The question whether other kinds of necessity and possibility have the same logical properties with respect to negation as aletheutic necessity and possibility is somewhat more controversial; and we shall come back to it presently.

The fact that aletheutic necessity and possibility are duals means that in this respect they are like the universal and existensional quantifiers $((x)$or, alternatively, $(\forall x)$: "all"; and (Ex) or

($\exists x$): "some") as these are standardly defined by logicians: $(x) fx \equiv \sim ((Ex)\sim fx)$, i.e. "For all x, x has the property f" is equivalent to "It is not the case that there is some x such that (i.e., there is no x such that) x does not have the property f". This parallelism between quantification and modality is by no means fortuitous. In traditional logic (based on a bipartite analysis of propositions into subject and predicate), modality was commonly described as quantification of the predicate. And, as we have seen, in some systems of modern intensional logic (including the one which underpins Montague semantics) necessity is defined (following Leibniz) in terms of truth in all possible worlds, possibility in terms of truth in some (i.e., at least one) possible world. Given that necessity and possibility are interdefinable, the question arises which, if either, should be regarded as being more basic than the other. Generally speaking, logicians take aletheutic modality to be necessity-based, rather than possibility-based. But from a purely formal point of view this is a matter of arbitrary decision.

Aletheutic modality, then, like propositional negation, is by definition truth-functional. But what about modality in the everyday use of natural languages? Let us take another of the examples used in section 6.5: the sentence

(17) 'He may not come'.

Now, there is no doubt that this sentence can be used to assert a modalized negative proposition (with either external or internal negation: either $\sim Np$ or $M\sim p$). In this case both the negative particle *not* and the modal verb 'may' are construed as contributing to the propositional content of the sentence.

But with this particular sentence (when it is uttered in most everyday contexts), the modality is more likely to be either epistemic or deontic than aletheutic. (The terms 'epistemic' and 'deontic' were explained in section 8.4. As we shall see, they are being used here in essentially the same sense.) Both kinds of modality may be either objective or subjective. If our sample sentence is given an **objective epistemic** interpretation, its propositional content will be

(18) "Relative to what is known, it is possible that he will not come";

if it is given an **objective deontic** interpretation, its propositional content will be

(19) "It is not permitted that he come".

Drawing intuitively and informally upon the notion of possible worlds (and neglecting the complications of tense) we can paraphrase (18) and (19), respectively, as:

(18a) "There is some epistemically possible world in which he comes"
(19a) "There is some deontically possible world in which he comes".

In both cases, it will be noted, the modality is represented as something that holds, as a matter of fact, in some epistemic or deontic world which is external to whoever utters the sentence on particular occasions of utterance. This is what I mean by objective (or propositional) modality. Both epistemic and deontic modality are always construed objectively in standard modal logic and in formal semantics.

However, independently of whether (17) is construed epistemically or deontically, the modality associated with 'may' can be **subjective**, rather than objective: that is to say, in uttering this sentence, speakers (more generally, locutionary agents) may be expressing either their own beliefs and attitudes or their own will and authority, rather than reporting, as neutral observers, the existence of this or that state of affairs. Subjective modality is much more common than objective modality in most everyday uses of language; and objective epistemic modality, in particular, is very rare. If (17) is uttered with subjective epistemic modality, it means something like

(20) "I-think-it-possible that he will not come"

(where the hyphenated "I-think-it-possible" is to be taken as a unit); if it is uttered with subjective deontic modality, it means something like "I forbid him to come".

When I used the terms 'epistemic' and 'deontic' earlier, in connexion with the notion of illocutionary commitment, I talked as if the only options open to the locutionary agent were those of expressing full commitment and withholding full commitment. We now see that this is not so. As far as making statements is concerned, there are various ways in which locutionary agents can qualify their epistemic commitment. They can indicate that their evidence – their **epistemic warrant** or **epistemic authority** – for what they assert is less good than it might be; that their commitment is tentative, provisional or conditional, rather than absolute; and so on. Subjective epistemic modality is nothing other than this: a locutionary agent's qualification of his or her epistemic commitment. All natural spoken languages provide their users with prosodic resources – stress and intonation – with which to express the several distinguishable kinds of qualified epistemic commitment. Some, but by no means all, grammaticalize them in the category of mood; and some languages, such as English, lexicalize or semi-lexicalize them by means of modal verbs ('may', 'must', etc.), modal adjectives ('possible', etc.), modal adverbs ('possibly', etc.) and modal particles ('perhaps', etc.).

Assertion, in the technical sense of the term, implies full unqualified epistemic commitment. Relatively few of our everyday statements have this neutral, dispassionate, totally non-subjective character. English, however, does allow us to make statements which can be reasonably classified as assertions. It also allows us, as we have seen, to objectify both epistemic and deontic modality – **propositionalizing** the content of modal verbs or adverbs and bringing this within the scope of the illocutionary agent's unqualified "I-say-so". But English is certainly not typical of the world's languages in this respect. It may well be true, as we assumed in Chapter 8, that all languages enable their users to make statements of one kind or another; it is not the case that all natural languages provide their users with the means of making modally unqualified assertions. Mood is by definition the category which results from the grammaticalization of modality (epistemic, deontic, or of whatever kind). In terms of this definition, it is a well-established fact that among the languages of the world there are many that have several non-indicative moods, for different kinds of epistemic modality, but do not have an indicative mood: i.e., they do not have what is traditionally regarded, both by linguists and logicians, as the semantically neutral (or unmarked) mood. It is arguable that this traditional view of what constitutes semantic neutrality is linguistically and culturally prejudiced. At the very least, the fact that there are languages with various non-indicative declarative sentences, but without indicative declarative sentences, reinforces the point made in section 6.6 about the necessity of distinguishing 'declarative' from 'indicative', and more generally of distinguishing sentence-type (or clause-type) from mood.

Let us now take up briefly the relation between mood and tense. Tense, as we saw in the preceding section, is the category which, in such languages as have tense, results from the grammaticalization of (incidental) deictic temporal reference. At first sight, it might appear that, since there is no obvious connexion between temporal reference and modality, tense and mood are quite distinct grammatical categories. However, as was noted in section 6.6 and mentioned again at the beginning of the present section, in all languages that have both tense and mood, the two categories are, to a greater or less degree, interdependent. In fact, it is often difficult to draw a sharp distinction, from a semantic or pragmatic point of view, between tense and mood. Even in English, where tense can be identified without much difficulty as a deictic category, there are uses of what are traditionally described as the past, present and future tenses that have more to do with the expression of subjective modality than with primary deixis. For example, in saying

(21) *That will be the postman,*

speakers are more likely to be making an epistemically qualified statement about the present than an unqualified assertion about the future; in saying

(22) *I wanted to ask you whether you needed the car today,*

they are more likely to be making a tentative or hesitant request than to be describing some past state of consciousness. Some of these modal uses of the tenses could perhaps be accounted for in terms of the notion of secondary deixis. But, as I mentioned in section 10.2, secondary deixis and subjective modality are often indistinguishable. Although I will not go into the question in this book, I should mention at this point that there are certain, untraditional and so far non-standard, but empirically well supported, theories of tense according to which, looked at from a more general point of view, tense itself can be seen as being primarily a matter of modality. For anyone who does take this view, the facts (i) that mood is more common than tense throughout the languages of the world and (ii) that both categories are in all languages more or less interdependent are only to be expected. Whatever view we take of the relations between tense and mood and between deictic temporal reference and modality, the fact that there are these interdependencies and difficulties of demarcation in practice, casts further doubt upon the applicability of standard systems of tense-logic to the analysis of the semantic structure of all natural languages.

There has been an enormous amount of work done in the last few years, from various points of view, on the analysis of modality in various languages. Among the general questions that have been addressed, one has been mentioned earlier in this section: given the interdefinability, or duality, of the modal notions of necessity and possibility in formal semantics, which, if either, is more basic than the other in natural languages (and in what sense of 'basic')? Another very similar question is the following: given that there is a distinction to be drawn between objective and subjective modality, what is the relation between them and which, if either, is prior to, or more basic than, the other in natural languages? So far, there is no generally accepted answer to either of these questions. This is hardly surprising. First of all, before they can be properly addressed, it must be established what is meant by 'basic'; and, as we noted in our discussion of lexical meaning and the role that the empiricist notion of ostensive definition has played in logical semantics, there are at least two senses of 'basic' which might be relevant and which cannot

be assumed to coincide (see 3.2). Second, scholars who are interested in such questions from a theoretical point of view tend to
be philosophically, or metatheoretically, prejudiced in favour
of one theory of linguistic semantics rather than another.

What can be said, however, is the following. There is a certain
amount of empirical evidence to suggest that, as far as the grammaticalization and lexicalization of modality in some, if not
all, natural languages is concerned, epistemic modality is
possibility-based, whereas deontic modality is necessity-based.
There is perhaps stronger empirical evidence to support the
view that in many, if not all, natural languages subjective modality, both epistemic and deontic, is diachronically prior to
objective modality and that, as has been mentioned earlier, it
is much more commonly grammaticalized and lexicalized
throughout the languages of the world.

It must also be noted, however, that (i) it is not always easy to
distinguish epistemic modality synchronically from deontic
modality and (ii) in English many expressions that were primarily deontic in earlier stages of the language are now used also in
epistemically modalized utterances (cf. 'must' and now 'have
(to)' in such utterances as *You must / have to be joking*). The fact
that epistemic and deontic modality merge with one another
diachronically and are often indistinguishable synchronically
confirms the view, now widely held by linguists as well as by
logicians, that they are rightly classified under the same term
'modality'.

But the most important conclusion to be drawn from recent
investigations of the grammaticalization and lexicalization of
modality in several languages is that objective (or propositional)
aletheutic modality, as this is formalized in standard modal
logic, should not be taken as basic – in any relevant sense of
'basic' – in the semantic analysis of natural languages. Subjective modality, like deixis (or, more generally, reference) is a
part of utterance-meaning. But, also like deixis, it is encoded in
the grammatical and lexical structure of most, if not all, natural
languages and, in so far as it is encoded, or conventionalized, in
language-systems, it is just as much part of sentence-meaning as
is truth-conditionally explicable objective modality, which, as I

have been emphasizing here, is less commonly encoded in natural languages and may well be inexpressible in some.

A further point to be made about natural-language modality is that, although it has here been explicated in terms of necessity and possibility, many linguists have felt that this does violence to the facts: that, for epistemic modality at least, a three-term system is required. This view is reflected in many traditional treatments, which deal with subjective epistemic modality in terms of certainty, probability (or likelihood) and possibility.

A similar point can be made about natural-language quantification. As was mentioned earlier, there is a well-known parallelism between modality and quantification: between necessity and universal quantification and between possibility and existential quantification. (As $\mathcal{N}$ and $M - \square$ and $\diamond$ — are duals, interdefinable under negation, so also are (x) and (Ex).) But in many natural languages, including English, the so-called quantifier system is not very satisfactorily handled in this way. In addition to 'all' and 'some', there are also such expressions as 'many', 'several', etc.: and 'some', in most everyday contexts, is not obviously related to the existential quantifier ("at least one").

Three kinds of modality have been discussed in this section: aletheutic, epistemic and deontic. Other kinds of modality (bouleutic, dynamic, etc.) have also been recognized in recent years by both linguists and logicians; and considerable progress has been made in analysing their diachronic and synchronic connexions. So far there is no consensus among either linguists or logicians on the establishment of a comprehensive framework which is both theoretically coherent and empirically satisfactory. At the same time it must be emphasized that the accounts of modality (and mood) given in up-to-date reference grammars of English (and of a limited number of other languages) has been immeasurably improved by the attempt to apply to the description of natural languages one or other of the standard systems of modal logic which were developed initially to handle aletheutic modality.

10.6 SUBJECTIVITY AND LOCUTIONARY AGENCY

In several sections of this chapter, especially in the preceding section on modality and mood, I have invoked the notion of subjectivity. I will now explain what is meant by the term 'subjective' in this context. This is all the more important in that the word 'subjective' tends to be given an irrelevantly pejorative interpretation in everyday English. It is also the case that the notion of subjectivity itself has not figured as prominently as it should have done, until recently, in works on linguistic semantics written in English.

Indeed, it is probably true to say that the majority of such works – and especially those which adopt, or are strongly influenced by, the viewpoint of formal semantics – are seriously flawed, both theoretically and empirically, by their failure to give due weight to the phenomenon of subjectivity. This failure is perhaps attributable to the empiricist tradition, which still bears heavily on mainstream British and American philosophy, psychology, sociology and, to a lesser extent, linguistics. The reassertion of so-called Cartesian rationalism, by Chomsky and others, over the last thirty years has done little to remedy the defects of empiricism in this respect. For British empiricism and Cartesian rationalism (in the form in which it has been taken over and reinterpreted by Chomsky) both share the intellectualist – and objectivist – prejudice that language is essentially an instrument for the expression of propositional thought. This prejudice is evident in a large number of influential works, which, though they might differ considerably on a wide variety of issues, are at one in giving no attention at all to the nonpropositional component of languages or in playing down its importance. The same intellectualist and objectivist prejudice is evident, as we have seen, in standard logical treatments of modality, in which objectivism is closely connected with propositionalization. But, as I have emphasized in other sections of this chapter, objectivism is also to be found in standard treatments of deixis (including tense), aspect, and other phenomena.

But what exactly is meant by 'subjectivity' (in the present context)? I have just mentioned Cartesian rationalism. What is now at issue is one of two historically connected, but logically separable, aspects of what is commonly referred to as Cartesian, or post-Cartesian, dualism. One of these is the doctrine of metaphysical dualism: the doctrine that there are two radically different kinds of reality, matter and mind. This is of no direct concern to us here. The other is the dualism of subject and object: in cognition, feeling and perception, on the one hand, and in action or agency, on the other. (It is this latter dualism, of course, which explains, ultimately, the grammatical opposition both of 'subject' and 'object' and also of 'active' and 'passive'.) Although metaphysical dualism is of no direct concern to us here, its historical connexion with subject–object dualism is worth noting. For it is this historical connexion, no doubt, which accounts for the pejorative associations of the term 'subjective'. 'Subjectivity' in the empiricist tradition was associated with a certain kind of unscientific and untestable mentalism; 'objectivity', with a sturdy nineteenth-century (now outmoded) scientific materialism. Without going further into this question, let me say that 'subjectivity', as the term is being used here, denotes the property (or set of properties) of being either a subject of consciousness (i.e., of cognition, feeling and perception) or a subject of action (an agent). It denotes the property of being what Descartes himself called a "thinking entity" (in Latin, 'res cogitans') and identified, as others have done, with the self or the ego. In saying this, I am not however committing myself to a sharply dualistic, Cartesian or post-Cartesian, opposition of the subject and object of cognition.

So much then for the general notion of subjectivity. What is of concern to the linguist is, more specifically, **locutionary subjectivity**: the subjectivity of utterance. If we accept uncritically for the moment the post-Cartesian (and post-Kantian) distinction of the (internal) subjective ego, or self, and the (external) objective non-ego, or non-self, we can say of locutionary subjectivity that it is the locutionary agent's (the speaker's or writer's, the utterer's) expression of himself or herself in the act of utterance: locutionary subjectivity is, quite simply, self-expression in the use of language.

Defined like this the notion of locutionary subjectivity might seem to be wholly uncontroversial, and neither novel nor especially interesting. After all, self-expression is something we talk about quite freely, non-technically, in everyday discourse. We say, for example, that X expresses herself well or that Y has difficulty in expressing himself; and we acknowledge that a capacity for self-expression is one of the dimensions of fluency in the use of language and varies from one speaker (or writer) to another. When we come to examine the notion of locutionary subjectivity from the viewpoint of modern linguistic theory, however, we soon discover that it is far from being as straightforward as it might appear to be at first sight.

As we have noted above, the standard, post-Cartesian, view of the self or the ego is that of a thinking being, conscious of itself as thinking, as it is also conscious of itself as having certain beliefs, attitudes and emotions; a being which is distinct from the mental activity of which it is the subject, or agent, and from the thoughts, beliefs, attitudes and emotions, of which it is the seat or locus. It has been responsibly argued, however, by many philosophers and psychologists that no such distinction can be drawn between the subject and the object of consciousness: more particularly, that Descartes, in his famous analysis of the (composite) proposition expressed in Latin in the sentence 'Cogito, ergo sum' (usually translated into English, as 'I think, therefore I am', but better translated in context with the aspectually different sentence 'I am thinking, therefore I am') was misled by the bipartite subject–predicate structure of Latin (and other Indo-European languages, including French, English, German, etc.) when he separated the ego from its cogitation. Linguists do not need to take a view on the validity of the philosophical and psychological arguments (although they can contribute relevant evidence based on the grammatical and semantic analysis of particular natural languages). But they must not accept uncritically what I am referring to as the standard, post-Cartesian, dualist view of the self, or the ego, as the subject of consciousness and activity.

Still less should they accept without question the view which underpins the currently dominant intellectualist and objectivist approach to formal semantics: the view which represents the self, implicitly if not always explicitly, as the reasoning faculty operating dispassionately upon the propositions stored in the mind (or the mind/brain) or brought to it for judgement from observation of the (objective) external world. Throughout this book, and especially in Part 4, I have been stressing the importance of the non-propositional aspect of language. The inadequacy of truth-conditional semantics as a total theory, not only of utterance-meaning, but also of sentence-meaning, derives ultimately from its restriction to propositional content and its inability to handle the phenomenon of subjectivity. Self-expression cannot be reduced to the expression of propositional knowledge and beliefs.

A second point to be made here is that the self which the locutionary agent expresses is the product of the social and interpersonal roles that he or she has played in the past, and it manifests itself, in a socially identifiable way, in the role that he or she is playing in the context of utterance. As I pointed out in the discussion of Austin's theory of speech acts in Chapter 8, the central concepts of epistemic and deontic authority have a social basis. But they are vested by society in particular individuals; they are part of the self that is expressed whenever the locutionary agent utters a sentence in some socially appropriate context.

As there are those who have argued that there is no sharp distinction to be drawn between the self that is expressed in language and the expression of that self, so there are those, especially anthropologists and social psychologists, who have argued that there is no single, unitary, self which is constant across all experience and, more especially, across all encounters with others, but rather a set of selves (not one persona, but a set of personae), each of which is the product of past encounters with others, including, crucially, past dialogic, or interlocutionary, encounters. Once again, there is no need for linguists to take a view on this issue. Even if there is such a thing as a monadic and unitary, Cartesian, self, ontologically independent of, and unaffected by, the language which it uses for self-expression, this self cannot but express itself (or be expressed) linguistically in terms of the grammatical categories and semantic distinctions that are made available to it by the language it uses for self-expression. It is generally accepted nowadays by linguists of all theoretical persuasions that there is, in reality, no such thing as a homogeneous, stylistically and socio-expressively undifferentiated, language-system. It follows that, for the linguist, philosophical and psychological arguments about the nature of the self and personal identity are of secondary importance. Subjectivity in so far as it is manifest in language – locutionary subjectivity – is situationally and stylistically differentiated. So too, demonstrably, is the degree of subjectivity that is expressed in different styles and in different situations.

We now come to another point. Earlier in this section, I defined locutionary subjectivity as self-expression in the use of language. I have now been talking about locutionary subjectivity as the subjectivity of utterance (and as combining the subjectivity of consciousness and the subjectivity of agency). I have also said that locutionary subjectivity is manifest, or expressed, in language. It is quite possible, of course, for the use of language – the activity of utterance – to be imbued or invested with subjectivity, and yet for this subjectivity not to be manifest in language: i.e., in the utterance-inscriptions (or utterance-signals) that are the products of the activity of utterance. It is also possible for locutionary subjectivity to be manifest in language in one sense, but not the other, of the ambiguous (and syntactically ambivalent) English word 'language': that is to say, it is possible for it to be expressed (for example, prosodically or paralinguistically in speech) without being encoded in the grammatical or lexical structure of the language-system.

For example, as we saw in section 10.5, it is arguable (though some might deny this) that a sentence such as

(23) 'He may not come'

is wholly devoid of subjectivity. In speech, however, it can be uttered with various kinds of prosodic and paralinguistic modulation by means of which the speaker – the locutionary agent – can, and normally will, invest the product of the act of utterance with various kinds, and different degrees, of subjectivity. In particular, it can be uttered as a more or less qualified assertion either of the fact that there is, objectively, a possibility that the referent of 'he' will come or of the fact that permission has been granted (by some deontic source external to the locutionary agent) for the referent of 'he' to come. In speech, the prosodic contour will usually make clear to the addressee that the utterance is to be interpreted as a subjectively qualified assertion; and, coupled with associated vocal and non-vocal paralinguistic information, it may also reveal something of the locutionary agent's attitude to what is being asserted as a fact or the nature or degree of the locutionary agent's epistemic warrant for asserting it as a fact. The distinction that we have drawn, in this book, between sentence-meaning and utterance-meaning enables us to make the point that has just been made in the way that it has been made. The point itself, however, holds independently of whether the theoretical distinction between sentences and utterances is drawn in the same terms, or at the same point, as it has been drawn here.

As I said at the beginning of this section, the subjectivity of utterance has not been much discussed, until recently, in the terms in which I have explained it here, in work on linguistic semantics written in English. More attention has been devoted to it by French and German scholars, possibly because the notion of subjectivity itself plays a more important part in the Continental philosophical tradition. However that may be, as I have been arguing in several sections of this book, there is much in the structure of English and perhaps all natural languages that cannot be explained without appealing to it. It is also arguable – though this is more debatable and I will not argue the point here – that, for historical and ultimately social reasons, some languages, including English, are less deeply imbued with subjectivity than others. It suffices to note that, as was mentioned in section 6.6 and again in section 10.5, there are many natural languages in which there are no indicative declarative sentences: i.e., no sentences with which it is possible to make subjectively unqualified (or unmodulated) assertions.

At the end of Chapter 7, I mentioned the notion of accessibility between possible worlds. I said that speakers must necessarily refer to the world that they are describing from the viewpoint of the world that they are in. I might just as well have put it the other way round, saying that speakers must refer to the actual or non-actual world that they are describing from the viewpoint of the world that is in them. But, whichever way these relations of accessibility are formulated, it will now be clear that they can be explicated in terms of the account that has been given in this chapter of indexicality and subjective epistemic modality.

There is no reason to believe that these notions are beyond the scope of formalization. Indeed, my reference to the notion of accessibility, at the end of Chapter 7 and again at this point, is intended to suggest that model-theoretic, or indexical, semantics is not necessarily restricted to the truth-conditional part of linguistic meaning. It could doubtless be extended to cover everything that has been discussed in this chapter, and more especially in this section, as part of the subjectivity of utterance. Of course, there are those who might prefer to refer to any such extension as pragmatics, rather than semantics. But that is neither here nor there. As we have seen on several occasions, there are many different ways of drawing such terminological distinctions. The view that we have taken throughout this book is that linguistic semantics should cover, in principle, (all and only) such meaning as is encoded in the lexical and grammatical structure of particular natural languages, regardless of whether it is truth-conditionally analysable or not.

Suggestions for further reading

As I said in the Preface, I expect this book to be read in conjunction with other introductions to linguistic semantics (and pragmatics) and with a selection of textbooks, monographs and articles which deal with the particular topics in greater detail. Many of these other works will adopt a different theoretical stance from mine. They may also use different terminological and notational conventions. Throughout this book, but especially in Chapter 1, I have tried to give readers enough guidance for them to be able to move from one theoretical framework to another without difficulty. Most of the books mentioned below have good bibliographies, which will usefully supplement the Bibliography given below.

Chapter 5 of Lyons (1981) contains a simplified exposition of linguistic semantics that is theoretically and terminologically compatible with the one given in this book: it also provides enough information about other branches of linguistics as is necessary for understanding any references made to them in the book. Readers with no previous background in linguistic semantics will find that Leech (1974), Nilsen and Nilsen (1975), Hurford and Heasley (1983) and Palmer (1981) provide them with a very good starting point. Two more recent introductory works, which take a radically different view from mine on some of the issues dealt with in this book, are Frawley (1992) and Hofmann (1993): the former gives examples from a wide range of languages and includes a number of discussion questions for each chapter; the latter contains a set of well-chosen exercises (with answers at the end of the book). Allan (1986) covers much the same ground as I do here, but in greater detail and with far more examples. Lyons (1977), though superseded by more recent works for particular topics, is still the most comprehensive general work.

For general surveys of the field and its several subfields and an up-to-date account of work on particular topics, not only in linguistic semantics (and pragmatics), but on other relevant branches of linguistics, Asher (1994) is invaluable. Also to be consulted from this point of view are Bright (1992), Collinge (1990) and Newmeyer (1988a, b, c, d).

On lexical semantics, the best textbook to use in conjunction with this volume is Cruse (1986): it generally uses the same terminology, goes into most of the topics in much greater detail, and has plenty of examples. Ullmann (1962) is still useful, especially for its account of early-twentieth-century work and its exposition of structuralism and the adoption of the Saussurean principle of the priority of the synchronic over the diachronic. Baldinger (1980) develops, in greater detail than Ullmann (1962), the post-Saussurean semiotic approach to semantics. Aitchison (1987) is an excellent general introduction to modern lexical semantics and deals with most of the topics discussed in Part 2 of this book with a wealth of well chosen examples: it is especially to be recommended for its account of recent psycholinguistic work. A very readable, deliberately non-technical and, at times, provocative, introduction to lexical semantics at an elementary level is Hudson (1995). For an up-to-date account of various modern approaches to lexical semantics, see Lehrer and Kittay (1992).

In addition to the works listed above: for componential analysis, see Nida (1975), Dowty (1979); for semantic fields, see Lehrer (1974); for prototype semantics, see Lakoff (1987), Taylor (1989). For influential modern versions of the cognitive approach to lexical semantics, see Jackendoff (1983, 1990) and Wierzbicka (1980, 1992). For the acquisition of lexical meaning by children, see Clark (1993).

There are no textbooks that deal exclusively with sentence-semantics (or grammatical semantics) as such. My own treatment of sentence-semantics in Part 2 is intended to introduce students, informally, to modern formal semantics: it can be supplemented with Cann (1993) and Chierchia and McConnell-Ginet (1990). For semantics within the framework of Chomskyan generative grammar of the classical (Chomsky, 1965) and immediately post-classical period, which prepared the way for the adoption by linguists of the ideas of formal semantics, see Fodor (1977); and for generative grammar as such see Lyons (1991a) and, for a more technical treatment, Radford (1988). For Montague's system of formal semantics, see Montague (1974), with its important 'Introduction' by Thomason. For standard modal logic, see the now classic Hughes and Cresswell (1968). For the basic concepts of formal logic (set theory, propositional calculus, predicate calculus, etc.) see Allwood *et al.* (1977).

For the grammatical structure of English, I have generally followed Huddleston (1984). But most of the terms I use are also compatible with those employed by what is currently the most comprehensive and authoritative reference grammar of English, Quirk *et al.* (1985).

For noun classes and categorization, see Craig (1986). For tense and aspect, see Comrie (1985, 1976), Dahl (1985). For mood (and modality): Palmer (1986), Coates (1983), R. Matthews (1991). On negation, see Horn (1989).

On morphology as the interface between grammar and lexical semantics, in English and more generally, see P.H. Matthews (1992), Bybee (1985), Lipka (1990). On the complementary notions of grammaticalization and lexicalization, see Hopper and Traugott (1993).

On the prosodic structure of spoken English, see Brown (1990), Crystal (1976).

For the topics dealt with in Part 4, under the rubric of utterance-meaning (or pragmatics), see, generally, Leech (1983), Levinson (1983), Horn (1988). More specifically: for illocutionary force, see Austin (1962/1975), Searle (1969, 1979), Katz (1972), Recanati (1987); for conversational and conventional implicatures, see Grice (1989); for relevance theory and neo-Gricean pragmatics, see Sperber and Wilson (1986), Smith (1982), Blakemore (1987), Huang (1994), Levinson (forthcoming). For deixis, see Jarvella and Klein (1982); for anaphora, see Cornish (1986), Reinhart (1983), Huang (1994); for metaphor in relation to semantics (and pragmatics), see Lakoff and Johnson (1980), Ortony (1979).

For the semantics of text and discourse (regarded in this book as an extension of linguistic semantics based on the analysis of the meaning of utterances), see Brown and Yule (1983), Halliday and Hassan (1976), Beaugrande and Dressler (1981), Seuren (1985).

For the philosophical background, reference may be made, in most cases selectively, to some or all of the following: Alston (1964), Lehrer and Lehrer (1970), Olshewsky (1969), Parkinson (1968), Potts (1994), Rorty (1967), Strawson (1971b), Zabeeh *et al.* (1974). Many of the classic papers (by Davidson, Frege, Grice, Kripke, Tarski, and others) in formal philosophical semantics are included in Martinich (1985).

Only a small number of the works listed in the Bibliography have been mentioned explicitly in these 'Suggestions for further reading'. This does not mean that the others are less important or less highly recommended. What they deal with is usually evident from their titles; and students are advised to consult at least some of them in order to acquire a sufficiently broad and balanced knowledge of the field.

Bibliography

The Bibliography lists all the works to which reference is made in the text, together with those mentioned in the 'Suggestions for further reading'.

Aitchison, Jean (1987). *Words in the Mind: An Introduction to the Mental Lexicon*. Oxford: Blackwell.

Allan, Keith (1986). *Linguistic Meaning*, 2 vols. London and New York: Routledge and Kegan Paul.

Allwood, Jens, Andersson, L-G., and Dahl, Ö. (1977). *Logic in Linguistics*. Cambridge, London, New York and Melbourne: Cambridge University Press.

Alston, W. P. (1964). *Philosophy of Language*. Englewood Cliffs, NJ: Prentice-Hall.

Anderson, Stephen R., and Keenan, E.L. (1985). 'Deixis'. In Shopen (1985a: 259–308).

Arnold, Doug, Atkinson, M., Durand, J., Grover, C., and Sadler, L. (eds.) (1989). *Essays on Grammatical Theory and Universal Grammar*. Oxford: Clarendon Press.

Asher, Ronald E. (ed.) (1994). *The Encyclopedia of Language and Linguistics*, 10 vols. Oxford and New York: Pergamon Press.

Austin, John L. (1962). *How To Do Things With Words*. Oxford: Clarendon Press. (2nd, revised, edn, 1975).

Ayer, A.J. (1946). *Language, Truth and Logic*, 2nd edn. London: Gollancz.

Bach, Kent, and Harnish, R. (1979). *Linguistic Communication and Speech Acts*. Cambridge, MA: MIT Press.

Baldinger, Kurt (1980). *Semantic Theory: Towards a Modern Semantics*, trans. (from 2nd Spanish edn, 1977) by W.C. Brown and ed. by R. White. Oxford: Blackwell.

Bar-Hillel, Yehoshua (1964). *Language and Information*. Reading, MA: Addison-Wesley.

Bar-Hillel, Yehoshua (1970). *Aspects of Language*. Jerusalem: Magnes.

Bar-Hillel, Yehoshua (ed.) (1971). *Pragmatics of Natural Language*. Dordrecht-Holland: Reidel.

Bar-Hillel, Yehoshua, and Carnap, R. (1952). 'An outline of a theory of semantic information'. (Technical Report, 257. MIT Research Laboratory of Electronics.) Reprinted in Bar-Hillel (1964: 221–74).

Beaugrande, Robert de (1980). *Text, Discourse and Process: Towards A Multidisciplinary Science of Texts*. London: Longman; and Norwood, NJ: Ablex Publishing Corporation.

Beaugrande, Robert de, and Dressler, W.U. (1981). *Introduction to Text Linguistics*. London and New York: Longman.

Benveniste, Emile (1966). *Problèmes de linguistique générale*. Paris: Gallimard. (English trans., *Problems in General Linguistics*. Coral Gables: University of Miami Press.)

Benveniste, Emile (1974). *Problèmes de linguistique générale*, vol. 2. Paris: Gallimard.

Berlin, Brent, and Kay, P. (1969). *Basic Color Terms*. Berkeley and Los Angeles: University of California Press.

Bierwisch, Manfred (1970). 'Semantics'. In Lyons (1970: 166–84).

Bierwisch, Manfred (1971). 'On classifying semantic features'. In Steinberg and Jakobovits (1971: 410–35).

Blakemore, Diane (1987). *Semantic Constraints on Relevance*. Oxford: Blackwell.

Blakemore, Diane (1988). 'The organisation of discourse'. In Newmeyer (1988d: 229–50).

Blakemore, Diane (1989). *Understanding Utterances*. Oxford: Blackwell.

Bloomfield, Leonard (1935). *Language*. London: Allen and Unwin. (American edn, New York: Holt, Rinehart and Winston, 1933.)

Bright, William (ed.) (1992) *International Encyclopedia of Linguistics*, 4 vols. Oxford University Press.

Brown, Gillian (1990). *Listening to Spoken English*, 2nd edn. London and New York: Longman. (1st edn, 1977.)

Brown, Gillian, and Yule, G. (1983). *Discourse Analysis*. London and New York: Cambridge University Press.

Brown, Penny, and Levinson, S. (1987). *Politeness: Some Universals in Language Use*, 2nd, enlarged, edn. Cambridge: Cambridge University Press. (1st edn, 1978).

Bühler, Karl (1934). *Sprachtheorie*. Jena: Fischer. (Republished, Stuttgart: Fischer, 1982.) (English edn, *Theory of Language*, trans. with introduction, by Donald F. Goodwin, Amsterdam and Philadelphia: Benjamins, 1990.)

Bybee, Joan L. (1985). *Morphology: A Study of the Relation between Meaning and Form*. Amsterdam and Philadelphia: Benjamins.

Cann, Ronald (1993). *Formal Semantics*. Cambridge: Cambridge University Press.

Carnap, Rudolf (1942). *Introduction to Semantics*. Cambridge, MA: MIT Press.

Carnap, Rudolf (1956). *Meaning and Necessity*, 2nd edn. Chicago: Chicago University Press.

Chafe, Wallace L., and Nichols, J. (eds.) (1986). *Evidentiality: The Linguistic Encoding of Epistemology*. Norwood, NJ: Ablex.

Chierchia, Gennaro, and McConnell-Ginet, Sally (1990). *Meaning and Grammar: An Introduction to Semantics*. Cambridge, MA: MIT Press.

Chomsky, Noam (1957). *Syntactic Structures*. The Hague: Mouton.

Chomsky, Noam (1965). *Aspects of the Theory of Syntax*. Cambridge, MA: MIT Press.

Chomsky, Noam (1972). *Studies on Semantics in Generative Grammar*. The Hague: Mouton.

Chomsky, Noam (1977). *Essays in Form and Interpretation*. Amsterdam: North Holland.

Chomsky, Noam (1980). *Rules and Representations*. Oxford: Blackwell.

Chomsky, Noam (1986). *Knowledge of Language: Its Nature, Origin and Use*. New York and London: Praeger.

Chung, Sandra (1985). 'Tense, aspect, and mood'. In Shopen (1985a: 202–58).

Clark, Eve. V. (1993). *The Lexicon in Acquisition*. Cambridge: Cambridge University Press.

Coates, Jennifer (1983). *The Semantics of the Modal Auxiliaries*. London: Croom Helm.

Cole, Peter (ed.) (1978). *Syntax and Semantics, 9: Pragmatics*. New York and London: Academic Press.

Cole, Peter (ed.) (1981). *Radical Pragmatics*. New York: Academic Press.

Cole, Peter, and Morgan, J.L. (eds.) (1975). *Syntax and Semantics, 3: Speech Acts*. New York and London: Academic Press.

Collinge, Neville E. (ed.) (1990). *An Encyclopaedia of Language*. London: Routledge.

Collins Dictionary of the English Language, ed. Patrick Hanks (1979). London and Glasgow: Collins.

Comrie, Bernard (1976). *Aspect*. Cambridge and New York: Cambridge University Press.

Comrie, Bernard (1985). *Tense*. Cambridge and New York: Cambridge University Press.

Cornish, Francis (1986). *Anaphoric Relations in English and French: A Discourse Perspective*. London: Croom Helm.

Coulthard, M. (1977). *An Introduction to Discourse Analysis*. London: Edward Arnold.

Craig, Colette (ed.) (1986). *Noun Classes and Categorization*. Amsterdam: Benjamins.

Cruse, D. Alan (1986). *Lexical Semantics*. Cambridge and New York: Cambridge University Press.

Cruse, D. Alan (1990). 'Language, meaning and sense: semantics'. In Collinge (1990: 139–72).

Crystal, David (1976). *The English Tone of Voice*. London: Edward Arnold.

Dahl, Östen (1985). *Tense and Aspect Systems*. Oxford: Blackwell.

Dowty, David R. (1979). *Word Meaning and Montague Grammar*. Dordrecht-Holland, Boston and London: Reidel.

Dowty, David R., Wall, R.E., and Peters, S. (1981). *Introduction to Montague Semantics*. Dordrecht-Holland, Boston and London: Reidel.

Dressler, Wolfgang U. (ed.) (1978). *Current Trends in Text Linguistics*. Berlin: De Gruyter.

Fodor, Janet D. (1977). *Semantics: Theories of Meaning in Generative Linguistics*. New York: Crowell; and Hassocks, Sussex: Harvester.

Fodor, Jerrold A., and Katz, J.J. (1964). *The Structure of Language: Readings in the Philosophy of Language*. Englewood Cliffs, NJ: Prentice-Hall.

Frawley, William (1992). *Linguistic Semantics*. Hillsdale, NJ: Laurence Erlbaum Associates.

Fries, Charles C. (1952). *The Structure of English*. New York: Harcourt Brace.

Gazdar, Gerald (1979). *Pragmatics: Implicature, Presupposition and Logical Form*. New York and London: Academic Press.

Geach, Peter, and Black M. (eds.) (1960). *Translations from the Philosophical Writings of Gottlob Frege*. Oxford: Blackwell.

Geckeler, Horst (1971). *Strukturelle Semantik und Wortfeldtheorie*. Munich: Fink.

Givon, Talmy (ed.) (1979). *Syntax and Semantics, 12: Discourse and Syntax*. New York and London: Academic Press.

Goody, Esther N. (ed.) (1978). *Questions and Politeness*. Cambridge: Cambridge University Press.

Grice, H. Paul (1957). 'Meaning'. *Philosophical Review* 66: 377–88.

Grice, H. Paul (1975). 'Logic and conversation'. In Cole and Morgan (1975: 41–58).

Grice, H. Paul (1978). 'Further notes on logic and conversation'. In Cole (1978: 113–27).

Grice, H. Paul (1981). 'Presupposition and conversational implicature'. In Cole (1981: 183–98).

Grice, H. Paul (1989). *Studies in the Ways of Words*. Cambridge, MA: Harvard University Press.

Halliday, Michael A.K. (1970). *A Course in Spoken English*. London: Oxford University Press.

Halliday, Michael A.K. (1978). *Language as Social Semiotic*. London: Edward Arnold.

Halliday, Michael A.K., and Hassan, R. (1976). *Cohesion in English*. London and New York: Longman.

Harman, Gilbert, and Davidson, D. (eds.) (1972). *Semantics of Natural Language*. Dordrecht-Holland: Reidel.

Hofmann, Thomas R. (1993). *Realms of Meaning: An Introduction to Semantics*. London and New York: Longman.

Hopper, Paul J. (ed.) (1982). *Tense-Aspect: Between Semantics and Pragmatics*. Amsterdam: John Benjamins.

Hopper, Paul J., and Traugott, E. C. (1993). *Grammaticalization*. Cambridge: Cambridge University Press.

Horn, Laurence R. (1988). 'Pragmatic theory'. In Newmeyer (1988a: 133–45).

Horn, Laurence R. (1989). *A Natural History of Negation*. Chicago: Chicago University Press.

Huang, Yan (1994). *The Syntax and Pragmatics of Anaphora: A Study with Special Reference to Chinese*. Cambridge: Cambridge University Press.

Huddleston, Rodney (1984). *Introduction to the Grammar of English*. London and New York: Cambridge University Press.

Huddleston, Rodney (1988). *English Grammar: An Outline*. London and New York: Cambridge University Press.

Huddleston, Rodney (1994). 'Sentence types and clause subordination'. In Asher (1994: 3845–57).

Hudson, Richard A. (1995). *Word Meaning*. London: Routledge.

Hughes, G., and Cresswell, M. J. (1968). *An Introduction to Modal Logic*. London: Methuen.

Hullen, W., and Schulze, R. (eds.) (1988) *Understanding the Lexicon*. Tübingen: Niemeyer.

Hurford, James R., and Heasley, B. (1983). *Semantics: A Coursebook*. London and New York: Cambridge University Press.

Jackendoff, Ray S. (1983). *Semantics and Cognition*. Cambridge, MA: MIT Press.

Jackendoff, Ray S. (1990). *Semantic Structures*. Cambridge, MA: MIT Press.

Jarvella, Robert J., and Klein, W. (eds.) (1982). *Speech, Place and Action: Studies in Deixis and Related Topics*. New York: Wiley.

Katz, Jerrold J. (1972). *Semantic Theory*. New York: Harper and Row.

Katz, Jerrold J. (1977). *Propositional Structure and Illocutionary Force*. New York: Crowell; and Hassocks, Sussex: Harvester.

Katz, Jerrold J., and Fodor, J. A. (1963). 'The structure of a semantic theory'. *Language* 39: 170–210.

Katz, Jerrold J., and Postal, P. M. (1964). *An Integrated Theory of Linguistic Description*. Cambridge MA: MIT Press.

Keenan, Edward L. (ed.) (1975). *Formal Semantics of Natural Language*. London and New York: Cambridge University Press.

Kempson, Ruth M. (1977). *Semantic Theory*. Cambridge: Cambridge University Press.

Kempson, Ruth M. (ed.) (1988). *Mental Representations*. Cambridge: Cambridge University Press.

Kripke, Saul (1972). 'Naming and necessity'. In Donald Davidson and S. Kripke (eds.), *Semantics for Natural Language*. Dordrecht-Holland: Reidel. (Revised version published separately as *Naming and Necessity*, Oxford: Blackwell.)

Ladusaw, William A. (1988). 'Semantic theory'. In Newmeyer (1988a: 89–112).

Lakoff, George (1987). *Women, Fire and Dangerous Things: What Categories Reveal about the Mind*. Chicago: University of Chicago Press.

Lakoff, George, and Johnson, M. (1980). *Metaphors We Live By*. Chicago: Chicago University Press.

Langacker, Ronald (1987). *Foundations of Cognitive Grammar, 1: Theoretical Preliminaries*. Stanford: Stanford University Press.

Leech, Geoffrey N. (1974). *Semantics*. Harmondsworth, Middlesex: Penguin.

Leech, Geoffrey N. (1983). *Principles of Pragmatics*. London: Longman.

Leech, Geoffrey N., and Thomas, Jenny (1990). 'Pragmatics'. In Collinge (1990: 173–206).

Lehrer, Adrienne (1974). *Semantic Fields and Lexical Structure*. Amsterdam and London: North Holland.

Lehrer, Adrienne, and Kittay, E. F. (eds.) (1992). *Frames, Fields and Contrasts: New Essays in Semantic Organization*. Hillsdale, NJ: Laurence Erlbaum Associates.

Lehrer, Keith, and Lehrer, A. (eds.) (1970). *Theory of Meaning*. New York: Prentice-Hall.

Levinson, Stephen C. (1983). *Pragmatics*. Cambridge: Cambridge University Press.

Levinson, Stephen C. (forthcoming). *Generalized Conversational Implicature*. Cambridge: Cambridge University Press.

Lewis, David (1969). *Convention: A Philosophical Study*. Cambridge, MA: Harvard University Press.

Linsky, Leonard (ed.) (1979). *Reference and Modality*. London: Oxford University Press.

Lipka, Leonhard (1990). *An Outline of English Lexicology: Lexical Structure, Word Semantics, and Word-Formation*. Tübingen: Niemeyer.

Longman Dictionary of Contemporary English. (1978). London: Longman. (2nd edn, 1987).

Lyons, John (1968). *Introduction to Theoretical Linguistics*. London and New York: Cambridge University Press.

Lyons, John (ed.) (1970). *New Horizons in Linguistics*. Harmondsworth: Penguin. (Republished as *New Horizons in Linguistics, 1*, London: Penguin Books; and New York: Viking Penguin, 1987).

Lyons, John (1977). *Semantics*, 2 vols. London and New York: Cambridge University Press.

Lyons, John (1981). *Language and Linguistics*. Cambridge, New York and Melbourne: Cambridge University Press.

Lyons, John (1987). 'Semantics'. In Lyons *et al.* (1987: 152–78).

Lyons, John (1989). 'Semantic ascent: a neglected aspect of syntactic typology'. In Douglas G. Arnold *et al.* (eds), *Essays on Grammatical Theory and Universal Grammar*. London: Oxford University Press, 153–86.

Lyons, John (1991a). *Chomsky*, 3rd, revised and further enlarged, edn. London: HarperCollins. (1st edn, 1970; 2nd, revised and enlarged, edn, 1977.)

Lyons, John (1991b). *Natural Language and Universal Grammar: Essays in Linguistic Theory*, vol. 1. Cambridge, New York and Melbourne: Cambridge University Press.

Lyons, John (forthcoming). *Semantics, Subjectivity and Localism: Essays in Linguistic Theory*, vol. 2. Cambridge, New York and Melbourne: Cambridge University Press.

Lyons, John, Coates, R., Deuchar, M., and Gazdar, G. (1987). *New Horizons in Linguistics, 2*. London: Penguin Books; and New York: Viking Penguin.

Martinich, A. P. (ed.) (1985). *The Philosophy of Language*. Oxford: Oxford University Press.

Matthews, Peter H. (1981). *Syntax*. Cambridge, New York and Melbourne: Cambridge University Press.

Matthews, Peter H. (1992). *Morphology*, 2nd edn. Cambridge, New York and Melbourne: Cambridge University Press. (1st edn, 1974.)

Matthews, Richard (1991). *Words and Worlds: On the Linguistics of Modality*. Frankfurt: Peter Lang.

Montague, Richard (1974). *Formal Philosophy: Selected Papers of Richard Montague*, ed. by R. H. Thomason. New Haven: Yale University Press.

Morris, Charles W. (1938). 'Foundations of the theory of signs'. In Neurath, Carnap and Morris (1938: 79–137).

Morris, Charles W. (1946). *Signs, Language and Behavior*. New York: Prentice-Hall.

Neurath, Otto, Carnap, R., and Morris, C. W. (eds.) (1938). *International Encyclopedia of Unified Sciences*. Chicago: University of Chicago Press. (Combined edn, 1955.)

Newmeyer, Frederick J. (ed.) (1988a). *Linguistics: The Cambridge Survey, 1: Linguistic Theory: Foundations*. Cambridge, New York and Melbourne: Cambridge University Press.

Newmeyer, Frederick J. (ed.) (1988b). *Linguistics: The Cambridge Survey, 2: Linguistic Theory: Extensions and Implications*. Cambridge, New York and Melbourne: Cambridge University Press.

Newmeyer, Frederick J. (ed.) (1988c). *Linguistics: The Cambridge Survey, 3: Language: Psychological and Biological Aspects*. Cambridge, New York and Melbourne: Cambridge University Press.

Newmeyer, Frederick J. (ed.) (1988d). *Linguistics: The Cambridge Survey, 4: Language: The Socio-cultural Context*. Cambridge, New York and Melbourne: Cambridge University Press.

Nida, Eugene (1975). *Componential Analysis of Meaning*. The Hague: Mouton.

Nilsen, Don L. F., and Nilsen, A. P. (1975). *Semantic Theory*. New York: Newbury House.

Ogden, Charles K. (1968). *Basic English: International Second Language* (revised and expanded edn of *The System of Basic English*). New York: Harcourt Brace.

Olshewsky, Thomas M. (ed.) (1969). *Problems in the Philosophy of Language*. New York: Holt, Rinehart and Winston.

Ortony, Andrew (ed.) (1979). *Metaphor and Thought*. Cambridge: Cambridge University Press.

Palmer, Frank R. (1981). *Semantics: A New Outline*, 2nd edn. Cambridge: Cambridge University Press. (1st edn, 1976).

Palmer, Frank R. (1986). *Mood and Modality*. Cambridge: Cambridge University Press.

Palmer, Frank R. (1990). *Modality and the English Modals*, 2nd edn. London and New York: Longman.

Parkinson, G. (ed.) (1986). *The Theory of Meaning*. London: Oxford University Press.

Partee, Barbara H., ter Meulen, A., and Wall, R. E. (1990). *Mathematical Methods in Linguistics*. Dordrecht-Holland, Boston and London: Kluwer Academic Publishers.

Payne, John R. (1985). 'Negation'. In Shopen (1985a: 197–242).

Pelletier, F. J. (ed.) (1979). *Mass Terms: Some Philosophical Problems*. Dordrecht-Holland: Reidel.

Perkins, M. R. (1983). *Modal Expressions in English*. London: Frances Pinter.

Potts, Timothy (1994). *Structure and Categories for the Representation of Meaning*. Cambridge: Cambridge University Press.

Pulman, Stephen G. (1983). *Word Meaning and Belief*. London: Croom Helm.

Putnam, Hilary (1970). 'Is semantics possible?'. In H. Kiefer and M. Munitz (eds.), *Languages, Belief and Metaphysics*. New York: State University of New York Press, 1970. (Reprinted in Putnam, 1975: 139–52).

Putnam, Hilary (1975). *Mind, Language and Reality*. London and New York: Cambridge University Press.

Quine, Willard V. (1953). *From a Logical Point of View*. Cambridge, MA: Harvard University Press. (2nd edn, 1961.)

Quine, Willard V. (1960). *Word and Object*. Cambridge, MA: MIT Press.

Quirk, Randolph, Greenbaum, S., Leech, G., and Svartvik, J. (1985). *A Comprehensive Grammar of the English Language*. London and New York: Longman.

Radford, Andrew (1988). *Transformational Grammar*. Cambridge: Cambridge University Press.

Recanati, François (1987). *Meaning and Force: The Pragmatics of Performative Utterances* (revised English version of *Les énoncés performatifs*, Paris: Minuit, 1981).

Reinhart, Tanya (1983). *Anaphora and Semantic Interpretation*. Chicago and London: University of Chicago Press.

Roget, P. M. (1852). *Thesaurus of English Words and Phrases*. London (Abridged and revised, London: Penguin, 1953).

Rorty, Richard (ed.) (1967). *The Linguistic Turn: Recent Essays in Philosophical Method*. Chicago and London: Chicago University Press.

Russell, Bertrand (1905). 'On denoting'. *Mind* 14: 479–93.

Russell, Bertrand (1940). *An Inquiry Into Meaning and Truth*. London: Allen and Unwin. (Reprinted, Harmondsworth, Middlesex: Penguin, 1962.)

Ryle, Gilbert (1951). 'The theory of meaning'. In C. A. Mace (ed.), *British Philosophy in the Mid-Century*. London: Allen and Unwin, 239–64. (Reprinted in Zabeeh *et al.*, 1974: 219–44.)

Saddock, Jerrold M., and Zwicky, A. M. (1985). 'Speech act distinctions in syntax'. In Shopen (1985b: 197–242).

Saussure, Ferdinand de (1916). *Cours de Linguistique Générale*, ed. by Charles Bally and Albert Séchehaye. Paris: Payot.

Schiffrin, Deborah (1987). *Discourse Markers*. Cambridge, New York and Melbourne: Cambridge University Press.

Searle, John R. (1969). *Speech Acts: An Essay in the Philosophy of Language*. Cambridge and New York: Cambridge University Press.

Searle, John R. (1979). *Expression and Meaning*. Cambridge and New York: Cambridge University Press.

Searle, John R., Kiefer, F., and Bierwisch, M. (eds.) (1980). *Speech Act Theory and Pragmatics*. Dordrecht-Holland: Reidel.

Searle, John R., and Vanderken, D. (1985). *Foundations of Illocutionary Logic*. Cambridge, New York and Melbourne: Cambridge University Press.

Seuren, Pieter A. M. (1985). *Discourse Semantics*. Oxford: Blackwell.

Shopen, Timothy (1985a). *Language Typology and Syntactic Description, 1: Clause Structure*. Cambridge: Cambridge University Press.

Shopen, Timothy (1985b). *Language Typology and Syntactic Description, 2: Grammatical Categories and the Lexicon*. Cambridge: Cambridge University Press.

Smith, Neil V. (ed.) (1982). *Mutual Knowledge*. London and New York: Academic Press.

Smith, Neil V., and Wilson, D. (1979). *Modern Linguistics: the Results of the Chomskyan Revolution*. Harmondsworth, Middlesex: Penguin.

Sperber, Dan, and Wilson, D. (1986). *Relevance: Communication and Cognition*. Cambridge and New York: Cambridge University Press.

Steinberg, Danny D., and Jakobovits, L. A. (eds.) (1971). *Semantics*. London and New York: Cambridge University Press.

Strawson, Peter F. (1952). *Introduction to Logical Theory*. London: Methuen.

Strawson, Peter F. (1971a). *Logico-Linguistic Papers*. London: Methuen.

Strawson, Peter F. (ed.) (1971b). *Philosophical Logic*. London: Oxford University Press.

Strawson, Peter F. (1975). *Subject and Predicate in Logic and Grammar*. London: Methuen.

Sweetser, Eve E. (1990). *From Etymology to Pragmatics: Metaphorical and Cultural Aspects of Semantic Structure*. Cambridge and New York: Cambridge University Press.

Tarski, Alfred (1944). 'The semantic conception of truth'. *Philosophy and Phenomenological Research* 4: 341–75. (Reprinted in Olshewky, 1969: 578–609; Zabeeh *et al.*, 1974: 675–712.)

Tarski, Alfred (1956). *Logic, Semantics, Metamathematics*. London: Oxford University Press.

Taylor, J. R. (1989). *Linguistic Categorization: Prototypes in Linguistic Theory*. Oxford: Clarendon Press.

Tedeschi, P., and Zaenen, A. J. (1981). *Syntax and Semantics, 14: Tense and Aspect*. London and New York: Academic Press.

Ullmann, Stephen (1962). *Semantics*. Oxford: Blackwell; New York: Barnes and Noble.

Van Dijk, Tune A. (1977). *Text and Context*. London and New York: Longman.

Wierzbicka, Anna (1980). *Lingua Mentalis: The Semantics of Natural Language*. London and New York: Academic Press.

Wierzbicka, Anna (1992). *Semantics, Culture and Cognition*. London and New York: Oxford University Press.

Wittgenstein, Ludwig (1953). *Philosophical Investigations*. Oxford: Blackwell; and New York: Macmillan.

Woisetschlaeger, E. F. (1985). *A Semantic Theory of the English Auxiliary System*. New York and London: Garland.

Zabeeh, Farhang, Klemke, E. D., and Jacobson, A. (eds.) (1974). *Readings in Semantics*. Urbana, IL, Chicago and London: University of Illinois Press.

Index

connexion with sentence-type,
177–80, 332
as a grammatical category, or as
mood of a proposition, 255–6
and interrogativity, 191–3
modal expressions and modality,
327–35
relationship with tense, 275, 319,
332–3
and sentence-type, 253
tense and aspect, 195–7
uses of term, 327
and verbal inflection, 179–80
morpheme-based grammar, 48, 66, 72
morphologically synthetic languages,
31, 313
morphology, 105; bibliography, 345
morphosyntactic identity, 56
morphosyntactic properties of a word,
24
morphosyntactically distinct forms,
53
morse-code, 34

naive realism, 90–1, 98, 324
names, 295
narrower scope, **175**
native speakers, 134–5, 308–9
difference between homonymy and
polysemy, 58–60
intuitive judgements of
meaningfulness, 148
unconscious rules and conventions,
9–10
natural kind expressions, theory of
(Putnam and Kripke), 92–3
natural kinds, **76**–7, 89–90, **91**–6, 325
natural languages, **6**
descriptive and expressive powers of,
209
formal semantics of, 201
naming in, 295
semantic structure of, 209
spatio-temporal deixis in, 306–7
without tense, 312
natural necessity, **121**–2
natural sign, **3**
near-synonyms, **60**–2
necessarily, uses of term, 121
necessarily true or false proposition,
117, **118**
necessity, 327–9, 333–5

definition of, 329
negation, **150**, **162**, 169–76
bibliography, 345
propositional, 328
negation-operator, **109**, 173
negative indefinite pronouns, 172
neo-Gricean pragmatics, **277**, 280,
292
bibliography, 345
neuropsychology, 73, 211
nominal negation, 171
nominalism, 82, 92
non-arbitrariness, 13–15
non-conventional behaviour, 13
non-declarative sentences, 185, 193–8,
224
non-deictic information, 307–10
non-descriptive meaning, **44**, 64–5,
130
non-detachability, **289**
non-factual significance, and emotivism,
144–5
non-human communicative behaviour,
12–13
non-indicative sentences, 224
non-inflecting languages, 67
non-intentional behaviour, 13
non-isolating synthetic languages, 31
non-lexical meaning xv, 104
non-linguistic semantics, 11–16, 101
non-natural metalanguages, **9**
non-progressive aspectual distinction,
195
non-propositional meaning, xiii, xiv,
8, **44**, 203, 291–2
neglect of, 336, 338
non-verbal component of natural
language utterances, 10, **14**, **36**
non-words, 46
notational conventions, 9–10
for distinguishing word form and
meaning, 23–30
noun classes, bibliography, 345
noun-headed noun-phrases, **296**–7
noun-phrases (NP), 296–7
quantified, 300–1
nuclear extension, 94, **96**–7, 116
number, **74**

object-words, and dictionary-words, 83
objective deontic interpretation, **330**

Printed in the United States
69348LVS00003B/1-39